Teaching Autoethnography: Personal Writing in the Classroom

Teaching Autoethnography: Personal Writing in the Classroom

Melissa Tombro

Open SUNY Textbooks

©2016 Melissa Tombro

ISBN: 978-1-942341-21-5 ebook
ISBN: 978-1-942341-31-4 print

This publication was made possible by a SUNY Innovative Instruction Technology Grant (IITG). IITG is a competitive grants program open to SUNY faculty and support staff across all disciplines. IITG encourages development of innovations that meet the Power of SUNY's transformative vision.

Published by Open SUNY Textbooks, Milne Library (IITG PI)

State University of New York at Geneseo,
Geneseo, NY 14454

This book was produced using Pressbooks.com, and PDF rendering was done by PrinceXML.

Teaching Autoethnography: Personal Writing in the Classroom by Melissa Tombro is licensed under a Creative Commons Attribution-NonCommercial-ShareAlike 4.0 International License, except where otherwise noted.

v 0.1

Contents

About the Book   x
Reviewer's Notes   xi
Carole Deletiner

Teaching Autoethnography

Introduction   3
1. Understanding our Students' Relationship to "I"   16
2. Getting Started in the Classroom   19
3. Writing Essays for Class: The First Steps   26
4. Workshop and Peer Review Process   32
5. Memory/Character Essays   35
6. Writing about Spaces and Events   39
7. The Autoethnography Project   43
8. Choosing Topics for the Autoethnography   53
9. The Interview Process   58
10. Conducting Observations   62
11. Putting It All Together   64
12. Challenges of Personal Writing   66
13. Concluding Thoughts   68
14. Sample Class Schedule   69
15. Additional Readings on Autoethnography   71

Deep Observation Assignment: Eleven Examples

Melanie   75
Joomi Park

Rattling Thoughts   77
Neziah Doe

Southern Belle   79
William Rossi

The Battle   81
Emma Suleski

The Woman with the Purple Mat *Heather Brackman*	83
David Everitt-Carlson *Anna Ehart*	85
The Man *Justine Giardina*	87
Colors, Lines, and Shapes *Jillian McDonnell*	89
Angelic Atmosphere *Chadbourne Oliver*	91
Sylvia *Tyana Soto*	93
One *Adriana Pauly*	95

Self-as-Character Assignment: Eight Examples

Sight *Neziah Doe*	99
Fastforward *Emma Suleski*	101
Reflections *Zachary Volosky*	103
Unfortunate Truths *Justine Giardina*	105
Hanatomy *Hannah Lajba*	107
What I Never Thought *Or Gotham*	109
Past Midnight *Jeffrey Cheung*	111
Five Feet Mighty *Joomi Park*	113

Memory Assignment: Six Examples

The Curse *Zachary Volosky*	117
Memory of the Maine *Joomi Park*	119

A Memory of Mr. Oko 121
William Rossi

Inhale, Exhale 123
Emma Suleski

An Honest Living 125
Justine Giardina

A-Relief 127
Hannah Lajba

Memory/Character Essay: Thirteen Examples

How to Survive 131
Or Gotham

A Living Contradiction 134
Mike Gomez

Georgia on My Mind 137
Joomi Park

To the Center 140
William Rossi

Growing Through Dirt 143
Magdalene Moore

Playbill 146
Hannah Lajba

I Told You So 149
Jillian McDonnell

Genetic Disposition 153
Emma Suleski

Shomer Nagia 156
Neziah Doe

Brooklyn, Madness, Lust, Death, and the Apocalypse ... 160
Chadbourne Oliver

Mommy 164
Katie Braner

The Job That You Want 167
Jeffrey Cheung

Self-Destruct 171
Danny Gomez

The Space or Event Essay: Thirteen Examples

In-Patient *Mike Gomez*	179
Daringly Different *Tyana Soto*	184
Two Places, One Home *Maria Beyer*	188
See the World *Adriana Pauly*	191
Manhattan *William Rossi*	196
November First *Neziah Doe*	199
Get a Grip *Emma Suleski*	202
Room in the Back *Justine Giardina*	205
Aging Not so Gracefully *Anne Ehart*	209
There and Back Again: A Comic-Con Tale *Hannah Lajba*	213
Sundays *Jillian McDonnell*	218
Family Ties *Zachary Volosky*	223
Focus *Erika Veurink*	228

The Autoethnography: Ten Examples

On Anarchism in New York *Adriana Pauly*	235
Allies, Advocates, Activists *Tyana Soto*	241
Unicorny, the Only Way a Coder Will Define Rails *Hannah Lajba*	245
Friendship Is Magic *Heather Brackman*	249
Gin and Tonic: A Look into the Subculture of Taxidermists *Jillian McDonnell*	254

Don't Judge the Bible by Its Cover: An Honest Story with a Cliché Title 260
Emma Suleski

Autoethnography on Manhattan Drag 264
William Rossi

NaNoWriMo 269
Joomi Park

Steel Paradise: The Hardcore Metal Aesthetic 272
Justine Giardina

YouTube: Science Isn't Just for Geeks Anymore 278
Neziah Doe

Works Cited 283
About the Author 289

About the Book

Teaching Autoethnography: Personal Writing in the Classroom is dedicated to the practice of immersive ethnographic and autoethonographic writing that encourages authors to participate in the communities about which they write. This book draws not only on critical qualitative inquiry methods such as interview and observation, but also on theories and sensibilities from creative writing and performance studies, which encourage self-reflection and narrative composition. Concepts from qualitative inquiry studies, which examine everyday life, are combined with approaches to the creation of character and scene to help writers develop engaging narratives that examine chosen subcultures and the author's position in relation to her research subjects. The book brings together a brief history of first-person qualitative research and writing from the past forty years, examining the evolution of nonfiction and qualitative approaches in relation to the personal essay. A selection of recent student writing in the genre as well as reflective student essays on the experience of conducting research in the classroom is presented in the context of exercises for coursework and beyond. Also explored in detail are guidelines for interviewing and identifying subjects and techniques for creating informed sketches and images that engage the reader. This book provides approaches anyone can use to explore their communities and write about them first-hand. The methods presented can be used for a single assignment in a larger course or to guide an entire semester through many levels and varieties of informed personal writing.

About Open SUNY Textbooks

Open SUNY Textbooks is an open access textbook publishing initiative established by State University of New York libraries and supported by SUNY Innovative Instruction Technology Grants. This initiative publishes high-quality, cost-effective course resources by engaging faculty as authors and peer-reviewers, and libraries as publishing service and infrastructure.

The pilot launched in 2012, providing an editorial framework and service to authors, students and faculty, and establishing a community of practice among libraries.

Participating libraries in the 2012-2013 pilot include SUNY Geneseo, College at Brockport, College of Environmental Science and Forestry, SUNY Fredonia, Upstate Medical University, and University at Buffalo, with support from other SUNY libraries and SUNY Press. The 2013-2014 pilot will add more titles in 2015. More information can be found at http://textbooks.opensuny.org.

Reviewer's Notes
Carole Deletiner

I would recommend this text to any undergraduate college instructor interested in developing and teaching a writing course that centers on using qualitative research methods to investigate, examine, reflect, and write about personal experiences. The strength of the text derives from how it can be used and the author includes precise and carefully considered "approaches anyone can use to explore their communities and write about them first-hand" (Tombro). Of particular use to a writing instructor is the step-by-step presentation of the author's research methods that "can be used for a single assignment in a larger course or to guide an entire semester through many levels and varieties of informed personal writing" (Tombro).

The text is clear and concise methodically laying out the steps necessary to complete a semester long project. Of particular value is the clarity of the assignments and how they build on one another helping to guide students through a sophisticated and challenging process.

Carole Deletiner earned a PhD in English Education at New York University. Until her retirement in 2014, she taught a variety of writing and literature courses at the college level for more than twenty-five years.

Teaching Autoethnography

Introduction

Goals and Uses of This Book

The purpose of this textbook, aimed at college-level teachers, is to present a unified approach to using personal writing and qualitative inquiry, specifically autoethnography, in the first-year writing classroom. Its use can also extend into any classroom where the instructor wishes to use personal writing. Compositionists and university composition programs have embraced aspects of personal writing and qualitative research with varying degrees of success for many years. My book is meant to be a practical guide to integrating many of these methods, with help from the field of creative writing, into a course that teaches all of the aspects of writing that students should practice before leaving the first-year writing classroom. The book can be used to structure an entire first-year writing course or creative nonfiction course or as a resource for individual assignments in any classroom when the instructor wishes to use personal writing critically. All writing assignments included here can be considered either building blocks for autoethnography or autoethnographic in nature.

Through conversations with colleagues over the past thirteen years, I have come to realize that many writing teachers need more opportunities to theorize properly and demonstrate the importance of the work they are doing with personal writing. Although personal writing remains a popular genre, varying opinions about its value and use keep it from being analyzed and studied in a way that allows its definitions to expand and evolve. The intention of this book is not to ask why personal writing has been such a contentious yet popular form in the field of composition but rather to trace its history in the field of composition and to explore how we can employ it critically and productively in our classrooms using qualitative inquiry.

In my introduction, I draw together a number of working definitions and methodologies to situate the approach to the teaching assignments I include in the rest of the book. For my purposes, the focus on personal writing will be on its position in the field of composition studies. Depending on the academic field of study, there is much disagreement about the definition of the term *autoethnography*. There are many valuable resources, including well-conceived literary reviews, on the use and differing definitions of autoethnography in the social sciences, a few of which I will contextualize for our purposes in Chapter 7. However, to maintain the focus of this textbook, I have limited my literature review to how qualitative inquiry has been appropriated and used in the field of composition studies. Additional readings from the social sciences on autoethnography can be found in the bibliography at the end of this book.

In this book, autoethnography is treated as personal writing in which the subjectivity of the writer is highlighted and experiences are understood through narrative exploration and storytelling, incorporating other voices, observation, participation, and larger cultural ideas. Using autoethnography in this way allows students to employ first-person research and analyze their own subjectivity in narrative form. The primary focus is on the value of storytelling and examining the self in relation to experience. This approach values the audience and considers the value of analyzing, reflecting on and narratively communicating personal experience, which I will refer to as the "Who cares?" factor in Chapter 3.

I hope you will find this to be an informative and user-friendly book that draws on my own experiences in the classroom. Rather than including a large number of professional examples, I include a variety of student contributions to demonstrate the products of this kind of work. During my years of studying this topic, I have come to realize that solid examples of student writing in response to these assignments are a major element that has been missing from our research resources. I am grateful to all of the enthusiastic student volunteers from my classrooms who have made this book possible. I encourage all teachers using this book to complete the assignments themselves, so they can understand the perspective of the student writers and share their writing in the classroom, guiding students in their own endeavors.

Informational sections will be addressed to the instructor, and assignments will be directed at the students. Please feel free to adapt any of this information as necessary for different audiences. The structure of this textbook in its entirety would be appropriate for a traditional 15-week course. I have included a sample timeline at the end of the book and timeline references in each chapter introduction. Any of the assignments can be excerpted for individual use.

I will not include readings for students in this textbook. Instead, I will include some examples in the chapters from texts I have used in class. While I hope this will be helpful, I encourage all teachers to choose readings they find relevant for students based upon their focus and desired outcomes.

A Brief History of Personal Writing in Composition Studies

Within the field of composition, personal writing—an umbrella term that includes any writing which draws on first-hand experience, including genres such as autoethnography, autobiography, and mystery—maintains a precarious position at best. I use personal writing both to provide a more general term that can apply to many kinds of writing and to avoid using terminology that has historically been problematic in this genre. Following a more general trend that started in the mid-1960s and flourished in the mid-1970s, personal experience has appeared in the academic accounts of scholars involved in the process of creating the field and expanding it to include disciplinary ideas from communication to cultural studies. The use of personal writing has become so ubiquitous that often it does not get the critical attention it deserves or it receives critique that is not productive. There are concerns that what is personal is not critical and that personal writing is therefore not what we should be teaching our students to use in the classroom.

Deriving knowledge from personal experience is risky for at least two reasons: (1) first-hand experience may have limited application or relevance in other situations—or as scientists and social scientists like to say, "Anecdote is not evidence"; and (2) display of the self can often elicit harsh personal and scholarly judgments from others. I is a well-established point of contention for the teacher, the researcher and the student—when to allow it, how to use it, whether it is critical, where its use can be rigorous. For most people, forbidding the use of I is an outdated notion (although the majority of students will still admit in their first college classes that at least one of their previous English teachers banned its use), but there seem to be gaps in the critical research supporting theories of the benefits of using I. Current personal writing terminology often carries negative connotations, encouraging scholars to redefine their terms, and in doing so splinters the definition of personal writing. As Karen Paley suggests in her study of I-Writing: The Politics and Practice of Teaching First-Person Writing, a book that came out of her dissertation exploring the implications of personal writing, "the sheer circulation of so many synonyms or near synonyms may be indicative of anxiety about the personal in the academy…. [O]n the other hand, the multiple names may reflect the versatility of the form itself" (10). I will break down current notions of I in this introduction; in later chapters I will include assignments that use I in the classroom both literally and metaphorically.

Tracing attitudes toward the personal and how they have evolved within the pedagogy and scholarship of composition can establish a working definition for the term and lay out the current stakes for personal writing in our departments and classrooms and its potential for interdisciplinary expansion. Practices associated with the expressivist movement, such as free writing, fast drafts and even performance, have made their way into the core curriculum of many English departments, according to composition scholars such as Paley (I-Writing) and Thomas Newkirk (The Performance of Self in Student Writing).

These two books thoroughly analyze the value of expressivist pedagogy as a basis for many popular composition practices. In I-Writing, Paley views the entire debate surrounding the use of personal writing through the history of the expressivist movement in composition, concentrating on the debate between David Bartholomae and Peter Elbow, and evaluating the classroom practices of Patricia Bizzell to discover what the expectations are for the personal in the classroom. After evaluating the relevant literature, Paley defines expressivism as:

> a pedagogy that includes (but is by no means limited to) an openness to the use of personal narrative, a particular type of the narrative mode of discourse. Personal narrative takes the writer's own experience as its focus. It involves the use of a narrational I that seems to be the actual voice of the person who writes. Sometimes the narrator may appear to isolate individual consciousness, and sometimes he or she may represent the self in one or more social contexts, such as the family or college community. The narrator may or may not explicitly link the particular situation with those experienced by others (13).

According to Paley, personal writing concentrates on the experience of the individual but may include outside perspectives.

Paley conducts her research on the premise that most literature denigrating the use of I is not based on qualitative research, a problem I will attempt to address in this introduction. According to Paley, "The misrepresentations of pedagogies that include the teaching of personal narrative are based largely on published writing as opposed to classroom observation" (13). In her own study, she spends time in classrooms and interviewing scholars to add to the body of scholarship on personal writing. In doing this, she can begin to break open the category by contributing new observations and insights.

The debate between Elbow and Bartholomae that Paley discusses may be the first thing composition scholars refer to when analyzing personal writing. The assumption that expressivism and personal writing are the same thing is so ubiquitous that in The Performance of Self in Student Writing, Newkirk assumes that the two discussions are identical, moving freely between analysis of self-writing and expressivist methodology. While the topics have abundant similarities, we need to push past many of the restraints of expressivist writing to make new strides in critical evaluation of personal writing. The ability of the personal narrative to allow students and scholars to be engaged readers and thinkers becomes apparent in Newkirk's study.

In addition to engaging expressivist pedagogy, composition scholars regularly publish personal writing that draws on teaching practices, literacy narratives, and case studies from classrooms. While composition literature has included many nods toward the personal in the teaching of first-year writing, concerns arise when first-person autobiographical perspective is employed in our publishing and when nontext-based models are used as research methodologies. An example of this resistance can be found in reviews of current autobiographical scholarship such as James D.

Williams' College English piece "Counterstatement: Autobiography in Composition Scholarship." Though he discusses the importance of the personal in the accounts of composition scholars, Williams ultimately chides the authors of the books under review, stating, "The key topics…must be pried from the personal history" (211). This simultaneous acknowledgement and rejection of the value of personal writing is not uncommon. As a whole, then, this book will analyze some of the origins of conflicting attitudes toward personal writing and how we can make these disagreements productive in creating new definitions.

In addition to academic writing, of course, there are many other ways to share personal stories, from casually recounting our day to our friends to sharing our own learning experiences in the ways we teach and write. In Getting a Life: Everyday Uses of Autobiography, Sidonie Smith and Julia Watson emphasize the consumer nature of the individual American, who naturally takes in the life experiences and stories of others on a daily basis while offering her own in return. Everything from popular memoir to reality television supports this kind of life sharing. As Smith and Watson put it, "In postmodern America we are culturally obsessed with getting a life—and not just getting it, but sharing it with and advertising it to others. We are, as well, obsessed with consuming the lives that other people have gotten" (3). We rely on personal stories to convey common messages and relate to one another. From the obsessive imbibing of celebrity gossip to sharing personal experiences in a conference presentation, we can involve the personal in our leisure activities and in our work. When considering how we contextualize the work we do in the classroom, it is important to be aware of how we as teachers use personal writing every day to create life narratives and how our students, whose lives are infused by social media, have learned to create public life stories.

Qualitative Inquiry and the Composition Classroom

Qualitative inquiry methods have grown in popularity in writing programs and universities over the past twenty-five years. Some universities have started programs that encourage students to engage in various kinds of fieldwork, interacting with and interviewing their communities as well as investigating university resources. Examples include the Center for Ethnography at the University of California, Irvine, created to support interdisciplinary use of ethnographic research and writing, and Harvard's Sensory Ethnography Lab to provide support for those combining visual media and social scientific practices. Among such programs is the University of Illinois' Ethnography of the University initiative, the first ethnography program I was a part of and one that encourages instructors in all disciplines to incorporate qualitative inquiry methods in their classrooms while helping students get to know the history and makeup of the university more intimately. Students are thus producing writing that is personally meaningful and contributing to an understanding of their position at the university while also contributing to the community through writing and inquiry. This can be an empowering experience for students and especially in first-year composition can allow them to feel they are an important part of their community. As I have mentioned, it is this concept of empowerment that can allow students and scholars to create and expand theories of the personal. According to the program's mission statement:

> The Ethnography of the University Initiative … engages students in research on what they know and care about: their own universities. Student work is public and preserved, housed in a dynamic on-line archive designed to encourage future generations of students to build on past student research. EUI guides students to think about colleges and universities in relation to their communities as well as in national and global contexts. EUI researchers reflect on their findings to identify concrete ways that the University can better fulfill its many missions. EUI leads students to become engaged citizens, actively and critically contributing to public life.

Student work is put into a publicly accessible database, which gives it a readership well beyond the confines of the classroom.

In addition to interdisciplinary programs like those mentioned above, the popularity of using qualitative inquiry methods to teach undergraduates research skills in composition is also evidenced by textbooks that have been widely adopted in composition classrooms. FieldWorking: Reading and Writing Research by Bonnie Stone Sunstein and Elizabeth Chiseri-Strater, two researchers who in their own scholarly lives employ qualitative inquiry methods as well as teacher research, is a textbook intended to help teachers walk students through the process of writing ethnography. The work is now in its fourth edition, and many articles have been written in response to its methods. The textbook takes students step by step through creating research proposals, mining and analyzing data and considering their own position in their research. For Sunstein and Chiseri-Strater, the value of the methods contained in the book is clear. In their notes to the instructor they explain:

> Fieldwork invites students to be more engaged and involved in the research process. To a much greater extent than their counterparts whose research activities are confined to the library and the Internet, students who work in fieldsites and archives learn to observe, listen, interpret, and analyze the behaviors and language of 'others' around them. Because doing fieldwork allows students actual contact with people and cultures different from their own, they will often be more invested in the topics they investigate. Doing fieldwork also encourages a greater understanding of self as each student reads, writes, researches, and reflects on relationships with 'others' in the culture. But the most compelling reason for any instructor to use this investigative approach is that through the process of fieldworking, a student will become a better reader, writer, and researcher (To the instructor, vii).

Sunstein and Chiseri-Strater also created the qualitative research network at the Conference on College Communication and Composition, and other major conferences in the field of composition have followed suit, devoting large sections of their programming to qualitative inquiry. In fact, a simple Google search for "ethnography and composition" leads to a large number of articles and Web sites dating to the early '80s that deal with the value and pitfalls of using ethnographic methods in the composition classroom. Of course, as in the rest of the history of composition, there are issues that arise in this teaching of qualitative inquiry and ethnography. These initial issues were hashed out as scholars began early in the field engaging in teacher research and other qualitative inquiry that involved their students and their communities. A number of edited collections have been published in the field of composition that explore the role of the teacher as ethnographic researcher, most notably Voices & Visions: Refiguring Ethnography in Composition and Ethnography Unbound: From Theory Shock to Cultural Praxis.

Voices and Visions focuses on the ethical dilemmas of the ethnographic researcher in composition studies. Editors Cristina Kirklighter, Cloe Vincent and Joseph M. Moxley attest through their research and call for papers that ethnography, despite the predictions of many, has continued to increase in popularity, prompting composition scholars to further explore the implications and value of this research.

In the first chapter of the collection, "North Northwest: Ethnography and The Making of Knowledge in Composition," H. Eric Branscomb begins with an overview of the reaction to Stephen North's 1987 book The Making of Knowledge in Composition—a book that, in addition to predicting the demise of the field and the imminent failure of ethnography as a methodology, set off a lot of the major ethical discussions of qualitative inquiry in the field of composition (2).

Since the publication of North's book, Branscomb argues, feminism and postmodernism "seem to be directing Composition studies away from paradigmatic models and toward narrative models, of which Ethnography is a prime example" (6). This, according to Branscomb, has led to the proliferation and flourishing of teacher research models and "polyvocality" (6-7). Besides briefly recounting a popular history of ethnographic methods in composition, this chapter signals the acceptance and growth of the valuation of teaching narratives and the methods used to conduct and write the research. This is followed in the rest of the volume by accounts of individual scholars' struggles in applying and theorizing ethnography, but always while ultimately assigning value to its processes.

In Ethnography Unbound: From Theory Shock to Cultural Praxis, editors Stephen Gilbert Brown and Sidney I. Dobrin strive to make the same assertion seven years later, that despite continued criticism and questioning, critical ethnographic inquiry seems to be growing in use and here to stay. The book focuses on the practices of critical ethnography, which implicate action, change, and citizenship in the actions of the ethnographer. The individual authors in the anthology explore their ethos, decision making and projects, but more importantly for my purposes here, they explore the student as ethnographic researcher and the implications of teaching ethnographic inquiry in addition to practicing it ourselves as scholars, something I would like to explore in more depth.

Almost every chapter in this volume discusses the important fact that doing ethnography ultimately changes the researcher and the researched. It is an involvement in a community, a change in awareness of positionality. In "Critical Auto/Ethnography: A Constructive Approach to Research in the Composition Classroom," Susan S. Hanson describes a classroom where she "had organized the order of the reading and writing assignments to demonstrate that autobiography and ethnography operate on a continuum and to suggest that the two forms of narrative are inextricably connected" (183). Here she explores the transition she made from being a graduate student with a traditional understanding of autoethnography, to entering the field as a scholar and developing her own definition of the term in relation to composition pedagogy. For her purposes in this chapter she postulates that "As a composition pedagogy, critical auto/ethnography enables subjugated others (read students) to do systematic fieldwork and data production about subjects other than themselves, but without concealing what they learn about themselves in the process" (184). She seeks to combine here two types of writing and research that have come under fire in the field for being too limited and generalizing, namely autobiography and ethnography. By combining the terms, she hopes to create a new way to view the possibilities for the integration of the personal and methods of analyzing communities. Hanson explains:

> My aim in this chapter is to propose that critical auto/ethnography emerges at the interstices of autobiography and ethnography. I incorporate the slash (/) as a way to emphasize that critical auto/ethnography is committed, as is ethnography, to studying other people, but as an account of that process, it bridges the chasm between the autobiographical Here and the ethnographic There and lays bare the dynamics of self-other engagement....I advocate developing a pedagogical practice that emphasizes what students bring to the classroom by encouraging them to contribute to the production of ethnographic knowledge by becoming participant-observers in discourse communities engendering communicative practices that reproduce or resist dominant notions of race, class, gender, and literacy. Critical auto/ethnography meets this need (185).

Hanson recognizes the interdisciplinary history of qualitative research and believes that because of the many connections that can be made, it is more successful for students trying to learn to write than simply asking them to read and respond to texts. Bringing experiences and multiple methods of knowing into classroom research can help expand their understanding of their communities and themselves. Also, understanding what goes into the creation of the texts they read from other authors can help them gain the necessary authority to create valuable texts. As she continues to explain:

> Critical auto/ethnography emerges at the interstice of autobiography and ethnography, but as a research, writing, and reading strategy it encompasses literature, folklore, anthropology, sociology, linguistics, social history, and cultural geography. Additionally, because ethnographic research is central to much of the work that goes on within the humanities and social sciences as well as across the arts, business, education, law, and agriculture, showing students how the kinds of texts that form the basis of much of the scholarship that we assign as reading are produced makes good sense. It is a premise of this approach, however, that while reading surely improves writing, it is not necessarily the best place to begin in college composition classes, because to read well, which is to say critically, one needs to understand how language works in writing, how texts are constructed, what the choices are, how the pieces fit together, and to what end. And to understand writing, one needs to write extensively (188-89).

Hanson gives an overview of how her class is laid out in a ten-week quarter moving from autobiographical narrative to a final auto/ethnographic essay. She starts with an autobiographical narrative because "it helps me get acquainted with the students and the students with each other; second, it helps me help the students select a research topic that intersects with their own experiences, concerns, and interests" (192). She connects these initial pieces of writing to potential topics for field research and moves through a series of assignments that will be familiar to qualitative inquiry practitioners, including writing on spaces and description, annotated bibliographies, interviews, "emerging themes," ethnographies, and self-reflections (192-97). This course plan creates an increasing level of success with qualitative inquiry assignments. As Hanson explains,

> When I started teaching composition I slipped a few field research writing assignments into the syllabus....(Students') response to the field note assignments, the quality and length of their writing compared to the rest of their work, and their level of curiosity about ethnographic methods confirmed my suspicions: student like writing when they "get" the point. The next year I based the writing and reading assignments on autobiographic and ethnographic methods, texts, and theory, believing that undergraduates might actually "take" to academic writing given the opportunity to approach it auto/ethnographically. They do (197).

Hanson contends, in fact, that using these methods has reaffirmed for her the potential of all students to be good writers once they realize their connection to the writing and "perceive of themselves as having authority" (198).

Hanson is not the only one to report success with qualitative inquiry in her classroom. In the chapter "Writing Program Redesign: Learning from Ethnographic Inquiry, Civic Rhetoric, and the History of Rhetorical Education," Lynée Lewis Gaillet describes her creation of a course based on the methods in Sunstein and Chiseri-Strater's textbook Fieldworking: Reading and Writing Research, discussed earlier in this section. "Inspired by metropolitan university philosophies," she says, she created an ethnographic writing course:

> The ethnographic approach in this course takes advantage of the unique research opportunities available in Atlanta and surrounding communities. Higher education task forces advocating a metropolitan university philosophy of education indicate that the quality of student learning is directly related to the quality of students' involvement in their education. It is not enough, in other words, to say that a writing curriculum will involve public issues or demand that students venture out into their communities (105).

Gaillet asks students to engage in projects that identify and investigate issues and groups close to home that have importance to them. For her, "the ethnographic-based writing class answers the call for incorporating community experience in the academic classroom. Those involved in this project are "inventing" a new curriculum and pedagogy – adopting an interdisciplinary approach to writing instruction that is new and exciting for teachers and engaging for students; moreover, we are creating scenarios for conducting primary research and producing writing assignments tied to community experiences" (106). She sees the direct community impact of these projects and the excitement of the students who get to pick their own field sites and engage in ethnographic assignments, portfolio work, traditional research, and self-reflective writing (107).

The value and success of this work come from students being encouraged to engage in the same kind of writing that teachers and scholars in the field are doing. This helps teachers to explain the process of writing to the students and communicate how it can best be researched. The time spent by scholars in the field to theorize and consider important applications has made successful community-oriented and student-focused inquiry possible. In "Anti-Ethnography?" Ian Barnard recounts his own experiences with the use of ethnography in the field and how he applied what he knew to a class he taught in social sciences. He believes in an ethnographic pedagogy that makes students aware of the impact of their research and of how media and political representations shape meaning and understanding. Barnard states:

> These understandings of the real material impact of ethnographic writing…inform students' reading of and participation in writing in their disciplines and in their larger social and political contexts. Once students realize the extent to which representations of the Other enform material reality, their own rhetorical work takes on added urgency. This, of course, is also a challenge to compositionists, writing teachers, and all teachers, to intervene into the ethnographic project as it is variously manifested in our cultures and curricula, and to conceptualize this intervention as a question of writing as much as it is a question of history, politics, and sociality (8).

This extension into concepts of citizenship or connectedness to community and the importance of student writers' contribution can be hard to communicate and assess and might not be a goal for all teachers. While this is not a necessary outcome of ethnography in all situations, finding ways to understand their work in the world outside the classroom allows students to have a sense of authority and to value their personal experiences in a broader context.

Looking specifically at how this writing can lead to larger ethnographic projects, Howard B. Tinberg in "Ethnography in the Writing Classroom" advocates ethnographic methods and the creation of projects relating to issues of language use, diction, vocabulary and the value of words culturally, as a way to make composition curriculum more inclusive. He explains, "At a time when students are bringing increasingly diverse backgrounds into the classroom, ethnography, which would take as its subject the communities from which these students have come, would not only educate faculty and students alike in the ways of such communities but would make the classroom a setting for genuine and committed research" (79). This bridging of the gaps between classroom and community is the cornerstone of a more effective and productive classroom for Tinberg, as he explains: "It is important to emphasize that in 'doing ethnography' students ...are actively and genuinely doing research and that they are connected to the research they do. Moreover, in using ethnography teachers send a clear message to students that their communities are worthy of study even in, of all places, the classroom" (82). In describing the project of one of his students, Victoria, he offers a tangible example of a project that fostered a greater understanding of the writing process, community awareness, and the value of personal experience.

Wendy Bishop, a compositionist recognized for her work as both an ethnographer and teacher-researcher, created an important resource for students and scholars attempting to make qualitative research accessible for all involved. Ethnographic Writing Research: Writing it Down, Writing it Up, and Reading It stems from her own experiences in doing research and writing as a scholar and teacher and provides an important set of guidelines for this emerging field in composition. She frames the goals for her study:

> This book, in a way, may be seen as one translation, or an introduction to translations. For those initiating smaller classroom-based ethnographies, this text may provide a fieldguide or blueprint, an initial talking-through of issues and decision points. For those already involved in a deeper, long-term engagement with the methodology, this book will serve as a part of the conversation, pointing you toward issues (that no one can resolve, however much we enjoy and need to talk about them) and sources as you make your own contributions to field discussions in the form of finished ethnographies and meta-analyses of your methodology (xi-xii).

Bishop attempts to keep the category fluid in order to engage multiple perspectives on the value and uses of ethnography. As she does this she proclaims proudly that the book is "personal and anecdotal" and avoids the "high academic road" in order to be a piece that helps in thinking through things rather than just instructing or providing evidence (xii). Both her concepts and the way she engages the "I" in her writing broaden the possibilities for qualitative inquiry.

Although many have theorized its value and application, there are still many stories that recount a marbled history, similar to the history of personal writing in the field, as scholars have battled at different points in their lives to integrate ethnography effectively and in a scholarly way. In her 1992 piece "Ethnography and Composition: Studying Language at Home," (in Methods and Methodology in Composition Research edited by Gesa Kirsch and Patricia A. Sullivan) Beverly J. Moss explores her decision as a graduate student to choose ethnographic research as her dissertation method. "I knew then that I need my scholarly life to have some real connection to my personal life, that I needed a bridge between what I saw as a rather large gap between academic research and real problems that affected the people where I came from" (153). She was inspired by Shirley Brice Heath's work on the African American church and how she engaged in an ethnographic project that had strong personal relevance (153-54). In later chapters, I include student ethnographic projects that show the connections their work has to their personal lives.

What each of these authors explores in his or her own way is the concept of critical ethnography. According to D. Soyini Madison in Critical Ethnography, a conscious awareness is required as we use these methods in our classrooms and our own scholarship. She asks us to consider that performance is not just the doing but also the awareness of doing. This is essential when we engage the larger community in ethnographic research, and it is important for that awareness to be passed on to our colleagues and our students as readers of our research. Madison explains:

> One important theoretical view of performance addresses the notion of experience. This view asserts that experience begins from our uneventful, everyday existence. Moving inconsequentially through the daily, colorless activities of our lives, we flow through moments of ordinariness, nonreflection, and the mundane. We brush our teeth, ride the bus, wait in supermarket lines, and generally talk about the weather without excitement or happenstance. But then something happens, and we move to moments of experience. At this point, life's flow of uneventfulness is interrupted by a peak moment that breaks through the ordinariness, and we think and consider what has just happened to us. We give feeling, reason, and language to what has been lifted from the inconsequential day-to-day. We bring experience to it. The experience is received in consciousness and reflected upon: while brushing our teeth this particular morning, we notice a gray hair growing at the top of our head; while riding the bus, we meet an extraordinary person; while in the supermarket line, the cake box jogs a childhood memory; and while talking about the weather, we discover disturbing news. The mundane becomes heightened when gray hair conjures thoughts of aging; when an extraordinary person brings new insight; when the egg carton reminds us of licking mother's cake pan; and when the rainy weather brings news of tragedy and loss. (151)

We can communicate this awareness in both our writing and our actions, whether we use simple exercises that move bodies around in the classroom to create connection between the physical and mental or we ask our students to interview members of their community to broaden their ideas about subcultures.

Teachers Including Student Voices: Scholarship and Practice

In *The Performance of Self in Student Writing*, Thomas Newkirk discusses personal essays and the difficulty of critiquing them, mentioning the fear of invading students' privacy and "assuming the role of therapist" as just two unsubstantiated issues critics dwell on when discussing personal writing (19). In fact, he draws on his own analysis of personal writing forms and teaching them in his classroom to clarify his point of view. Although he is ultimately celebrating their value, he does discuss other potential problems.

Perhaps these concerns do go back our own classrooms, where it can be difficult to evaluate the personal writing efforts of our students, even though that is what many of us strive to elicit from them. How can we ask our students to be creative learners, perhaps participating in a composition classroom where we ask for alternative methods of inquiry, when we as scholars are often wary of how similar efforts outside the classroom will be evaluated by our peers? Since this use of the personal and qualitative methods is debated pedagogically within the classroom, perhaps it should come as no shock that it is debated outside it.

Including students in scholarship, as I do in this textbook, and teaching them the methods we theorize can be the first step for creating more space for those who do not necessarily have the power to create it for themselves. For Kirsch, "It is exactly this kind of change—a move away from competition and toward building connections between lived experience and academic subject matters—that educators…advocate in their model of connected education" (133). The people with whom we have the most interaction and share the most personal experiences are often in our own classrooms.

Qualitative inquiry can still be considered risky, but in discussing the successes and failures we can establish critical value and theory. Teaching as a practice in and of itself is not always easy, and perhaps one of the things teachers are most loath to discuss are failures in their classrooms. They are certainly not as likely to publish articles about failure, unless the lack of success was ultimately overcome. For Susan Hunter, "Even within our field there are dangers associated with talking and writing about teaching unless we authorize it in relation to some mode of inquiry" (Hunter 80). Hunter says composition teachers are constantly engaging in teaching practices that make us prone to failure because students are unused to methods, we are inexperienced, or we are relying heavily upon writing our students have had no prior exposure to. But admitting problems, especially in published articles, and telling others about our personal struggles in the classroom might be difficult.

> While theoretical perspectives, programmatic and disciplinary histories, and success stories are informative and necessary, we also need to credit the personal histories of teachers, even if they are less than encouraging about where the field of composition stands in relation to the center and the margins of the academy. Their accounts can give us a localized perspective, which we should value on a par with other kinds of perspectives because they capture the reality of the composition classroom. I know I would like to read what some of my freshman students clamor for: stories written by better storytellers than I am with characters and situations I can identify with (82-83).

Just like our students, we may find it valuable to read how other people are experiencing their jobs and their classrooms so we can better understand where we stand in relation to our peers, perhaps finding kindred souls and personalized advice. Engaging in teacher-research and recounting personal experiences in the classroom are important steps to creating a body of knowledge and the groundwork to critically appreciate our students' personal writing.

How to encourage students and ourselves to share these experiences without fear of failure is perhaps the most difficult part. In "Student Voices: How Students Define Themselves as Writers," Carol Lea Clark says the best way is to get students to write and be involved with us in the writing process. "Whether these students know it or not, or whether anyone else recognizes it or not, that pride in their words does make them writers" (228). It is important not only to ask our students to consider their personal experiences but for us as scholars and instructors to place the work of our students in the context of our own professional writing. Instilling a sense of authority in personal writing can demonstrate the critical value of this writing. Students can learn a lot by reading about the experiences of other students, as in the examples I provide in this textbook, and since we ask students to read much of what we ourselves are writing, students' stories are a valuable addition. This kind of incorporation can be a first step to recognizing the value of their personal participation and writing.

In "Students' Stories and the Variable Gaze of Composition Research," Bishop is able to clearly articulate the potential value of student stories. She explains:

> This kind of research will change composition studies. When teachers become researchers and students' stories, interpretations, and contributions count, then knowledge making and professionalization come into balance....And I do not believe a research methodology is useful unless it encourages and achieves some degree of methodological metaknowledge. Without such self-knowledge, something gets lost (210).

This "metaknowledge" can come from the ways that we actively theorize our expectations for student writing, both for them and for ourselves. This student writing we encourage is often not preserved; they submit portfolios and never collect them, drafts are lost, and we are forced to throw away thousands of papers if only for room on our desks. We are constantly bombarded with writing from our students that never makes it past our classrooms. Bishop discusses the need to have student voices in all research in order to make it valuable for the field and warns against the dangers of "student vacant" research (197).

> A research report based in student writers' experiences, which respected students' views, gave my students support for exploring their own writing. They felt that their dirty linen could finally be aired and the generally not-talked-about-but-important aspects of writing, like procrastination or grades, could be raised. They were pleased to encounter a composition article that spoke to them and appeared to detail student writing experiences authentically (199).

The kind of research and writing that includes student concerns and writing can encourage student interaction and empower us as researchers by demonstrating how we value this work. The key to the success of any methodology is theorizing our successes, failures and actions. This is not only important in our own scholarship but an essential thing for our students. Providing models will give the methodology the groundwork it needs to be critically successful. For Bishop, "Listening to students' stories helps me to remember that we occupy only a small portion of their lives, while they loom large in ours" (212).

Janice Hays notes that our ability to learn and interact begins when we are children and believes that merely staying aware of our natural tendencies will allow us to be effective instructors (161). This awareness is something that allows us to realize our own transformation along with the transformation of our students (161). Hays believes instructors must "support and challenge" simultaneously (168). She observes, "In teaching writing, such a pedagogy would regard discourse as a meaning-constructive activity, dialogic, a mutual construction of 'truth'; included in this dialogic process is the instructor's parental status as one who has greater knowledge and experience to share with students, while recognizing mutual participation in the process and mutual transformation in the process" (161). In this way you are not divorcing yourself from what you know; you are building upon it. As with Bishop's concept of "metaknowledge," you are tracking not only developments in student writing but your reactions to this development and how it shapes your teaching practices. As Andrea Lunsford suggests when talking about this student-teacher awareness, "Within this context, the embodied practices that dropped out of composition's regular curriculum in the nineteenth century (i.e., the recitation, declamation and speech making, extended reading aloud, and other oral forms associated with rhetoric) become significant tools for working powerful classroom transformations" (Lunsford 232-33). As I have explored in this introduction, it is a reintegration of the self and outside experiences in the classroom that can lead to the success of methodology that encourages teachers to clearly identify goals and values for personal writing, verbal sharing and qualitative research methods in the classroom and in our writing. This definition of criteria is the first step in creating a clear vision for how we value our own experiences and those of our students.

Compositionists strive to position themselves in the field among their students and to thus broaden the "academic community" to include the classroom. The teacher of composition is unique, as Hunter points out, in that she is constantly involved in "[c]onferencing, responding, collaborative learning, peer review, portfolios, journals, dialectical notebooks, freewriting, writing to learn, workshops—…the currently preferred ways of teaching writing that I use enable my students to form a community of writers, collaborating to make knowledge" (70-1). As we encourage students to tell their own stories, we can help them by devoting publishing space to them and their writing, as I do in this textbook. This can also help us to demonstrate how our life stories work and combine with the experiences of our students.

In looking at my own classroom practices, I demonstrate the value and potential for these kinds of projects in expanding our ideas of personal writing and the use of personal experience in the classroom. I contend that the melding of our traditional composition practices and new ideas from qualitative inquiry can help our field strike an ethical balance and critical awareness in teaching and utilization of personal writing in our classrooms and scholarship. We can combine writing intensive assignments with community engagement and analysis of positionality to create a holistic education model.

1. Understanding our Students' Relationship to "I"

Histories of individual relationships with writing, family histories and educational histories are just a few examples of what students may have been asked to write in order to ease into writing "formal" or "academic" essays in high school. In other words, personal writing is often used in the classroom as a warm-up exercise for "real academic writing." Using personal writing only as an untheorized method of introduction to other kinds of writing can distance students from their experiences and from their subjects of study. When these activities are not given critical attention, the result can be that although personal writing is used in the classroom, the manner in which it is critically considered may not be clear and thus most of its value can be lost for the student and for the teacher as well.

While the personal obviously is thought to have some value, since it is used so frequently in writing classrooms, many teachers may be missing numerous opportunities to draw on the personal critically. Personal writing does not necessarily describe deeply emotional and private moments, as many may assume. Instead, as I demonstrate throughout this book, the personal is a representation of individual and collective experience, sometimes serious, sometimes playful, but always rooted in ideas that are valuable and meaningful for the writer.

Among the possibilities for this kind of writing and for expanding the way personal writing is treated and theorized is using the classroom as a place for students to connect to each other and their teacher—to create a classroom community and even connect to the larger university community through extended critical projects that simultaneously engage personal interests and expand the potential consequences of these interests. Experiencing ideas in action can help you understand your positionality and the consequences of your positionality.

Activities and methods can be devised to help students and teachers build critically on the personal, by grounding it in method and theory, thus allowing first-year students to bring what they know to the classroom while simultaneously empowering them and allowing them to connect to other new students. For students who are already established in the university, the personal can enable them to contribute to their community. For teachers, the personal can create richer connections for building community in the classroom and can provide insight into the students' interests and connection to their academics and outside lives. It can encourage scholars to value our own personal experiences, positive and negative, and share them with the field in our own writing. Building a critical framework for the use of personal writing in the classroom can thus empower both students and scholars, who can then situate their work in a larger body of theory and scholarship. While not without its problems and complications, the introduction of verbal sharing into writing classrooms can provide valuable examples for this kind of engagement and expansion.

Min-Zhan Lu's essay "Reading and Writing Differences: The Problematic of Experience" portrays a pattern that appears within composition again and again; the desire for an ability to re-envision the classroom through our experiences and thus revise our understanding of one another as parts of the classroom community. According to Lu, "We need to imagine ways of using experience critically: experience should motivate us to care about another's differences and should disrupt the material conditions that have given rise to it" (239). When we can identify with certain elements of a story or piece of writing, we tend to focus on those experiences at the expense of other important elements and veins. Lu offers a concrete set of "exercises" for her students that will allow them to read and interpret a story based on their own experiences first, then take part in reading critical feminist discourse, and finally "re-vision" and rewrite their initial interpretation of the story from new perspectives, incorporating the viewpoints they have read about in order to learn how this can change their initial readings and help them see from new perspectives while analyzing their old perspectives (240). Exercises like the ones that Lu discusses, which encourage students to integrate real-world experiences into their academic writing, provide the basis for performance studies methodology and can foster positive effects on personal classroom writing practices.

Teachers have tried to build in the personal in direct and theorized ways. In "Personality and Persona: Developing the Self," Walter S. Minot discusses the value of building the self-esteem of his students through writing assignments that interrogate the concept of persona (353). He encourages the use of one form of performance, drawing on research suggesting that if we repeat something often enough or use a certain voice, we are more likely to accept it as our own. He argues essentially that embracing the concept of I, using it in speech and in writing, makes one more assertive (355). In other words, practicing something and utilizing it in multiple ways can make you believe in its value and applicability in a way that just writing it cannot.

But much confusion remains about the kinds of assignments we can use to engage students on a personal level while allowing them to develop their writing skills. Nancy K. Miller brings this issue to light in her discussion of teaching an autobiography class. What we need to ask of our students and what then to do with what we get is not always easy to figure out and value. Miller writes:

> So, on the assumption that the main thing was to write something, instead of a second critical essay I assigned the writing of what I called "autobiographical fragments." My notion in asking for short takes of personal experience was to bypass both the problem of institutional writing, with its canonized standards of correctness, and the plot of becoming that characterizes canonical autobiography (466).

While Miller encourages experimentation, she found herself afraid to read stories that were too personal and having a hard time determining how to grade and value a student's life. This is an issue that comes up often as scholars struggle with how to evaluate and teach personal writing, and it is something I will discuss in later chapters. Teachers have come up with their own ways of rationalizing and evaluating personal writing based upon individualized criteria and expectations. It is this kind of consideration of goals and value that can mitigate nervousness about evaluation. Miller also considers all personal writing to be something that requires a kind of secret-telling, which minimizes what I have defined as the personal throughout this study.

Ultimately, Miller realized the value by watching the reactions of her students and noticing how she reacted herself. It was valuable both for others in her class and for herself as an academic to hear other people's stories, no matter how well-written, touching or painful. She explains:

> Teaching autobiography provides texts for reading that engender the coming to writing in others. Perhaps the essence of autobiography as a genre—or rather one of its most valuable effects—is to enable this process. To say this is also to say that autobiography in its performance as text complicates the meaning and reading of social identity, and hence of the writing subject (468).

The students were able to analyze their positions in the classroom and relate to each other through the writing of the personal. This was not only empowering for them but enabled Miller to write her own piece for publication based on her experiences, thus helping her enact what she was teaching. In this way, Miller was able to analyze the situation and find value in the experience, thus contributing to a larger framework for the analysis and valuation of the personal.

Other scholars such as Janice Hays recommend programs of teaching in which students are encouraged to be personal and reflect on their experiences and then "branch out" from there. According to Hays, "The use of personal narrative as topic material or as a springboard for more analytic writing can ensure that students do not find analytic writing irrelevant and dull, even though it may be general or abstract" (174). As I have mentioned, for notions of personal writing to be valued and expanded, scholars need to move away from the concept of the personal as simply a "springboard" to more important or critical writing and understand what function it serves in their classrooms. Although problematic, Hays' view does still show that in the classroom, many academics believe in the value of "writing ourselves," even if their criteria and analysis of goals are underdeveloped.

Min-Zhan Lu suggests that often we create exercises for our students that allow them to experience what they read on a personal level, although we leave little room for this in our own professional scholarship. She says, "The task facing a teacher is to help students rethink ways of using personal experience so that readings through the personal will not be at the expense of other stories and selves" (242). If we use the personal only as a "step" to other things, we are not valuing it in and of itself for our students or ourselves. We are unable to understand our environment in a critical way if we are unable to understand how we are situated within it. Lu thus believes:

> We need assignments that ask students to explore the analytic possibilities of experience by locating the experience that grounds their habitual approach to differences; by sketching the complex discursive terrain out of and in which the self habitually speaks; by investigating how that terrain delimits our understanding of differences along lines of race, class, sex and gender; and by exploring personal and social motivations for transforming one's existing self-location in the process of rereading and rewriting (243).

Instead of using the personal only as a set of uncritical stepping stones, we need to theorize its function and application.

We need a methodology for theorizing the personal that is applicable in the classroom as well as in our scholarship. Such a methodology has to extend beyond limited notions of personal writing and evaluation and include theoretical value for the entire academic community. In the next chapter, I will provide ideas for how to introduce students to interacting with their audiences. I suggest throughout this chapter that the practice of these methods as well as the teaching of them will provide the consistency and connections necessary to make the personal productive for both students and teachers.

2. Getting Started in the Classroom

Overview

In this chapter, I will demonstrate how you can begin a semester-long class that draws on personal writing and qualitative inquiry. I will break down a number of ideas and small introductory assignments in detail. All assignments will be in a form that you can distribute to students.

I will not be including readings for students in this textbook. I encourage all teachers to choose readings that they find relevant for students, based upon their focus and desired classroom outcomes. I will make reference to value I find in a few pieces I regularly include in my classroom. These assignments would be appropriate for the first one to three weeks of class.

The Public Nature of the Classroom

Before I start any writing in the classroom, I introduce a few concepts about the nature of nonfiction writing. Probably one of the most important things to note, and one of the first things I say to students, is that all writing in the class should be treated as public. This means that no writing should ever be considered for my eyes only. Each student should expect to share personal writing with classmates at some point.

This is important to note for a number of reasons. In treating every piece of writing as public, students become aware that they are talking about real people, the self included, and that they have an obligation to consider their writing and their audience carefully. This also helps students to become aware of what they are willing and not willing to explore when the interaction is more than the private back-and-forth with their teacher. It is an important first lesson in taking ownership of content and voice and considering a broader perspective (particularly one that is not giving them a grade).

Given the public nature of their writing for class, I emphasize that being mindful of feedback and commentary is very important, since all writing is about real people. I encourage students to be honest and specific in their feedback as readers and open and willing recipients of critique as writers. They need to make ethical choices about how they portray people, being mindful of the opinions of the subjects. This discussion sets a tone of respect and openness that will guide the rest of the course.

Warm-up Exercises

Here I will give a few examples of early semester exercises that will prepare students to engage in personal writing and qualitative inquiry in a critical and productive way. Starting off with fieldwork and discussion sets a tone that can be carried throughout the semester, one that values individual voice, audience, and research. For each assignment, I will offer an overview of the exercise, details of the task and, in the results section, reflection on the value of the assignment.

The First Day of Class

On the first day of class, I ask students to do a freewrite about what the terms personal writing and academic writing mean to them. This is a great jumping-off point in that it allows you to learn what students have been taught over the years about the value of the self, the use of I and which writing has value. It can be the start of a discussion about how they might come to understand these terms differently in their college-level writing classes. It also creates a great moment for you to share your knowledge and perspective on the terms and how they will be used in your course.

In addition, freewrites are a great tool to use throughout the semester when you are introducing a new topic for discussion. They allow students to pause and engage the idea before sharing their thoughts with the class. This often gives them more confidence to participate and more ideas to contribute to discussion. Try to include freewriting in your course plan each time you introduce a new topic.

Freewrite Assignment

What is personal writing? What is academic writing?

Over the course of the semester, I will be asking you to create responses through something called freewriting.

Freewriting is also known as stream-of-consciousness writing—essentially writing whatever comes to mind on a particular subject. The theory behind freewriting is to allow your mind to make connections among given topics and your own thoughts and experiences. It is not meant to be an edited piece of formal writing, but rather an exploration of your responses to a particular topic.

Throughout this course, it will be necessary to make connections with one another and focus on communicating clearly and effectively with classmates. This first exercise will help you get to know your fellow students, consider the focus for the class, and also to get acclimated to sharing your writing with your peers.

For this exercise, I would like you to write about the terms personal writing and academic writing and what they mean to you. You will be writing continuously for twelve minutes.

The goal of a freewrite is to keep your pen or pencil to the paper for the entire length of time I give you to write. It is natural for the mind to wander. Often in life we are thinking of many things at the same time: class, how hungry we are, what time it is. When you feel as if you have run out of things to say or you find you can no longer focus on the topic, don't stop writing! Simply continue to write about what is distracting you and carefully make your way back to the topic. These pieces are not collected or graded, so do not edit yourself. Write whatever comes to mind in response to the prompt. Be prepared to read this writing out loud for the class. We will define the two terms as a group based on your contributions.

Results

Typically, students will be very flustered by this exercise. They will feel that you want a specific answer from them and will struggle with how they view each term. Usually, I find that students have still been encouraged to keep the personal out of the academic and have a hard time understanding how the two might be combined. It always creates a fascinating discussion and an opportunity to share stories about rules for writing and how students might reconsider some of the things they've been taught. I have the students share pieces from their writing and use the board to create lists of ways we currently think about our writing and ways we might adjust our perspectives in this class. As the discussion progresses, I add my own ideas for how these terms will be treated in our classroom.

The Importance of Observation

How to properly use and conduct observations will be one of the most important skills your students will acquire in this course. Having strong observational skills is key to being a successful writer, but for many people this does not come naturally. In a busy world, we often block out a lot of our daily experiences in order to focus on what we perceive as more important tasks. Many of the exercises for this course will encourage students to pause, take in these small moments in everyday life, and reflect on them.

When students think about observation, many will go directly to the idea of visual observation. This is not surprising, since we live in a visually oriented culture. However, when trying to convey an experience to someone who is outside of the experience, it is important to consider the value of other senses. For example, if someone visually describes a cafeteria, many of us will flash back to our own experiences in cafeterias. But if the writer is careful to share the smells, sounds and textures of a particular space, people will be able to relate their own experiences but understand how their environment differs. This exercise will help students focus on using their five senses to describe a situation.

The Deep Observation Assignment

Spend at least twenty minutes in a public space, observing one person you have never seen or met before. The person need not be someone who strikes you as interesting. In fact, somebody who appears to be less than interesting to you is often the best choice for this assignment.

This is a difficult assignment for a number of reasons. It is hard to find someone who will be still and accessible for twenty minutes; if the person moves, move with him or her. The subject also might become aware of being observed. This is not a problem; simply talk to the person if he or she inquires, or move on to another observation if it seems at all bothersome to the person being observed. Your goal is not to make someone uncomfortable but to pause and consider your environment and those who inhabit it.

Using your five senses, take notes on everything around you and everything about the person, focusing on the subject's appearance, how she carries herself, her actions and interactions, the way she interacts with her environment, any speech you might overhear, the feeling, look, smell and feel of the space your subject inhabits.

After you have finished taking notes, as close to the observation time as possible, construct a narrative description of this person and his or her life based on the details you have recorded.

This is an assignment you may enjoy doing more than once. If you are riding public transportation or have free time in a public space, you can practice your observational skills and storytelling abilities by basing pieces on this real-life observational note taking.

This is a fiction-writing assignment based on real observation and will be shared during class discussion.

Results

These are the strongest initial pieces of student writing in my class for a number of reasons.

Writing anything personal can be very challenging at first, since students can feel vulnerable and unsure about how they portray themselves and those they know. Starting with a fictional exercise that draws on real, observed detail opens up student writers to discussing all aspects of a person without fear. They do not feel as exposed personally or as bad about making judgments because their pieces are not intended to be truthful. Here they have the luxury of writing about a stranger in a fictional way.

In addition, the exercise allows students to take observed information and create a story from it, and that skill will be immensely helpful in their research as they amass notes and have to make sense of the information they have collected, identifying threads and narrative connections as well as contradictions and dissonance.

Since the exercise is based on limited information, it makes students rely on their own points of view and recognize how judgment and stereotyping play a role in their research and observations.

I encourage students to pick someone not particularly noteworthy, which forces them to be creative. They probably would have an easier time writing about things that are "striking" rather than commonplace. In general, when we conduct any sort of research, we are more likely to end up with many run-of-the-mill details and few aha moments; it is important to recognize the necessity of both in a narrative.

Students will quickly realize how much information they can gather in a small amount of time when they focus their attention. This will be useful in all other assignments that ask them to gather information and re-create experiences.

On a practical level, students will begin to practice taking notes and converting them into text. They will recognize the value of spoken language they might hear while conducting observations and will practice how to become an unobtrusive part of an environment they are observing.

The process will show that research is messy and often does not produce the result we assume or intend. That does not mean it is a failure. It means they will need to practice and improve their observation skills so they are able to draw on their surroundings and become more observant on a daily basis.

In sharing these pieces orally with classmates, they will be able to hear other student narratives and participate in a discussion about varied approaches to observation. You as the teacher can fill in any gaps and provide information that you feel was not covered in the discussion of their writing.

Examples of this assignment can be found in Chapter 12.

Writing from Other Viewpoints

It is often difficult for us to put ourselves in someone else's shoes. Training students to consider things from other peoples' perspectives is essential when they are writing about people as characters qualitatively. If they cannot imagine that other peoples' perspectives differ from their own and are informed by different life experiences, they will not be able to write successfully about themselves or the people they research.

This is an assignment students can do in class or at home. I think it works best the first time in a group so they can compare and analyze what they have written and see how the versions differ. Unlike deep observation, this assignment does not require that they observe as outsiders; instead they must try to put themselves into the heads of the people they are considering.

> ### Point-of-View Writing Exercise
>
> As a class, go to a place outside the classroom. If you do not have access to any outdoor space, which would be the best choice for this assignment, simply choose a space where you will be able to sit comfortably and observe other people. Sometimes a cafeteria or a study lounge will work for these purposes.
>
> As an individual exercise outside of class, you can do this in any public space where you plan to spend a long period of time.
>
> Once you are comfortably situated in the space, use a notebook with four separate pages to freewrite from at least four different perspectives about the space around you. The intention behind this exercise is to look at the same space and group of people but to adjust your viewpoint. You are not allowed at any time in the writing to mention directly what perspective you are writing from and what your viewpoint is or to use any word given in the prompt. Instead, you must use your five senses and try to imagine writing about the environment as if you were a different person.
>
> You can write based on mood: angry, sad, pensive, joyous. You can imagine a life situation: just fell in love or broke up with someone, just got a new job or lost a job, just returned from overseas or are eager to travel. You can write from almost any perspective imaginable, influenced by factors like socioeconomic status, gender, age, work title, and countless others.
>
> Later, when you are in class, take one of the pages you think is your strongest and hand it to the teacher, who will mix up all the pages and redistribute them. Students will then read aloud the pieces they have been given and will discuss what point of view they think each is written from and why. Once all the pieces have been read, there can be a discussion of the similarities among the pieces that were from a particular viewpoint, the ways in which they differed and why.

Results

This exercise, much like the deep observation assignment, is all about stereotypes and judgment. Where do students draw their assumptions about what it might be like to see the world through the eyes of someone with a different gender identity or different amount of wealth? Ideas can come from personal experience, what they see in the media and the kinds of expectations they have from life. Usually a pattern of similarities emerges in writing from the same perspectives but styles of approach differ greatly, depending on the group. Students can learn a lot about how their own life experiences affect the way they perceive others and what it might be like to experience things in others' positions. Recognizing their own prejudices and assumptions is essential to being open to other peoples' points of view.

Keeping a Writing Journal

As students begin to practice their observational skills, I encourage them to keep a journal, whether it be a paper journal or just notes on a phone or tablet. This allows them to practice being aware of their surroundings and to take time to reflect on daily experiences. I never collect or grade these journals, but I encourage them to write often to practice for larger assignments. They are a great space to practice the first two writing assignments on their own time outside class.

> ### Journal Guidelines/Assignment
>
> For many, journals are a way to share or express emotions in private. People can come home from a long day, sit down and just let all their stress flow onto the page. For other people, journals might act more like a scrapbook for keeping sketches, photos, pieces of paper that could serve as inspiration for art projects, designs, or writing a book.
>
> Consider your own experiences with journaling. Have you ever kept a diary? When you were young? Recently? Was it consistent? Sporadic? Did you write only when you were feeling emotional or nostalgic?
>
> Today there are a lot of options for journaling, and it can be private or very public. If you are part of any social networking site, you are probably aware of how personal thoughts, emotions or actions make their way onto the Internet. Many people choose to keep blogs that cover adventures, traveling, daily life, and relationships. They may chronicle small adventures on social media like Twitter, Facebook, Instagram or Tumblr. Sites like Livejournal have provided a direct forum for those who want to go public with their most private thoughts.
>
> Publishing a diary is no new concept, however. Thinking historically and from our individual pop culture knowledge, there are a great number of examples of people publishing private journals. Famous writers, like Sylvia Plath and Anais Nin, have had their journals published in their entirety. Musicians such as Kurt Cobain and artists such as Leonardo Da Vinci and Vincent Van Gogh have made the form important, and so have a few people who have gone through harrowing experiences, such as Anne Frank.
>
> Consider the value of keeping a journal. How can you use this form to help in your other writing? To reflect on experiences? To sharpen your observational skill and engage your world on a daily basis?

Results

Students find that practicing daily observation and reflection allows them to develop their writing voice. Most students will not keep a daily journal, but even if they make a few entries over the course of semester, this can improve the ease with which they approach their larger, more formal writing assignments and may develop into a valuable writing habit well beyond the scope of your class.

Intro readings

In the first few weeks of class, I use a few foundational texts to give students an overview of the field of creative nonfiction, the broad category in which personal writing is usually placed.

Becky Bradway and Douglas Hesse's Creating Nonfiction: A Guide and Anthology offers a nice overview of the variations in the genre. I have students read the first two chapters from this because it gives a nice, if dry, overview of the many types of creative nonfiction while providing a brief analysis of relevant examples. By also defining what creative nonfiction is not, it helps students get an idea of the wide range of disparate texts that fall and don't fall within this category. Bradway and Hesse write: "Creative nonfiction allows for a certain looseness of exploration. Some writers…are attracted to creative nonfiction for its very lack of definition. Over 250 years ago Samuel Johnson defined the essay as 'a loose sally of the mind; an irregular indigested piece; not a regular and orderly composition.' This very irregularity is what makes creative nonfiction so much fun to write, if the writer is comfortable with that openness" (8).

In their survey, they include memoir, essay, critiques, rants, reviews, lyric and reflective essays, place writing, the city essay, and literary journalism. This is a list I will include examples from but also deviate from when I include more qualitative examples later in the course. Bradway and Hesse make important points for students starting off, who need to consider objectivity and truth telling as foundations for all personal writing.

The authors state: "It is supposed to be true to the author's best ability. The story and people in creative nonfiction are based upon actual events, people, and information" (7). Yet at the same time, unlike what students might have experienced previously in their research, "Creative nonfiction makes no pretense of objectivity; the writer admits that she is coming from her own point of view" (7).

Lee Gutkind's "The Five 'R's of Creative Nonfiction" is a great starter piece as well. In his essay, Gutkind creates scenes, showing us his "fly on the wall" approach while discussing the importance of critical elements in creative nonfiction writing. Students enjoy the way Gutkind employs the strategies he suggests in his own essay. It's a fun and engaging piece, and I find that with the more instructional pieces, it is useful to see the authors using the methods they suggest. The five Rs Gutkind discusses are real life/immersion, reflection, research, reading and (w)riting (3-6). He stresses the need for students to read other writers, to reflect on the value in their writing, and to research experiences, even their own. He encourages students to step outside of the classroom to recognize the importance of the larger world in their writing. "I design assignments that force my students out into their communities for an hour, a day, or even a week so that they see and understand that the foundation of good writing emerges from personal experience" (9). By demonstrating the value of action in an essay, he highlights the importance of scene: "The creative nonfiction writer will show…subject, place, or personality in action" (9). His organizational ideas on creating narrative frame are also very useful.

Conclusion

These initial exercises should open up discussion for the students and allow them to examine their own perspectives on the outside world. They will begin to practice skills that will be essential to their longer essay writing and also make small realizations about how others view the same thing in different ways. You do not have to do all of these assignments, but I find that in conjunction they provide a great basis and important tools for the upcoming larger essays.

3. Writing Essays for Class: The First Steps

Overview

In this chapter, I will focus on a few ideas that will inform the students' formal writing for the semester. I will begin by reviewing concepts that may be confusing for students creating personal nonfiction and qualitative narratives. These will be in a form that you can distribute to students, much like the assignments of the previous chapter. I will also include more difficult exercises that ask students to establish themselves as interesting parts of the narratives they are creating. These are important steps moving toward the larger, longer autoethnographic writing they will be doing for their research assignment. This work should appear in the third and fourth weeks as preparation for the larger essay. For all extended writing assignments, especially longer essays, I encourage using a drafting process that allows students to work with classmates from invention of concept, to initial draft, to final version and rewrite, if necessary.

The "Who Cares?" Factor

In all classroom writing, one of the biggest issues is what I like to call the "Who cares?" factor. It is a rude question that I often pose to myself as a writer and feel is important to pose to my students. Sure, I can write a piece about this or that, but who cares? Inherent in this question are many considerations about audience. In all of their writing, students should have an intended audience. Audience is often dictated to us, whether by a professor, peers, a boss, a colleague, a friend or a family member. Just as students adjust their writing style to suit each occasion when they are directly aware of their audience (I would assume most of us would not write an email to our boss the same way we might to our great aunt), they need to have an audience they have identified for their formal writing in class. This intention is key to the success of their pieces. In addition, creating something they care about is essential to the success of any piece of writing. If they cannot include themselves in the answer to "Who cares?" nobody will benefit. Sure, they may care to the extent that their teacher is making them write something and will be assigning them a grade on that piece of writing. Above and beyond that, though, what do they want to accomplish in their essays? Outside of school, students will often be asked to develop ideas and pieces for intended audiences they have identified as important. They will be filling a hole in research, trying to reach a certain demographic, marketing themselves as artists, or applying for jobs. This same motivation, beyond pleasing the teacher, has to guide all of their writing, so this is a good time to practice. And as their teacher, you want them to care about their writing because it makes your work that much more interesting.

Creating Subtext

Subtext is one of the most difficult concepts to grasp. I repeatedly ask my students, once we have taken into account the "Who cares?" factor, what the subtext is. For instance, a piece of writing could be about home, but what other themes emerge in the piece? A good piece of writing is always complex, just like a good movie or television show. There are many links, many story lines that come together within the main narrative. Nobody just writes a piece about home. Often, when they write about home, people are also writing about many other things such as loss, moving, change, growing up, familial relationships, rituals, traditions, and the importance of objects and spaces. Subtext is created by being specific about experiences and observations. The more specific a writer can be, the more effective the writing. In wholeheartedly trying to capture the detail and nuance of their own experiences, students are more likely to hit upon ideas that will resonate with a more diverse audience. That is because everyone can identify with a good story that has many themes running through it. The more well-defined themes the writer has, the more potential there is for a wider interested audience. One of my favorite pieces to share with students in the first days of class is "Maternal Connections" by Carolyn Ellis. Ellis is an ethnographer who has written a number of textbooks on the process of autoethnographic and ethnographic writing, as well as many first-person autoethnographic pieces. This particular piece is only four textbook pages long and very similar in size and scope to the types of assignments students will be doing. It is a master class in how much can be accomplished in a very short span of time (measured in both pages and experience). In this piece from her book Composing Ethnography, Ellis describes four nights taking care of her mother, who is ill and hospitalized. In it, she uses all of the elements you want students to understand how to use in a piece of autoethnography or personal writing. She includes brief dialogue to give her mother a voice, detailed descriptions, well-defined themes and subtext. The themes in the piece are somewhat mature and may not have been readily experienced by the students. Taking care of an older relative in an intimate way, the unpleasantness of illness and hospitalization, aging, the body, and confronting life choices involving having a family or remaining childless are all parts of the narrative. Although they are not things most students of traditional college age have experienced, a few will recognize them as familiar and all can imagine a future in which they will be confronted with many of the questions and themes that arise. Ellis' writing is a great example of how being very specific to one's own experiences can end up being more universal than a piece that is trying to appeal to everyone. Throughout, she builds up to questions about her own potential for motherhood and desire for it. Asking questions of herself in the text allows the reader to question the choice of motherhood. Ellis is able to accomplish a tremendous amount very quickly. She describes the experience:

> Taking care of her feels natural, as though she is my child. The love and concern flowing between us feels like my mom and I are falling in love. The emotionality continues during the four days and nights I stay with her in the hospital. My life is devoted temporarily to her well-being. She knows it and is grateful. I am grateful for the experience. I do not mind that she is dependent on me. I am engrossed by our feeling, by the seemingly mundane but, for the moment, only questions that matter. Are you dizzy? In pain? Comfortable? Do you want to be pulled up in bed? Can't you eat one more bite? Do you need to pee? Have gas? Want water? Prefer to sleep now? As I help with these events, I do not question their meanings, as I so often do about most things in my life….Experiencing unconditional love for my mother makes me, for the moment, crave to feel it toward and from a child as well. Do I just want someone who will wash me when I'm 79? What if something is wrong with the baby? What about my career? Travel plans? Yet how can I omit this meaning-giving experience from my life? (242-3).

The difficulties and rewards of writing about her relationship with her mother have also been described and analyzed by Ellis. She considers the ethics of writing about her mother in "With Mother/With Child: A True Story." This companion piece is a great way to introduce the necessity of considering the people you are writing about and allowing them to view pieces you plan to make public. While this piece is brutally honest, it is also very carefully considered by its author and its subject.

Writing the Self as a Character

In another one of my favorite readings to share in the first weeks of class, Philip Lopate describes obstacles facing the student writer of personal essays in "Writing Personal Essays: On the Necessity of Turning Oneself into a Character":

> ...I am inclined to think that what stands in the way of most personal essays in not technique but psychology. The emotional preparedness, if you will, to be honest and open to exposure.

The student essayist is torn between two contrasting extremes:

> "I am so weird that I could never tell on the page what is really, secretly going on in my mind."

> "I am so boring, nothing ever happens to me out of the ordinary, so who would want to read about me?" (40)

This and a companion piece by Lopate that I will discuss are important because they encourage the student writer to think about herself as a topic of interest. Finding the self interesting and being able to write about the self as a theme are challenging for anyone. How often are we turned off by a piece because someone seems to have too high an opinion of herself? Or how often do we become frustrated because an author seems unable to understand his own circumstances and how they affect his interpretation? How often do we find people's stories boring or irrelevant when socializing, or think we have nothing interesting to contribute about our own boring lives? Then there are the people who can make every day seem like an adventure, in which tales of buying groceries, riding the train, or getting a haircut all seem like the most interesting things you've ever heard. Some people who have survived plane crashes or accomplished extraordinary things still seem rather dull. Creating interest is all about choosing the right details and establishing voice.

Lopate says in his piece that both of the student writer's contrasting extremes—"I am so weird" and "I am so boring"—reflect a lack of understanding that we are all inherently weird and normal. "In short, they (students) must be nudged to recognize that life remains a mystery—even one's own so-called boring life. They must also be taught to recognize the charm of the ordinary: that daily life has nourished some of the most enduring essays" (40).

It is interesting, after reading this process piece, to have students read and examine Lopate's "Portrait of My Body," in which he describes his own features at length as a way to present himself as a character. Notably, while he is self-deprecating, Lopate is careful never really to say anything negative about himself. Each thing he points out as a flaw is later redeemed, leaving readers ultimately confused and feeling the ego need to engage in such an undertaking, with each aspect of a rather ordinary body being compared to a celebrity or author such as Sandy Koufax or Cesare Pavese. It is this fluctuation between narcissism and self-deprecation that is so fascinating and revealing. Some examples are charming, such as the aura a student describes seeing around his head, while some are off-putting, notably a few pages discussing his penis.

With statements such as "They claim that men who have long, long fingers also have lengthy penises. I can tell you with surety that my fingers are long and sensitive, the most perfect, elegant, handsome part of my anatomy," (222) a vibrant discussion of how to write about the self is sure to follow. As Lopate says, most students find themselves at one of two extremes, immensely entertaining or terribly boring. In reality, most of us probably fall somewhere in between.

The Ellis and Lopate pieces are also interesting in considering the differences between nonfiction and fiction. If might be uncomfortable enough to read a piece describing intimate parts of anyone's body, but to know that is supposed to represent the truth is an entirely different story. It is an important reminder that personal writing is a vulnerable task, one that lays us on the table to be seen and judged. Writers are not, however, passive victims in this process. They have to choose what they put out there and recognize they are discussing real people who are vulnerable and need to be treated with respect.

I often ask my students how they would feel if they knew someone had written a nonfiction piece about them for a class, or how the people they write about would feel if were given the pieces to read? Something that might initially seem like a good idea, in fact, may be hurtful to the subject, who can feel vulnerable or even humiliated by another's characterization. That's why the most important first step in writing anything in nonfiction and personal writing is to make the self vulnerable, to more fully understand what it feels like to be the focus of truthful scrutiny. Through this process, students can begin to understand how to use the tools they have at hand to guide readers to the conclusions they wish to reach while treating their subjects, including themselves, carefully and ethically.

Self-as-Character Assignment

We all love a good character, someone who is complex yet relatable, full of all of the human foibles we are aware of, who may act differently from what we could ever anticipate.

This is by far the hardest assignment of the semester and also your first major assignment. Unless you have been honing your persona in writing for many years, you will have a hard time with this piece.

For this assignment, you will need to write a self-portrait. There are many ways you can do this. You can identify a structural element that allows you to move through personality traits, use interesting qualities or amusing actions to form a story or create narrative story lines that let us see you at your best and worst. So much of writing this piece is about making choices. Lopate chose to write about himself using his body as a device to make different kinds of observations about his character and personality. Other writers, like Geeta Kothari, chose food to talk about themselves as characters.

Choose a device that you can use to explain yourself as a character. A device is something we will practice with in many of the writing assignments—a tool that allows you to tell a story in a logical way when you might not otherwise have been able to tell it organically in the structure of your narrative.

However you approach this piece, make sure to focus on yourself in an interesting way. In other words, for better or worse, make yourself a character we want to hear and care about.

This work will be shared with classmates during class discussion.

Results

This is usually a breakthrough moment in class. Everyone, including the teacher, is made completely vulnerable at the same time as they present portraits of themselves for the group to hear and discuss. Before the sharing process, I ask students to take note of what stands out to them in other students' narratives. The students and the teacher then share, without pause for comment, and the class has a follow-up discussion about what was noteworthy.

This exercise, including the sharing process, is important because students will begin to understand the parts of themselves that resonate with their peer audience and how they might use these elements to their advantage as they create their voice in other, longer essays. Usually this is the first time students have tried, perhaps outside of social media, to make themselves cohesive characters. Some will share their doubts and struggles, while others will celebrate their quirks and accomplishments. Developing an individual voice and a sense of self will be important for all of their other writing during the semester. By establishing themselves as figures of authority who are self-aware and have valuable perspectives, they will communicate more effectively with their intended audiences.

Additional Readings

When the class works on defining character, I like to include pieces that examine different elements of experience and memories that authors use to do so. These authors use everything from cultural experience to food and schooling to define important moments in their lives and character development.

I use Geeta Kothari's "If you are what you eat, then what am I?" because it has an easily relatable topic with an unusual structure. Kothari uses a broken-up style, recounting a series of related instances involving food. Having grown up with a first-generation Indian mother who worked hard to make simple "American" food such a tuna salad, and having a meat-eating life partner, she finds herself constantly at odds with the food cultures around her. She recounts her own childhood experiences in traveling to India and her lack of interest in Indian cooking until she became an adult and tried to re-create memories of childhood. Kothari requires the reader to make her own connections by juxtaposing these related but different moments in time. This is both a stylistic choice and a stumble in the piece. I suggest students bridge the difficult territory of filling in the connections for their readers, rather than making the readers figure it out for themselves. Students will, however, readily relate to the significance of food in culture, memory, family structure and relationships.

In her piece "Talking in the New Land," Edite Cunha draws on a lot of ideas that can be very inspiring for students. Having immigrated to the United States as a young child, she uses three main examples to show the challenges she faced. She begins this essay by talking about how her first teacher changed her name to "Americanize" it and demonstrates how names can identify us. Most students will be able to trace a connection to their own names, whether those names are inherited from relatives, have religious meaning, were inspired by love for a celebrity, or causeds problems because of spelling, pronunciation, or assumptions made by those who heard them. Cunha explores how as she a child she had to take care of very adult things on behalf of her parents, who were not as proficient in English as she. At ten she was trying to get money for the family and negotiating with a woman who wanted heirlooms she had left behind in the house Cunha's family purchased from her. Her struggles with language and cultural identity as a child are obviously relevant for many young writers.

Although Jamaica Kincaid's "Girl" is a prose poem, it is a strong stylistic example of how character is and is not defined. In a series of directives, the main character is told how to do a variety of tasks and how not to do others. There are hardly any moments of pause, and the onslaught of advice is overwhelming. The voice of the girl is barely heard, yet at the end we get a clear picture of who the girl is supposed to be and who is there to guide her.

In a similar vein, Margaret Atwood uses lists and scenes in "The Female Body" to demonstrate the way the female body has been used for everything from advertising to patriotism. She reflects on the importance of the Barbie doll, the modifications women make to their bodies and the function of the male brain. This piece is quite aggressive and can spark a lot of good discussion about gender roles, how bodies define us, and how culture determines value.

Conclusion

These initial longer writing assignments will help students find a voice and consider the importance of intention and perspective in their writing. If they are able to master the exercises in Chapters 2 and 3, they will be well prepared for the larger essay assignments in the remainder of the class.

4. Workshop and Peer Review Process

Overview

It is essential as the instructor to create space in the classroom for the students where they feel free to comment on and discuss each other's work. Your feedback is important, and so is the feedback they receive from their peers.

For all major assignments, I give students narrative written feedback. I do not copy edit or make a large number of marginal comments. I find in my experience that the more you can tell a story in your feedback, the easier it is for the students to process and incorporate your comments. This may not be a method that works for everyone, but I have found it to produce the best conversations and results.

In the remainder of this chapter, I will outline the two major methods I use to help students give peer feedback.

Workshops

As often as possible, I try to make time in the class schedule for a large class workshop. This means each student will get to read her or his entire short work to the class for feedback. At my home institution, we are lucky to have a manageable class size of eighteen or twenty for our writing courses, making the full class workshop possible for everyone. If you have a larger class, you can alternate workshopping assignments, splitting up students so that only a few read each class period, making sure that everyone gets at least one chance to receive a full class workshop on a piece over the course of the semester. Another alternative when time in limited is to ask them to engage in a common practice of sampling sections of their longer pieces to share with the entire class. This mimics the process of a public reading in which authors are often asked to share pieces of longer works in hopes of encouraging the audience to want to read more. It is an important skill to develop and helps students see where the heart of a piece lies.

The rules I use for a workshop are common practice for many creative writing classes. Students are asked to read their work as written without any explanation. This helps the class hear the work as it appears on the page, closer to the experience of an outside reader unfamiliar with the person behind the writing and that person's reasons for writing it. We have the added advantage of hearing each student's voice, and this is also good practice for students who might want to share their work in a larger forum.

When students first share their work with the class, we follow a few simple rules. I draw a lot of principles for initial workshops from the Amherst Writers & Artists method. Pat Schneider's book *Writing Alone and With Others* is a great resource and includes guidelines to build support and community in writing groups. Drawing on Schneider's book, we offer only positive feedback to each other initially. This kind of feedback can include what we liked about the text, what stood out to us, what we remembered. This creates a safe space for the students to share first drafts of their writing. This work has not been critiqued or significantly edited, so sharing out loud and commenting in this way helps build student confidence. Students read in succession without pause.

I encourage them to jot down things they like during the readings or to just take careful notice of what stands out to them. We then share our thoughts as a group. I also participate, reading work of my own and taking notes to model the behavior. This is a great way for students to get to know and trust each other and you. They start building community by referring to each other by name with the aid of name tags they keep on their desks for the first four weeks of class. If room allows, it also helps to have everyone sit in a circle when sharing.

Peer Review

Peer review is an essential part of the writing process. To facilitate review beyond the larger class workshop, which is not possible for extended pieces due to time constraints, I break students into small groups of three to five members, depending on class size, and have them exchange drafts. The first thing students do is write down concerns they have about their own writing. These concerns may include doubts about whether the text is cohesive, anyone will care about the topic, or a particular sentence is properly structured. Each then shares these concerns with a peer reviewer, who takes them into account when reading and reviewing the essay. The reviewers are asked first to read the writers' concerns, second to put down their pens and read the entire draft from top to bottom, then third to respond in writing to the writers' concerns and a sheet of peer review questions. I have included sample questions here that can work for any of the extended drafts with minor modifications. I help students keeps track of time and encourage them to spend forty to fifty minutes with each draft, especially the first time they are doing this. The students usually finish at about the same time with my help. Once they have finished, they exchange written comments. The writers then read the feedback they were given and talk with their peer reviewers to clarify questions they have about the feedback and discuss overall impressions.

By doing peer reviews this way, students are able to have meaningful conversations with peers about their work, have the opportunity to see in detail how someone else chose to approach the assignment, and have written feedback and notes to take home for reference as they revise. Although students may understand feedback at the time of review, they may have forgotten much of the conversation by the time they are able to revise the paper. Having the written notes helps with this problem. As previously mentioned, I also always provide detailed feedback on student drafts of longer papers.

A sample three-week timeline for the formal paper might look like this: I ask students to turn in a draft for peer review during the first week. I ask students to bring two copies of their drafts so that during the class session I can do my first read of their work. This allows me to answer any immediate questions that come up during peer reviews or address concerns they want to begin working on right away. I provide detailed student feedback in the second week. I have a larger class discussion with the students about patterns I see in the writing so that we can have an open dialogue and share concerns. The final draft is due in the third week. Students are asked to submit the original draft, my comments, both peer reviews and their final draft. This way I can evaluate the process from top to bottom. For instance, if both peer reviewers and I suggest a revision to the introduction, I will expect a student to address this concern. In reviewing feedback, I encourage students to listen to their peers and to my feedback but ultimately to make their own decisions about how they want to revise their essays. The grade I assign is an assessment of where each essay is in relation to the progress I think it should make in the class.

Because of its creative nature, many students are interested in the prospect of publishing their personal writing. This may be different from what you have experienced in a typical first-year writing classroom. At this point, the students will have read a wide variety of pieces from essayists, fiction writers and journalists. With a variety of topics and perspectives represented, students will be able to identify with some of the writers and wish to join the conversation in a more public way. In class, I explain that publishing an essay requires another process, one that would take considerably more time and different audience awareness to achieve. We strive for progress within the limitations and scope of the semester, and I offer to meet with students individually to discuss paths to publication.

Peer Review Sheet (Sample)

Writer:

Reviewer:

Writer, please identify any issues you feel you are currently having with this piece of writing so that your reader/reviewer can focus on these issues.

How well does the author set up the idea of place/event in this piece? Point to specific details that give the concept of character dimension or stifle it on the page.

Are you able to get a clear sense of setting? How well do you feel situated in the environment of the piece? Explain how this feeling is achieved, citing details from the writing.

Does the author give enough personal background to situate the importance of the place/event as well as his or her own point of view? If so, what details help the author do this? If not, what do you think is missing?

Does the piece seem to flow from beginning to end? Is there a natural progression of characters and story line? If so, how is this accomplished? If not, how can the author make the piece flow more effectively?

Where does the story begin, and where does the story leave you? Do you feel you are able to enter the narrative easily and let it end where it does? Why or why not?

Is there specific language that you feel is particularly expressive and effective in this piece? If so, point it out here.

Is there specific language that you feel is somewhat stilted or dragging the narrative pace? If so, point it out here.

Do you have any additional suggestions or comments for revision? Please also feel free to use this space to express what you like best about the piece of writing.

Readings

I use a variety of readings to demonstrate different forms to the class. Even in a short period of time, it is important to expose students to many forms of personal writing, not just one. I also include forms other than nonfiction, such as fiction and poetry, to demonstrate writing styles. I cannot encourage you enough to choose readings that are appropriate for your own student body. What works for my students may very well not work for yours. My advice would always be to represent a diverse range of experiences to give students more opportunity to find a voice they can relate to and possibly identify with. I will include some sample readings throughout the chapters to give examples of readings that have worked in my classroom.

5. Memory/Character Essays

Overview

One of the hardest things to master, and a hurdle to overcome for many students, is learning how to show and not tell. This may seem like a tired subject, but it is an important one. Most students—who at this point have written many documents in their academic lives to prove they have read something, done research or are worthy of attending a college, receiving a scholarship or getting a job—have a hard time mastering techniques that allow experiences to "speak for themselves." It's clear why this is so hard for them to understand: In college writing classes, we are not asking them to prove they are doing or reading something. We assume they have done their readings and preparation. We are asking them to take the next step and to create meaning, a new skill for many college student writers and one that takes time to master.

When much of your writing life has been devoted to summing things up and proving things, it can be hard to avoid the habit. I prohibit students from "summing up" their essays for class. How tiresome the world would be if everyone constantly had to sum up their purpose in life. So my students are never allowed to tell their readers what something means. They must create strong enough connections and reflections so that by the end of the writing, readers understand the significance of their narrative. A lot of developing this skill is learning to choose details, identify the "So what?" factor of the writing, and, most importantly, trust the reader.

Through using devices and cues and most importantly creating scenes, writers are able to convey ideas and messages to us without thrusting their purpose in our faces in the form of summaries and underlined theses. Students can do the same thing by coming to understand that once they know and explore the purpose of their writing, others will be able to follow their meaning. As I mentioned in the "Who cares?" section, if students don't know why they are writing something, most often their audience will not know either. Intention in writing is key. Students must work on understanding why they are choosing a topic, other than that they need to complete an assignment to earn a grade. That way, they can work as they write to tease out important ideas and themes through the details they choose to include and the voice they use to convey it to their intended audience.

Students must also understand that memory is fallible. As a rule, people remember only a very small amount of what they experience. If this were not true, we would not be able to function on a daily basis. I often ask students in class if they have a memory of something that others dispute—maybe something that happened in childhood or an experience with a friend on which they disagree about what actually occurred. Most students will raise their hands and acknowledge that this has happened to them, and I invite a few students to share these stories with the class.

It is important to establish that just because memories differ does not mean they are invalid. There is a fine line between remembering something to the best of our ability and willfully misremembering something. In class, we work on remembering to the best of our ability and intending to be truthful. Talking to others who were involved in memories, if possible, can be helpful in fleshing out details. Readings in which authors use examples of childhood memories can be helpful in understanding the finer points of these distinctions, especially with memoir.

Joan Didion's essay "On Keeping a Notebook" is very effective for helping students analyze the concept of truth and what that means for the reader. Our class is not studying philosophy, but I try to devote a fairly large amount of time right off the bat to discussing how and what truth means to us as writers. Didion both lies to her readers and convinces us of her truthfulness. How does she achieve this?

In this essay, Didion cleverly analyzes her reasons for keeping a journal, holding on to notes and images from her life. She shares some of the stories she has created from these moments and how they differ from the recollections of her family and friends. This reading usually makes students reflect on what the term truth mean for them in their everyday life and what power it contains. Didion reflects, "Not only have I always had trouble distinguishing between what happened and what merely might have happened, but I remain unconvinced that the distinction, for my purposes, matters" (333). In discussing her process of journaling and creating stories, she aims for a specific kind of truth, "How it felt to me: that is getting closer to the truth about a notebook" (333). Didion explains that the truth in her writing is how a situation felt to her at the time; in this way she is being accurate to her experience. This highlights an important aspect of all nonfiction writing—an obligation for the writer to maintain an ethical regard for the reader and represent the experience in a way that is true, not always to facts and chronology, but to experience. It is a thought Carolyn Ellis uses to define autoethnography in a piece I will analyze in Chapter 7.

I also use this discussion as a time to ask people if they have ever journaled, blogged, or maintained Twitter or Facebook feed. We discuss the importance of capturing important moments in our lives for personal reasons while also tailoring them to elicit a response from an audience.

As a warm-up exercise to practice showing and not telling, I ask students to draw on a specific memory and try to re-create it vividly for the reader. I keep this first assignment short and vague, to allow them to approach it informally and organically. They are encouraged to use their five senses as well as to incorporate any remembered dialogue in the writing. This work should be conducted in weeks five to seven.

The Memory Assignment

Briefly describe a memory that is important to you. Try to avoid explaining why the memory is important and focus on showing the importance of the memory. Use your five senses, and include dialogue, if possible.

Results

Sometimes these initial memory pieces will be very difficult for the students to share. Reading them aloud can be the first time a student cries in the classroom, since when asked to remember something, many students will reflexively turn to difficult or painful experiences, such as the death of a family member or a humiliating incident. On the other extreme, this writing can be very generic and predictable and involve topics such as being accepted to college or any event of achievement that might appear in a college application essay.

This is an important exercise because it often demonstrates that while a memory seems significant to an individual writer, it will not necessarily seem important to the audience. Students may have accomplished something very impressive, but there must be a point of entry for an audience to understand the value of this achievement as a topic for reading. Also, when writing about difficult situations that are intensely personal, we have to find ways to allow an audience to relate to the narrative.

I use the results of the shorter assignment as a way to introduce more details for students to consider as they write longer memory pieces. In extending their writings, students will need to take the time to explore the subtext of the memory, the details, persons involved, dialogue and settings to demonstrate the meaning for the reader. The longer memory essay will be a chance to practice these skills. Using the examples students generate in the shorter assignments is an effective way to point out strengths and weaknesses before moving forward in the writing. I invite students to use the ideas from this short assignment in the longer essay or to feel free to choose a completely new topic for the extended essay. I emphasize focus on the creation of characters for their first extended essay. The focus will be on incorporating the skills they have worked on in their deep observation, perspective and self-as-character assignments.

Examples of these essays can be found in Chapter 12.

The Importance of Creating Scenes and Using Dialogue

One way to strengthen the showing-and-not-telling aspect of writing is to create scenes. In creating a scene, it is important not just to describe what is seen with the five senses, as students practiced in their observation exercises, but also to let the people in the scene speak for themselves. This is not always possible, but using dialogue is an important skill to master, and the extended memory assignment will be a great place to try it out. This will be the first time students consider how they can create a perspective that readers will trust by incorporating other voices.

Using dialogue in nonfiction writing for the first time can be tricky and unnerving. Re-creating conversations, allowing people's speech to come through, using direct quotes or overheard language can help students see that it is important not only to present their take on the event but to let readers experience the direct voice of the players. This will allow a piece to seem more balanced in perspective. Readers are often turned off if writers are not able to present a measured view or confident voice. Students need to convince the reader that they are truthful, believable, worthy of trust. By allowing more voices to speak, they are insinuating the veracity of the situation through no insistence of their own. A very small amount of well-chosen dialogue can go a long way.

As with anything involving memory, it is important to urge students to be as accurate as possible when using speech. Including speech in projects researched in real time is easier than writing about dialogue in the past. Encourage students to do their best to re-create moments of speech accurately and to keep voices consistent.

Researching Your Own Experience

The memory essay is also a good place to introduce the idea that many memoir writers research their own pasts. Since memory is fallible, interviewing others who were present at important events or speaking to multiple people directly involved in the memories can be an important part of the writing. It will come as a surprise to many students that writing about their own lives can require research.

That research won't necessarily be essential for this essay, but it is important to inform the students that for extended and complicated pieces they intend to publish, drawing on multiple sources for accuracy can be informative and essential to ensure the veracity of details including timelines, locations, and players.

> ### The Memory/Character Essay Assignment
>
> A memory is not necessarily something that happened a long time ago. Rather, a memory is something that is past, something that is reflected upon. It can be something that happened last week or a moment from your childhood, but for our purposes, it is something that has happened before this assignment was given.
>
> For this assignment, choose a memory that has multiple levels of meaning for you. It is important not just to create a narrative about one particular thing but to think about the complexities of the memory and why you find it worthy of exploring in an essay. Subtext and intention are crucial.
>
> You should re-create details as accurately as possible, even talking to friends or family members who might help you remember aspects of a memory. All good writers of memoir research their own histories. This is because memory is fallible and other people might be able to shed important light on our experiences.
>
> Focus especially on re-creating characters, yourself included, who were involved in the memory. Use dialogue to let these characters speak, and choose details to convey the nature of relationships.

Results

As with the shorter memory assignment, students will often use the memory/character essay to explore something that has become a part of their rehearsed life narrative. It may be one of the hardest pieces for them to revise, since it may be based on a story they have repeated many times. Getting students to reconsider a somewhat fixed narrative to demonstrate its potential for expansion can be challenging. As with the shorter piece, the range of experiences is likely to go from the very sad and tragic to the mundane. It will be important for the students to share these pieces with one another through the drafting process so they have models to consider for expansion of their ideas. This also will allow them to see that memory does not have to be something very large to be important and can be very small if treated properly.

Examples of these essays can be found in Chapter 12.

Conclusion

With the assignments in this chapter, you might have some setbacks in the quality of the students' writing in initial drafts. When asked to put together all of the elements for the first time in larger, extended pieces, students may feel overwhelmed. The extended memory essay is the first time they are attempting to employ everything they have learned simultaneously. It is natural, therefore, that this will be difficult for them. By working from invention to draft to final version and possibly revision in peer groups and one on one, students will gain confidence and start to master the voice they will need for the next series of assignments.

6. Writing about Spaces and Events

Overview

This chapter's focus will be on writing more specifically about space and environment. The students, who until this point have focused mostly on character, will now concentrate on how space and objects work as important elements in their narratives. They will already have completed the deep observation assignment from Chapter 2 and have spent time discussing the value of using the five senses in their writing. To continue with this process, each of the exercises in this chapter asks students to develop different writing techniques that will assist them in understanding the importance of objects and environment as players in their larger narratives. The goal is to treat spaces and events as characters in the narrative and use sensory elements to structure and organize the final narratives.

Also, for the first time, students will be asked to engage a space or event in real time specifically to have a subject to write about. This will be a major change from relying only on memory and will require students to use the skills they have practiced, employing observation in conjunction with memory and applying them to a new subject. In some class situations, having students do real-time observation will not be possible. In these cases, this project can be very successful as a memory piece that focuses on the value of space and event as equally important to character. This work should happen in weeks eight to eleven.

Writing About the Classroom

This exercise is one of the more boring exercises we do over the course of the semester, and that is the point. I ask students to write about our classroom. Some of you may be lucky and have beautiful rooms with windows overlooking lush green quads and bustling student life. Often my classrooms are four concrete walls, devoid of windows or with the shades down to block out city street noise. How can students make a space interesting when there is nothing inherently interesting about it? This is great practice in figuring out how to do a lot with very little, and the exercise is similar to the deep observation assignment with the focus changed from people to space.

> ### Writing About the Classroom Exercise
>
> Take ten minutes to create an in-class narrative about your current classroom space, without talking about the people in the room. Objects, colors, anything observed with the five senses—except people—are all valid.

Results

Ask students to share with the class both the experience of writing this as well as excerpts from the writing. This will start a dialogue about the challenges of using space and objects as important players in narratives and what space can tell us about people. It will also encourage students to create narratives based on moments specifically chosen as topics for writing, rather than relying on a memory as a point of reflection. Turning the uninteresting into something interesting is an important skill and can help students develop topics when they do not have any readily apparent ideas. In other words, anything, if treated correctly, can be a good and valid topic for writing.

Using Devices

When writing about space and event, students will be focusing on how to use devices to tell a story. For our purposes, the use of devices refers to using objects or sensory information as an excuse to tell a story. This allows the writers to move around in time or "flash" between time periods to provide information you otherwise wouldn't have an excuse to include. The readings by Lee Gutkind, Philip Lopate and Carolyn Ellis all provide great examples for this technique.

For example, referring back to the Ellis piece I discuss in Chapter 5, we can see how she uses many devices throughout her narrative to tell stories. She uses her mother's body as a way to discuss her own. Also, as she looks at her mother's body she talks about a Caesarean scar, which she uses to mention a brother who has since died. This is an "information drop" and is a common device for writers. Lopate does something similar when he briefly mentions but then fails to reflect upon a suicide attempt. This does a few things: it demonstrates the complex lives of the characters and instantly shows that there are serious experiences that inform even mundane stories. Devices have endless possibilities and will be explored in more detail in the autoethnography chapters.

Describing a Room That Is Not Your Own

Describe a room that is not your own but that is occupied by a character you have created. At no point should you mention anything directly about the character you have created. Instead, try to convey who lives in this room by describing in detail the objects contained in the room and the room itself. Make sure to use your five senses to flesh out this description.

Results

This exercise helps students to continue the process of realizing how much we identify people's personalities by the things that surround them. Some of these things are chosen by the person; others are a product of circumstance. Students will use many cues from popular culture, personal experience and media to clue in their readers to the identity of the inhabitants. Pause and focus on the processes they have used to make these choices. This is another opportunity to assess how judgment and stereotyping play a part in how we view the world.

Space and Event Writing

For this next extended essay, students will be writing about a space or event that they enter strictly to write about it. If this is not possible due to time constraints, students can certainly write about a space or event from memory. In the examples at the end of this book, I will provide both types. Ideally, this can be an extended opportunity for them to practice having an intended topic for an essay, conducting the research, and then writing up the results in a cohesive narrative. It is an important step in building up to their final autoethnographic essays.

> ### The Space or Event Essay
>
> Unlike the memory essay, the space or event essay will require you to write about something you will be experiencing for the first time as you write. This does not mean you cannot employ elements of memory as you investigate and discuss your topic. What it means is that you will be writing in "real time," experiencing something with the intention of writing about it.
>
> Until this point, many of our pieces have relied strictly on memories. Going into a new environment or experience with the intention of writing about it will change the way you experience and record the event. I am asking you to enter the moment or space with a writer's eye, using powers of observation to both participate in and find the significance of a space or event you enter purely for reasons of creating this essay.
>
> If you are choosing a space, choose one you have easy access to and will be able to visit readily. If you are choosing an event, make sure it is happening within the confines of the essay dates. Keep in mind that an event need not be something large. It can be something small, a gathering, a visit, or it can be a concert or a lecture. Any of these ideas and other choices will be relevant if written about in a thoughtful and prepared way.
>
> In this essay, whether based on a new experience on not, the space or event should be a main character. Space or event can be important for structuring a narrative, and objects and surroundings can communicate a lot about the experience to the reader. Focus should be on the power of these elements to act as characters in the narrative alongside descriptions of the self and other people. Space and event are not necessarily separate. Your piece may focus on both; do not feel the need to separate these concepts artificially.

Results

For many students, this will be a departure from how they are used to approaching an essay topic. The focus on using space or event as an element equal in importance with character will be a new way for them to view the potential of personal writing. Also, having an intended topic and conducting research specifically for the purpose of writing will be new and will introduce them to a new approach to personal writing that will be necessary for extended autoethnographic research. I will elaborate on this exercise's connection to the autoethnography in Chapter 10.

Readings

Building up to this second essay, I try to choose pieces that show how events and spaces can be used to structure narratives. Use of objects and devices also is key to understanding how things other than character motivate narratives.

Judith Ortiz Cofer's "More Room" is an excerpt from her memoir Silent Dancing. The essay is a good example of using home as a device. The rooms in the house represent the expansion of the main character's family and her ultimate decision to claim a space of her own. Students will often choose to write about their homes. The concept of home is imbued with meaning. Home can be nostalgic, painful, loving, a place of solitude, used as a structure to reflect on the nature of relationships or the difficulty of change.

Rebecca Skloot's essay "The Truth About Cops and Dogs" is much more journalistic in tone. Skloot is better known for her book The Immortal Life of Henrietta Lacks. In this, a much earlier piece, Skloot engages in a bit of reportage and recounts a harrowing story involving a pack of dogs that attack and almost kill her dog in New York City. Skloot is able to offer a balanced account of the dogs' homeless owner. An important lesson for students is that to get readers on your side and to have them dislike a person or the person's actions, you have to help them see something compelling or good in that person. The best movie villains have a backstory about where and when things went wrong. By understanding a person's complex humanity, we become more invested in the character as real and three-dimensional and then increasingly disappointed or incensed at that character's wrongful actions. This piece is particularly effective in my classes because I teach in New York City. I would encourage you to search out regional pieces when looking for class readings.

"Consider the Lobster" is arguably one of David Foster Wallace's most pedantic pieces. With its heavy use of footnotes and sometimes dry scientific rhetoric, it is a beast of a read for almost anyone. I have students read it as they prepare to write place/event pieces. Wallace is invited to cover the Maine Lobster Festival for Gourmet magazine. He uses the event as an excuse to take a look at animal rights in a very prescient way and consider how we choose which animals deserve what kind of treatment.

Choosing excerpts from Jack Kerouac's *On The Road*, I show both the success and downfalls of stream-of-consciousness writing. In one passage, Kerouac fetishizes the native innocence of girls while celebrating his own form of white masculinity. He uses the road as metaphor and the characters as touchstones for his own ego expansion.

Conclusion

After completing the assignments in this chapter, students will have had practice in many of the basic techniques they will be asked to use in the autoethnography assignment, the final project of the semester. Beyond what has already been explored, in the final assignment students will add research skills including conducting formal and informal interviews, identifying and engaging a subculture, and becoming a part of a larger informed narrative undertaken for the sole purpose of writing about the subculture.

7. The Autoethnography Project

Overview

In this chapter, I will offer an analysis of the autoethnography assignment and give detailed consideration to student examples from my classroom. After this overview and analysis, I will use the remaining chapters to outline to step-by-step process for teaching the paper using assignments and techniques for weaving all of the elements together.

Defining Autoethnography

In the social sciences, there has long been a debate over criteria for traditional ethnography and alternative or evocative ethnography. In recent years, social scientists have sought a more inclusive model that allows for relaxing some of the rigid scientific constraints of ethnography in favor of the impact of more literary forms.

In "Evocative Autoethnography: Writing Emotionally About Our Lives," Carolyn Ellis describes her gradual departure from traditional sociological methods into an approach that is more personally meaningful. She achieves this balance in her writing by using multiple voices, starting and restarting to establish her point of view through both analysis and storytelling. "I made myself begin again in an autoethnographic voice that concentrates on telling a personal, evocative story to provoke others' stories and adds blood and tissue to the abstract bones of the theoretical discourse" (117). Throughout the piece, she clearly establishes a point of view, which she emphasizes in many of her works about autoethnography, "I think that sociology can be emotional, personal, therapeutic, interesting, engaging, evocative, reflexive, helpful, concrete, and connected to the world of everyday experience" (120). She aims to be true to her feelings, move away from time ordered structures and convey her emotions (128).

Ellis draws on interviews, notes, conversations, and diaries to construct her writing and seeks to find herself in the context of a larger world. "The inner workings of the self must be investigated in reciprocal relationship with the other: concrete action, dialogue, emotion, and thinking are featured, but they are represented within relationships and institutions, very much impacted by history, social structure, and culture, which themselves are dialectically revealed through action, thought, and language" (133).

She seeks to find value in autoethnography through the impact it has on her audience. "A story's 'validity' can be judged by whether it evokes in readers a feeling that the experience described is authentic and lifelike, believable and possible; the story's generalizability can be judged by whether it speaks to readers about their experience" (133). She believes that by sharing stories this way, we open up a world that allows others to share their stories (134).

In her piece "Evaluating Ethnography," Laurel Richardson examines the divide that has persisted between literary and scientific writing (253). This is similar to the division that has existed between academic and personal writing. She notes the "oxymoronic" naming of genres that have tried to bridge this gap, thus blurring distinctions among categories such as "creative nonfiction; faction; ethnographic fiction; the nonfiction novel; and true fiction" (253). And she seeks to lay out the criteria she uses to judge ethnography's success.

In attempting to create new standards that allow writers to move more freely in their ethnographic work, Richardson establishes the following as important evaluative criteria. She believes the work should: make a substantive contribution, have aesthetic merit, have reflexivity, make an impact, and express a reality (254). In this way, Richardson intends to show the related nature of scientific research and creative expression.

Arthur Bochner responds to Richardson in "Criteria Against Ourselves" and sets up his own evaluation criteria for what he terms "alternative ethnography," another name often assigned to ethnography that deviates from traditional social science norms. He sees alternative ethnographies as "narratives of the self" that "extract meaning from experience rather than depict experience exactly as it was lived" (270). When looking at this personal writing, he wants abundant concrete detail, structurally complex narratives, emotional credibility, a tale of two selves, and ethical self-consciousness (270-71).

In these three pieces, we can see how social sciences have laid a path for our work in composition studies, to examine the value of the personal and use traditional modes of research to flesh out the narrative of the self.

The Autoethnography

One of the biggest problems with teaching ethnographic writing can be having students understand their own positionality in the research being conducted. For this reason, in my own classroom I have decided that a form of autoethnography provides one of the clearest ways not only to analyze a subculture or aspect of society but also to investigate one's involvement in that community. I define autoethnography in this case as a qualitative investigation of a subculture the writer is currently involved in. Students are asked to analyze their position in the subculture as well as the positioning of others and how this affects attitudes. Autoethnographic analysis in this case includes interviewing other members of the subculture, conducting field observation, analyzing textual materials, investigating histories, and engaging in self-reflection. Previous involvement in or attachment to the subculture gives students a vested interest in the project, a sense of authority, and a position from which to analyze.

When conducting autoethnographic research, as opposed to traditional ethnographic research, students are somewhat empowered in that their personal involvement enables them to start out with a certain amount of knowledge about the subculture they are investigating. At the same time, because it is necessary for them to explain the subculture to those who are unfamiliar with it, they must learn how to translate their knowledge to an outside audience. In addition, when conducting observations they need to look at the subculture afresh and describe elements they have taken for granted. They must account for rituals, language and subtleties that make it operate as something unique and situated. By interviewing members of the subculture who inhabit a different position, they are confronted with new perspectives from insiders that will help them to further articulate their own ideas and question their own authority in communicating exactly what the subculture is. Interviewing and conducting observations both empowers them and decenters them from their own experience, forcing them into a position of questioning and representation to an intended audience (their instructor and their classmates, who will see this writing at multiple stages).

Asking students to draw on visceral experiences as well as textual evidence complicates their analysis and keeps them constantly involved in what is being communicated. Students come out with a richer understanding of the subculture, an ethical responsibility to convey its multiple facets and to avoid being reductive. This often has the effect of increasing students' understanding and involvement in the subculture and produces a new appreciation for an activity that perhaps had been an unexamined part of their lives outside the classroom. In this way, the writing carries an impact that extends beyond the scope of the assignment and its evaluation against classroom standards.

In "Making the Personal Political," Stacy Holman Jones points out the major differences between telling and showing that are key to successful autoethnographic research. She notes criticism of autoethnography and advocates for performance that not only expresses but employs mimesis, poesis and kinesis, moving from a stage of recognition to action, as performance scholars such as Victor Turner and Dwight Conquergood have suggested. Jones uses stories of her grandfather to show how she was engaged in this kind of autobiographical and autoethnographic knowing and text from an early age. She points out that many of us have been involved in this kind of appropriation of ourselves in texts we have written throughout our lives, making them somewhat autoethnographic even if they were not originally intended that way. It is important to remember, Jones says, that all of these texts are partial views and that is OK: "You can't do it all, you need to do a version" (760). When students are made aware of their presence in already-constructed texts and the places they currently hold in the subcultures they are investigating, this kind of project can be more organic.

In the classroom, you can show students they are already involved and invested in subcultures but investigating these different versions and helping them recognize that they have an immediate investment in the ethnographic research and potential to develop their perspectives. Making students aware that autoethnographic research involves focus and decision making, like all other writing, allows them to understand they are creating a version and not representing every aspect of their subculture.

For their final projects, my students are required to choose subcultures they are part of or feel connected to. In addition, there must be a field site for the subculture that the students can visit in person at least twice during the semester to make detailed observations. Accessibility is a key factor in that students have only six weeks to conduct the research and analysis necessary to complete their assignments successfully. Any documents related to the subculture are analyzed and reviewed so that students can work from both written history and their own experiences. Students also are asked to interview at least two people who hold different positions in the subculture in order to get different perspectives. They have the opportunity to practice interviewing skills and writing questions to elicit the best information for their projects. They also have the option of interviewing or surveying people outside of the subculture to incorporate more positions on it. Again, because of time constraints, they are not required to do this.

Each aspect of the project is conducted as a separate assignment, and students are asked to amass the data in a portfolio and create a final autoethnographic piece of writing that draws on their accumulated research and analyzes the process of creating the materials and writing the paper. Analysis of rituals, language and routines is part of these small assignments, and self-reflection, reflection on the process, and analysis of research are all important elements of the final project.

Requiring students to investigate a subculture in which they are involved enables them to choose from among many different topics. Some students chose subcultures that are very personal and involve family, friends and religion, while others prefer to study school clubs, hobbies or neighborhoods. In each case, students can pursue a topic that interests them and increase their understanding of the subculture while staying within their comfort zone.

Student project topics have included "cosplay" (costumed role-playing), singles culture, and specific academic clubs. The two projects I have chosen to discuss are striking because they are strong examples of an evolution that can happen during this kind of research. Each involves a subculture that has had a major impact on the student's life, yet each student had not had any sort of formal opportunity to reflect on this impact. The two writers reflect on subcultures that involve family members, giving an immediacy to the writing and analysis. Here I give an overview of the student projects, excerpts from their writing and analysis of the process of each student.

Sheila

Sheila decided that her autoethnographic project was a great opportunity to investigate a subculture that she had been involved with as something of an outsider for her entire life. Her her brother, her father and their large friend group, which spent a lot of time at Sheila's home, engaged in drag racing. Sheila had always been present but not involved in the activities surrounding it. It was mostly the domain of the men in her family, and while she was not a direct observer or participant in the racing, the drag racers, their friends, and the conversations and lives of her father and brother affected every aspect of Sheila's daily life.

Starting the project, Sheila had hesitation and curiosity. She thought it would be a great opportunity to participate, but with a degree of distance. Sheila had always wanted to know more about the subculture but found she had no real excuse to enter it. She talked to her father about going to an event one night, and to her surprise he was very excited about the prospect . What happened that night was the catalyst for Sheila's paper and her final performance piece.

In preparation for her project, Sheila conducted interviewed her father, brother, sister, and two friends who were also involved in drag racing. She also solicited opinions from people outside the subculture for perspective analysis. Her research culminated in observation of a race with all of the preparation and aftermath. Her interviews, observations and final paper all share a common awareness of her place as both outsider and insider with respect to the subculture. Her final paper starts with a kind of blunt factual interaction between her and her father, and it shows her constant reflection on her position while conducting the research. She moves between narration and observation, bringing us into the story while making us aware that she is outside of it.

> November 28, 2007 and it's 10:45 p.m. 'Sheila, come on. There's a race going on tonight,' my father says grinning. I've been asking him if a race will ever happen before my project is due, so I know that he's happy I can get off his back. I rush to put on my sneakers and coat because I'm so excited and I don't want to miss anything. I walk to the window in front of my house, and I see a crowd of over fifteen people. Seeing all of the people outside of my house made me realize that a race will happen. 'Make sure you have your camera and everything,' my dad blurts out. Quickly I run back to my room to get my camera, but when I reach back to the window in the front of my house, no one is there….

> It's brisk and very cold. It's dark out, with a little light coming from the street lights that line my block. With my pen and pad in hand, I take a seat on the stoop in front of my house. I see about four cars pull up, there's a group of ten males, and they come to my right. One of them is very loud and active. My dad is sitting down on the opposite side of the stoop, so all of the guys stand around him. 'He got the break. You gotta put the money up.' he screamed. 'What is that about?' I ponder. I have no clue. 'Gimme my money,' he blurts out. 'Stop bitching' follows. I observe and listen to what he says. As I write some of what he says in my note pad, some people in the group of guys look at me and then turn away. A few

> minutes passed and I realize that the group moved further away. They were on the sidewalk when I first came out to observe, now they're practically in the middle of the street....
>
> I focus on a group of seven different males to my left, in the middle of the street. The scent of cigarettes fill my nostrils. One of the guys looks at me as I write, so I stop. When he looks away I continue. As I write, my leg starts to shake.

Sheila's writing is filled with a kind of immediacy. It's easy to see her thinking through the process as she writes: her circumstances, identity through cultural markers, language, actions. She in constantly present and aware in all aspects of her writing, and the people she writes about are constantly aware of her, whether her father is telling her to get her camera or a guy is staring her down as she writes notes on him.

This project is interesting for a number of reasons, not least of which is that Sheila's family, participating in illegal drag racing, never actually gets to race. Instead, there is a showdown with police right in front of her house, people flee, and nobody ever gets to drive. The real interest in the piece, however, comes from Sheila's growing awareness of this world that has for as long as she can remember been a part of her life. Although always present, she never really asked any of the people in her house or in her family what it was all about and managed to avoid ever watching it happen.

In her reflection, Sheila was surprised by how eager those around her had been to share what they knew about drag racing and how excited her own father had been to have her watch and take an interest in what was going. Throughout her transcripts of interviews, she commented on her need to brush up her interviewing skills, always maintaining a dialogue with herself and with her readers. She chose to do many more interviews than the assignment required and got perspectives from those who race, those who are fans and those who are outsiders to the entire subculture.

Sheila was very quiet and often kept to herself in class, although she was always the one to participate in a thoughtful way when the rest of the class was unprepared or silent. She was reserved but very energetic in her own way, usually sitting to the side of the room in a zippered hoodie, smiling the smile of someone who always did her work and fully understood what was going on but didn't let others know that. Because she had been rather quiet, the nature of her project and the language she presented in her spoken-word piece came as a surprise to her classmates, who were fascinated by the scenario and the action. Sheila's piece was informed by a sensitivity to character and surroundings, to identities and the positionality of herself and those otherwise involved in the subculture.

For her final presentation, Sheila performed snippets of the dialogue she overheard at the race, giving a spoken-word performance that was often brazen and confusing in its meaning. After her performance of the fast-paced language, she stopped to explain to her classmates what the words meant and where they had come into play in her observation of the evening of the drag race.

> He got the break, you gotta put the money up
>
> Gimme my money
>
> Guaranteed break means he has to leave
>
> He's scared

> I'm not taking no 500
>
> Anyway, I'm a get my money
>
> They getting money up right now

The fast-paced dialogue, the unfamiliar vocabulary and the nature of the activities interested Sheila and her classmates. The performance engaged her peers and made them consider how their classmate had come to be involved in this subculture and what that meant. Sheila felt she had found a way to bond with her father and brother yet keep her distance, just as she did in the classroom.

Considering my goals for the assignment, Sheila's writing became increasingly critical and experimental, allowing her to express herself on multiple levels. She had an opportunity to explore a subculture she had otherwise been too timid to enter and created a stronger relationship to the members of the subculture as a result. The experience thus extended into her daily life and helped her produce insightful writing and analysis for her peers.

Kelly

Kelly was struggling with her first semester at a college, wondering where she really fit in. Her father was a graffiti artist and her mother and siblings also were visually artistic, so she felt pressure to show her own artistic talents. She shone in her writing ability and decided for her project to investigate her own neighborhood and the influence it had on her life. She struggled a long time to figure out what kind of project she wanted to do, feeling as almost all of the students do in the beginning, that she was not part of a subculture and didn't know where to begin.

Through numerous conversations with Kelly, I came to understand her ambivalence about college and her difficulty in negotiating her situation. She was constantly trying to balance her family's goals for her with figuring out where her own talents and ambitions were. When Kelly decided to focus on Brooklyn, she was able to deal simultaneously with her family and where she had been raised. It is not uncommon for students to do their projects on a neighborhood where they were raised or a childhood home or some aspect of family life. What made Kelly's project interesting was the way she was able to engage her surroundings and through the process learn what her neighborhood meant to her on a deeper level.

In her paper, Kelly looked through the lens of her family—people with strong artistic abilities and a desire to be free from the housing projects where they lived. Recounting episodes from her childhood, talking through her father and brother and mother's perspective, Kelly was able to give a picture of an identity in flux—a person who had difficult interactions with drug dealers, was a high achiever in school, and struggled to earn family approval with academic achievements. She conducted interviews with her father, mother, and brother and explored her own memories of her neighborhood. She did observations in the areas surrounding where she grew up and drew on texts that reflected on the nature of home to develop her final project. She began her piece like a much older person reflecting on childhood experiences:

> I always knew that one day I would be writing about Brooklyn, I just didn't know how soon. I connect Brooklyn with who I am and who I am becoming like every hair on my head, it's just natural. Even though I've lived in Brooklyn for all eighteen years of my life, I still feel like a part of me is indifferent. I think it's really me searching for the true me.

In the piece, Kelly embodies her environment and analyzes her relationship to her surroundings by looking at Brooklyn as a home, something that cares for her and something that keeps calling her back, inviting but also disingenuous. In her reflection, she discusses how the project gave her the opportunity to reflect on her surroundings, how she felt about school and her family, how her identity was tied to her neighborhood and the way in which she had been raised. The interview with her mother and father gave her the opportunity to talk to them about their goals and background in Brooklyn and the way they felt about their relationship. Kelly's reflective observation paints a picture of the connection she has with her surroundings as well as how she struggles to bridge the gaps.

> I am a little hesitant to approach my mother to do the interview, especially while she's watching the news, but I should get it done since it is due tomorrow. I tell her what I have to do and she gives me that look. It's a special one that only mothers can do or just the women in my family, and I know I already have it, people told me. While I asked her the question, she looks up at the ceiling for answers, like clouds are floating with memories on them, only if it was that easy. Her gestures are flowing and have movement like a mob boss. It scares me a little bit. She smiles at me but she is really looking through me. She sees someone else with every question, I was a new person, and maybe I was her. She was free within me, the youth that just disappears after a while, without saying goodbye. I got to not only see another side of her, I felt like I was like her. Everything she was and everything she could have been. I wished that we could have talked more, but it was time to go to sleep.

> My father and me just finished the beginning of the food for Thanksgiving, even though we don't celebrate it. He is obviously tired and that usually happens when he has his drink. We're watching television and I pop the question. He looks at me as if I am crazy. Well I believe that I am for helping him with cramps, so I think he can do this for me. He takes a sip of his drink and motions me with his eyes for me to begin. I start off with the questions and he grows sleepy. I was dual thinking at the time, I could clearly remember when he suggested that journalism wasn't for me, and this interview proved that for him. I guess when he said that all of the questions sounded the same, it wasn't good enough, I'm not sure if it ever is. We go through the questions and I know he loves to talk about his lifestyle and former adventures as a graffiti artist. I could see from the pictures that I found of the family how things really used to be and he misses that. He is frustrated by the change in the environment, but if anyone knows best he does, that things are bound to change. He looks at the television while he is talking to me and always has that know it all, catch me if you can smile on. Hey, what can you say that's his signature, just like Brooklyn is for all of us.

For Kelly, the interviews with her parents both reaffirmed her assumptions about their attitudes toward the importance of her schoolwork and at the same time made her long to make more of a connection with them and understand how their worlds have changed. She uses her parents as representative of the fabric of Brooklyn, at once engaged in memory and reality, standoffish but reflective of herself and her life.

For her presentation, Kelly decided to do a spoken-word poem that explored her feelings for her home and her family while also showing her struggles to identify who she is and negotiate this with her environment. She performed a five-minute poem, which I have excerpted here.

> Every word I write

> The way I speak
>
> The style I have
>
> You're a part of me
>
> It originated, generated, and
>
> Cultivated from you
>
> You first rated and now it's dated
>
> Never hated—maybe a little
>
> People played it
>
> They're all jaded
>
> Soon you'll be faded
>
> Hopefully not so much
>
> I hope you'll remember me
>
> And everything I aim to be
>
> Who I once was
>
> The transition you see
>
> Cause like you we all change
>
> It would be a shame

Kelly's dialogue with Brooklyn, incorporating her memories, aspirations and hopes for the future, was touching for the whole class to hear. She was able to effectively translate the emotion and exploration of her written project into a piece that engaged and excited her audience. It was a thoughtful reflection of the changing nature of her subculture and her changing place in it: while she would always maintain a connection to Brooklyn, she didn't know if Brooklyn would always be there for her. Her nostalgia for a past recounted by her mother and her father reflects an uncertain connection for Kelly with Brooklyn in the future.

The goal of this project was not to come to any conclusions about her upbringing, but rather to explore a place that informed her life and her goals. Kelly's relationships to Brooklyn and her family remain unresolved and thus realistic. She doesn't try to force any conclusions on her project, but rather embraces it as an opportunity to explore, connect and share her subculture with her classroom community.

Concluding Thoughts

The critical writing in all of its varieties that emerged from students demonstrates that there is a good deal of potential in the mixing of qualitative inquiry and personal writing. Developing classroom methods that allowed students to understand their personal connection to what was happening in class, engage in meaningful writing, workshop and collaborate with peers, and create projects extending into the community and their lives beyond our classroom was the ultimate goal.

At the end of the semester, after grades had been submitted, I asked students to do an anonymous freewrite that reflected on their experiences in the class, including the topic, projects and texts. Most of them found the curriculum surprising for a writing class but were pleasantly surprised by how much their writing and critical thinking had improved. While some thought the subject matter had been somewhat repetitive, many felt it had helped them stay invested in all of the projects for the class. Overwhelmingly, students appreciated the opportunity to pursue personally meaningful subjects and share their insights with classmates.

Of course, not all student projects were successful and my instruction was not always clear. Especially when investigating personally important subcultures in the autoethnographic projects, students can become frustrated by a lack of progress. They may feel initially as if they are not part of any subculture, as I mentioned earlier in my analysis of Kelly's project, and a constant conversation with peers and the instructor can guide those students who have a harder time choosing a topic. The opposite problem also occurs: students get so excited about a project that they want to go way above and beyond requirements with their research. It is important to remind students that it is only a one-semester assignment and that an adjustment in goals can be necessary and beneficial. As a class, we tried to plan for the inevitable, including unwilling or reticent interview subjects, cancellations, and restricted access to field sites. Teaching autoethnography requires a lot of adaptation on the part of the instructor and student and a willingness to adjust expectations based on unpredictable circumstances.

The benefit in all projects was that the students created large amounts of critical writing, and many student projects allowed an engagement with an aspect of a larger community and an opportunity to analyze their positionality in these communities. My suggestion is that we have an obligation to prepare our students by devising courses that can allow them to engage in personally relevant research and then share it with larger audiences. I believe students benefit from having the opportunity to think through the subcultures and communities they are part of, creating not only personal writing but personally invested writing and performance. Often the process leads them to ideas and feelings they have never fully analyzed before.

My favorite example of the personal performance projects leading to new insight is the case of Charles, a middle-aged man with a military background who sat among the otherwise traditional students in my Rhetoric 243 class at the University of Illinois at Urbana-Champaign in the fall of 2006. He was clearly and rather vocally resistant to the work we were doing. He did not believe in sharing the self and thought the assignments were fluffy. He consistently showed he was simply not interested through both his body language and his participation. However, his attitude evolved when he was asked to engage in the autoethnographic inquiry project. Charles decided to talk about deer hunting, something everyone knew he liked because of the sweatshirts and t-shirts depicting deer that he regularly wore to class. Through his paper, he questioned why hunting was so important to him. To his surprise, as he shared with the class, it turned out that deer hunting was so important to him because it was the primary way he bonded with his father. He continued the tradition with his two little girls, enjoying the ritual of waiting to get deer in their sights but often going home without firing a shot. He explained described to the class that he found out deer hunting was a way for him to bond with his children as well, and he shared their pictures with me on his way out of class on the last day, his pride in his family obvious in his expression.

Charles is an example of a student who realized something about his own community by engaging in personal writing that gave him the ability to analyze his subculture and communicate the depth of the experience to his obviously moved peers and instructor. During the process of conducting qualitative research, interacting with his audience and sharing his subculture with classmates, his writing gained dimension and richness and became part of the process rather than simply a product of it. My point here is that despite difficulties and successes, I believe all students and instructors can find a way to benefit from this kind of work and evolve as writers and critical thinkers. While not all projects will be as intimate, this is not the point. Projects vary as much as individuals do, sometimes inviting new emotional insight and sometimes producing equally meaningful insight about the individual's role in society. This kind of work can be engaged on many different personal levels and have varied meaning for each participant.

8. Choosing Topics for the Autoethnography

Overview

Throughout the assignments up to this point, students have been investigating different ideas about and definitions of identity through character creation, observation, and treatment of space and event. After defining identity for themselves and discussing the identity of others in smaller qualitative and personal pieces, students will now take a look at how identity is created in chosen subcultures in their final autoethnography assignment.

Through readings and experiences over the semester, students will have considered a broad range of subjects that include childhood memories, relationships with family, questions of race and religion and the importance of experience. In each of these pieces, culture has played a pivotal role, defining the circumstances in which they and the authors have created individual notions of the self.

Culture in these cases does not have one singular definition. It can be a multitude of things that influence lives. As they progress through research, students will consider how each person defines culture for herself and what the implications of this kind of definition are. I encourage students always to think about the larger societal consequences of the things our participants experience.

Their goal in the autoethnography assignment should be both to read individual experiences and to decide for themselves which aspects of culture are affecting identity formation. To do this, they will make connections between their gathered research and their own experiences to better understand identity and culture through multiple perspectives. This work should happen in weeks ten and eleven.

Choosing a Topic Assignment

A subculture is a smaller cultural group—a group that can be distinguished from a larger societal group based on a host of factors. Subcultures can be almost anything that we are currently involved in; there are subcultures we choose to be a part of and subcultures we are part of without any consent. They can be based on hobbies, religion, location, friends, family, race, gender, ethnicity, sexual preference—just about anything that creates identity.

For our final project for the class, you will be asked to select a subculture that you have currently chosen to be a part of or one that you will choose to connect yourself to and to investigate this subculture in a larger research paper called an autoethnography.

For this immediate assignment, I would like you to identify two subcultures that you are currently a part of and that you would find interesting to research. For each of the subcultures you identify, I would like you to give a brief description (three to four lines or more if necessary) that gives an overview of what the subculture is and your position in the subculture (how long you've been a part of it and how you feel about it).

From these two options, you will be choosing a topic for your final research paper. We will be sharing these ideas with the entire class. Please be as specific as possible. Your topics must fulfill the following criteria:

- You must be able to do background and preliminary research on your topics. In other words, written and visual material must be readily available for analysis.
- Topics must be local and accessible.
- There must be a place, field site, or event space for the topic that you will be able to visit at least twice during the semester.
- There must be at least two people you can interview who have different roles relevant to the topic.
- Topics must be new and cannot overlap with research topics in any other course work.

Results

This initial stage of the assignment is very important in that it will give students the one-on-one attention and grounding necessary to start successful extended projects. You may find that students have a hard time identifying subcultures that they are interested in or intentionally part of. That difficulty can be addressed by having students share their ideas in a class discussion. In this setting they can help others define their ideas more specifically, inspire one another by explaining their own choices, and provide tips to one another about resources. As the teacher, you also have a chance to intervene immediately and offer helpful suggestions, indicate ways students might make projects more specific or manageable, and dissuade students from projects that might be overly complicated or inappropriate due to topic or time constraints. These are concerns I will discuss more specifically in later chapters.

Objects for Storytelling

Once students have identified a subculture they are interested in investigating, I begin to introduce new ideas they can use to identify the significant aspects of the subculture. Objects can inspire students to tell great stories. When they look at a photograph, pick up a memento or keepsake, flip through a playbill, or look at a trinket in a junk drawer, they can be transported back to another place, another time and can re-create a memory that is sparked by their understanding of that object. Objects will be used as devices in the final autoethnography to tell stories and share important ideas. This initial assignment will help students understand the value of objects in their narratives.

Show-and-Tell Assignment

For this assignment, identify an object that you believe is representative of your subculture. For class, prepare a story behind the object that you will present orally. Make sure to choose something that will allow you to explore a specific idea tied to your subculture. If possible, please bring a physical object to class and try to avoid photographs or images on a mobile device or computer.

Results

This assignment should be familiar to the students from childhood. In this case, they are using a well-worn activity to learn how objects can be great jumping-off points to tell stories or explain insider knowledge of a subculture to an outsider. For instance, a pair of dance shoes might represent a ballerina's connection to her family, her passion for dance, successes and failures, exhilaration on the stage, specific performances, or nostalgia for youth, while for an outsider they may seem merely utilitarian, common, or worn.

Rituals and Routines

In our lives, we all participate in daily routines, whether brushing our teeth, making our beds, or following a complicated set of steps before preparing meals or going to sleep at night.

We also participate in larger rituals. Rituals have a history beyond the self and can be understood by a bigger group. They are based on a larger cultural meaning or understanding. Often we participate in rituals and aspects of rituals without fully understanding the meaning behind certain aspects. This can be true of religious rituals, cultural rituals, rites of passage such as parties, graduations, weddings, and even holidays, just to name a few.

In the following exercise, students can analyze how rituals and routines play an important role in their lives and how meaning is created through repetition.

> **Rituals and Routines: Freewrite**
>
> For ten minutes, freewrite on the following questions: What are rituals and routines? What is the difference between them, and what can we learn by examining them?

> **Rituals and Routines Assignment**
>
> Make a list of all of the rituals in which you have participated over the past year. From the list, choose two rituals to examine in detail. When you are breaking down the aspects of the two chosen rituals, consider the following: the reasons for participation, who else was involved in the ritual, your understanding of the different aspects of the ritual. Are there parts of the ritual you had a problem with? Thought were silly? Thought were really satisfying and important? Was there anything beautiful? Particularly complicated?

Results

Both assignments, the freewrite and the detailed examination of two rituals, are great ways to help students understand how rituals and routines are important parts of culture. By looking at those they engage in personally, they will come to understand how individual perspective as well as larger cultural perspective are important. They will familiarize themselves with identifying routines and rituals in their subculture and analyzing the importance of them.

Insider-Outsider Knowledge

At this point, you might want to introduce the concept of insider and outsider knowledge. Students should be prepared to use all exercises to identify information that would be readily understood by participants in the subculture but potentially misunderstood by those outside it. Rituals, routines, language, and the importance of space and objects can all be subjects on which insider and outsider knowledge vary. Reminding students about earlier work on perspective can help emphasize the difference.

Autoethnography Project Guidelines and Assignment

The autoethnography is an extended research project that allows you to investigate a subculture you have chosen to be part of or will choose to be part of and critically assess this subculture from both outsider and insider perspectives. To do this, you will be relying on your own experiences as well as assessing the experiences of other members of the subculture.

Based on our discussions and class projects related to culture and identity, you will be focusing now on a larger investigation of one subculture.

Your project will include information you collect in observations, interviews and interactions with your subculture. I expect you to draw on personal experiences, history, friendships, emotions and responses to both your participation in the subculture and your research into it. This is not different from your previous assignments; it is an extension of the work you have been doing all semester.

In your final project, I would like to see evidence of critical thinking about what makes your subculture a subculture and what you think your place is in it. The final format of the project is largely up to you. The only requirements are listed below.

- Your final autoethnography essay should be a minimum of six pages but can be as long as you need it to be, although more than ten is not advisable.
- You must conduct at least two formal interviews and include a written copy of each with your final essay. Additional informal interviews are recommended. Also, you must do at least one observation, and two or more in the space are recommended. Within the text, I would like to see you use artifact description as we worked on it in class.
- I encourage you to approach this final project as creatively or traditionally as you would like, but always critically. In addition to the written project, you will be required to do a presentation of your project for your classmates on the last day of class. Your reading should last three to five minutes.
- Consider these questions as you write: What have you learned about your subculture from this process? If you could share anything about your subculture to explain it to an outsider, what would it be? How would you like your final project to look and read? Based on your research, have you changed your mind about any aspects of your subculture? If so, which and why? What do you think the value of a project like this is or can be?

Conclusion

This initial groundwork will be essential to ensuring that your students pick appropriate topics that can be researched in the time available. Each step will allow them to think through the elements of their chosen subculture so that their formal interviews and assignments that I discuss in the following chapters will be productive.

9. The Interview Process

Overview

People are inherently lazy. That is the first thing you want to help students learn about interviewing anyone. It is not necessarily a malicious laziness. Most people just want to get to the point quickly and to finish the task at hand. This is the reason that when I ask my students how they are at the beginning of class, they say they're good, fine. It's not that they are bad people; I am asking a bad question that invites them to get to the point as quickly as possible. In this chapter I offer a few tips on how to help students conduct effective interviews.

When I was a graduate student writing my dissertation, I had an amazing experience. I was interviewing the head of a very large writing program in New York City. I knew this man had a long history of supporting personal writing in the composition classroom, which was the topic of my dissertation, and that he had great success with his methods. He seemed to me a kindred spirit, and I was excited to hear his thoughts on the state of personal writing in the field. When I asked if he would be willing to be interviewed, he agreed.

Before meeting him, I followed the procedure I had for all the interviews I had conducted up to that point. I sent him the outline of my dissertation project and some questions I intended to ask him. We met in his office, and during an informal discussion in which I was laying out my hopes for the interview before it started, he told me that he thought my project was naïve and uninformed. He did not want to be recorded and seemed resistant at best. It was in this moment that I learned my first important lesson about conducting interviews: The interviewee is always right.

Sure, this man was not saying what I wanted to hear. Above everything, I wanted people to respect me and be impressed and interested in my project and the contribution they could make to it. Being quick on my feet, I told my interviewee the best thing I could muster, that I agreed with him. I, too, thought my projected was naïve and perhaps misguided. I invited him to show me the error of my ways by imparting his experience and answering my questions. I invited him to stop at any time. I explained that the recording would be heard only by me and would be used in an honest manner.

Having assuaged his ego, I got one of the best interviews of my project—honest, direct, and informative. I realized that I was fallible and that as a researcher there was a large chance that the premise for all my work was not what I hoped it would be. That is part of the risk involved in any kind of research. It is important to have goals and to set up expectations. It is important to do background reading, be prepared with intelligent questions, and have a purpose and narrative behind a line of questioning. It is also important to remember that everything students know and think they know may crash and burn when the time comes to talk with a primary source. This is the joy and pain of creating knowledge. Teaching students to accept that they may be wrong and expect that they may be right will help them end up somewhere in between. This work should happen in weeks twelve and thirteen.

Setting Expectations

Making sure students know why they are choosing to interview someone and what they expect to get from the interview is extremely important for their research process. Although their expectations might not be met, it is important for them to have a strong plan so they are able to adapt to any situation.

How to Write Effective Questions

Not only are people inherently lazy, but they also have low self-esteem. They are not sure what interviewers want to hear from them unless those interviewers tell them what they want to hear. When I converse with people, my first assumption is that they do not want to hear me prattle on and on in great detail about myself. But the opposite may be true during the interview process. Since much of the success of the interview depends on getting stories and as much detailed information as possible, students will want to encourage interviewees to create narrative arcs in their answers that can be easily adapted to fit in the structure of their projects. As I tell my students, one great interview can make an entire project successful. So the key is letting people know that, yes, this is a time when I want to hear all about you, as much as you can tell me—stories, anecdotes, everything you want to share.

Besides mannerisms, there are linguistic ways for students to make it clear to interviewees that for this moment in time, you think they are the most interesting people on the planet. Including phrases that invite interviewees to speak at length—"Can you tell me a story about…," "In detail describe…," "From the beginning explain…"— and avoiding yes-or-no questions are good ways to get lengthy, informative responses.

Choosing People Who Occupy Different Positions in the Subculture

Since students are doing these interviews in a short period of time, initially identifying people to interview who occupy very different positions in the chosen subculture is a quick way to get varied viewpoints. Of course, as with all other assumptions, the interviewee responses, despite intentions, may end up remarkably similar. There are ways to try to ensure that you will be getting varied viewpoints.

Encourage students to consider how long chosen interviewees have been involved in the subculture, approaching persons who occupy different positions of authority, those that seem heavily involved versus those who seem on the outskirts, and urge them to make note in their observations of any other characteristics or participation that may identify people as holding different roles.

Interviewing People You Know

Sometimes the people students know best end up being their worst interviews. There are a number of reasons this is true. Since the student already knows the person, a formal interview can seem awkward and uncomfortable, almost artificial, and can keep the subject from expressing himself or herself effectively. Depending upon the relationship, the person being interviewed might not be used to talking to the interviewer in a formal way.

If students choose to interview somebody they are already familiar with, it is important to include their knowledge in the interview and not to pretend that they do not know what they actually know. For instance, if a student grew up with a twin sister and upon interviewing her asked what day or where she was born, it would be pretty ridiculous. The interviewer would clearly already know this information. Although this is a silly example, it is important. Making sure that students let their interviewees understand their knowledge base is important to getting good responses. A conversation in everyday life often takes off when people find they have something in common or share a similar experience. Interviewees like to know upfront what interviewers' intentions are and what the interviewers already know about them and their experience.

This will also help the subject to take the interview more seriously. When an interviewer makes clear to the subject that the questions will not cover a bunch of stuff the interviewer already knows, but instead will focus on getting to know unfamiliar things in a deeper way, it can help move the interview from friendship to research.

Previously known information might actually appear in the language of the question. For instance, one might ask, "I already know this about you; can you explain in detail why you might have made those choices?"

Conducting Interviews Assignment

An essential part of your final project with be conducting interviews with members of your subculture. Experience doing fieldwork has shown me that it is best to interview people who you are less familiar with. For instance, if you interview a very close family member or friend, you may not get the same kind of information you would get from someone you do not know. For this reason, I would recommend that you try to interview an acquaintance or someone you have had lesser, looser contact with for this portion of the project.

For each scenario there are important things to consider. If the person you choose is relatively unknown to you, be sure to make the interviewee feel comfortable sharing information and answering questions at length. Keep your manner genial and open, and encourage storytelling. Good stories from interviews can end up being riveting narrative elements in your final piece. In other words, great interviews can structure a great paper.

If you chose to interview someone you are familiar with or know a lot about, make sure to incorporate that knowledge into the questions you are asking. For instance, it would be silly to ask a sibling you grew up with "Where and when were you born?" Instead, include what you know when asking questions.

The purpose of the interview is to help you gain insight into the perspective of another member of your subculture. This can be valuable on a number of levels and for a number of reasons. It can help you understand the subculture more as an outsider, offer additional information you can use to examine your own positionality, and provide interesting narrative content for the final project.

As you plan for your interview, consider what information you would like to get out of the interview, and write out your questions accordingly.

For this assignment, write up a minimum of ten questions you plan to ask your interviewee. Make sure the questions are in an order that is logical. This will allow you to know what you intend to get out of an interview and enable you to adapt when an interviewee inadvertently answers more than one question at a time or shares information you would like to ask about in greater depth.

Make sure you ask leading questions rather than questions that can be answered with one-word responses. It is helpful to incorporate phrases such as these into your interview questions: "Tell me a story about the time…"; "Can you explain in detail when…"; "Describe your favorite memory about…" ; "At length, describe…."

This kind of questioning will help your interviewee to feel comfortable and willing to share more information about which you can then ask follow-up questions.

> Interviews can be conducted in various ways: through online chats, via telephone or in person. Each method has its own plusses and minuses, so be aware that they will yield different products.
>
> In-person interviews are usually the most productive in that they allow you to take notes on the interviewee's manner, dress and composure in addition to getting your verbal answers. The benefit on online interviews conducted in writing is that they are already written up for you, and the task of writing up in-person interviews is time-consuming. You will miss out on observation details, however, in any form that is not face-to-face.
>
> Please bring to class at least one set of questions with a brief description of whom you will be interviewing, what you already know about that person and what you would like to learn from her or him. Ultimately, you will be picking two people to interview and writing questions for each interview.

Results

Once students have picked two people they want to interview and written up their questions, they are asked to bring them to class. I then ask three or four student volunteers to write their questions on the board. As a class, we workshop the questions, analyzing their overall structure, considering what the student hopes to get out of the interview, and changing questions to help get the most out of the experience.

Students really appreciate the workshop aspect of this assignment and learn a lot about something they may have experienced as an interviewee but not as an interviewer. You will not be able to workshop all of the students' questions, but the examples can open up discussion that will apply to any student's interviews. Often students will interject with concerns about their own plan, and by the end of the session most questions will be answered.

Conclusion

Conducting interviews can often be the hardest part of the process for students. Interviews will sometimes fall through and even when they don't, not every conversation will be useful and productive. Helping students think through their goals and to anticipate many common issues faced in the interview process will ensure they have a number of options when they face challenges.

10. Conducting Observations

Overview

In earlier chapters, I discussed the importance of observation and using the five senses. Up to this point, students have done many assignments that rely on observation and analysis. For this chapter regarding the final autethnographic project, I will not reintroduce these previous assignments, but will add a small amount of information about ways students will be using observation to do three additional things: describe the person they are interviewing, describe an event they attend, and describe a meeting space for their subculture. This work should happen by week 14.

Observing an Interviewee

As described in Chapter 9, while interviews can be conducted in many different ways, the most productive results will come from in-person interviews. If your students are able to conduct their interviews in person, it is important to remind them of the importance of taking notes on the process rather than just recording the interview. Observing the physical space where the interview is conducted can help the student writer create a scene later in the narrative. Taking note of the diction of the interviewee, emotions, mannerisms and physical appearance can also help the student re-create the person as a dynamic and complex character in the final narrative. The more information the better!

Observation Assignment

When we engage in autoethnographic writing, it is important to try to re-create the spaces we are visiting—in other words, to explore the field sites where we are spending our time.

As part of our larger assignment, you need to identify a field site that will be relevant for your subculture. This can be a location where it meets, a place where history, event or memory is held.

For this assignment, I want you to walk into a space or event related to your subculture and spend at least twenty minutes there. You will be engaging in a stream-of-consciousness freewrite, making notes on everything you experience with your five senses. As in earlier assignments, I will then ask you to create a narrative from the details you have noted.

Rely on all five of your senses to convey not just what the space looks like but what it feels like. Sight, smell, touch, sight, sound are all important to consider as we try to re-create an environment we are experiencing for an outsider. Do not edit! Just write for the entire twenty minutes in the space without picking up your pen or pencil or relinquishing your keyboard, and see what you come up with!

As you did with earlier assignments, you should write the narrative version of your notes as close to the time of observation as possible.

Results

As in previous observation assignments, students will be gathering information to use space and event as characters in the final assignment. Focusing on working in spaces in real time will help students gain new insight and obtain copious amounts of information they can use to create subtext, support themes, frame and introduce their final narratives.

Conclusion

Observational information will add the rich sensory detail students need to make their projects accessible and interesting for their audience. Building on these skills throughout the semester and expanding their applicability in the autoethnographic project ensures students are attuned to the importance of their surroundings.

11. Putting It All Together

Overview

Now that students have finished the research for the final project, they need options for putting it all together. As in every other paper they have written this semester, they are a large part of the paper and will use their own experiences, gathered observation, interviews and reflection to create their narratives. In identifying themselves as both members and observers of a subculture, students should communicate a message about the subculture to an outside audience. To be successful, his message should be layered and make use of multiple themes, claims and subtext.

Have students consider the readings they completed and the writing they shared over the semester; any of these pieces can serve as a model for the final format. This is an extended exploration that will add elements to previously practiced forms. This final product's look is dependent upon the nature of the information they have collected. This work should happen in weeks fourteen and fifteen.

When to Quote, When to Paraphrase from Interviews

One of the first things you can practice when assembling your paper is how to excerpt and interpret texts. This is an essential skill as we begin to incorporate voices more specifically in our larger formal writing assignment.

For our purposes, quoting means taking language directly from the text or interview and including it in a piece of writing you have created. Use MLA or other appropriate citation methods to give credit to the author of the language you are excerpting.

You quote for a number of different reasons. Most notably the reason you quote is that the speaker or author has articulated a concept in a specific way that helps you understand a point you otherwise could not understand. For this reason, the author or speaker's language is intrinsic to the point and thus you need to quote it directly.

When you are reading the texts you have gathered and reviewing your interviews, you will have to make choices about when you think the author's language is important to the point and when you can make a valid argument by summarizing and rearticulating this language yourself.

This is where paraphrasing comes in. To paraphrase is to take an author's idea—still giving credit using appropriate MLA or other citation methods—and put it completely in your own words. This is a useful practice if you want to demonstrate your understanding or interpretation of an author's point but you don't think the precise language of the quote is necessary to its meaning.

Whenever you include a quote or paraphrase in the text you are writing, it is important to fully interpret the quote or idea and make sure the reader will know what it means and how it is of value. A quote or paraphrase should never be any longer than is necessary to support the views that you want to explain. The reason for this is that you must be sure to address all language and claims the quote makes in your own interpretation of it.

You should introduce the content of the quote before you bring it into the text. In addition, you will need to explain the quote's relevance to the surrounding argument.

Observations as Frames and Introductions

Observations can be used in a number of very important ways in final papers. A good observation can act as an introduction that brings the reader into the subculture. Observations can also frame an entire narrative, providing important details and jumping-off points for exploration of subthemes. Sometimes a good observation can conclude your narrative and provide a lovely replacement for a summary.

Observational detail about interviewees can help to contextualize the information you gather in your interview. Also, artifact, space and event analysis can all be used as devices to structure a final narrative and as ways to fill in important information about your chosen subculture.

> ### Drafting Your Final Autoethnography Assignment
>
> When trying to incorporate your research into a final paper, it is important to realize that you will not be using all of it. As in our essays earlier in the semester, you will be drawing on important pieces of it to make your larger arguments (parts of the observation, pieces of the interview, etc.). You should not try to use all of the information you gathered in the final paper. Any kind of personal and qualitative writing is about making choices and creating narratives and subtext while maintaining your own voice as a participant-observer.
>
> The most important thing to do is to find common threads in your research, identify your main themes and use the information you have gathered, combined with your own narrative understanding or experience, to create your final piece.
>
> Your final paper will end up being roughly six to ten pages long, given the amount of data you have collected. It is important to ask questions as you go through this final drafting process, so please feel free to contact me at any point about concerns and ideas.
>
> When transcribing interviews, please include only your questions and the full responses that will appear as quotes or paraphrases in your final paper. Since transcribing is time-consuming, this will be the most efficient use of your time. I ask you to attach these documents as well as the observations you completed to the final paper.
>
> You will be asked to present your findings and read a brief piece of your project on the last day of class.

Conclusion

The final assembly of the paper will be a challenging process for everyone. I encourage you to allot at least six weeks in your syllabus for successful completion of the final papers from start to finish. Students will need one-on-one attention to work through specific questions, so in those six weeks I encourage setting up individual meetings and making sure students have peer groups in class that they can trust to assist them in the final stages of writing.

12. Challenges of Personal Writing

Overview

As I said in the introduction of this book, issues or questions can arise when using personal writing in the classroom. In this chapter, I will try to review situations I have experienced and how to deal with some of these issues or questions.

When to Say No to a Project

I personally employ a fairly liberal policy when it comes to choosing topics for writing in my classroom. This is because I feel confident from years of experience helping students tackle most topics. If you are new to this kind of writing, consider what you as a teacher feel able to handle and make these limits clear to your students early on. Sometimes writing is uncomfortable, and that is OK, as long as you are comfortable handling the messiness of this as a teacher.

For the most, part students will self-censor unless they are very comfortable or interested in pursuing a particular subject. Often discomfort can occur because of emotions that are brought up when a student is writing about a topic that is close to the heart or very recently experienced. Some students are able to write about very tough experiences very beautifully; for others, writing about a death in the family or being victimized can cause them to relive experiences in a negative and potentially damaging way. It can be hard to ask students who are having a hard time with a subject to then revise and revisit writing that serves as a painful reminder or opens old wounds.

When students decide to write on a topic such as abuse, sexual violence or experiencing the death of someone close to them, I try to have a one-on-one conversation about the choice of topic early in the drafting process. In no way do I wish to discourage students from choosing a topic if they feel this is a good time to explore it. Instead, in these meetings, I invite them to write about these topics and also advise them that sometimes exploring these topics can be difficult because they will relive them again and again as they revise their writing. They will even be critiqued on how they recount something very personal and painful, which can be difficult. Ultimately, I leave the decision to the students. Most of the time, they will decide fairly quickly upon embarking on the writing of the essay whether the topic is indeed too hard. As long as you employ a drafting process that allows students a number of weeks to work on their essays, any student who decides to change a topic will have ample time to do so without negative consequences. In my class, students are also always invited to rewrite an essay if they were unable to complete the essay to their liking because of a difficulty with the topic.

There have been times when personal writing has brought to light issues for which students might benefit from having support services. We are there to create a supportive environment where they can explore issues in their writing, but professional services should be utilized when a student has a serious concern. I have found that students appreciate information about available services. I try not to pry, but because the writing is personal, when I see any warning signs or become concerned, I offer all of the available information about our student counseling services and explain what support the university can provide. I also offer to help make an appointment if that is something they would like. Some students will simply accept the information, while others will ask you to help set up an appointment. This will allow you to be supportive without having to become a counselor or get intimately involved in the matter. Your school may have its own process for handling cases such as these. I encourage you to speak with your department chair and to understand school procedures before intervening in any such situation.

Questions to Ask Students

For all projects, it is important for students to consider the ethical implications of their writing. For this reason, any group that cannot be a willing and capable participant in the research will not be a good choice for the assignment. Since I teach in New York City, I have had a few students come up with problematic topics for study, including the homeless, survivor groups, or even drug dealers they know.

To avoid some of these issues, I encourage students to pick subcultures they have chosen to be a part of. This often automatically rules out groups that could be inappropriate subjects because of circumstances such as mental or physical illness or drug-related activities.

How You Can Help with the Process

Sometimes it is very difficult to find something interesting to say about ourselves or our environment. One reason I include so many student examples in this book is to give new teachers an archive of potential topics and ways to steer students into topics they might find interesting. Initially I try not to give direct suggestions to students; instead I use the exercises I have included here to get them started with ideas that I can then help them refine and tailor.

On rare occasions, students will simply give up. Sometimes you can refer to earlier writing from the class to spark their interest, but it is always good to have in mind a few local organizations or events to help that rare student in a pinch.

Permissions

All students conducting interviews are asked to get permission from subjects to quote them in the writing assignments. This can be done a number of ways. Some schools will require you to use the institutional review board and develop a permission form that students must have participants sign. This is necessary if the writing will be published outside the classroom. Otherwise, make sure students know they must get oral consent from interviewees after clearly explaining the scope and audience for their writing.

Students are encouraged to use false names for people interviewed to make sure they will be comfortable sharing and answering questions and to protect everyone's privacy.

13. Concluding Thoughts

Throughout this textbook, I have engaged historical viewpoints and examined the possibilities for future expansion of personal writing's critical application in composition scholarship and pedagogy using qualitative inquiry. Through my classroom research, I have attempted to address the possibilities for critical written engagement from the student body, when invited to invest their time in writing projects that draw on the self and personal experience. I hope I have offered multiple models for this kind of personal engagement in the classroom as well as in Composition scholarship and teacher training.

Despite the productive possibilities for personal writing, there are still many difficulties to be addressed. As I interview fellow Composition scholarship teachers, despite their own successes and willingness to use the personal in all aspects of their careers, their stories remain fairly similar. Failure to have proper support and thus, to have widely accessible models, has made engaging the personal in a meaningful way a consistently uphill battle, one that requires constant risk-taking and a willingness to search for support in unlikely places. I hope this is a resource that offers you and your students' ideas, information, examples, and support.

Student Examples

The remainder of this textbook will be devoted to examples of writing I have received from students in response to the larger assignments described in previous chapters. For each assignment, I will provide a brief annotation that demonstrates the topics and scope of the included samples. All samples included are with full student permission; names have been changed where appropriate to ensure the anonymity of writers and subjects who wish to remain unidentified.

I recommend handing out more than one example to your students from your chosen category. This will allow you to have a group discussion about the ways in which the pieces work differently. While these are all good examples of the assignment, their different strengths and weaknesses are valuable to look at in comparison. Encourage your students to analyze the student writing as they would any other text you have looked at in your class. It is important to look at these samples with a critical eye, identifying elements of effective writing you will be discussing over the course of the class.

14. Sample Class Schedule

The following schedule would be for a class that meets once a week for approximately three hours.

Week 1

- In-class Writing: Freewrite Assignment – What is personal writing? What is academic writing? (Workshop)
- Introductions to each other and class content
- In-class Writing: Point of View Writing Exercise (Workshop)

Week 2

- Writing Due: Memory Assignment (Workshop)
- In-class writing activity: Writing About the Classroom Exercise

Week 3

- Writing Due: Self as a Character Assignment (Workshop)

Week 4

- Writing Due: The Deep Observation Assignment (Workshop)

Week 5

- Writing Due: Essay #1 Draft Memory/Character Essay (Peer Reviews)

Week 6

- In-Class Writing: Describing a Room That is Not Your Own Exercise

Week 7

- Writing Due: Essay #1 Final Memory/Character Essay (Workshop)

Week 8

- Writing Due: Choosing a Topic Assignment – Autoethnography

Week 9

- Writing Due: Essay #2 Draft The Space or Event Essay (Peer Reviews)

Week 10

- Writing Due: Show and Tell Assignment (Workshop)

Week 11

- Writing Due: Essay #2 Final The Space of Event Essay (Workshop)

Week 12

- Writing Due: Conducting Interviews Assignment (Workshop)

Week 13

- Writing Due: Observation Assignment (Workshop)

Week 14

- Writing Due: Autoethnography Draft (Peer Review)

Week 15

- Writing Due: Autoethnography Final (Class Presentations)

15. Additional Readings on Autoethnography

Denzin, Norman K. and Yvonna S. Lincoln, eds. *Handbook of Qualitative Research.* 3rd Ed. Thousand Oaks: Sage, 2005. Print.

Ellis, Carolyn, and Arthur P. Bochner. "Autoethnography, Personal Narrative, Reflexivity: Researcher as Subject." *Handbook of Qualitative Research.* 2nd ed. Eds. Norman K. Denzin and Yvonna S.Lincoln. Thousand Oaks: Sage, 2000. 733-68. Print.

Ellis, Carolyn. *Revision: Autoethnographic Reflections on Life and Work.* Walnut Creek: Left Coast, 2009. Print.

—-. *The Ethnographic I: A Methodological Novel About Autoethnography.* Walnut Creek: AltaMira Press, 2004. Print.

—-. *Final Negotiations. A Story of Love, Loss, and Chronic Illness.* Philadelphia: Temple University, 1995. Print.

Goodall, H. L., Jr. *Writing Qualitative Inquiry: Self, Stories and Academic life.* Walnut Creek: Left Coast, 2005. Print.

Jones, Stacy Holman, Tony E. Adams, and Carolyn Ellis,eds. *The Handbook of Autoethnography.* Walnut Creek: Left Coast Press: 2013. Print.

Mitchell, Claudia, Sandra Weber, and Kathleen O'Reilly-Scanlon,eds. *Just Who Do We Think We Are?: Methodologies for Autobiography and Self-Study in Teaching.* New York: Routledge Falmer, 2005. Print.

Deep Observation Assignment: Eleven Examples

Instructions

Spend at least twenty minutes in a public space, observing one person you have never seen or met before. The person need not be someone who strikes you as interesting. In fact, somebody who appears to be less than interesting to you is often the best choice for this assignment.

This is a difficult assignment for a number of reasons. It is hard to find someone who will be still and accessible for twenty minutes; if the person moves, move with him or her. The subject also might become aware of being observed. This is not a problem; simply talk to the person if he or she inquires, or move on to another observation if it seems at all bothersome to the person being observed. Your goal is not to make someone uncomfortable but to pause and consider your environment and those who inhabit it.

Using your five senses, take notes on everything around you and everything about the person, focusing on the subject's appearance, how she carries herself, her actions and interactions, the way she interacts with her environment, any speech you might overhear, the feeling, look, smell and feel of the space your subject inhabits.

After you have finished taking notes, as close to the observation time as possible, construct a narrative description of this person and his or her life based on the details you have recorded.

This is an assignment you may enjoy doing more than once. If you are riding public transportation or have free time in a public space, you can practice your observational skills and storytelling abilities by basing pieces on this real-life observational note taking.

This is a fiction-writing assignment based on real observation and will be shared during class discussion.

Student Samples

These assignments are based on a two-tier process of taking notes first and then crafting a story.

Because of the narrative nature of this assignment, although these samples are first drafts, they are quite strong.

Joomi describes a young woman eating alone.

Neziah describes a couple in love riding the subway.

William describes an ill-fated encounter at a bar.

Emma describes a young man visiting her ailing father in the hospital.

Anne describes a man arriving at a homeless shelter.

Heather describes a woman reflecting on her relationship on her way home from yoga.

Justine describes a man reflecting on others accepting his relationship.

Jillian describes a woman struggling to finish her work.

Chadbourne describes a man singing for donations.

Tyana describes a woman selling jewelry on the sidewalk.

Adriana describes a woman anxious about her relationship.

Melanie

Joomi Park

She loosened the neckline of her gray hoodie before picking up her spoon for another rich mouthful of Japanese katsu curry. She knew she shouldn't be eating past six to keep her promise of a healthier diet, but she had already broken so many of her New Years resolutions that this one felt just as harmless. Besides, she felt like if she didn't get food inside of her right that minute, she would deflate into a pile of gunk. Every time she put down her spoon, thoughts of the midterms and finals she had to study for, the never-ending calls from her overprotective mother that she had to pick up, and the rude, good-for-nothing customers she had to cater to flooded her mind. And so she frowned, and ate, and ate and for once she felt in control of her life, like her food could solve all her problems.

But of course, it always hit her, how pitiful she must look to other people. Melanie Tubbs—a young, 20-year-old girl sporting a matching set of gray sweatpants and a hoodie, eating alone next to a heart-eyed couple, and staring at the chair in front of her, all on a Friday night. She noticed a group of girls in the corner, and the Asian one with brown hair kept looking up at her every so often. "I bet she thinks she's better than me. I don't need her pity," she thought spitefully. Melanie tuned the girl out and let her mind wander. Soon she envisioned herself in a dramatic movie scene. The whole thing would take place in this very restaurant, and it would tell the tale of love, drama, and breakup. All she'd have to do is sit there and say a few different lines each time. Now that'd be the life. She wanted to laugh but she didn't want to seem crazy, so she sat there in silence the whole time. Her spoon scraped the plate, indicating that her food stress session was over. She wondered if there was anything good about her moving to the city for school. Would she even get anywhere when it seemed like so many of her peers already knew what they were doing? She frowned and asked for the check. Her movie idea didn't seem too funny anymore, so she paid and she frowned. At least her stomach was full.

Discussion Questions

- Why would somebody want to read this piece (the "Who cares?" factor)?
- Can you clearly identify the author's intention for the piece?
- How well does the author support the intention of the piece? Cite specific details that support or take away from the author's intention.
- Is there information missing from this piece that would make its intention clearer? What else would you like to know?
- Does the author portray herself as a round character? How does she do this?
- Do you trust the author of this piece? Why or why not?
- How clearly does the author establish a sense of setting/space in this piece? Cite specific details that support your claim.
- How clearly does the author establish characters other than the self in this piece? Cite specific details that support your claim.
- Did you learn anything new from reading this piece? If so, what?

- Are there particular passages with engaging language/description that stood out to you? Describe the appeal of these passages.
- Would you read more writing from this author? Why or why not?

Rattling Thoughts

Neziah Doe

The 1 Train rattles on in the depths of the infamous New York City subway system. I rest my hand on my girlfriend Maria's knee as we sit down in the corner, my clean, well-cut, square-shaped fingernails trailing along the thin ochre squares that pattern her business slacks. I remember her hands shaking with nerves and she showed them to me, her crooked smile telling me in that soft-spoken voice in our trashy apartment of the time, "I have a job." But that was three years ago, in the beginning. I rub my fingernails on her slacks, she fidgets as she leans on my shoulder, her body unsure whether she could rest all that weight upon me. Whether she should, I see this in her, that hesitation, it bothers me, consumes me. Ever since the beginning, I wanted her to crawl towards me like melting butter, like rain flowing down a clean drain. I kiss her, lightly, looking around the train smugly—this beautiful woman is mine, for as long as I live.

She flickers again and I look down at her curvaceous body. A red knitted zip-up she got for Christmas, with black designs of snowflakes and reindeer. I teased her when she left the house today wearing that so early on, it not even being close to winter. She raised her well plucked eyebrow at me, defiantly. It was my favorite look on her face, it compelled me to send her back into the bedroom, crashing against the mismatched furniture we have accumulated over the years, making sure she knew she was mine.

She whispers in my ear in Spanish teasing me about my wrinkles, the spiderweb thin lines etching themselves, claiming my skin as a canvas for their greater design, the artist of age. People said I look like my father, now sometimes when I pass mirrors I see him in there. But Papa would never come to such a big city like New York, he prefers the sweet quiet of his remote cabin in Texas. Looking in the mirror scares me sometimes.

I stare blankly at the wall behind those people I front of me, as I've been taught from ten years of living here—ignore all the people. Don't ever smile—they may see your weakness. They will look at you and destroy you when they see the weakness in your eyes. I smirk. I look down at Maria, she looks pensively at the ground with her sad brown eyes, picking at her cuticles sub-consciously, her smooth ponytail grating against my skin. She looks upset, they cut her hours last week by over half, she thinks they're going to fire her soon. Downsizing. Everyone wants more for less, she's been scorning at random intervals for the past few days, tutting like her mother used to.

"Is it here?" she asked, out of focus with the rattling car, craning her neck.

"No, next one," I sigh, "relax." We hold hands, or we have been for awhile, that simple pleasure doesn't send a parade of adrenaline down my arm every time the way it used to. The train stops. 168th, one more to go.

We shift from sitting to standing, not sure after all of these years what is the proper decorum for getting up for your stop. We smile, finally standing as the train begins to slow, Maria slips a bit.

"Wanna get up?" I tease her. She rolls her eyes. The doors open. I walk out, hoping that she has followed, I stick out my hand for her to take. I wait for her to take it.

She does.

> **Discussion Questions**
>
> - Why would somebody want to read this piece (the "Who cares?" factor)?
> - Can you clearly identify the author's intention for the piece?
> - How well does the author support the intention of the piece? Cite specific details that support or take away from the author's intention.
> - Is there information missing from this piece that would make its intention clearer? What else would you like to know?
> - Does the author portray herself as a round character? How does she do this?
> - Do you trust the author of this piece? Why or why not?
> - How clearly does the author establish a sense of setting/space in this piece? Cite specific details that support your claim.
> - How clearly does the author establish characters other than the self in this piece? Cite specific details that support your claim.
> - Did you learn anything new from reading this piece? If so, what?
> - Are there particular passages with engaging language/description that stood out to you? Describe the appeal of these passages.
> - Would you read more writing from this author? Why or why not?

Southern Belle

William Rossi

She isn't from here and God only knows why she dragged herself here for him. Their chance encounter in Miami was probably more romantic as a result of booze, sun, and recreational drugs. They were side by side their whole spring break, apart from the times they were on top of each other. They both took the trip down with their friends for spring break in their senior year of college. She must've been wild then; compared to the conservative schoolteacher she is now.

"Gonna miss you, Kaitlin," he mumbles to break the silence that ensued since they got on the train. Her blouse is buttoned all the way to the top; the buttons enclosing her breasts are one breath away from flying into the seat in front of her. She wraps her yellow cardigan around her body and fidgets in the seat due to the lack of space between them. He rests his hand on her thigh and rubs it softly. The fact that he's still interested astounds her. Her eyes roll up in a plea to God to end the torture. She's still heated over the fight and argument that ensued Saturday afternoon, after Chris recovered from his hangover and Kaitlin packed her bags up.

The monthly bar crawl that Chris and his friends avidly participate in, conveniently fell on the date of Kaitlin's arrival. The problem with drunken, male twenty-somethings from Long Island is that they are bestial beings, whose brains stopped growing in the early stages of fetal development. Their alcohol tolerance is at a maximum but that doesn't stop them from hitting peak intoxication by 9 p.m., thirty minutes into the bar crawl. With multiple bars to continue, the group of beefed up morons fumbled down the pavement until they managed to plant themselves on a stool at the next bar. They all neglected the small, southern blonde until her face smacked the pitcher that Chris swung over toward his table of brutes. Her hair turned a dark brown and her curls fell loose as the Budweiser dragged her makeup down her face. Any sober gentleman would have grabbed as many napkins as he could, apologized profusely, and left with his "date." However, Chris was not sober and not a gentleman. "Fuck! The beer," he shouted with a slurred Long Island accent. As Kaitlin ran out, he returned to the bar where he slugged back what was left in the pitcher and slammed it on the counter, demanding a refill, and reporting a spill on aisle three.

Once she gets back to North Carolina she'll send a text, a call if he's lucky, explaining how the distance is too much and they're both clearly in different stages of life. She has a career ahead of her, and he won't make it much further than the futon he tried to seduce her on in his parents' basement. How could she possibly commit to someone with no goals, aspirations, or even a job?

She educates children, in a town no larger than the one she grew up in. Her parents live five minutes from the apartment she shares with a nurse named Liz. Liz accompanied her on spring break in April, and saw Chris and Kaitlin's relationship develop. She helped Kaitlin pack for the trip and dropped her off at the airport Friday morning. Now Liz will have to listen carefully, as Kaitlin speaks between spoonfuls of Ben & Jerry's chocolate ice cream.

Discussion Questions

- Why would somebody want to read this piece (the "Who cares?" factor)?
- Can you clearly identify the author's intention for the piece?
- How well does the author support the intention of the piece? Cite specific details that support or take away from the author's intention.
- Is there information missing from this piece that would make its intention clearer? What else would you like to know?
- Does the author portray herself as a round character? How does she do this?
- Do you trust the author of this piece? Why or why not?
- How clearly does the author establish a sense of setting/space in this piece? Cite specific details that support your claim.
- How clearly does the author establish characters other than the self in this piece? Cite specific details that support your claim.
- Did you learn anything new from reading this piece? If so, what?
- Are there particular passages with engaging language/description that stood out to you? Describe the appeal of these passages.
- Would you read more writing from this author? Why or why not?

The Battle

Emma Suleski

She smacked together cherry red lips and turned her head towards the window. Boston's underground tunnels reflected fleetingly in her polished sunglasses before she put her head back down to her phone. She lifted her sunglasses to push back ashy-blonde curls. She stared at the screen of her phone then shut her eyes momentarily. Her posture was unflinching, shoulders remained poised, neck taut, chin up, yet her lip quavered and her eyes weren't simply shut, they were squeezed tight. After a sharp inhale, she looked back down at her phone and typed a reply. A short, "okay" or maybe, "on my way."

The T jolted back and forth on uneasy tracks and her eyes darted from person to person, scanning unfamiliar faces, seemingly wanting to get lost in their stories and away from her own. Her heavy lids fell back down and she imagined better days. She dreamed of spring break in Mexico three years ago where she acquired the small bird tattoo on her left forearm. She could've sworn she was breaking free that year. She let memories of her childhood flurry around her crowded mind. A smile crept across her face thinking of her dad, much younger back then, tossing her up and down in the living room, making her believe she could fly. Her mom, listening to music as she cooked in the kitchen until Dad interrupted her by asking for a dance. Her younger brother walking in the door triumphantly parading his basketball and a smile on his face, "I beat Dad this time! By a whole six points!"

The train jolted her out of her dreams and the mechanical voice indicated, "Longwood." She gathered her belongings, a black backpack and small duffel, and stepped out of the train car. Walking quickly she dialed a number on her phone.

She spoke quickly and clearly, "Hey, Kathy? I just got off the T. Yeah I'll be there soon. What room number?" Her Aunt Kathy was always in charge of any family emergency. She had an incredible levelheadedness about her that nobody else seemed to possess. It would be a comfort to see her and hear another of her timely updates.

Blond curls tangling in the city wind, she turned left into Massachusetts General Hospital's driveway. Ironically, at this point she pulled out a cigarette and stopped to smoke. She had planned to quit the habit but then all of this happened with her dad and she needed a simple comfort, no matter how unhealthy. She tossed the cigarette to the ground and used the tip of her nude flats to extinguish it. She couldn't put this off any longer. She walked up to the big revolving door and entered the hospital.

The elevator took exactly twenty-four seconds to arrive. When it did, she traveled up eight floors and down a long hallway. It was the typical hospital scene; nurses power walking this way and that, doctors in lab coats updating patients. She finally entered room 815 and looked at her sickly father on the bed in front of her. He looked just as he always did, yet totally different. The peaceful rise and fall of his chest indicated a sleep she hadn't had in days. Kathy greeted her with a sympathetic smile that spoke for itself; there was no news.

She let her bags drop to the floor and took over the seat closest to her dad. She smiled briefly, then picked up his hand and rested her head on his shoulder. This battle had only just begun.

> **Discussion Questions**
>
> - Why would somebody want to read this piece (the "Who cares?" factor)?
> - Can you clearly identify the author's intention for the piece?
> - How well does the author support the intention of the piece? Cite specific details that support or take away from the author's intention.
> - Is there information missing from this piece that would make its intention clearer? What else would you like to know?
> - Does the author portray herself as a round character? How does she do this?
> - Do you trust the author of this piece? Why or why not?
> - How clearly does the author establish a sense of setting/space in this piece? Cite specific details that support your claim.
> - How clearly does the author establish characters other than the self in this piece? Cite specific details that support your claim.
> - Did you learn anything new from reading this piece? If so, what?
> - Are there particular passages with engaging language/description that stood out to you? Describe the appeal of these passages.
> - Would you read more writing from this author? Why or why not?

The Woman with the Purple Mat

Heather Brackman

Light blond hair tightly twisted in a bun on the top of her head, Hadley carefully eased herself onto the gray plastic bench that connected to the side of the car. Sliding her tote bag to rest on her lap, Hadley pushed a rolled up purple yoga mat between her legs. She crossed her ankles, tightening her knees on either side of the foam, and pulled a pair of white earbuds out of a small pocket on the outside of her bag. The fluorescent lights of the subway car irritated her still sleepy brain and she slowly shut her eyes. Until her phone made a *ping* noise. Jolting her head up from resting on the wall, Hadley was quickly mesmerized by the message on her phone. Hadley's fingers furiously punched the screen of her device then paused. This man hadn't even waited an hour to text her. A smile crept onto Hadley's face and she recalled the off balance, barely flexible Mark who had insisted on coming to yoga with her.

They had met when he stole her coffee off the counter a few weeks back at a Starbucks and took it as his own, even though Hadley was clearly written across the white paper cup. On edge from her lack of caffeine, Hadley tapped him on his gray suit covered shoulder.

"Excuse me, sir," she snapped. "I'm running really late and you took my coffee, see?" She forcefully pointed her finger at her cup, hoping her glare would be enough to get the liquid addiction in her hand. Hadley's sneakered covered foot tapped with agitation as she awaited his response. Her tote slowly started to slip off her shoulder.

"Oh, you are so right." He smiled, the corners of his eyes crinkled. Hadley huffed in frustration. She raised her eyebrows.

"Wow, sorry." He sensed her irritation. "I already put some extra cream in here. But you can have mine if you want." He suggested, raising his voice at the end. "Just wait here, I'll go get it." Hadley pulled out her phone to check the time. She was going to miss the first part of class.

"Here you go," The man handed Hadley an identical cup to his. He grabbed his coffee and started to head towards the door. "Let me know how I can make it up to you," he yelled over his shoulder. Left by herself, Hadley looked down at her cup where the name Mark was scribbled. But Mark wasn't the only thing written on the cup.

Hadley waited a few days before texting him, but eventually she told Mark that the only way he could make it up to her was to buy her another coffee and accompany her to the same yoga class that he made her miss. Now, as Hadley stepped off the subway, she hit the send button, replying to Mark. Her loosely fitted purple long sleeved shirt slid off one shoulder and barely protected her skin against the chilled air that blew down onto her as she walked up the stairs to the street. Crossing her arms, Hadley briskly walked towards 30th street then took a sharp left, letting her bun out. Loose curls bounced to her shoulders. Opening a worn down, rusted metal door, Hadley stepped inside and ran up to her one bedroom studio. She had a date to get ready for.

> **Discussion Questions**
>
> - Why would somebody want to read this piece (the "Who cares?" factor)?
> - Can you clearly identify the author's intention for the piece?
> - How well does the author support the intention of the piece? Cite specific details that support or take away from the author's intention.
> - Is there information missing from this piece that would make its intention clearer? What else would you like to know?
> - Does the author portray herself as a round character? How does she do this?
> - Do you trust the author of this piece? Why or why not?
> - How clearly does the author establish a sense of setting/space in this piece? Cite specific details that support your claim.
> - How clearly does the author establish characters other than the self in this piece? Cite specific details that support your claim.
> - Did you learn anything new from reading this piece? If so, what?
> - Are there particular passages with engaging language/description that stood out to you? Describe the appeal of these passages.
> - Would you read more writing from this author? Why or why not?

David Everitt-Carlson

Anna Ehart

David Everitt-Carlson arrives at the 30th Street men's shelter with his black rolling suitcase and a rolled up tarp under his arm. The gray mop of hair on his head is greasy and unkempt and the denim of his gray skinny jeans is torn in places. He hasn't bothered to put his only pair of shoes on for the long walk from the High Line to the shelter, his calloused feet tough from years of treading the Manhattan streets. The night is warm, and today October felt like mid-June. He pushes open the iron gates and the ivy covered brick of the old psychiatric hospital seems to be consuming him as he approaches the door. Inside there is the familiar filth and stench of unbathed men, which he's grown accustomed to over the years.

"Hey, Carlson, how'd the interview go today?" The employee guarding the door asks.

"It was useless, thanks for asking." He's been applying for jobs in HR, but no one is hiring. He's been applying for jobs since his advertising agency went bankrupt after 9/11. He enters the dimly lit stairwell, his bare feet making a soft, thumping echo. He turns down the long white hallway to his usual room on the third floor, where six cots are made with thin cotton blankets. He sets his tarp on the cot and begins to unfold it.

Orange and yellow boards of plastic cut in panels of various sizes and shapes have managed to arrive at the shelter just a little bent. The boards are covered in small paintings, all on squares of cardboard of the same size. Contorted and monster-like portraits are shadowy in the partially illuminated room. One square reads "Make Peace Not War" and others have colorful peace signs. Geometric compositions painted by children and detailed mini artworks by practiced artists are displayed together on the panels. He unzips his suitcase and takes out the containers of paints, brushes, and palettes encrusted with dried colors and places them on the metal set of drawers next to his cot.

Before he stows away the street art for the night, he stops and puts his rough hands on his hips. He's been setting up his miniature city on the High Line for a few years now, drawing in small crowds of tourists and locals alike who stop to look. The traveling structure has grown as more and more people have sat down to paint with the barefoot man with the yellowing teeth. Children ask their parents if they can paint and ask "What does art mean?" He tells the children it's "anything you can get away with." He's hardened and gnarled compared to the young innocence of the children, like different species unsure of how to interact. The children kneel on the mats that he lays out along the edge of the green tarp covered in paint and use his globby acrylic paints. When they're finished he tells parents that he is accepting donations for supplies in a small box attached to the structure. The box is labeled "I Think Outside the Box," a phrase he turned into a movement that started with the Occupy Wall Street protests. He protested with his artwork, painting his slogan on a box and getting recognized by the Wall Street Journal. In Zuccotti Park, he protests the causes of his unemployment with his talent of sign painting.

He packs up the panels, carefully tucking his most valuable possession away. He strips down to his soiled boxers, his calloused feet on the cool tile floor and eases his aging and thin body into bed. He sighs with relief, muscles relaxing. The only thing he has is his art. No family, no job, no house. He finds joy in painting signs for his traveling art, and spreading art around the city by having people paint. The support of his fellow protestors makes him feel at home, a support that money can't buy.

> **Discussion Questions**
>
> - Why would somebody want to read this piece (the "Who cares?" factor)?
> - Can you clearly identify the author's intention for the piece?
> - How well does the author support the intention of the piece? Cite specific details that support or take away from the author's intention.
> - Is there information missing from this piece that would make its intention clearer? What else would you like to know?
> - Does the author portray herself as a round character? How does she do this?
> - Do you trust the author of this piece? Why or why not?
> - How clearly does the author establish a sense of setting/space in this piece? Cite specific details that support your claim.
> - How clearly does the author establish characters other than the self in this piece? Cite specific details that support your claim.
> - Did you learn anything new from reading this piece? If so, what?
> - Are there particular passages with engaging language/description that stood out to you? Describe the appeal of these passages.
> - Would you read more writing from this author? Why or why not?

The Man

Justine Giardina

He stumbles, clumsily, onto the dirty subway car. His sleeves are rolled up and he's clutching a cloth bag to his chest. The man situates himself next to a sticky rail beside a tired-looking Latina woman and her small son, and grips the unwashed pole just as the train sets into motion, staggering back one or two steps. It's hot on the subway and he, having lived in New York since he was seventeen, knows better than to drag his heavy coat along with him for the ride. He rocks back and forth on his feet, shifting his weight from one foot to the other, discontent with the anticipation for his next transfer, three subway stops away. He's late already and he still has two more transfers to make. Gathering all of his items into one arm, he reaches for his phone with the other, and upon seeing the number of missed calls present on the cracked screen of his mobile, puts the phone back into his pocket without opening it.

His partner, Nick, would have been much more on top of this than he would. Nick was thorough and organized about everything, the kind of person who wrote a list before going to the store and calling twice to confirm evening plans. Nick was especially thorough today, one might even say unreasonably so, because his mother was coming to visit. Having dated Nick for five years and knowing exactly how anxiety-inducing his parents are, he couldn't seem to really blame his partner. It wasn't that he didn't like his mother-in-law, but at times she could be slightly overwhelming. Like last Christmas, when she knitted them each rainbow scarves, and then decided it would be appropriate to place a smaller scarf wrapped around an adoption brochure at the bottom of the gift box. Or, two Thanksgivings ago when she rooted through their cabinets, collected all of their cigarettes and left sticks of chalk in the crisp Marlboro boxes. When Nick next went to light one up after that he had been so drunk that he didn't realize he had drawn out chalk until thirty seconds of holding it between his teeth.

These antics on occasion proved to be annoying, but the main thing that bothered him about Nick's mother was the degree of frivolity with which she regarded their relationship. Nick is one of three, junior to two habitually drunk sisters. Nick's mother regarded both of his, admittedly bland, sisters as valid candidates for marriage and a serious life, whereas she regarded Nick as kind of a fun accessory to the family that could bring boyfriends to holidays. When he and Nick brought up having a wedding one night at a dinner she had invited herself to, she laughed and asked why they couldn't just have a party. In addition to this, she bought into every single gay stereotype she could. Unsatisfied with her wardrobe, she one day dragged Nick into a Macy's for some sort of revamping act. Nick is a lawyer who plays Jeopardy and reads *Reader's Digest* and has no love for shopping, and frankly, he thought she would probably need some sort of miracle worker to fix even a single outfit of hers. She signed Nick up for salsa dancing classes with her for Christmas one year, and then the year after she took him to a Broadway show. Nick went on and on about how he hated each, but the idea of his partner salsa dancing with his mother was too disturbing to process so mostly he just tuned Nick out. He had always secretly blamed *Glee* and *Modern Family* for perpetuating those kinds of things.

As the train reared to a stop, he clutched tightly to the cloth bag and gripped the metal pole closest to him. She was overwhelming, but Nick's mother had never referred to him as Nick's "friend" or "roommate" and that said something, he was sure. As the subway doors open he quickly steps off, ignoring the sixth consecutive buzz from his pocket in less than thirty minutes.

> **Discussion Questions**
>
> - Why would somebody want to read this piece (the "Who cares?" factor)?
> - Can you clearly identify the author's intention for the piece?
> - How well does the author support the intention of the piece? Cite specific details that support or take away from the author's intention.
> - Is there information missing from this piece that would make its intention clearer? What else would you like to know?
> - Does the author portray herself as a round character? How does she do this?
> - Do you trust the author of this piece? Why or why not?
> - How clearly does the author establish a sense of setting/space in this piece? Cite specific details that support your claim.
> - How clearly does the author establish characters other than the self in this piece? Cite specific details that support your claim.
> - Did you learn anything new from reading this piece? If so, what?
> - Are there particular passages with engaging language/description that stood out to you? Describe the appeal of these passages.
> - Would you read more writing from this author? Why or why not?

Colors, Lines, and Shapes

Jillian McDonnell

She holds her pencil lightly gripped but it taps with a surprising thud as the eraser hits the table. More of a thump rather than a tick. She holds it in between her index and middle fingers and allows gravity to pull one side down. Over and over. *Thump, thump, thump.* She looks anxious and perplexed. Perhaps unable to discover the solution to her assignment in a sketch book. Blonde with one colored streak in her hair, a bright green so she could make that big statement to her parents. "I can do whatever I want to my hair, and no you cannot stop me," but now she twirls it and sighs, *"Why green? I don't have anything that matches this thing. Of course I couldn't have used my head and gotten something a bit easier to work with."* Like any of the trends and statements she had to make, she got bored with this one and dreams of change once again. She keeps tapping the pencil. *Thump, thump, thump.* How could she have been so stupid?! This assignment was given over a week ago. She did have time to do it that one day…but she did enjoy that night out with her friends. She looked great that night, no one could take her eyes off her. All done up in the form fitting little black dress, and she felt good. Her green streak shown in the light at the club and for once went with the brightly colored room and even her outgoing personality of the night. *Come on come on*, she thinks. She is unable to think of one design. One sketch, anything, that's all she needs.

Now with the thump of the pencil comes the jangle of her foot as it swings swiftly back and forth. *Thump, ching, thump, ching, thump.* Only so much time left until she has to tell the teacher what she has done. She thinks of her excuse. "I was, um, in the hospital. No! My aunt's sick, or my sister had her dance recital now how could I miss that?!" But no, she had all those days to do it, even start it, and the made up excuses work for only an allotted time, certainly not to excuse a completely blank page. *Thump, ching, thump.* But wait, an idea. Wait, no. Just a line, and then the faded mark of it left by the eraser unable to completely fulfill its job. "*C'mon, c'mon, anything will do,* anything." She thinks back to all of those PowerPoints from class, but again, nothing. *Thump, ching, thu-* "Hi Sarah," she sighs as her classmate walks over. "*Here we go*," she thinks as Sarah begins to speak: "Did you finish the assignment? I could not believe how long it took me!" She answers yes as she slowly closes her sketchbook to hide her false reply. "Cool so I'll see ya in ten then!" "*Ten minutes?!*" Sarah panics. Nothing on her paper she knows she has to at least start something. "*I can't, there's not a chance.*" Now the wheels are turning. *Anything will do, anything.* Another line but again another eraser mark to replace it. She thinks back to the class. All of the colors and lines and shapes and names zigging and zagging across the board. *Thump, thump, thump.* "Wait…what was that one slide he showed us?" As if going through the slides she shifted through each one with her memory as the screen and shut her eyes to bring silence to the eating area. *Yes.* Finally, her eyes lit up. She knew what she must do. But with her next class coming up, mine did as well. And as we both got up to throw out our trays, she ran ahead of me out of my sight. *Ching, ching, ching, ching.* And that was that for the blond girl with the green streak.

Discussion Questions

- Why would somebody want to read this piece (the "Who cares?" factor)?
- Can you clearly identify the author's intention for the piece?
- How well does the author support the intention of the piece? Cite specific details that support or take away from the author's intention.
- Is there information missing from this piece that would make its intention clearer? What else would you like to know?
- Does the author portray herself as a round character? How does she do this?
- Do you trust the author of this piece? Why or why not?
- How clearly does the author establish a sense of setting/space in this piece? Cite specific details that support your claim.
- How clearly does the author establish characters other than the self in this piece? Cite specific details that support your claim.
- Did you learn anything new from reading this piece? If so, what?
- Are there particular passages with engaging language/description that stood out to you? Describe the appeal of these passages.
- Would you read more writing from this author? Why or why not?

Angelic Atmosphere

Chadbourne Oliver

The door at the back of the car slides left, and in reels a bent old man. Dark are his sunglasses, his weathered boots, his skin. Pale and dirty are his shirt and hair, neither of which retain their presumptive original color. His torso leans forward of his legs at an obtuse angle that flirts cruelly with ninety degrees. A short cane of gnarled and polished wood bends a little under his right hand. About his neck is harsh cord that pulls tightly on the red indented skin it touches, supporting a large gray bucket wherein the hearts of artichokes once dwelled. With his left hand he lends some support to the bucket and his strained neck upon which it weighs. Where the brine of vegetables once sloshed there now comes the muted drum of filthy coins oiled by thousands of hands. The bucket is his wallet, his salvation, and above the reckless rumble of the Q train he gives it yet another purpose.

With a laborious step he heaves the bucket up and lowers it with a clunk; the entrance of his solemn percussion section. With another he thrusts the cane towards the floor and it resonates loudly. And then, with a passion that suggested the car from whence he has just come contained a yawning chasm that plunged down beneath even the loneliest depths of the New York City subway, his voice erupts forth from somewhere within that bony breast and spills into the atmosphere like smoke into fog. His rich voice is loud and unrestrained, uninhibited by the angle at which he projects towards the floor. He is an itinerant Stevie Wonder, complete with clouded, unseeing eyes and an angelic voice.

Step by step he moves arduously through the car, each left foot in sync with his coin-and-bucket bass drum, each right foot with his makeshift snare. His pace surpasses slow. It is rhythmic, it is careful, it is burdensome. It is the backbeat to a hymn, a funeral procession trudging along a path thickened by rain. And yet it is no dirge that the bent man with his gilded vocal cords does intone, but an air of rather different morals. "If you want my body, and you think I'm sexy, come on sugar, let me know," he cries. Rod Stewart's piece has never been spewed from unlikelier lips. Could he have picked a better song? Could he have picked one worse? All the passengers are awestruck. Their eyes are transfixed, their jaws sag. Several bohemians aboard the train are practically groveling. Coins and bills are drawn forth hastily and thrown into the bucket to swell the tide of metal that breaks with each thunderous step against the plastic sides. The bent man issues appropriate thanks for each donation between lines, "If you really need me, God bless, just reach out and touch me, God bless, come on honey, tell me so, God bless." He reaches the end of the car. The door slides right and then left, wavers, and then shuts fast.

Discussion Questions

- Why would somebody want to read this piece (the "Who cares?" factor)?
- Can you clearly identify the author's intention for the piece?
- How well does the author support the intention of the piece? Cite specific details that support or take away from the author's intention.

- Is there information missing from this piece that would make its intention clearer? What else would you like to know?
- Does the author portray herself as a round character? How does she do this?
- Do you trust the author of this piece? Why or why not?
- How clearly does the author establish a sense of setting/space in this piece? Cite specific details that support your claim.
- How clearly does the author establish characters other than the self in this piece? Cite specific details that support your claim.
- Did you learn anything new from reading this piece? If so, what?
- Are there particular passages with engaging language/description that stood out to you? Describe the appeal of these passages.
- Would you read more writing from this author? Why or why not?

Sylvia

Tyana Soto

Sylvia's hands shook as she gently placed an embellished gold necklace into its felt box.

It was beautiful to her, so beautiful that she almost didn't want to sell it. She placed it on the table next to the other necklaces and admired how stunning it looked in the morning light. After staying up for hours polishing and cleaning it carefully she couldn't help but smile at the sight of it. It was perfect, and she was so glad that she was able to put it on her table next to all of the other knickknacks. She straightened a golden frame with an antique picture, and looked around at the crowd that was beginning to come already.

She felt her heart beating.

Oh, how she loved these mornings; the weekends of the flea market, the weekends of her life. All week her hands would flutter around her precious trinkets with anxiety, just waiting and longing for the weekend to arrive. On Friday night she would lie in bed extra early with her eyes shut tight hoping that the next morning had arrived. She loved waking up and hauling her things to the small white tent. It was magic seeing the different people come, and the way that they swarmed to her table and admired all of her things. She was a big seller, and seemed to be one of the most successful ones in the market.

Pulling the soft cloth from her pocket, Sylvia walked over to her porcelain section and began wiping off the dust fondly. Even though she had done it before she left she still felt it necessary to do it again. If something looked clean people were more likely to look and possibly buy. There was nothing worse than something dirty and uncared for. People wanted bright and shiny. It was the first rule of the flea market.

When she was finished buffing and cleaning all glass objects, she slowly shuffled to the center of her square of tables and sat down slowly into her green and yellow lawn chair. She remembered when she had first started selling at flea markets. Her kids were young, her marriage had just begun, and life was good. She and John would load the kids in the van with things they had bought at garage sales, and they would sell all day. John would be the ultimate salesman, bringing people over with his magnetic smile, and always making a sale no matter how big or small. The kids would gallop through the streets like horses, talking to vendors and playing games with the other children. They were all so happy, and so drawn to the life of buying and selling.

But then the kids got older, the van was traded in for a newer car, and John got sick. The weekends at the flea market were scarce, and eventually they stopped going. Now that everyone was gone she could do that again.

No, she was not that vibrant woman she once was. The one with jet black hair and a tiny waist who would always catch stares on the streets. Her clothes were looser, hair grey, and body a little slower. She used to be able to haul everything from the van into the tent with no problems at all. Now she needed help. But life was just the same, and Sylvia could almost hear her kids running towards her, mouths stained red and blue from the ice pops they had eaten. Smiles big as the sun. She may be alone now, and her life may consist of tiny porcelain dolls with perfect faces, but that life made her happy.

"Excuse me, but is this real gold? Its beautiful."

Sylvia glanced up to see a woman holding the gold necklace in the velvet box. With a smile she slowly got up from her chair and said, "Yes honey, 100% authentic 14-karat gold. A special necklace for a special woman like you."

Life was going to be all right.

> **Discussion Questions**
>
> - Why would somebody want to read this piece (the "Who cares?" factor)?
> - Can you clearly identify the author's intention for the piece?
> - How well does the author support the intention of the piece? Cite specific details that support or take away from the author's intention.
> - Is there information missing from this piece that would make its intention clearer? What else would you like to know?
> - Does the author portray herself as a round character? How does she do this?
> - Do you trust the author of this piece? Why or why not?
> - How clearly does the author establish a sense of setting/space in this piece? Cite specific details that support your claim.
> - How clearly does the author establish characters other than the self in this piece? Cite specific details that support your claim.
> - Did you learn anything new from reading this piece? If so, what?
> - Are there particular passages with engaging language/description that stood out to you? Describe the appeal of these passages.
> - Would you read more writing from this author? Why or why not?

One

Adriana Pauly

She closed her eyes. Just a second. One tiny moment. One pause. One breath. It was as if she could see and feel how gravity was pulling her mentally and physically to the ground. Her eyes were turned downward, her lids hung heavy over the ends, her cheeks had reached her chins, making their way towards her collarbone.

When had this change occurred? Had it been gradually, below the surface of her consciousness? Had it been hiding this whole time, only to come out under the harsh lighting of the subway, like a monster hiding in the dark? Once more, she looked at her reflection in the window across from her, only to turn her eyes back to the ground and into emptiness.

She touched her wedding band, twisting it a few times, reassurance, a solid reminder of their promise, their companionship. Twenty-seven years. Twenty-seven years, stuck, the one with the other, nowhere else to go anymore. She still liked him and she was sure he still liked her, now that the children were old enough, finally he wasn't merely father and she wasn't merely mother anymore. They had regained their independence finding their way back to each other.

She fidgeted in her seat. She was anxious to arrive. These seats, this light, these bodies pressed against each other, establishing an awkward intimacy. She kept her hands folded in front of her belly holding on to her city guide while trying to avoid immediate physical contact with her neighbors. A task made virtually impossible thanks to her body. She was round, her breast were big, her belly was big, her thighs were big. She had given up being a regular weight after her children had been born. It did not matter, for now anyway.

She had been walking around all day. Well equipped with her sneakers, her windbreaker jacket and scarf. The scarf. She subconsciously touched it. It was knitted out of brown wool, circling her short neck and ending in the shape of a fox head. She had bought it a long while back thinking it was a clever design, she knew it was not up to speed with the newest fashion trend, but she liked it anyway. As a matter of fact, she even felt like it embodied her personality. Round, warm, comforting and a bit goofy on the one hand, a little worn out and with some loose stitches here and there on the other.

She suddenly felt self-conscious. She felt like she was being watched. She held on tight to her city guide, avoiding eye contact with the other passengers. There were two theatre tickets stuck between the pages from the play they'd gone to see.

Discussion Questions

- Why would somebody want to read this piece (the "Who cares?" factor)?
- Can you clearly identify the author's intention for the piece?
- How well does the author support the intention of the piece? Cite specific details that support or take away from the author's intention.

- Is there information missing from this piece that would make its intention clearer? What else would you like to know?
- Does the author portray herself as a round character? How does she do this?
- Do you trust the author of this piece? Why or why not?
- How clearly does the author establish a sense of setting/space in this piece? Cite specific details that support your claim.
- How clearly does the author establish characters other than the self in this piece? Cite specific details that support your claim.
- Did you learn anything new from reading this piece? If so, what?
- Are there particular passages with engaging language/description that stood out to you? Describe the appeal of these passages.
- Would you read more writing from this author? Why or why not?

Self-as-Character Assignment: Eight Examples

> ### Instructions
>
> We all love a good character, someone who is complex yet relatable, full of all of the human foibles we are aware of, who may act differently from what we could ever anticipate.
>
> This is by far the hardest assignment of the semester and also your first major assignment. Unless you have been honing your persona in writing for many years, you will have a hard time with this piece.
>
> For this assignment, you will need to write a self-portrait. There are many ways you can do this. You can identify a structural element that allows you to move through personality traits, use interesting qualities or amusing actions to form a story or create narrative story lines that let us see you at your best and worst. So much of writing this piece is about making choices. Lopate chose to write about himself using his body as a device to make different kinds of observations about his character and personality. Other writers, like Geeta Kothari, chose food to talk about themselves as characters.
>
> Choose a device that you can use to explain yourself as a character. A device is something we will practice with in many of the writing assignments—a tool that allows you to tell a story in a logical way when you might not otherwise have been able to tell it organically in the structure of your narrative.
>
> However you approach this piece, make sure to focus on yourself in an interesting way. In other words, for better or worse, make yourself a character we want to hear and care about.
>
> This work will be shared with classmates during class discussion.

Student Samples

These assignments are single drafts. This means that students did not revise these pieces. Rather, they turned them in as practice assignments for larger essays.

Neziah uses her history with eyeglasses to define her character.

Emma chooses defining moments from a series of ages, presented chronologically, to define her character.

Zachary describes his struggles with low self-esteem to establish his character.

Justine examines her history of relationships with others and her tendency to cry to examine her character.

Hannah uses humor to examine her body and define her character.

Or describes how his experiences at his local bar define his character.

Jeffrey shows himself as an overworked student in order to define his character.

Joomi uses her height as a frame to examine her character.

Sight

Neziah Doe

0. The only thing I got in trouble for as a child was hiding under my covers and reading horribly written children's fiction into the cold depths of the school year nights. I could barely wake up in the morning, shirt buttons incestuously snuggled up in the wrong slits as I made fresh squeezed orange juice stains worthy of Jackson Pollock. My mother would scold me as she gave me the smallest piece of toast: you're going to ruin your eyes like this.

1. Sevens and ones, o's and u's, m's and n's were interchangeable. I couldn't see the monochrome letter sheet on the doctor's grey door, the strong slab serifs blending into indiscernible shapes, an astroid belt of "umm"'s, "I dunno"'s and the all too bold "can YOU read that"'s? The thick nurse in her rubber ducky scrubs sighs and taps her bitten pen against my medical records, facing my mother and I she says "You definitely need glasses. It's written that you needed them last year too. Why don't you have glasses?"

2. Later that week the nice eye-doctor lady with the *Highlights* magazines in her lobby tells me and my dismayed mother after a few minutes of "can you read that—no? No." that a lovely pair of sight-enabling magic lenses are in my future. With a melodramatic sigh my mother asks if contacts are an option and the doctor's eyebrows shoot up past her enviable thick frames. "She's only twelve you can't give her contacts just yet." I am internally jumping with joy, thinking of finally looking like as much of a loser as I know I am. My mother yells at me for my eye abusing ways as we go to Costco to pick out the perfect pair. After much arguing (I wanted the grandma frames), I go with a brown pair with wire detail on the side, like a stained glass frame that had yet to be completed.

3. The Stained Glass Frame. The ones that sang a solo for the first time, thought they fell in love, cried drugstore eyeliner onto their shininess. Had their first kiss: a nauseating, saliva filled fifteen seconds of "This is what everyone was waiting for? Seriously?" The glasses had their first holidays with extended family—drinking instant coffee and cracking open salt crusted sunflower seed pods with front teeth. The ones that attempted writing and failed, the ones that had the clarity to look in the mirror and see it was an artist. And a mess worth cleaning up. They barely got through the ninth grade, friends all fleeing their disarray of a life one by one, it was torture, like pulling off fingers, a Venus fly trap of a glove. May the noble pair rest in peace, lying on the briny lake floor of Camp Ramah in the Berkshires since that spring day.

4. The Replacements. Bought in a frenzy because I refused to get the same pair as before, letting them have their run. Glasses don't get a 2.0. Black on the outside, pink on the in. Their face never really suited them, warped into someone else by the beach-ball shaped flesh they rested on. They were smart and calm. They went to San Francisco, they were neglected on every surface as they realized that all boys are really good for are kisses. They tried unkosher food, they tried not believing in God. Oh how this pair tried, the glasses were reminded what they were there for, and they looked in the mirror and only saw a floating disembodied version of themselves, were flung to the bed and sighed.

5. The Replacement Replacements. They were free. They were there. Left behind in my dresser for the contacts that just did their job better. The obsessive glasses cleaning tempest was vanquished.

They came out of hiding for dark days, test days. I couldn't go to sleep last night days. I want to go to design school why I am I taking Math days.

6. The David Tennant. They look nothing like David Tennant's 10th Doctor glasses but I thought they did and that is what counts. They were sexy, sophisticated. They got into Design School. They were short haired. They went to Israel and miraculously changed their vision.

7. The Henna Glasses. Bought in a rebellious state of spending twenty dollars past what the insurance gives. They were bought to clash with the growing mane of henna'd hair that surrounded them.

They don't have a story yet.

It's too bad I always wear contacts.

Discussion Questions

- Why would somebody want to read this piece (the "Who cares?" factor)?
- Can you clearly identify the author's intention for the piece?
- How well does the author support the intention of the piece? Cite specific details that support or take away from the author's intention.
- Is there information missing from this piece that would make its intention clearer? What else would you like to know?
- Does the author portray herself as a round character? How does she do this?
- Do you trust the author of this piece? Why or why not?
- How clearly does the author establish a sense of setting/space in this piece? Cite specific details that support your claim.
- How clearly does the author establish characters other than the self in this piece? Cite specific details that support your claim.
- Did you learn anything new from reading this piece? If so, what?
- Are there particular passages with engaging language/description that stood out to you? Describe the appeal of these passages.
- Would you read more writing from this author? Why or why not?

Fastforward

Emma Suleski

When I was seven years old I tried to scratch off the beauty mark below my left eye. It bled and I cried. I hated my freckles and that one stupid bump never made me feel any better. I didn't understand why it was called a beauty mark anyway; I always thought whoever named it that just felt bad for people who had moles on their faces.

My oldest brother Patrick left for college in New York when I was ten. I cried again and wrote him tens of e-mails. He faithfully replied with "I'll see you soon" and "hang in there, kiddo." When we finally took a family trip to visit him, I realized why he never came home. The City was intoxicating and from that moment on I was love drunk.

At twelve years old I had a brilliant idea. I found going to the hairdresser to get my bangs trimmed every few weeks tedious and unnecessary. Instead of growing them out, I decided to cut them myself. There were many messy attempts, including the time I trimmed them to half way between my hairline and eyebrows, and the time the trim was so uneven I wore a headband to school for two weeks until I could try again. Eventually I mastered the task enough for my friends to ask me to trim their hair too.

On my thirteenth birthday I received what is still today my most prized possession, my iPod. I loaded 645 songs onto it and bragged to all of my friends about how much music I could listen to, anytime, anywhere. Five years later it has several scratches, a chipped screen, and approximately 5,500 more songs. I love it even more.

I experienced true pride for the first time shortly after my fourteenth birthday. I stood on the podium with my first place trophy at the USA Gymnastics state championship and smiled for my mom's Nikon. I worked for a moment like this at All-Star Gymnastics for ten years. Nothing could ever take that away from me.

My life came to a screeching halt when I was fifteen and experienced my first heartache. The words "it's time to quit gymnastics" echoed in my head in a way that made tears well up in my eyes but I did not cry. I heard those words not only from my parents, my coach, and my doctor, but the bones in my body too.

Sixteen and seventeen were an exploration of how to rebuild myself. It was a blur of hard work, sometimes resulting in disappointment, sometimes yielding a beautiful result. It involved a lot of red hair dye, a few too many piercings, a tattoo on my ribs, and one very specific way to make the wings on my eyeliner match. I was always convinced I needed to be one thing in order to be recognized as a person. I needed something to make people get me, my own personal punch line. I wanted a simple defining word, an adjective that made me make sense.

Now, at eighteen years old I am both trial and error. I am success and failure. I am simply a work in progress.

Discussion Questions

- Why would somebody want to read this piece (the "Who cares?" factor)?
- Can you clearly identify the author's intention for the piece?
- How well does the author support the intention of the piece? Cite specific details that support or take away from the author's intention.
- Is there information missing from this piece that would make its intention clearer? What else would you like to know?
- Does the author portray herself as a round character? How does she do this?
- Do you trust the author of this piece? Why or why not?
- How clearly does the author establish a sense of setting/space in this piece? Cite specific details that support your claim.
- How clearly does the author establish characters other than the self in this piece? Cite specific details that support your claim.
- Did you learn anything new from reading this piece? If so, what?
- Are there particular passages with engaging language/description that stood out to you? Describe the appeal of these passages.
- Would you read more writing from this author? Why or why not?

Reflections

Zachary Volosky

I am not an attractive person. I do not think so at least. I am sure there are people who look worse than I do, but I cannot think of a time when I have looked in the mirror and thought "Zach, you're a good looking guy." In fact, I remember a time in the seventh grade when I looked in the mirror and thought just the opposite. I do not say things like this to fish for compliments from others (although that is something that someone who fishes for compliments would say,) but I say this because it is what I think.

Yes, I have low self-esteem. Perhaps it is a radicalization of the humility I was raised to have, just taken to the extreme by some other fault in my personality. Or perhaps it is the fact that I was bullied by a friend I had from the first to the seventh grade, who made my life miserable in order to feel better about the problems he was having at home. It is likely the latter although it really does not matter; the effect remains the same. My self-esteem has never been a personal quality I have been proud of. Maybe it is why I have found an interest in fashion; to dress myself up and look fabulous on the outside so that I could feel fabulous on the inside. That makes the interest sound shallow and superficial which is something that I have also been struggling with. When you dedicate your life to studying a superficial and materialistic industry, you tend to run into some conflicts with your Catholic-raised morality.

I guess I do have good qualities as well. I am remarkably average. I do not mean "average" in the "I'm just an Average Joe doing Average-Joe-things" kind of way. I mean I am five-foot-nine and one-hundred and fifty pounds, the average height and weight of an American man that is eighteen to twenty years old. I am decently strong and fit but I do not look like Ryan Gosling when I take off my shirt no matter how many crunches I do. I have long legs and a short torso which has always given me luck when running. I also cannot hear out of my left ear. This is something that I act like bothers me less than it really does. Having people run to my left side upon learning this and saying ridiculous things followed by "Did you hear that?" does get frustrating after the first fifty or so times. It's something that I have learned to deal with since the fifth grade and I believe that I have dealt with it quite well. Unfortunately, when I am in large groups at parties or any other place with significant background noise and a conversation is happening around me that I cannot participate in because I cannot hear, I happen to feel quite alone. It is an odd feeling but one that is able to be dealt with. Apart from my body, there are aspects about my personality I do rather like.

I try to be really nice to people, especially females. No, that is not just a ruse to try to get them to like me and sleep with me or something, as some people think. It is because I refuse to let chivalry die. I like to fantasize that I am one of those cute, short, bald monks that don't say much and live like hermits and I would just travel the country and tell women that they were pretty. I feel like some women deserve to be told that because they do not hear it enough.

I also have this overwhelming urge to help people. I remember on the first date I went on with my current girlfriend, a waiter at the restaurant we were at dropped a tray of plates and they shattered at his feet. I got down to help him pick the pieces although I did end up cutting myself on one of the pieces. I just could not see not helping him. This sounds like a good quality but it does usually end up with me getting hurt in some way. I do not mind though. Someone has to do the things that others might not want to do, even if it does mean hurting themselves. It might as well be me getting hurt.

> ### Discussion Questions
>
> - Why would somebody want to read this piece (the "Who cares?" factor)?
> - Can you clearly identify the author's intention for the piece?
> - How well does the author support the intention of the piece? Cite specific details that support or take away from the author's intention.
> - Is there information missing from this piece that would make its intention clearer? What else would you like to know?
> - Does the author portray herself as a round character? How does she do this?
> - Do you trust the author of this piece? Why or why not?
> - How clearly does the author establish a sense of setting/space in this piece? Cite specific details that support your claim.
> - How clearly does the author establish characters other than the self in this piece? Cite specific details that support your claim.
> - Did you learn anything new from reading this piece? If so, what?
> - Are there particular passages with engaging language/description that stood out to you? Describe the appeal of these passages.
> - Would you read more writing from this author? Why or why not?

Unfortunate Truths

Justine Giardina

I had a lot of anxiety in public when I was little, which is why I think that in my late teen years I have made a hobby out of unabashedly having breakdowns in public. I will walk right into stores like I belong there, tears streaming down my face and sticky black eyeliner marring the backs of my hands and I will make purchases as though I am not even a "hot mess." I've cried in restaurants, on subways, in parking lots, on the corners of sidewalks, between library shelves, in convenience stores, under bridges, on buses and behind cars all with a certain degree of shamelessness that is typically reserved for people who aren't bawling their eyes out. The only exception to this rule is Toys R Us. Anyone really can cry in Toys R Us and still get fairly normal customer service. Once on a sidewalk I overheard a man walking by me say "I'm tired of seeing prostitutes crying on the street" and for whatever reason that made me feel a little better.

I feel as though the person who knows me best is my mother, which is definitely strange because she is the person who I most often feel misunderstood by. My mother is a somewhat typical suburban mom, she works in a preschool and has a favorite coffee mug and yells "No one cares!" at reality television shows but continues to watch them anyway. My mother always wanted a girl, but I don't think I turned out as she expected because she is frequently pushing the idea of being "like all of the other girls." Unfortunately for my mother, in addition to sobbing on public transit I have a slew of other atypical hobbies, none of which she is particularly fond of. I once spent a month drawing tampons and sanitary napkins and I could see a little piece of her die inside as she slowly began to realize that we would never bond over reality television together.

The people who are most honest about what I am like tend to be on dates with me and their unfortunate truths always come veiled as some sort of passive-aggressive compliment. "You were even more jaded when I first met you than you are now," someone said to me once over cheap Chinese take-out. He didn't say anything after that for a little while, and I think that was because he was waiting for me to thank him. "That was cute," another once said to me, "like in the way a baby horse tries to walk for the first time," this was followed shortly after by "Your bangs actually look straight today" and "I bet you don't even wax your eyebrows." I think the reason why this happens so frequently is because I have a very specific type, and that type is metrosexual with moderate to severe mommy issues. Mostly these instances are ok but usually when they occur the date ends at dinner.

If I were asked to describe myself to someone I would probably leave out the fact that my bangs don't fall perfectly straight and probably wouldn't think to disclose any information about my eyebrows. I would describe a person who doesn't really know how to balance things in her life and I would describe someone with a deep restlessness that I guess I could call a "Wanderlust" if I felt the need to romanticize it. I would talk about how I find little things about people endearing, like how they talk about their sister or the way they write their name, and I would also talk about the way that I am repulsed by, without exception, every single person on the subway and will whisper "How dare you" under my breath if anyone so much as looks at me. Sometimes this is difficult because when someone is bawling on a subway like they are in the privacy of their own home a lot of people, for whatever reason, want to watch.

I sometimes wonder if that is because they are bored of watching the crying prostitutes on the street.

> **Discussion Questions**
>
> - Why would somebody want to read this piece (the "Who cares?" factor)?
> - Can you clearly identify the author's intention for the piece?
> - How well does the author support the intention of the piece? Cite specific details that support or take away from the author's intention.
> - Is there information missing from this piece that would make its intention clearer? What else would you like to know?
> - Does the author portray herself as a round character? How does she do this?
> - Do you trust the author of this piece? Why or why not?
> - How clearly does the author establish a sense of setting/space in this piece? Cite specific details that support your claim.
> - How clearly does the author establish characters other than the self in this piece? Cite specific details that support your claim.
> - Did you learn anything new from reading this piece? If so, what?
> - Are there particular passages with engaging language/description that stood out to you? Describe the appeal of these passages.
> - Would you read more writing from this author? Why or why not?

Hanatomy

Hannah Lajba

Let's skip the hair.

I've been told I have a heart shaped face, the most attractive of the face shapes, the cutest, and most appealing to boys. I would like to think it's that simple, but seeing as this face hasn't attracted any boys in my eighteen years I assume that my brain shaped itself into a heart to accommodate for that small, black bicycle pump in my chest. My over thinking, whimsical, self indulging brain, that Igor would have for sure taken as a replacement to the one he dropped. I new there was always a reason my dad told me they wanted my first name to be Abby and my middle name be Normal.

You know what's a fun makeup trick, putting the eye shadow beneath your eyes instead of on the lid, I think it could really be a cool new trend. I would suggest using purples and blues, but make sure to put a nice dot of red towards the inner edge of your eye. Also, if you're feeling crazy, add in some lines with blue eyeliner. I pull it off pretty well, don't I?

My humps, my humps, my uneven lady lumps. Chicken cutlet is my right boob's best friend. I never thought they would be so close, they just bumped into each other one day and since then they've just been two peas in a pod. They always greet each other with a bear hug and they always have to sit next to each other on the bus(t).

My hands always like to crack jokes. The worst part is that they do it at the most inappropriate times. During church, especially during the homily, Right Hand loves to tell inappropriate jokes that leave Left Hand cackling for minutes. In reply, Left Hand will make a lewd comment that chokes out a short laugh from Right Hand that he tries so hard to contain he usually ends up overextending himself. The worst is during class when a joke will be so funny that the entire body starts cracking up.

My legs have been defined by dermatologists as chicken legs. You know when you look at raw chicken skin and it has all those dots where the feathers were plucked from, that's me. I am speckled all over with little red dots. I cannot remember not having these speckles, I must have been born with feathers.

Yeah, I work out, you surprised? I usually do a lot of muscle-focused mouth training. I start off with breakfast, really more of a warm up to the intense weightlifting that I do during the rest of the day. Lunch is usually my rest period, more mumbles to myself, nothing that requires any effort. After dinner is when I go hardcore. The exercise includes singing, gossiping, blabbing, whispering, laughing, questioning, and joking.

I've always wanted to visit the desert, so on one cold, winter's day I traveled down to my hand. I immediately felt parched, the cracked lines opening up for some small droplet of water. The red sand radiated with streaks of pink and white. As I traveled farther, becoming more parched I came to an oasis. There was pool of red water on the top of a great hill, but as soon as I arrived it dried up and seeped back into the cracks.

Still ignoring the hair.

> ### Discussion Questions
>
> - Why would somebody want to read this piece (the "Who cares?" factor)?
> - Can you clearly identify the author's intention for the piece?
> - How well does the author support the intention of the piece? Cite specific details that support or take away from the author's intention.
> - Is there information missing from this piece that would make its intention clearer? What else would you like to know?
> - Does the author portray herself as a round character? How does she do this?
> - Do you trust the author of this piece? Why or why not?
> - How clearly does the author establish a sense of setting/space in this piece? Cite specific details that support your claim.
> - How clearly does the author establish characters other than the self in this piece? Cite specific details that support your claim.
> - Did you learn anything new from reading this piece? If so, what?
> - Are there particular passages with engaging language/description that stood out to you? Describe the appeal of these passages.
> - Would you read more writing from this author? Why or why not?

What I Never Thought
Or Gotham

Everything worth knowing in life I learned sitting behind a bar. I go to a bar every night after work, or class just to wind down. It's on the corner of 4th and 2nd. It's not a nice bar, either. 'Divey' would be a euphemism. It always smells like old beer and rotting wood and inadvertently, a little like home. Time for a drink. I have a usual depending on the day of the week or time of the night I stroll in. The weekday bartender, Mark, greets me with a smile and a hug from across the bar. He generally has forgotten deodorant that day. He asks about life and school. Topics that are place holders till I have a husband and kids. "Makers, neat?" he asks. The answer is always "yes, sir."

Maybe I'll have just two for that night. If I don't have much to do the next day, I'll keep drinking until Mark stops offering. It's always so hard for me to tell how drunk I am at this bar. They don't have mirrors in the bathroom and looking at my sloppy ass in the mirror gives me a more accurate reading than a breathalyzer.

The first thing I've learned is that I look great in dim bar lighting. No mirrors in the bathroom, but plenty behind the bar. Counterintuitive, I know. I also understand that most people probably do look better in the absence of light, but I think I gain at least three points on the 1–10 scale of attractiveness. Maybe the average person gains only one or two. I don't know what this says about me in full spectrum lighting, but you can't win 'em all. I think I just called myself ugly. It took coming to this bar for a couple months to start to feel like I was at least over a 6. Having guys come up to me and want to buy me a drink is very validating. I generally don't need the drink. (I have one in my hand.) And I certainly am not looking for someone to take me home. (I like my bed just fine.) But, I'm no stranger to the fact that having someone size you up really makes a night feel worth it. Makes the pleat in my pants worth my time, so to speak.

The second thing is everyone likes "Easy" by Lionel Richie. I always throw a buck in the jukebox and play this song. Even if all seven of the people in the bar decided to be a square that night, like most nights, people will start toe tapping, mouthing lyrics or even bobbing their head. Maybe they think it's "Midnight Train to Georgia" by Gladys Knight & the Pips, which if you aren't really paying attention sounds just like "Easy."

Thirdly, the more people know your name at a bar, the more your life is like a movie. I once pulled out my ID at the door to show the bouncer as a mindless formality, even though he is the same bouncer that I deal with on a daily basis. He said "what the fuck do you want me to do with this?" It was awesome. I've made friends with the bartenders. We catch up on life between drinks as they mop the bar down with a rag. I know about their break ups, they know about mine. And if they have to step away to get someone a drink, they always remember were we dropped the pin in the conversation.

I never thought that I'd end up spending my nights at a shitty dive in the East Village. I never thought I would be one of those people who would "wind down" with a drink at the end of the night. Everyone needs their own way of healing. From an actual event or just from the long day. Everyone needs shelter. Some people go out and spend money they don't have, or clench their fists and slam their silverware. I just have a drink. I let it bloom in my chest until it feels like I just put on a blanket. I also never thought I would be this much like my father. But, I also never thought I would enjoy it so much.

> ### Discussion Questions
>
> - Why would somebody want to read this piece (the "Who cares?" factor)?
> - Can you clearly identify the author's intention for the piece?
> - How well does the author support the intention of the piece? Cite specific details that support or take away from the author's intention.
> - Is there information missing from this piece that would make its intention clearer? What else would you like to know?
> - Does the author portray herself as a round character? How does she do this?
> - Do you trust the author of this piece? Why or why not?
> - How clearly does the author establish a sense of setting/space in this piece? Cite specific details that support your claim.
> - How clearly does the author establish characters other than the self in this piece? Cite specific details that support your claim.
> - Did you learn anything new from reading this piece? If so, what?
> - Are there particular passages with engaging language/description that stood out to you? Describe the appeal of these passages.
> - Would you read more writing from this author? Why or why not?

Past Midnight

Jeffrey Cheung

A young man sits, staring into one of the two monitors that occupied his dark wooden desk. Littered across his desk are various loose bits of paper, coins, BASIC acrylic paint tubes, brushes, two tall glasses and half a cup of tea that had long lost its steam. One of his speakers is faced towards the wall, pushed there by the disarray on his desk while the other is obscured behind a various boxes and jars. On top of his computer tower is another mess of papers, all sticking out in different directions. To speak frankly, although the desk was, in actuality, rather spacious a claustrophobic person would never sit anywhere near it.

Only the light from the monitors and one dim ceiling light lit the desk. It was dark, past midnight but he was still up and awake. Nighttime was the best time to work. The world is quiet and there is no one to distract you from your work, except for the occasional sibling on a trip to the lavatory. Although usually easily distracted and lax, at this moment he sat there and worked in fervor. He had his headphones on his head, but there was no sound from them; the music program had crashed a few hours ago. His eyes shifted from one monitor to the next and to the illustration board in front of him with a nearly completed painting. The work has to be done, he thinks to himself. Occasionally he glances at the window, making sure that the first light of dawn has not yet arrived. Seeing as it was still dark, he continues painting while checking the references on his monitor. Even though there are still many hours before the sunrise, he worries, after all incompletion would most definitely spell doom after all.

Raising the cup to his mouth, he notices that it had already chilled down to room temperature. He quickly gulps it down, not one to waste all the energy that it offers. Still it wasn't satisfying, the tea was meant to be drunk hot after all. Well, now's as good a time to get a new cup of tea as any, he thought. Working overnight is tiring and taking a small nap is not an option. He tried that before, vowing to nap for an hour but always he would find himself sleeping as if in a coma. Yes, tea was a much safer option. Still hopped up from that last gulp, he moves energetically to the kitchen and boils some water. In the meantime he puts a tea bag and sugar into his cup. One scoop. Two scoops. Three scoops. At those times, he likes his tea rather sweet, though quietly laments about how he's sure to get diabetes from doing this one day. Still that's the only way he can survive through the night. Sitting back at his desk with a steaming hot cup of tea, he continues to work on his painting. He fidgets more, an effect of both the tea and also of the deadline that's drawing ever so closer.

Breathing a sigh of relief, he manages to clear the task just moments after the sky outside started to lighten. There isn't anything left to do, and there was at least an hour and a half to spare. If he does nothing now, he might fall asleep, so for the moment he keeps himself occupied with some games until it is time to leave the apartment and make his way to the subway. On the subway, he stands up regardless of the number of available seats; if he gets too comfortable he could fall asleep and miss his stop. Although it is embarrassing to have his knees partially give way occasionally when he dozes off while standing, at least that jolts him back awake and prevents him from missing his stop. The assignment has to be handed in after all.

Discussion Questions

- Why would somebody want to read this piece (the "Who cares?" factor)?
- Can you clearly identify the author's intention for the piece?
- How well does the author support the intention of the piece? Cite specific details that support or take away from the author's intention.
- Is there information missing from this piece that would make its intention clearer? What else would you like to know?
- Does the author portray herself as a round character? How does she do this?
- Do you trust the author of this piece? Why or why not?
- How clearly does the author establish a sense of setting/space in this piece? Cite specific details that support your claim.
- How clearly does the author establish characters other than the self in this piece? Cite specific details that support your claim.
- Did you learn anything new from reading this piece? If so, what?
- Are there particular passages with engaging language/description that stood out to you? Describe the appeal of these passages.
- Would you read more writing from this author? Why or why not?

Five Feet Mighty

Joomi Park

My body is a five feet piece of double sided tape, drifting through Georgia and New York while memories, feelings, and lessons stick to me, capture who I am today.

Start from the bottom with two feet ten inches. My feet are a size six in women's, a size four in men's, and my toenails are never perfectly shaped because clipping them is a wild adventure, especially when I can't see my toes very well without my glasses on. Yet my feet have confidence etched into them after experiencing the conservative streets of Georgia in five-inch platforms. My ankles are, to put it nicely, utterly fucked up. After a few sprains and a stretched ligament, I can no longer run without a brace on or walk a mile without them snap, crackle, popping. My legs are short and chubby, and due to the fact that I have yet to get over my fear of razors, they're also a little stubbly. However, these are the same hairy legs that shook as I made my way to the podium to welcome and introduce everyone during graduation. Unfortunately, my vagina isn't as interesting as Phillip Lopate's penis, but at least I know I'm not as egotistical as he is. My buttocks are not in the nice shape that one would expect from a young eighteen year old girl; I suppose I've simply yet to pick up on the idea of working out for fun. Thankfully these buttocks have cushioned me on countless public education chairs and communal toilets and that, I'd say, tops off two feet ten inches of bravery and strength.

Move up one foot and four inches; stop at my shoulders. At the center one will find the flab that is my stomach—a side effect from my addiction to bread and cheese. This stomach once consumed only 140 calories, or one granola bar, which had me bed ridden because my body refused anything I tried to put in my mouth the next day. It was an incredibly valuable lesson for me. My breasts are the embodiment of myself in one word: small. But I've come to accept it and manage to still feel damn good in Aerie bras. My hands are my favorite, and it's almost obligatory for me to have on nail polish, just to adorn my fingers. I've played violin, guitar, and the ukulele, flicked off those who weren't worth wasting my breath over, and held the sweaty palms of close friends on our first rollercoaster rides. My back remains a land unknown, but it's received enough congratulatory pats to know appreciation. That's one foot and four inches of self love and love from others. That's four feet two inches of me.

The remaining ten inches come from my head. My teeth are crooked, I wear lipstick religiously, and I'm pretty sure my tongue is too big for my mouth. With it, saying "y'all" is my guilty pleasure. Of course, cursing up a storm, singing some tunes, and giggling at hands getting cut off make me pretty happy, too. I have two moles above my upper lip that remind me of Pikachu because they're so symmetrically placed. My nose has my father's slight bump and it's also smelled the most awful stenches when my class visited a wastewater treatment plant and we were graced by the presence of other people's feces. My eyes always have on double eyelid tape and they are completely mismatched: one has perfect vision and the other can barely see across the room. Through them I've seen my father hunched over English workbooks and I've witnessed movie scenes of characters' eyes being ripped out. My ears are pierced and they've heard so much music that if I were a body part, I would be an ear just to channel lovely sounds into my body. My hair has been intoxicated with straightening chemicals because I have naturally curly hair, to the point where I had an Asian afro going on when I was younger. Ever since I got to FIT, I've wanted to cut it short and dye it dark blue. My head is a mystery even to me, and all I know is that my thoughts are incredibly odd. I think about death, I think about love, I think about my future. In all honesty that's ten inches of twisted.

But in one piece, I am five feet. And five feet may not be tall or grand but I know that I am comprised of many parts that make me whole. At this point in life it seems impossible to go through much more, but I'm still that double sided piece of tape—a bit tattered, a bit small, but sticking with a whole lot of might.

Discussion Questions

- Why would somebody want to read this piece (the "Who cares?" factor)?
- Can you clearly identify the author's intention for the piece?
- How well does the author support the intention of the piece? Cite specific details that support or take away from the author's intention.
- Is there information missing from this piece that would make its intention clearer? What else would you like to know?
- Does the author portray herself as a round character? How does she do this?
- Do you trust the author of this piece? Why or why not?
- How clearly does the author establish a sense of setting/space in this piece? Cite specific details that support your claim.
- How clearly does the author establish characters other than the self in this piece? Cite specific details that support your claim.
- Did you learn anything new from reading this piece? If so, what?
- Are there particular passages with engaging language/description that stood out to you? Describe the appeal of these passages.
- Would you read more writing from this author? Why or why not?

Memory Assignment: Six Examples

Instructions

Briefly describe a memory that is important to you. Try to avoid explaining why the memory is important and focus on showing the importance of the memory. Use your five senses, and include dialogue, if possible.

Student Samples

These assignments are single drafts. This means that students did not revise these pieces. Rather, they turned them in as practice assignments for larger essays.

Because of the narrative nature of this assignment, although they are first drafts, they are quite strong.

Zachary reflects on his time as part of his high school crew team.

Joomi reflects on her experiences as a self-described "fangirl."

Will reflects on a small experience with a regular customer as his supermarket job.

Emma reflects on waking up from major back surgery.

Justine reflects on an injustice experienced by her fast food coworker.

Hannah uses humor to reflect on having shy bladder syndrome.

The Curse

Zachary Volosky

I closed my eyes as I listened to the splash of the oars sink into the water around me. I could feel the boat lunge forward and slow down as the six rowers behind me moved up their slides to take the next stroke. These were the only sounds anyone made. All nine members of Central Catholic's Second Varsity crew, myself included, had been dreaming about this moment and were speechless as we made our way up to the starting line of the Grand Final of the Scholastic Rowing Association of America's national championships. Nine months of training had been spent in preparation for this one race and not a single member wanted to go home with anything less than a gold medal. Not only would it be a feat to accomplish in itself, but winning nationals would mean that we would have officially broken "the curse."

"Bow pair out, stroke pair add in in two. One…two." My coxswain, Nick, counted from two seats ahead of me. Stroke pair was my pair, I was rowing now. I effortlessly moved into the same pace as the rest of my crew, moving us slowly forward to the start of what would be the most taxing race of our rowing careers, and the last one of mine.

This so-called curse was the idea that any Second Varsity crew from our team was destined to accomplish one thing: second place. Countless crews from years past set out to achieve the same goal but came up one place short. I was in one of these crews my sophomore year and my older brother his sophomore year. I planned to change that record.

"Way-enough, in two. One, two," counted Nick and simultaneously all eight oars lifted toward the sky. "Down." The blades slammed down to the water just as quickly as they had risen up. "Okay, we're just going to wait here until they call us up." Nick's voice crackled through the sound system that was wired through the boat.

He could tell that I was looking at him through my sunglasses and met my gaze. I could tell that he was nervous and he could tell that I was terrified. He had been my coxswain the season before and our performance at nationals then was nothing short of embarrassing. I nodded at Nick to let him know it would be all right, to comfort him. He returned my nod and comforted me more than I could ever comfort him.

The clouds had dissipated and the sun began to beat down on our backs. The five other crews had pulled up beside us in the staging area, each in their respective lane. No one spoke a word besides the occasional coxswain having his bow or second rower take a stroke to keep the boat straight in the lane.

The wait for the race marshal to call us up was painful and what had started as a comfortable warmth from the sun now was an unbearable heat. I began to lightly sweat and I swear I could feel the sunburn coming onto me. And then we heard the megaphone blare from some twenty-odd meters behind us: "All crews, approach the starting line please." My stomach dropped a few feet.

Nick had all eight rowers take a couple strokes to get us to the line and we moved into the starting block, or "stakeboats" as they are called in rowing. All eight rowers moved into the starting position as the rest of the crews around us did the same. In a matter of seconds, every single possibility of something going wrong flashed through my head; I did not know if I was going to pass out, throw up, or both. And then the countdown began: "All crews ready. Five. Four. Three. Two. One. Attention....Row!"

> ### Discussion Questions
>
> - Why would somebody want to read this piece (the "Who cares?" factor)?
> - Can you clearly identify the author's intention for the piece?
> - How well does the author support the intention of the piece? Cite specific details that support or take away from the author's intention.
> - Is there information missing from this piece that would make its intention clearer? What else would you like to know?
> - Does the author portray herself as a round character? How does she do this?
> - Do you trust the author of this piece? Why or why not?
> - How clearly does the author establish a sense of setting/space in this piece? Cite specific details that support your claim.
> - How clearly does the author establish characters other than the self in this piece? Cite specific details that support your claim.
> - Did you learn anything new from reading this piece? If so, what?
> - Are there particular passages with engaging language/description that stood out to you? Describe the appeal of these passages.
> - Would you read more writing from this author? Why or why not?

Memory of the Maine

Joomi Park

The lyrics, "we're all monsters living in a dream," resonated through the car as my mother drove down the highway. The cars rushed by us and I wondered if they could feel the anxious teetering of a seventeen-year-old girl on her way to see the loves of her life for the second time live. One glance into my life was all it took for someone to see my undying love for the Maine. My walls were covered with their posters and I knew exactly what tattoos the lead singer had and where he had them. I collected their band tees and merchandise galore and I bought magazines I had never heard of before, all because they would be featured on half a page. When the Maine released new albums I would listen to them start to finish in the darkness of my room; by the end I would be crying tears of pride and joy. My friends and family called it an unhealthy obsession. I called it the life of a devoted fangirl.

This particular day was special to me because it was the first concert I was going to alone. I asked two of my friends to come with me to the previous Maine concert, and they ended up vomiting in the restroom throughout the whole thing. Filled with guilt, I decided that if anyone was going to puke while listening to amazing music, it would and should be me. By the time I reached the venue I was an hour and thirty minutes early, but the line was still snaked around the building. I initially felt out of place because I was the olive green outlier in a sea of heavy black leather jackets. The nipping November wind showed no mercy to the queue; fortunately, I was able to make small talk with the people in front of me until we were finally admitted into the building.

After what seemed like an eternity, the Maine finally strode onto the stage and the room exploded with satisfied screams and outstretched arms. I found myself holding my breath because it was unbelievable seeing them in person after watching hours of YouTube footage. The concert in its entirety was beautiful and peculiar: head banging along with the band, hearing the room fill with a chorus of passion as everyone sang along, witnessing bras being thrown on stage and getting hung off of microphone stands, and looking on in amusement as the bodyguards grabbed the crowd surfers down, only to have them riding the hands of the group once more. As the Maine reached their final song on the set list, we put all we had in joining the heavy guitar riffs and strong vocals singing, "stay away, sweet misery."

Knowing that the Maine meets with their fans after every show, I ran out of the building as soon as the concert ended. I met the guitarist Jared Monaco, and the biggest smile lit up his face when I told him he was my inspiration while I showed him my guitar necklace that he had signed at the last concert. I also met John O'Callaghan—the lead singer and by far the most popular. As the line to meet him dwindled down, I could hardly breathe and I couldn't remember what I wanted to say to him. When my turn arrived and he landed his eyes on me and said, "hey," I rambled with something along the lines of, "Hi I'm Joomi and this is my second time seeing you guys live but my first time meeting you and y'all are really great live and you guys are my favorite band and could you sign my notebook and could I also get a picture and hug, please?" He complied with all my requests and it was spectacular because anyone could have a normal conversation with these band members. They were so grateful for us as we were to them.

Before I went to sleep that night, I opened my notebook of signatures and found that John

O'Callaghan had written, "Always love." And it was then that I realized that the Maine not only created music, but also a safe haven for fans to connect and experience life together. The little things that day had radiated so much kindness. When a petite lady asked if she could move up a row, everyone let her all the way to the front. Since I had gone to the concert alone, random fans offered to take photos of me with the members, as well. It didn't take much reflection to see that the Maine is constantly growing through their music, and that their fans are growing up with them. From light lyrics in their earlier albums such as "sunlight, sunshine, all for you my daisy" to heavier lyrics in their more recent ones like, "I don't think I'll ever be happy," the Maine offers a raw understanding of every mood and situation. I finally dozed off that night knowing that there are Directioners, there are Beliebers, and then there are Maineiacs, and my heart swelled knowing that I was one of them.

Discussion Questions

- Why would somebody want to read this piece (the "Who cares?" factor)?
- Can you clearly identify the author's intention for the piece?
- How well does the author support the intention of the piece? Cite specific details that support or take away from the author's intention.
- Is there information missing from this piece that would make its intention clearer? What else would you like to know?
- Does the author portray herself as a round character? How does she do this?
- Do you trust the author of this piece? Why or why not?
- How clearly does the author establish a sense of setting/space in this piece? Cite specific details that support your claim.
- How clearly does the author establish characters other than the self in this piece? Cite specific details that support your claim.
- Did you learn anything new from reading this piece? If so, what?
- Are there particular passages with engaging language/description that stood out to you? Describe the appeal of these passages.
- Would you read more writing from this author? Why or why not?

A Memory of Mr. Oko

William Rossi

My first month at King Kullen, I collected shopping carts from the parking lot. Carts that your average American was too lazy to put back in front of the store after the brutal 20-foot walk to deliver their groceries to their car. Rain, sleet, snow, or hail, I was out there pushing carts. I would collect them in small groups of five and hurl them up the curb and into the neat rows directly next to the front wall of the store.

From my constant time outside against the stone wall watching customers enter and exit the store, you begin to smile at the ones you see most often. Occasionally, I would take their carts from them or go out of my way to get them a cart, merely in an act of friendly interaction. Few would stop to thank you, even fewer would stop to talk to you.

There were regular customers, whose faces became familiar and whose conversations would drag on much longer. They would come in every other day, pick up a few groceries and leave. Mr. Oko was one of them.

He was a small, frail Oriental man. His face was sunken with wrinkles and he always wore a baseball cap with a globe on the front. The globe was always visible because he crouched as he walked, back hunched and knees bent. He wore orthopedic shoes, and one sole was taller than the other. His skin was dark, tanned, and covered in liver spots. His hands were bony, covered in a thin layer of nearly translucent skin. His veins pressed against the skin as he gripped the handle on a shopping cart and pushed it past me.

After he was done shopping, he came over to me and asked if I would help him carry his bags to his car. I loaded my arms with his few bags, to assure he wouldn't have to carry any at all. We walked to his small, white car. It was covered in a layer of dirt that was lifted with the swipe of a finger. He opened his trunk and allowed me to place his groceries down carefully as he began to introduce himself. He told me his full name, which I wouldn't be able to pronounce, and he acknowledged this from the blank stare I gave him as I told him my name.

"Call me Mr. Oko," he said, "That's what everyone calls me here." He closed the trunk and placed his hand delicately on the top of the trunk. He looked at me and released a small laugh and continued to say, "You know, I have seen you pushing carts, my boy. You are a very hard worker." Slightly confused and a little embarrassed, I replied, "Thank you. It's not the best job, but I get a good paycheck." He laughed and began to walk the cart back toward the store. I grabbed the handle, assuring him that I would take it for him. He placed the hand covered in the layer of dirt onto my shoulder and said, "Hard work will pay off, my boy. You have success in your blood, I see it in your eyes."

I didn't know what to say, so I smiled and walked off with the cart, placing it back into the row and removing the sales circular that was left inside.

The next time I saw Mr. Oko, I was behind the counter of the bakery, putting out a sample for customers to enjoy. He stopped in front of the sample dish and shouted, "My boy, you see what hard work gets you? The rewards are sweet!"

Discussion Questions

- Why would somebody want to read this piece (the "Who cares?" factor)?
- Can you clearly identify the author's intention for the piece?
- How well does the author support the intention of the piece? Cite specific details that support or take away from the author's intention.
- Is there information missing from this piece that would make its intention clearer? What else would you like to know?
- Does the author portray herself as a round character? How does she do this?
- Do you trust the author of this piece? Why or why not?
- How clearly does the author establish a sense of setting/space in this piece? Cite specific details that support your claim.
- How clearly does the author establish characters other than the self in this piece? Cite specific details that support your claim.
- Did you learn anything new from reading this piece? If so, what?
- Are there particular passages with engaging language/description that stood out to you? Describe the appeal of these passages.
- Would you read more writing from this author? Why or why not?

Inhale, Exhale

Emma Suleski

"What is your name and date of birth?" a voice asked me from a distance. As I struggled to lift my eyelids, I shuddered; bright white light flooded my eyes. I shook my head left to right, left to right, left to right. What was happening?

"I know," the voice said, "but I need you to tell me, what is your name and date of birth?" I struggled to make the thoughts in my head into sentences. I had never been so keenly aware of every centimeter of my body. I had never had my senses flooded, not with pain, not like this. The word I expected to come out as "Emma" came out as a muffled groan.

"Okay," the voice sighed, "can you feel this?" A finger traveled down my big toe, towards the back of my heel. Every time I had been asked that question, the answer was always yes. Every time I said yes, I felt lucky. I had numerous back problems since the age of thirteen and there was no saying when a disc in my back might give, causing nerve damage or even paralysis. Every step I took, seat I sat in, bump I drove over, I was in danger. Safety just wasn't a part of my everyday life. I nodded and I felt the movement migrate from my neck to my feet. I made myself a mental note: don't move.

"One more time, what is your name and date of birth?" I squeezed my eyes shut and used whatever strength was left in me to force out, "Emma Suleski, six-three-ninety-six."

"Good!" the voice called back to me. "Now, can you tell me, on a scale of one to ten, what is your pain?" I struggled to open my eyes a second time, only seeing blurry figures traveling around me; everything and everyone was drenched in white. In the background I heard the hum of machines, a steady bee-beep, and the shuffle of feet following familiar paths. I squeezed my eyes shut again. I wanted to go back to sleep.

"Come on, Emma, stay with me. One to ten, how are you?" I shook my head back and forth, back and forth again. Tears flooded my eyes. The thing they don't tell you about spinal fusion surgery is that to check for paralysis, they have to bring you out of anesthesia without any painkillers. So, in essence, they cut you open, drill into your spine for a few hours, sew you back up and let your body be its own rude alarm clock. "Ten" I choked out.

There was a scurrying of feet and I felt a pull on the IV in my left wrist. Broken conversations followed.

"Am I touching your right foot or left?"

"Right," I said aloud as I wondered, "Was this worth it?"

"We're going to scrape the bottom of your foot."

I mumbled, "okay," while thinking to myself, "Yes. You didn't want permanent damage, did you?"

"I'm going to turn you and check your incisions."

Hands gripped my shoulder and hip, pulling me onto my side. Inhale, exhale, throbbing pain. I winced as the IV in my left wrist began to move again and the beeping began to fade. I felt myself drifting, wondering, "Am I going to come out of this?"

My eyes shot open and my heartbeat raced. To my left my mom was sprawled out in a chair, snoring softly. "Mom?" I asked, "am I okay?" She lifted her head up and quickly rushed over to me. She squeezed my hand.

"The doctors said you had a rough time in the recovery room. You've turned a corner Em; you're safe now."

> **Discussion Questions**
>
> - Why would somebody want to read this piece (the "Who cares?" factor)?
> - Can you clearly identify the author's intention for the piece?
> - How well does the author support the intention of the piece? Cite specific details that support or take away from the author's intention.
> - Is there information missing from this piece that would make its intention clearer? What else would you like to know?
> - Does the author portray herself as a round character? How does she do this?
> - Do you trust the author of this piece? Why or why not?
> - How clearly does the author establish a sense of setting/space in this piece? Cite specific details that support your claim.
> - How clearly does the author establish characters other than the self in this piece? Cite specific details that support your claim.
> - Did you learn anything new from reading this piece? If so, what?
> - Are there particular passages with engaging language/description that stood out to you? Describe the appeal of these passages.
> - Would you read more writing from this author? Why or why not?

An Honest Living

Justine Giardina

They didn't actually pay us on our breaks, but typically if you were in a rush to get back to work, especially on a Saturday night during rush hour, it wasn't out of eagerness to collect an extra five minutes' pay. The sixty-six cents that one could make working five minutes on minimum wage was not worth any extra time spent having to serve fast food. If you came back early from the safe haven of the crusty McDonald's break room, it was usually because you cared about whoever was stuck alone at the front counter and understood the insufferable experience they were probably having with the entourage of impatient customers.

The particular coworker I was going back for was my favorite coworker—a tiny Hispanic woman named Virginia who always wore a black polo from the uniform for a different fast food company and had a charming, wide smile filled with crooked teeth. Late on a Tuesday Virginia told me that she was a single mother and hadn't spoken any English when she landed in the US, carrying nothing but one bag and her fatherless infant son. She told me how hard it was to learn English and she told me that I'd better go to school and make something of myself and then she told me that I had brewed the coffee wrong again and certainly wouldn't last there much longer, repeating again that I'd better get myself into school.

When I got to the front counter there was some sort of scene unfolding. I wasn't outrageously surprised, and I shouldn't have been because throwing a tantrum at McDonald's is the only thing upper-middle-class people like more than coffee. I still hurried over, motivated by a curiosity I can only compare to the way that people driving cars slow down to stare at a car accident like it's some sort of show.

The woman on the opposite side of the counter was blonde and white, a scarf tied fashionably around her neck and a tan pea coat knotted fashionably around her waist so tight that it seemed if you untied it the top half of her body would fall right off the bottom half. When I approached the counter a smile of relief spread across her face and she looked up at me thankfully, as though we were on the same tag team and I had finally come to relieve her and let her step out of the boxing ring.

"What's wrong?" I asked a haggard Virginia, but the blonde woman answered instead, jumping up like a child answering a petty question in a classroom. She answered with great zest, as though she had been eagerly waiting for someone to listen to her talk all day.

"She's trying to take extra money for herself," she said, matter-of-factly. She spoke to me as though I am in charge of Virginia, a woman fifteen years my senior with years more work experience than I have.

Virginia said nothing. I looked to the register, a glaring "$7.87" staring back at me. I then turned my eyes to her order, a large cappuccino with some sort of specialty sauce drizzled over a layer of whipped cream at the top, and a meal enclosed in a white bag. I begin to sort through her items and before I can finish she has shoved the screen of her iPhone on the counter saying, "I added it up. It should be seven dollars."

Later I would pick out exactly what words were apt to yell across the counter. Later I would list vocabulary just harsh and true enough to hurt. "Entitled" would be at the top of the list. "Insufferable little priss" would be somewhere down the line. Later I would think about standing up to that woman and calling out her bigotry, protecting someone who didn't have the privilege to protect herself. I would think about all of the contents of the scene *I* would throw at McDonald's. But in that moment I did nothing. I was not a hero.

"Tax." I replied quietly. Her determined look melted to an expression of realization. "You didn't factor in tax."

The woman stuttered something and fished out the remaining change, something you might give to a child to buy milk with or put into a gumball machine, but of course something my coworker, a woman working two eight-hour shifts at two disgusting fast food restaurants each day to make an honest living, would try to steal out of her cashmere pockets.

"Have a nice day." Virginia said. I wished she hadn't, but the store's pleasantry policy does not make exceptions for racists.

That night an article about the bystander effect would come across my computer screen and I would close the window and pretend I hadn't seen it at all.

Discussion Questions

- Why would somebody want to read this piece (the "Who cares?" factor)?
- Can you clearly identify the author's intention for the piece?
- How well does the author support the intention of the piece? Cite specific details that support or take away from the author's intention.
- Is there information missing from this piece that would make its intention clearer? What else would you like to know?
- Does the author portray herself as a round character? How does she do this?
- Do you trust the author of this piece? Why or why not?
- How clearly does the author establish a sense of setting/space in this piece? Cite specific details that support your claim.
- How clearly does the author establish characters other than the self in this piece? Cite specific details that support your claim.
- Did you learn anything new from reading this piece? If so, what?
- Are there particular passages with engaging language/description that stood out to you? Describe the appeal of these passages.
- Would you read more writing from this author? Why or why not?

A-Relief

Hannah Lajba

Everything is white and my leggings are pulled down to my kneecaps. Artificial florals invade my nostrils at every breath I take, which is many, short gasps urging myself to just forget where I am, what is happening just outside that door. I am nervous, a ball of sweat drips from my temple, can they hear me if I can hear them? The clamoring of the kitchen staff cleaning up our latest meal combined with the laughing and yelling of the girls just on the other side make me clench.

Hello, my name is Hannah and I, for the most part, am no longer a shy bladder sufferer. It started my junior year when going on a class trip to the Renaissance fair. It was the midway point of the three-hour journey and, to be blunt, I had to pee. Getting up from the polyester printed bus seat the urge became full force. I went to the last open stall and, unfortunately, it was the handicapped stall. We all feel guilty when using that one; what if someone needs it and then here we are, using it? I think it was the regret, and also that large gap in the door, anyone could just look in and see me center front. It was a good five minutes of thinking of waterfalls, lakes, and streams while trying to use my imagination to hear the dripping of a tap, but nothing, and I gave up. Surprisingly, at my body's dire need of relief, I was able to go into the dirt-floored fly mating ground that is a Renaissance Fair toilet. Luckily my stall at least had toilet paper.

Funny how the exact same thing happened the next year, but no longer—or that's what I tried to tell myself. I pondered my condition, even Googled and Yahoo answered it, and the revelation came: if I drink more liquids, my body will learn to retain them better. Fun fact: I also suffer from small bladder syndrome. The thing is though I never got around to testing out my theory; who would want to deal with having to pee every half hour?

There is a fell voice in the air—no, not Saruman but Zac Efron. I listen closer, arching my body towards the door, "Bet on it, bet on it." Suddenly my mind is filled with the rolling green hills of a golf course and young, shaggy-haired Troy Bolton dashing about in all black. I hear my internal voice say 'Do it for Zac, Hannah' to which I reply, 'Please God let me pee!' and He answers. It is my own little golden waterfall; the sigh of relief that leaves my lips comes out like music to the heavens. 'T-God for Zac Efron.' I pull up my leggings, the sweat evaporating and the nerves going down the drain with the soapy suds. I do one final touch-up on my hair before exiting, seeing the line of bladder-exploding girls my untimely visit has caused.

Discussion Questions

- Why would somebody want to read this piece (the "Who cares?" factor)?
- Can you clearly identify the author's intention for the piece?
- How well does the author support the intention of the piece? Cite specific details that support or take away from the author's intention.
- Is there information missing from this piece that would make its intention clearer? What else would you like to know?

- Does the author portray herself as a round character? How does she do this?
- Do you trust the author of this piece? Why or why not?
- How clearly does the author establish a sense of setting/space in this piece? Cite specific details that support your claim.
- How clearly does the author establish characters other than the self in this piece? Cite specific details that support your claim.
- Did you learn anything new from reading this piece? If so, what?
- Are there particular passages with engaging language/description that stood out to you? Describe the appeal of these passages.
- Would you read more writing from this author? Why or why not?

Memory/Character Essay: Thirteen Examples

Instructions

A memory is not necessarily something that happened a long time ago. Rather, a memory is something that is past, something that is reflected upon. It can be something that happened last week or a moment from your childhood, but for our purposes, it is something that has happened before this assignment was given.

For this assignment, choose a memory that has multiple levels of meaning for you. It is important not just to create a narrative about one particular thing but to think about the complexities of the memory and why you find it worthy of exploring in an essay. Subtext and intention are crucial.

You should re-create details as accurately as possible, even talking to friends or family members who might help you remember aspects of a memory. All good writers of memoir research their own histories. This is because memory is fallible and other people might be able to shed important light on our experiences.

Focus especially on re-creating characters, yourself included, who were involved in the memory. Use dialogue to let these characters speak, and choose details to convey the nature of relationships.

Student Samples

These essays went through two drafts. This means that students revised these pieces with peer and instructor feedback.

Or examines an interaction with a man in a bar who claimed to be his future self.

Mike examines his experience of his mother's death.

Joomi examines her feelings about moving from Georgia to New York City.

Will examines visiting his father in a rehabilitation center.

Magdalene examines the experience of growing up female.

Hannah examines her wardrobe and its relationship to important moments in her life.

Jillian examines her relationship with her legs and her mother.

Emma examines her struggles with depression.

Neziah examines her relationship to her religion and to men.

Chadbourne examines his relationship with his sister.

Katie examines her relationship with her mother.

Jeffrey examines his relationship with his father and his profession.

Danny examines his struggles with drugs and relationships.

How to Survive
Or Gotham

I once met myself fourteen years into the future.

It was a complete accident that I met him, because he was so not my type and I wouldn't normally have entertained the idea of having a conversation with him. But, as I said: a total fucking accident. The wrinkle in time wrinkled, or time travel was invented and legalized in the not-too-distant future and older Or managed to wander from his continuum and into mine. When he introduced himself to me, I forgot his name literally immediately after he told me. He actually asked me my sign. Clenching my jaw and motioning to the bartender for another drink, I said "Capricorn."

"Yeah?" he asked excitedly. Apparently, we were born in the same moon cycle, or something. He asked my birthday, and after we swapped our licenses, it was confirmed – we had the same birthday, fourteen years apart.

The more I squinted at him in the unconducive-to-seeing-anything bar lighting, the more I saw my hairline, and my forehead wrinkles and the same sad hooded eyes I see in every mirror. I don't really remember what my father looked like, but he came pretty close. He also didn't look bad for 36, in the way that at 22, I still look like I'm 17. Fairly spry, it seemed, with how often he spoke with his hands. Almost spry enough to match the fact that he was dressed like he was nineteen fucking years old. And it was this 36-year-old wearing a college freshman's outfit that began to reveal that he knew everything about me, which made the previous coincidences that much stranger.

"The thing about us (He kept saying "us" instead of "you") is we build fortresses around ourselves." He drank his scotch and soda in between long-winded thoughts, furrowing his brow as he sipped because he knew it made him look cool. I recognized it immediately, because I am no stranger to doing it. I made a mental note that he was drinking scotch. I like scotch, but have always been more of a bourbon man. But, maybe that changes in the next decade and a half. He continued.

"We put up these walls to every single person we meet, not because we're afraid or wounded. Damaged, maybe. But being damaged can actually be a powerful thing. Because we're damaged, we know how to survive." Fuck. He sipped and furrowed. "But it's a test. It's how we find out who is good enough to keep around. And we just want someone to call our bullshit. It's so much easier to be alone than hurt, right?" He spoke softly, which at first was a nuisance, because I had to lean in. He also spoke declaratively, which is daunting when a stranger tells you things about yourself. He spoke like it was unquestionable truth. Because, as I found, it was.

"You want someone to get past those walls and just grab and hold you. Hold you until you push back and tell them to stop, and even then they still won't." I could feel myself stop breathing. "You're smart. And you want someone who can keep up with you. You two will bump heads and argue, but that'll work for you guys. That will be your foreplay."

This shit continued on for almost two hours. I barely spoke. For a number of reasons, really. I was speechless with how much he knew about me and with how much he knew about my past without me telling him a single thing. He knew about Adam, down to how long we dated, the color of his eyes and even the day he was born. He knew that I am the way I am because, as he put it, "you didn't get to have a childhood." For a second I felt my composure crack. My throat tightened and I had to break eye contact with him. Suddenly, I was a kid again, spitting blood into the bathroom sink.

"You've been thirty since you were thirteen. The way you talk, the way you hold yourself, the way you dress. Look at yourself! You're thirty. Something happened to you and you had to grow up faster than you should have." He used his hand to cover the fist I didn't notice I was making, as if to apologize. "But, the great thing is, when you actually are thirty, you get a chance to be a kid again. Why do you think I dress like this?"

As incredulous as I am capable of being, I sat earnestly in front of him. This man who had my hands. This man who closed his eyes when he spoke. This man who had nothing to gain from these things he said. I took a large sip from my drink, catching myself while furrowing my brow, and asked, "What happens to me?"

He had a smirk across his face as he began to map out invisible timelines on the table, or in the air between us. He told me about traveling, domestically of course, because I've always felt like I should see the country I live in before I go explore other ones. He somehow made absolutely no mention of my career. Which maybe would be strange to anyone else, but my goal in life has never been to be rich, or well known. I've always cared more about starting a family, building a home, and living somewhere off the grid and having a garden with the right guy. He told about a man I meet at 25. A man who I fall in love with and a man that loves me in return. He paused, as if to remember. "He's good to you."

I leaned in to hear him recount stories of a his-and=his bed and breakfast in the Appalachians. But, the story ended as quickly as it started. "You are going to be very happy with him," he declared. I beamed momentarily. He then added, "and it will be devastating when it ends. But, it is the breakup that will shape you into the man you become for the rest of your life."

That night I walked myself home. I paced slowly to navigate around the patches of ice, occasionally laughing at the idea that I actually entertained the idea of time travel. His name was Hardy. I suddenly remembered that on my beer-drunk walk back to bed. I toyed around with ideas of why he would come up to a stranger in a bar and tell them the things he told me. He didn't want anything from it. Not my number, or a drink. Nothing. And just before I began to write it off as one of the stories I will tell my kids, I thought about how I found Hardy. Standing alone on a Monday night at a bar. Just like I was. Maybe he wished he could tell twenty-two-year-old Hardy all the things he told me. Maybe he needed to be told that his father leaving had nothing to do with him. His mom would remarry and his new dad will call him "buddy" and take him camping like he always wanted. Maybe he needed to apologize for not standing up to fight when he was thirteen and getting his face kicked into the snow. He was young. He didn't know how. Maybe he needed to forgive himself for forgetting how to sleep after that breakup. His body didn't know how to be alone. His head just felt too heavy to even live. Maybe he needed to remember that the guy he fell in love with at twenty-five wasn't a bad guy. Just human. I could still taste blood in my mouth on my whole walk home.

Discussion Questions

- Why would somebody want to read this piece (the "Who cares?" factor)?
- Can you clearly identify the author's intention for the piece?
- How well does the author support the intention of the piece? Cite specific details that support or take away from the author's intention.
- Is there information missing from this piece that would make its intention clearer? What else would you like to know?
- Does the author portray herself as a round character? How does she do this?
- Do you trust the author of this piece? Why or why not?
- How clearly does the author establish a sense of setting/space in this piece? Cite specific details that support your claim.
- How clearly does the author establish characters other than the self in this piece? Cite specific details that support your claim.
- Did you learn anything new from reading this piece? If so, what?
- Are there particular passages with engaging language/description that stood out to you? Describe the appeal of these passages.
- Would you read more writing from this author? Why or why not?

A Living Contradiction

Mike Gomez

It's weird to look at yourself from the exterior while remaining inside. Throughout our lives humans perceive the world from the little man in our heads controlling the show. He gathers all the information within the range of your pupils' sight, vacuums the scents of circumstance, tastes the flavors of now, translates every vibration flowing into the ear's canal, and recycles the energy of physical and emotional encounters. There's a strangeness of sharing this world with the others. The many other protagonists we establish as secondary and impartial to this movie of life. Frame by frame we intersect and cross-pollinate realities affecting the trends of decision. What's amazing to me are the screens we use to separate the big picture. A mass collection of individual filters, perpetually blurring and masking an original image of collective experience. How weird is this? I'm trying to explain the obvious when really I've just made it more obscure. My human being lives a daily flux of contradiction. Yeah, I'd say this is a good place to start.

In the midst of fall in 1994, my mother passed away. She was thirty-four years old. Shortly after my younger sister Michelle was born, my mother was diagnosed with breast cancer. Actually, she had been diagnosed during the pregnancy. The doctor had given her the option of starting chemotherapy while it was still early, but such a decision would mean giving up my yet-to-be-born sister. For my mother, this was a no-brainer. A few months later Michelle would be born, but the odds for my mother's life consequently favored the opposite. Her funeral was held at her place of birth, upbringing, and final farewell, Puerto Rico.

Her name was Irma Doris Gomez. She grew up in a large family on the countryside of Puerto Rico, Guayama. When she was 22, she came to East New York to visit her sister, Maria, as a graduation present. She had just received her bachelor's degree in communication at the University of Puerto Rico. Then she met my dad. At the time, my mother hadn't yet learned English and my dad couldn't speak a word of Spanish, so naturally it was love at first sight. For months my mom and dad communicated via Maria, until they both had established a common ground of communication. My dad describes her as one of the smartest, most beautiful people he's ever come across. Needless to say, my mother decided to stay in New York and start a life with him.

We moved to Puerto Rico when my mom started her treatment. A paradise it was indeed; I look back and think about how she always just smiled through it all. Early mornings of waking up and running into her room just so we could lie next to her. My memories of her paint an image of soft joy. She loved her munchkin offspring and never once wore a face of discontent when we were around. She was wonderful for that.

At age 4, your understanding for the world is fantastic. Everything is the greatest thing ever and all you have to do is look, point, smile, and run to get there. The sun shines for you. The wind runs and laughs with you. After she had gone, it all seemed to look at me with sympathy rather than adventure. I didn't know what this thing was that I was feeling. It wasn't sadness. I'd been sad before. Sad is walking into a toy store to find the greatest of the most awesome Marvel superheroes pristinely packaged, ready to start adventures with its potential new owner, only to be told "no, you can't have it." Sadness is that passing feeling you experience while watching the evening news of tragic school shootings and an impending tropical storm that'll surely ruin your three-wee- planned

Saturday night out. This thing that was happening to me was different. It was too close to fade away, too real to let go of. I had lost the person who made it all happen for me. The woman who held me close with genuine warmth and wiped my tears with whispers that said, "It's okay, I'm here."

I don't remember crying during it at all. I remember the silence. Everyone had left the cemetery after the burial. The sun was teasing dawn and the wind made the leaves dance. There he was, my father standing a few feet away from her gravestone, holding my sister in a trance. I remember the stare he wore, the void he had fallen into. I can't even begin to imagine how he felt. Such heavy eyes had played many games with life already, had lost more times than won, but wore everything with pride. Today there was no lion of a man, just a shell of hollow echoes. My older brother Steven kicked rocks around him, head down as he slumped his shoulders into his pockets. His cheeks were moist and his eyes drained of tears. Something had changed in us all. A connection had scrambled. White noise replaced the frequency of a mother's kinetic nurture. I don't know how long we stood there, but we longed for a sense of admittance to leave her. We didn't want to go anywhere, do anything, but be there. She was gone and we began missing her forever.

Growing up, I still didn't understand exactly how her death had affected me. We moved back to New York and picked life back up from where we left it. Although Michelle, Steven, and I had been staying in Puerto Rico, my other siblings, Mark, Josh, Christal, and Nadia, were still in the city. They had a different mother than we did, but they welcomed us back with open arms and headlocks.

In a house where a moment alone didn't exist, boredom was a rarity and everyone cared for one another, you'd figure there would be a lot of consolation and openness to talk with someone about how you were feeling. But at that age, I just didn't know how. From early on as far as I can remember, I've always kept to myself. My father taught me that a man should always be headstrong and ready to do anything and everything himself, because it would always fall on just you to decide how your life will unfold. At age seventeen, my dad immigrated from everything he ever knew in his home of Guyana and moved to Canada on his own. His only possessions were will and desire to start a new life in a new world. Hands down, I consider my dad to be the strongest, wisest man I know. And it's because of this that I always wanted to be just as strong and ambitious as him.

My father would be gone most of the day, due to singlehandedly trying to maintain a household of seven children, and left our care to my older sisters. They worked as well, and when they didn't, they worked at home. So since I was a kid, I developed an early sense of independence. Some days we would be left home entirely to watch over ourselves, and of course on these days we would have the most fun. The outside world instantly became a distraction and foreground to the realm of my inside life. Nothing can ever replace the allure of my childhood shenanigans. I would spend hours on end outside just running around, losing myself in imagination and play. This allowed me to express myself and sedate the emotions that slept at the base of my heart. I had created a duality with the physical, manipulative nature of life, the world I could change and assimilate into, and the intangible, sensual repressions of my mind, the inner feelings and desires I was scared of embracing.

Such a relationship between me, myself, and I gave way for insecurities to develop. In order to preserve and keep secret what was happening inside of me, I became all too conscious of my actions and surroundings. I always monitored myself, constantly checking to ensure that I didn't give away too much information or say anything that might trigger concern in someone. If I was feeling a certain way, I did my best to conceal it. I didn't want anyone to give me any more attention than I was comfortable with. This is something that has been with me through the entirety of my life. One of my mottos for this thing called living is not to influence and not to be influenced. I think in terms of how I affect other people and catalyze their course of action. People tend to emotionally burden themselves with the dilemmas and personal happenings of another when it isn't needed or rather consensual, and this causes turbulence for all involved. With this kind of rationale, however, you inadvertently push people away. The more I kept to myself and steered shy of letting other people in, the easier it became for people to look past me and not want to involve themselves. It's funny because at a young age I didn't realize I was causing that result. I didn't realize how much I actually wanted to open myself up to other people. I didn't and couldn't relate my personal experience with someone else's because I didn't allow it. I made myself a lone stranger with alien feelings when really I was a lonely, embarrassed child seeking the approval to let it all go. It's taken all that's happened and everything I've dealt with up until now for me to honestly grip the complexity of my person.

So let's attempt to sum up this person I've introduced as a living contradiction. I bottle up and cope with lingering emotions inside of myself to not appear weak or bestow stress onto someone else. Through this I've developed a demeanor of nonchalance and indifference, in turn coming off cold to those around me. People get a feeling that I've got it figured it out somehow for myself and they leave me be. But then I ask myself, why don't people want to get to know me? If there's one thing I've learned, it's that no one will ever know who you are, until you get to know yourself.

Discussion Questions

- Why would somebody want to read this piece (the "Who cares?" factor)?
- Can you clearly identify the author's intention for the piece?
- How well does the author support the intention of the piece? Cite specific details that support or take away from the author's intention.
- Is there information missing from this piece that would make its intention clearer? What else would you like to know?
- Does the author portray herself as a round character? How does she do this?
- Do you trust the author of this piece? Why or why not?
- How clearly does the author establish a sense of setting/space in this piece? Cite specific details that support your claim.
- How clearly does the author establish characters other than the self in this piece? Cite specific details that support your claim.
- Did you learn anything new from reading this piece? If so, what?
- Are there particular passages with engaging language/description that stood out to you? Describe the appeal of these passages.
- Would you read more writing from this author? Why or why not?

Georgia on My Mind

Joomi Park

Brace yourself. One step on the gray bleak concrete will be the end of you. Your feet will become infected with the crushed dreams of the city that never sleeps, and you'll fall into the slums, into your own despair. Take one wrong corner and you'll be kidnapped and thrown into a dark van that reeks of ambiguity and you'll never see light again. Every single person on the street is your enemy. The men want to grope you, the women want to scam you, and the people there are the meanest in the world. So why on earth, Joomi, would you want to live in New York? Well I'm just wondering why Georgians who have never once set foot in the city feel compelled to fill me with their fear while they can nestle softly back into their sheltered beds.

My friend told me about her coworker who was kidnapped on the streets of New York and had barely made it out alive. She often liked to end her story with, "My coworker said she was never the same, and she still has traumatic bruises on her body." Shortly after that tale spread around, my boyfriend gave me a pink bottle of pepper spray to ward off any unwanted people around me. Though it was small and light, the emotional fear weighed so heavily. I contemplated if moving to New York was a bad idea, especially when I had lived in the comfort of a suburban environment all my life. I always talked about leaving Georgia, and I saw college as an outlet for me to finally start fresh anywhere other than the peach state. However, with the opportunity right in my face, I drowned in worry—95% came from the courtesy of all my friends, teachers, and parents. They called me a potential target for the evil New Yorkers because I am a "short little Asian girl." And it felt like everyone had gotten a note to call me that because I was never described as anything else.

I'll admit that the streets aren't as great as I had thought they would be. They don't sparkle and gleam with the magic of the city, but I have noticed that they are adorned with the occasional dog poop that fled the grips of the blue dog waste bag. Instead of glitter falling from the sky to indicate that I am in the perfect place to be, cold water droplets bombard my head from some unknown source on these buildings. It also wasn't a dream come true when I heard, "Look at those bodies. Damn, those tits....Did you see those tits? And man, her ass," on the streets at night. Regardless of whether those comments were directed at me or some other woman, I was appalled at hearing an incredible amount of inappropriate comments by men in the span of only a few blocks. I wanted to shove cacti all over their bodies, but when I was reminded that had the roles been switched, I might not have reacted as strongly to a woman speaking about a man in such a way, I guiltily tried to erase my dreamland streets filled with my man candy. Still, I've grown a fondness for walking down the streets. I'm pretty sure I've mastered my "I'm not interested in a trip to the Empire State Building so stop asking" bitch face, and surprisingly, a twenty-minute walk feels like nothing now. A twenty-minute walk in Georgia consists of trees, trees, and more trees. The streets would be lazy, save for the future fraternity boys who would roll out of their immense country club houses in their red pickup trucks with Confederate flag stickers on the bumper and country music blasting through the windows. Here, I take a few steps and I'm in front of a completely different store each time. I keep walking and I'm on a whole other street and I get to see almost every different kind of person in his or her own little world.

In its own ways, Georgia has its bad sides, too. I lived across from a very crowded Korean supermarket and in the other direction was a hog and horse farm. Almost everyone drove around, even if it was only a ten-minute walk, and maybe that's why traffic was always the biggest problem. Perhaps I've grown to love the state more than I thought, because right now all I can think of is nighttime in front of my house. I would walk outside and hear toads and crickets making a ruckus across the lake, look up and see the most beautiful scenery of stars, and breathe in the freshest air my lungs have ever felt. And then a dozen mosquitos would attack and the biggest moths would fly into the light and I'd scream while running back into the house. Sometimes I would spot deer calmly making their way across lawns and then unfortunately see them again as road kill, and the occasional comedian will tie a "get better soon" balloon on their bodies. Rabbits always inhabit the grass and little critters are afraid of humans but kind enough to give us our personal space. The best thing is that there's also a kangaroo conservation center where I've seen and petted all types of kangaroos, so even I have to ask myself what else I could possibly want. And then I find that I can answer my own question in a heartbeat. I want people who don't dress like carbon copies of each other and I want to be around people who aren't afraid to take a risk. I want to be able to roam the streets without seeing at least three images of Confederate flags. I want to live at a fast pace and put myself in situations that could only happen in New York.

I'd be lying if I said I'm not afraid of walking on the streets anymore. I never leave my dorm without my reassuring pepper spray, and there are times when I get super paranoid and look over my shoulder one or two times just to be safe. But currently, I can't possibly think of having a future anywhere other than here. I might cry a little inside when I think of how I only had to pay seven dollars for Chipotle in Georgia, but I suppose dollar pizza makes up for it. I haven't found any cool secret locations, but I've come to appreciate tourist scenes. At a certain time of the day, when the light hits just right, the Flatiron Building makes my head spin. My roommate and I stumbled upon Bryant Park late at night, and my eyes were coated with an infatuation so great that even a fountain blew me away. And I will never tire of looking up at the buildings, at the details, and sometimes at the solemn statues and gargoyles that are almost out of sight.

Georgia, this is not a goodbye or a breakup letter. It's a harsher "I'll only need you on vacations but I guess you're okay, too." Without a doubt I miss Chick-fil-A, sweet tea, and Coca-Cola. I miss going to breakfast restaurants like Cracker Barrel and ordering pancakes, grits, biscuits, gravy, eggs, and bacon. I miss school cancelling because of the first snow in five years and just on odd days when it was deemed too cold and dangerous. But don't confuse my nostalgia for love. New York will always beat you, and I now consider this my home. Sorry, it's not me; it's you.

Discussion Questions

- Why would somebody want to read this piece (the "Who cares?" factor)?
- Can you clearly identify the author's intention for the piece?
- How well does the author support the intention of the piece? Cite specific details that support or take away from the author's intention.
- Is there information missing from this piece that would make its intention clearer? What else would you like to know?
- Does the author portray herself as a round character? How does she do this?
- Do you trust the author of this piece? Why or why not?
- How clearly does the author establish a sense of setting/space in this piece? Cite specific details that support your claim.

- How clearly does the author establish characters other than the self in this piece? Cite specific details that support your claim.
- Did you learn anything new from reading this piece? If so, what?
- Are there particular passages with engaging language/description that stood out to you? Describe the appeal of these passages.
- Would you read more writing from this author? Why or why not?

To the Center

William Rossi

It wasn't that I hated *this* car ride; it was the fact that I hate any car ride over fifteen minutes. Yet still, an argument ensued about why we have to go and what exactly we would be doing once we got there. Then my mother snapped back with a response about my father, and his "facility," figuring once my brother and I got confused we would stop arguing with her. This was the first trip of many and it was the longest. We left the house late because my mother had to toggle getting my brother and I ready. It was too early, especially for a day when I didn't have school.

It was Saturday, the day for families to visit the patients: we only ever visited on Saturdays. To my surprise, the facility wasn't a huge brick building with a nice silver and granite sign adorned with a palm tree. Instead it looked like a residential community center, like the one I used to visit my great-great-grandma in when she was on hospice. There were two small buildings; one was full of offices, comfy chairs, and motivational posters. The other was where the patients lived. It was a small building that made a U-shape around an ornate garden. There was a sizeable waterfall in the center, surrounded by bright green shrubbery that always looked the same. The rooms were all dull shades of blue, the stable color palette used for the facility.

My mom parked in the gravel parking lot, and took my brother and I out of the minivan. Her light-brown hair got caught on her sunglasses as she slammed her door shut. She delicately pulled them from her face and untangled her hair, while she shuffled through the gravel kicking it around then complaining there were rocks in her sandals. We huddled into concourse of the center where we heard the low, monotone beginnings of a prayer. In a drab unison, "In the name of the Father, Son, Holy Spirit" echoed out of the small rear door to the gathering room.

"Goddamit. We're fucking late," snapped my mother as we crept through the white paneled door. In the large square room, we saw an array of other children who were all seated on the floor in front of their parents. Everyone else sat in chairs that lined the walls. We found our seats next to my father who was relieved to see us after our delay led him to believe we weren't going to come.

He stood up to hug us, his tall and lanky stature towering over my brother and I. He wasn't shaving in rehab so his kisses were scruffy. His stomach protruded his waist in a hard, solid bubble, but it contrasted his skinny silhouette. He had the same "beer belly" all my uncles had, protruding only forward and not out toward the sides. His hands were thick, unproportional to the rest of his body. They were the hands that built the tire swing in our yard, the hands that fixed boats and cut meat, the hands that held ours when we crossed a street. His hands were somewhat unsteady, along with the rest of his being. It wasn't a shock, or a shake, but a shiver. His body trembled in small jolts of muscle tension as we sat throughout the meeting.

He was always happy to see us, because it was those Saturdays that we were able to see him for a few hours every week. It was those Saturdays that kept him going through the 3-month process. The gathering consisted of men and women discussing their triumphs, and downfalls. They shared the best techniques of overcoming the battle, and told of ways to persevere through the challenges of withdrawal. Sometimes the family members spoke alongside their loved ones and sometimes even the leader of the center would join in the conversation. This was the solemn melancholy that began every Saturday and it remained stagnant throughout the duration of my father's rehabilitation program.

My father's roommate, Mike, sat with my brother and I while my parents sat in a small room in the other building. He told me how he plays his small guitar a lot when he's bored, or when he needs to take his mind off things. The same "things" everyone was trying to keep his or her mind off of. My brother sat and toggled with a leapfrog toy as we waited for the return of my parents. My parents sat through a half-hour-long initial therapy session, while I plucked the strings of the guitar. They met with the director of the program and then the special counselor who would specialize in my father's therapy sessions. He would meet the personal counselor shortly after the director finished his speech on the benefits of the program, the success rates, and the payment plans.

We stayed in the room most of the time. If it were ever nice outside, we would spend time in the grass yard. As the first month passed, my father's wall became decorated with postcards, letters, and photos exchanged with the members of his family. This mural of memories served to keep his thoughts positive and unwavering. Throughout the three-month program, he became humble and vulnerable. He wasn't as stern as I once knew him as. A stern where muscles would tense, but his arms wouldn't swing. Where the authority came up from his throat, like a vomit of demand and muted aggression. His progress to transformation began to impress me. Not enough to transform my opinion, but enough to make me question how I now felt about him. This place, where he remained for three months, had changed my father. It stripped him of his firm shell and diluted the heroic vision of my father that always clouded my mind. My father was not a villain, because although his actions might project otherwise, he was truly ordinary. He made a mistake; he was conflicted, and in constant war with an affliction deemed hereditary. This place had taken my father from his demons and reinvented him. For a while he was actually unrecognizable.

The center was where my father learned the twelve steps to a better life. There he learned the prayer to combat his desire for toxic sips from green glass bottles. It was there my father learned how to control his temptations and comprehend the consequences of his actions. This center was where I first saw my father cry. It was where I first understood what had happened the night a couple weeks ago when my brother and I were taken across the street to stay with the neighbor for the night. We carried over our blankets and pillows, laid on the couch, and listened to my mom yelling. She was angry, upset, and distraught. She stood on the front stoop while my father lurked in the garage. He rummaged through his crafts and tools, not to avoid my mother, but to hide his embarrassment. My eyes welled from severe allergies to the cats my neighbor bred, and I sat up watching the red and blue lights reflect around the room. Rhythmically they danced against the wall till I heard three doors slam and the lights descend back into the darkness they came from.

And there I was, in my father's 3-month crypt, grasping the fact that the incident was a drunken mistake. I had experienced the fourth step of my father's drunkard progress, drunk and riotous. He was not the man that taught me how to ride a bike, to catch a fish, or to throw a ball to the dogs. He was his own father; repetitive in the nature of DNA. Repeating the steps that sparked the cancer in my grandfather's liver; the cancer that killed him just before I was born. It was an addiction to malts, liquors, booze, and brews; little glass bottles of dissatisfaction. A battle I too may have to come to terms with in my future. That's where, unknowingly, our relationship changed; that's when my father and I lost our bond.

Discussion Questions

- Why would somebody want to read this piece (the "Who cares?" factor)?
- Can you clearly identify the author's intention for the piece?
- How well does the author support the intention of the piece? Cite specific details that support or take away from the author's intention.
- Is there information missing from this piece that would make its intention clearer? What else would you like to know?
- Does the author portray herself as a round character? How does she do this?
- Do you trust the author of this piece? Why or why not?
- How clearly does the author establish a sense of setting/space in this piece? Cite specific details that support your claim.
- How clearly does the author establish characters other than the self in this piece? Cite specific details that support your claim.
- Did you learn anything new from reading this piece? If so, what?
- Are there particular passages with engaging language/description that stood out to you? Describe the appeal of these passages.
- Would you read more writing from this author? Why or why not?

Growing Through Dirt

Magdalene Moore

Sanitary napkins are to be rolled in tissue three times before they are placed in a garbage pail so that they become unidentifiable among the rest of the trash. This is partly for sanitary reasons, but the reason my mother stressed was that other people in our house shouldn't have to see menstrual pads.

When I was eleven my cousin told me about the menstrual cycle because her mother had told her about it and, feeling betrayed that this seemingly impossible, repulsive thing was going to happen to me and no one had so much as mentioned it, I cried. She showed me diagrams of how a tampon was to be inserted in an American Girl book on women's hygiene that her mother had bought for her. My mother came home with the same book from a public library a few months later but I told her that I already knew about the menstrual cycle so we didn't open the book and we never talked about it. Ten days later I bled through white clothes.

At twelve I began describing myself as "more like a boy than a girl" because I did not want to be seen as dramatic, petty or ridiculous. Boys at school did not have any interest in me because I was not pretty, and I did not have any interest in them because my mother had told me that being interested in boys at my age was absurd and I wanted to be taken seriously. My mother became nonsensically accusatory when she found me holding hands with a girl, but she could have caught me kissing one instead, and it would have given her a much better case.

I was thirteen the first time I saw a porn film. The girl on the screen was white and blonde and her skin, tanned golden and unmarred by hair or razor burns, looked like that of a plastic doll. Her eyes were thickly lined with black makeup and her lips wet with a pink gloss. Her thighs did not touch and her stomach was a flat plane beneath her breasts. She had no pubic hair and her skin made me feel like my skin was wrong. When my mother caught me I was punished for a week. Girls aren't supposed to look at pornography, she said. I knew that she meant that girls aren't supposed to masturbate.

When I was fourteen I didn't wear makeup. I had long, mousy hair, freckles, and pale, imperfect skin. My mother complained of my attitude each time I spoke something that was not pleasant or agreeable and yelled if I cried. In December she took me to see her family up north and cheerfully laughed when her friend's son tugged at my arm and pulled me along throughout the evening. When he took me into the trees and threw me down in the snow there was no audience so no one laughed at that. Having never been kissed by a boy before and having already been told exactly what it was supposed to be like, I writhed and struggled to get away, knowing that this was not how it was supposed to happen. The thought of truly being overpowered by a man had never really occurred to me and, face up on the cold forest floor, I felt every notion of control slip from underneath me. "I've never kissed a redhead before," he said to me. Words would not come. As someone shouted his name in searching for him, I pulled myself up and stumbled away. He looked startled and quickly collected himself, as though he knew then what he had done was wrong, composing himself like nothing had happened. I did not have red hair.

When I was fifteen I tried inserting a tampon for the first time. It's easy, Becky Nicholson, a sweet, patient girl from school said. She noted the frustration twisting deep within me, coiling tighter with desperation, and she spoke gently. Use a mirror, put it into the opening. I could not make it work no matter how many diagrams I looked at and I could not understand why. What opening? It was months before my rigid body let any tampon enter, but not before a boy forced his fingers deep within it. I let him force his fingers into me and when he did I was in pain. The boy paid me more attention than I thought anyone would ever give to an ugly girl who spent her time thinking about not eating, but when he left he told me that I would never stop being a mess and that shattered me. With false promises of love, he sometimes called requesting to slip his hands beneath my waistband in the two years after that and, hungry for his attention, sometimes I let him.

The first time I tried to have sex was when I was sixteen years old. I was in a dimly lit bedroom a twenty-minute train ride from my own and the sheets beneath my fingers felt clean. I had stopped menstruating sometime earlier that year so there had been no need to try with tampons, and I was not prepared for the disappointment that, even then, my unrelenting body would not grant entry whether I wanted it to or not. I put my clothes on and rode the train home feeling dirty.

Later that year, in a parking lot of decent vacancy, a police car sat twenty feet away from a car in which I would have more than a kiss forced upon me. As I watched the police car pull away and turned to stare upward toward the sky I would think about how I deserved this. I would think about how I hadn't followed the instructions laid out for me in black and white, and how I was a slut and I owed my body to this man. When he was done I refused his kiss and he asked me if I liked him. I turned my head away and closed my eyes and did not answer. Nails driven into the material of the car seat, I silently willed him to look away from my exposed skin, unshaved and unfit for his viewing. Shame washed over me and, outside of his field of vision, I began to shake my head slowly. Lights moved through the dark in the distance and I, unmoving, watched without processing them, indiscernible thoughts buzzing discordant within my mind. I had never felt so cold. Slowly, I leaned over to the car floor and began collecting my clothes off the floor. *Because I like you,* he said.

Later in the night, washing the event from my barren body with water hot as the rusty shower would allow, I sank to the floor and felt myself shake. The overwhelming nausea I would feel for the next week had not yet begun, nor did the crying spells that would accompany it. I was not yet sad or angry, desperate or volatile. In that moment, crumpled on the white floor as water ran down my aching pale flesh, I felt almost nothing at all. In the years following I would spend countless hours reliving the event, face twisted with emotion, desperately trying to force back tears, but on the floor of the shower, only hours after its occurrence, I felt almost nothing at all. Eyes closed, I sat wordlessly, consumed by a certain emptiness that felt like, perhaps, it had been there all along.

> **Discussion Questions**
>
> - Why would somebody want to read this piece (the "Who cares?" factor)?
> - Can you clearly identify the author's intention for the piece?
> - How well does the author support the intention of the piece? Cite specific details that support or take away from the author's intention.
> - Is there information missing from this piece that would make its intention clearer? What else would you like to know?
> - Does the author portray herself as a round character? How does she do this?
> - Do you trust the author of this piece? Why or why not?

- How clearly does the author establish a sense of setting/space in this piece? Cite specific details that support your claim.
- How clearly does the author establish characters other than the self in this piece? Cite specific details that support your claim.
- Did you learn anything new from reading this piece? If so, what?
- Are there particular passages with engaging language/description that stood out to you? Describe the appeal of these passages.
- Would you read more writing from this author? Why or why not?

Playbill

Hannah Lajba

I am the lead in an eternal, external, internal performance. I do comedy, romance, heartbreak, tragedies, indie one-acts, one-person plays, monologues, asides, music videos, and sometimes even the occasional musical. Shakespeare was right when he said the whole world's a stage, with avenues where the spotlights shine bright and center, waiting for me to make my entrance from the side street wings. Once that light grazes over my face and blinds out my eyes I know I am ready to perform, to become what I am for that day, not what others are expecting me to be.

I write my own scripts, and like that of a stereotypical artist my best work comes out in the late night and early mornings when my mind becomes fogged of logic and my heart beats out pure emotion into my veins. For the trees' sake they are written down into the pages of my dreams, lucidity does come in handy, the lines are practically memorized by the time she wakes up. I am hair and makeup. Does this character not care that the baggage from late last night and days of worrying over the smallest of comments still appears on her face with Miley buns or would she rather have that hard edge of black around her eyes and a sinister ruby red lip with the perfectly greased quiff? Maybe she's sweet and is going to play the innocent card that she does so well with candy apple cheeks and a natural side part that must always be finger-combed back into place giving her awkward hands something to do during a conversation. I may just do the usual, standard stage makeup, enough to let her stand out from the other characters that may enter on to her stage combined with a seamless, frozen-into-place pompadour. I am the director. I tell her how to walk for the day, to come in center stage right or upstage left. I let her know her cues on when to enter and walk to certain places, what routes someone like her would take. I make sure that she knows when to say her lines and what inflection she will use. Will she be snarky, bold, daring, shy, flirtatious, or will she just not talk at all and mime her way through the daily grind that is her routine? I am the composer of my own orchestra and sound tech supervisor. Each playlist is perfectly arranged with songs for the side streets where emotions can be concealed and rhythms with a strong beat for the avenues where her walk of the day, whether it be a full-on strut or a downcast head stride.

Character Study No. 1 from *Heart's a Mess*. Hannah's a young midwestern girl who's come to the Big Apple to follow her lustful passion for fame and glamour in the fashion industry as a designer. Stress came as a tsunami her first week, and the unrelenting workload of draping and sketching occupied her late nights but soon came her character flaw, boys. Like Ophelia her life and choices have been driven by boys, always following her older brother's taste in music (the shows music will include Beck, Eels, Future Islands, and Yeah Yeah Yeahs), she joined an art studio that led to amazing fashion opportunities because of a high school crush which turned out he was gay, and now here she sits in the opening scene in front of the hottest boy on campus. Being bold she cracks out of her four-year shell of an all-girls education and talks to two boys, one of which becomes a true crush, taking its hammer to her heart and head. She works many late nights trying to get him off her mind only to think about him the moment she lays her head down for a restless sleep. The wardrobe consists of mismatched combinations of what she considers pjs: leggings, boxers, Levi's cutoff shorts, oversized sweaters, and men's flannels as the majority of the play is set in the hot, bland basement of coed. The hair is this outrageous big up do with a giant pale pink bow in the back; I think we're going to have to use a wig just to conserve the actress's hair. Hannah's awkward, her mouth murmuring out stuttered compliments, but how many changes will she make to herself to get the one she wants? With only a year before he leaves can Hannah seal the deal with pies?

Character Study No. 2 from *Suck It and See*. Hana is an "I don't give a shit, where's my cigarette?" rockabilly kid with plenty of snarky remarks just waiting up her leather jacket sleeve. Her wardrobe is an array of blacks and leathers with a few of her signature jumpsuits thrown in for good measure. She's always in her black skinnies, openly and obviously too tight to be comfortable, but somehow she still manages to walk down the street with long strides and ruggish pickups of her knees. She has this British grit to her, probably comes from having 25% Manchester blood in her. The night is where she feels safe, silently prowling the streets for secret corners of inspiration while she nervously inhales deeply on the last of her Parliaments, trying to cope with the stress of the day. She fears the future and will do anything to maintain that she knows what is exactly going to happen every day. She wakes up every morning, no matter how late she stayed up, to do her short hair in that perfect greasy coif. Luckily the actress agreed to chop her hair off without even telling her mother just so her method acting could be that much more on point with Hana. She carefully paints her face with black and red before doing her signature slick back with her hands, ignoring the new tackiness they possess. When she rarely goes out during the day her emotionless eyes are shielded by the mirror lenses of her sunglasses and with a smug grin into the corner of her mouth and proceeds on with her day. Her external soundtrack is a combination of The Horrors album Scary House and a culmination of every Arctic Monkeys love song, her tragic downfall, once again, is a boy. What happens when all her routine comforts become a disarray of uncalculated circumstances and she's just OD on Diet Coke?

Character Study No. 3 from *Work Bitch*. Hannah Lajba is a bitch. A stone-cold, get out of my face, do what I told you to do; don't think I'm going to repeat what I just said for the eleventh time that's it you're fired—and she likes it that way. I will slick her hair back into that perfect pompadour, it isn't greasy, it is stiff and sharp, just like her makeup that extenuates her cheekbones with strong contouring and a brow that is so intimidating one must look away in her presence. She only wears black and white. Even if her internal life isn't balanced she can at least be balanced on the outside. Her music is a complicated composition; she is never one mood, though you would never be able to tell. Her title track is Brittany Spears, but inside her internal radio plays Perfume Genius and Keaton Henson. Her face is what she would consider neutral, but to others it is a silent declaration of "Yes, I know, I'm better than you, now leave me alone" and that's how she feels after a euphorically productive day at the office, she just wants to be alone. Even with this demeanor, Hannah Lajba still doubts herself on the inside. She tries to hide her weak heart that falls prey too easily to the man of the hour, day, week, or month. When she scowls it isn't because she doesn't like what she is seeing, it is because she doesn't like what she isn't seeing. Her imagination is constantly playing tricks on her; what happens when the muse that inspired her becomes the muse that will be her downfall? Will she do anything to get ahead and take over what she has already claimed as hers?

"Five minutes to curtain call!" Our hero begins the day as usual, her script is memorized and she is well rehearsed. She steps into costume after spending hours in hair and makeup to get that perfect look before heading to the stage. As she makes the walk from the dressing room to the wings she prepares her mind and body for the stage. She lip synchs a few songs from the soundtrack and moves her body, letting loose all the unnecessary tension. She closes her eyes and thinks of the struggles her character is having and finds a face to match those hardships. "Places everyone!" She walks onto stage and positions herself at downstage center, waiting for the curtain to rise.

Discussion Questions

- Why would somebody want to read this piece (the "Who cares?" factor)?
- Can you clearly identify the author's intention for the piece?
- How well does the author support the intention of the piece? Cite specific details that support or take away from the author's intention.
- Is there information missing from this piece that would make its intention clearer? What else would you like to know?
- Does the author portray herself as a round character? How does she do this?
- Do you trust the author of this piece? Why or why not?
- How clearly does the author establish a sense of setting/space in this piece? Cite specific details that support your claim.
- How clearly does the author establish characters other than the self in this piece? Cite specific details that support your claim.
- Did you learn anything new from reading this piece? If so, what?
- Are there particular passages with engaging language/description that stood out to you? Describe the appeal of these passages.
- Would you read more writing from this author? Why or why not?

I Told You So

Jillian McDonnell

When I was a baby my legs were *really* big, especially my thighs. My mom said everyone commented on them, "Look at her thighs. They're huge!" I look at pictures of them and agree. They look like the Michelin Man or the Pillsbury Doughboy, chunky and wide. My eating habits were testimony to those meaty limbs, as it is claimed that I ate eleven pieces of lamb in one sitting at my aunt's house at age two, everyone gawking at me certainly did not faze me as my hands moved from one bone to the next. My legs were chubby, but like most baby fat they faded away over the years.

Jump to elementary school and I am tiny. Small all over, my legs nowhere near as plump as they were before. I am short and I am very thin. I don't like the sandwiches Mommy makes me every day so I eat everything but the crust (a whopping three whole bites with my teeny mouth). These legs are petite and as thin as toothpicks, covered weekly with a new scab here and a new scab there. One day before school in first grade I shake with excitement while my mom ties my brand new Keds on. They're pink with letters on one face of the shoe and green zigzags on the other. I hop up after she's done, sprint down the two flights of stairs and I'm off, headed for Baba's green Civic so ready for school and—BOOM—I'm down. I'm sobbing and Mom's carrying me in and my knee's bleeding a whole bunch and she's cursing those new Keds because she "Knew it, I just knew they were too big Jillian I should have never let you get them in the first place." I walk in late to school and stroll into class with a big gash in my knee once embedded with rocks now instead covered by two Band-Aids. One just wasn't thick enough to cover the battle scar.

Cuts are not the only thing that shift places and show up on my legs. I have hair, blonde and brown but thin, too young for me to shave yet so they streak and shine in the light. Past the little hairs are mosquito bites. *Always* there, never to leave. Not because they bite me all year round, rather my fingers scratch them again and again. So close to healing but then my nail feels one scab, and off it goes again, destined to never disappear as they should and instead leave a pinkish mark faded but always there. These marks that make my mom tell me "You look like a leper," or "Well there goes your leg modeling career," (which we all know is a joke because I don't grow past five foot three after tenth grade) and the most popular, "Jillian Mary! Stop scratching those things they are going to scar. *Forever.*"

I have a birthmark on my ankle. Not a dark one like the ones women draw on their face, but instead a little brown freckle slightly raised, and I hated it. It was always there and so, of course, it always bugged me. One day at a family dinner party it peeked right above my sandal strap and that was it. The nails equipped to pick at scabs upon scabs were ready, and they went at it. I picked at that thing for an hour, and finally, it gave in. The little brown fleck gave way and slowly raised. Alas it ripped off, but to my horror it started bleeding. I panicked and didn't want anyone to see, especially Mommy, so I covered it with my hand as my eyes searched frantically for a napkin. Good, I had replaced the millimeter-wide freckle with a gush of blood and a napkin and a hand, much less noticeable, much less eye- attracting. That night, once the bleeding had stopped, I looked at the little dig out on my ankle and cried. How could I have been so stupid?! That freckle was a part of me and I had erased it, what if it never returned? So I waited, checking the scab nightly, but unlike the mosquito bites this would not be touched, I needed it to go back to its normal form. Finally after fourteen days of care and caution, I looked and sighed a big happy sigh of relief. It had returned, and it is still there now, located on my right inner ankle, approximately half an inch below that knobby bone that juts out.

I look back through a photo album of my fifth-grade graduation. My mom walks by and she cringes, "God you were so thin. You look sickly." I gaze at pictures of me beaming ear to ear next to teachers and friends and I have to agree. The angles of my face are far too chiseled for the face of a child. My chin juts out like a sharp knife and the tendons on my neck are far too visible. That was the outcome of me not eating those sandwiches, those were pictures taken only a month before my doctor told my mom I was severely underweight. The night after the doctors I sit down for dinner. That night, like most nights, the food stares back at me for one, two, three hours. Everything is eaten but my salad, and now it is soggy with dressing that I don't particularly like. My mom gets tired of waiting to do the dishes, but this time it's different. She comes back and she's crying and she's screaming. She's scared for me, blames herself because I refuse to take care of myself. And then I'm crying, I don't want her to be upset. I sit on her lap and cry and she looks at me, "That's it. This is done. No more of this you have to eat so we don't have to get in trouble with the doctor again." I agree and sit down. I eat my salad piece by piece and ignore the feeling in my stomach that says, *"No more. No more."* This night is followed by the constant nag and worry of my mom. A yearly finger crossing when I step on the scale at the doctor's office is expected and fear of me ever leaving her watchful eye becomes quite apparent.

I ran track in sophomore year, against my mother's wishes, "You lose one pound and you're off the team, I'm not joking." Nervous to keep my mom happy, I kept the weight from runner's highs and Friday night pasta parties. So yes, I ran. Well, I ran half of the season anyways. Midway, Coach Kaminski yells, "McDonnell, you're signed up for the walk Sunday." Everyone laughs and I argue but he won't change his mind. So that Sunday I speed walk one mile in the correct form. Legs landing unbent, nineteen other girls and I get to waddle around an indoor track for ten minutes in spandex that rides up your butt. It's walking, but it's sure not easy, I get off the track grateful that my torture has ended. My legs feel like noodles, I don't know how to walk the right way again until the next morning, a morning teamed with lots of Advil to kill the pain, the pain from walking. Each morning after an intense workout or a race my mom laughs and then nags, "What's the point? You don't need to run track you're just killing yourself for nothing." Yet I get sucked into doing the walk again and again, and finally am granted the high and prestigious honor of "Dobbs Ferry's Number One Speed Walker" out of the whole two girls doing it (me being one of them). After every race my legs feel like noodles, and they look like them too, the petite shape from elementary school never went away, but now two friends are added and during that sophomore year of winter track, I get the nickname Boobs and, even more clever, Boobian.

My mom doesn't want me to leave for school. Why would she when I'm a "Train ride away Jillian everyone does the commute. You could even get rides from Mr. Scroope he is right next door!" These comments result in constant fighting and constant tears. I am so frustrated with my mom, how could she not trust me to leave, I can take care of myself I am not an infant. I beg and plead and finally I get the monotonous answer a thousand times, "Do what you want, but you can pay for dorming yourself." And to her surprise I do.

I don't feel pain like the speed walk again until college, in a spin class I was talked into going to by my roommates. I take the class as a newbie, I don't know what's going on, but I do it all the same. My legs continue to bounce out of the feet holders and I keep pausing and going, a perfect forty-five minutes of *"When is this over?"* and *"How did I end up in the front? I look like a complete fool."* Finally it's over, and I feel the noodle legs once again, but the pain was not contained in that forty-five minutes. My legs can't move, they are so sore I limp through my week of classes, and finally they have me in an ER. That's right, like a great TLC special, *Spin Class Sent Me to the ER.* I go expecting three hours of fluids, because they say I have something called Rhabdomyolysis and I am probably dehydrated. After sitting on the bed for two hours with an IV in one arm and a needle puncture in another, I feel a smile of excitement come on because I can't wait to get out of the place. But no, I get to stay overnight because the last blood test shows elevated levels. The doctor tells me this bad news and now I'm scared. I call the house phone and dread the answer I'll get but, "We'll be right there Jill." I have to keep sitting like this, trapped to the IV that keeps beeping, my "dancing partner." I feel fine physically, but I can't help but keep tearing.

I cry when my mom comes in, she looks so frightened for me, "How did this happen?! I don't understand." And runs over to me arms outstretched crying just as much. I keep tearing the entire night, my eyes redder and puffier each time my dancing partner and I wheel ourselves over to the bathroom. During one trip I don't sit down right away, and instead fling my fists around to no destination and think loudly, "*This doesn't happen to anyone what the* fuck *is happening to me.*" Finally my mom looks at me and pleads, "Please talk to me Jillian," and I throw the covers over my face curl myself up into the tightest ball possible and release. I sob big heaving sobs and in between each I admit word by word I can't stay overnight and I just want to go home. I hate letting her see me like this, this is just the thing she needs, the "I told you so" of the century, but I can't help it. I need her, I know I do. So when she offers to stay overnight I quietly say, "No it's ok, you need your sleep," but I know she'll ignore me and answers to the nurse, "Can we get another pillow please? I feel fine, but I'm stuck, no way to get out of it. That night my legs start to swell, they feel worse than they ever have. My little toothpick legs swell so large they are touching each other just like they did when I was a baby, but this time I'm hurt. I'm crying and the ice packs aren't working, the Advil's not working and the hot packs aren't working. I keep feeling them tighten and tighten, my body squirming with an endless discomfort. Finally the doctor comes in and says, "Ok go give her the heavy stuff." I don't even know what it is until I'm injected with a clear liquid when I hear the nurse say to my mom "morphine" and then I'm out.

I wake up the next morning and my IV's pinching me. I'm a bit dazed, but Mom's right next to me. She's sleeping but she's doing so much more. She's just…there. As always, but now she's just the only comfortable thing in this room. This room where they stick me with needles every six hours. This room where they come back with good and then terrible answers leaving me confused and disappointed. She's here like she always is, and there is nothing more comfortable then feeling her warm figure against mine in this tiny hospital bed.

Another nurse comes and she fixes the IV but a spurt of blood comes out. She sighs and starts removing the sheets so she can bring me a clean set. She lifts the covers off of my now semi-swollen legs, looks at them and says, "What are these, mosquito bites?! Don't you know if you keep scratching them they're gonna scar?" I look over at my mom and she looks right back with a look of, "I told you so."

Discussion Questions

- Why would somebody want to read this piece (the "Who cares?" factor)?
- Can you clearly identify the author's intention for the piece?
- How well does the author support the intention of the piece? Cite specific details that support or take away from the author's intention.
- Is there information missing from this piece that would make its intention clearer? What else would you like to know?
- Does the author portray herself as a round character? How does she do this?
- Do you trust the author of this piece? Why or why not?
- How clearly does the author establish a sense of setting/space in this piece? Cite specific details that support your claim.
- How clearly does the author establish characters other than the self in this piece? Cite specific details that support your claim.
- Did you learn anything new from reading this piece? If so, what?
- Are there particular passages with engaging language/description that stood out to you? Describe the appeal of these passages.
- Would you read more writing from this author? Why or why not?

Genetic Disposition

Emma Suleski

One foot in front of the other I slowly stepped off the bus. Boston is different than New York City. Maybe it's because I grew up minutes away from this city, but Boston always seemed so quaint and charming to me. It used to feel like home. Now it just felt small.

I shuffled silently through the bus terminal. For the first time in months I was in plain leggings and a hoodie, hair thrown carelessly on top of my head, eyebrows un-tweezed, makeup undone. I wasn't myself; I wasn't put together; I didn't have the same look on that earned me the nickname of "Barbie" in high school. I adjusted my backpack's straps on my shoulders, letting out a breath as I felt the books inside bounce on my lower back, just inches above the fading scars that marked where the screws went in. The books' presence was heavy, weighing down my body and my brain; they were a reminder of what I left and what I was going back to in just one week. The pocket of my sweatshirt buzzed and I pulled out my phone to read, "Inside the terminal. Downstairs."

I shifted my backpack on my shoulders one more time, hoping for an instant that their weight was transferring to my chest and that was the only reason for its constant aching. No luck, the weight redistributed but my chest remained tightly bound with fraying rope. Rounding the terminal corner, I saw him standing at the bottom of the steps. He looked just the same, the same worn Levi's, the same old flannel shirt, and the same salt and pepper hair. I shot my head back down to the ground, keeping it there as I trickled robotically down the stairs and bit the inside corner of my cheek in every effort to delay the tears. I held this position until I was standing in front of his ugly gray crocs. God I hated those things. I looked up, "Hi Dad."

He pulled me in for a tight hug and I felt my whole world stop. My brain rushed through all the thoughts I spent the last four-hour bus ride contemplating. See, people have this romantic idea of depression. It's the pretty girl weeping quietly as her make-up pours down her cheeks in her boyfriend's arms. It's the boy who just needs love to be saved. But it's neither of those things. It's coming home a month after starting college for your own health, it's greasy hair and red eyes, it's crying while hugging your dad in a bus terminal at eighteen years old. It's so many things and none of them are pretty.

Releasing from his embrace, my dad grabbed my backpack and threw it over one of his shoulders. I pushed open the door and we stepped into a Massachusetts September night. The chill left my eyes stinging so through squinted lids I looked around me at the pedestrian traffic, bustling in and out of South Station's doors. I smiled at the young girl, seven or eight years old, struggling to keep up with her family. I was familiar with her place as youngest and commiserated with having little legs that could only move so fast. I pivoted and followed my dad to his car and tossed myself into the front seat.

Watching city lights rush past, I sat in the silent car and thought. I won't, because it would be, well, depressing, but I could write fifteen thousand different words describing how dull and dark lacking serotonin can make your head. That's what it is too. It's a chemical imbalance. It's not some deep seeded Mommy or Daddy issue, the only thing my parents ever did wrong was pass down a genetic disposition.

My dad finally spoke, "How are you feeling Em?" No one ever wants to talk about how they're feeling. In public, it's taken as dramatizing teen angst. In pastel painted offices with ticking clocks, it is answering, "How does that make you feel?" over and over again. I've been taught to analyze every thought and to go against what my brain is telling me because if I had just a few more chemicals, well, it wouldn't be saying that. I can't answer the question in a simple few words; it takes weeks of hour-long sessions. In fact, how I'm feeling often doesn't even make sense to me. So, I'm lucky. I can simply sigh, "I'm doing okay, Dad" and he understands the message, leaving me back to my thoughts and watching the familiar scenery pass me by as I leave the city and approach my little suburb in the woods. He doesn't ask again today, but I know someday I'll need to give him and everyone else in my life a solid answer. Just like me, they're struggling to understand.

So I've learned. I learned to deal with it. After years of closing myself off and forcing myself to survive undertreated, I learned to ask for help. I went home because for just a few days, I needed the help of my biggest supporters. Like I said, it's not pretty. I cried and my mascara didn't run in little streams down my rosy cheeks, instead, snot dripped out of my nose. I learned that the best way to remember to take my medicine is to set an alarm on my phone and that even in 2014, not everyone is going to understand that I have a medical illness. I learned to talk, to express, to breathe, and to write. When I say write, I don't mean a beautiful poem; depression isn't writing words that rhyme or a symbolism that makes any sense. I mean writing an essay that is painfully raw and real. But getting those words down on paper, those real thoughts and feelings, that's how I've learned to cope.

The car made a smooth right onto Buttercup Lane. When we moved onto that street eleven years ago I remember how excited 7-year-old Emma was to be living on Buttercup Lane. It doesn't get more fairytale than that. That night I just chuckled, thinking about my poor teenage brothers who had to deal with living on such a flowery street. We pulled into my driveway and my dad yanked his keys out of the ignition. He sighed and put his hands in his lap, tossing a sympathetic smile in my direction. I nodded back to him and opened the car door.

I had been here a thousand times before. Not simply opening a car door in my driveway, but stepping out onto the pavement with a million thoughts rushing around my brain. Depression didn't exactly surprise me when I got to college; it had been creeping up on me for years, slowly changing my thoughts and actions, slowly changing me as a person. A typical day after high school consisted of stepping out of my car, walking into my house, taking a nap in my bed, waking up, doing my homework, eating dinner, and going back to bed. Most of the time, sleep was my only escape from my daily demons. Due to an injury, my back physically ached, day in and day out. The chronic pain had taken away so much from me: my favorite hobbies, my strength, and my energy. I was struggling with who I used to be, who I was, and who I wanted to be.

The sickly sweet smell of wild grapes warmed by the sun flooded my nose as I got out of the car. I opened the back door to grab my backpack. Stuck between the back seat and the passenger seat, I struggled to pull it out. My dad nudged me aside and in one simple motion pulled the black bag off of the floor and onto his shoulder. I followed him silently up the stairs of our farmer's porch and he opened the screen door. I pushed on our big front door, hip checking it twice as I always do during the humid months when its wood swells.

I trudged up the stairs and lay down on my bed, sinking deep into the foam that did, in fact, remember me. My thought then became, "what now?" I was home, I was safe, but I was still sick. I rolled over and on my nightstand still sat my old orange leather journal. It was a mess of impulsive scribblings and quotes I had found that resonated with me when I first slipped into the slump, thinking I was entering a phase of simple teenage insecurity.

My uncertain fingers opened creased pages. I turned randomly to an entry dated June 3rd, 2012: my sixteenth birthday. In hardly legible scrawl I read, "my second birthday I didn't have fun. This isn't just a phase." I cringed, remembering myself, ninety-two pounds, shuddering as I kept a poker face while eating my birthday cake. My friends laughed around me, piling plates with ice cream and cookies. I pushed cake frosting around my plate and just laughed along.

I flipped pages to a year later, the summer before my senior year. Months and months of sickness had pushed me to cross lines I never thought I would even approach. I read, "He asked me where the faded pinkish lines on my hips came from and I laughed and said, 'they're stretch marks, you asshole!' He traced one with his finger, looked at me with sad eyes and said, 'they look more like the physical result of all those nights you told me you hate yourself.' And I knew he had figured me out." I closed my eyes, remembering that night. Sitting on a dock in nowhere, New Hampshire, breathing in the scent of forest and lake. I felt the knot in my gut, the pain in my chest. I felt as if I had been caught in a crime I never meant to commit.

I scanned pages one more time and read and reread a quote from one of my favorite anonymous online poets. Tears rolled down my cheeks as the words struck me in a new way. "Drinking cough syrup when you didn't have a cough is ironic because in reality, you're sicker than you thought."

Discussion Questions

- Why would somebody want to read this piece (the "Who cares?" factor)?
- Can you clearly identify the author's intention for the piece?
- How well does the author support the intention of the piece? Cite specific details that support or take away from the author's intention.
- Is there information missing from this piece that would make its intention clearer? What else would you like to know?
- Does the author portray herself as a round character? How does she do this?
- Do you trust the author of this piece? Why or why not?
- How clearly does the author establish a sense of setting/space in this piece? Cite specific details that support your claim.
- How clearly does the author establish characters other than the self in this piece? Cite specific details that support your claim.
- Did you learn anything new from reading this piece? If so, what?
- Are there particular passages with engaging language/description that stood out to you? Describe the appeal of these passages.
- Would you read more writing from this author? Why or why not?

Shomer Nagia

Neziah Doe

I don't touch boys now. Not because they have cooties or anything, but more accurately I do. Trying to explain Jewish law to someone in only English is like, well, saying I have cooties. At least no one is going to ever date me for all of the hot sex we have. Or at least that's the case now, I definitely wasn't like that in junior year of high school, maybe I am like this because of my experience in my junior year in high-school.

"I am scared of him," I admitted to pre-clown-punk Leor, my school-bus companion and greatest school friend on the school bus two days after I broke up with him, "I don't know why, something makes me uneasy." It was a wet cloudy November day, I could feel the wheels skid over leftover fallen leaves from the fall, nearly losing control. I loved this weather, the drowsy ambiance giving more space for my manic enthusiasm. When he asked me out, my first thought was "yeah, sure, why not?"

"You're being overdramatic," smirked my brother, always assuming the best of people, always amused by my skepticism and neurotic paranoia, "he lives in Chicago, it's not like he's going to come here and hurt you." Daniel was always so uncomfortable with the idea of anyone doing anything badly, he refused to imagine a world where people would hurt others intentionally. It got him in a lot of trouble, I was always there to get him out of it.

I touched my newly shorn hair. I cut it with arts and crafts scissors after he hung up, looking blankly at the mirror as the long strands of split ends from the sixten years of growing my hair out fell to the ground. It tickled my shoulders, my hairdresser of a mother tearing up as she straightened up my raggedy hair that she insisted upon keeping long for so many years. She admitted that it looked healthy when she was done. But doing something spontaneous in a bout of emotional intensity is just something high-school me did. It took me two weeks to get over him. People telling me that my hair looked beautiful short, that I looked more like myself, was comforting.

He kept on texting me, saying he was sorry—that he misses me; that I shouldn't make promises that I cannot keep. As I cried in the library, my very happily not single friend looked upon me sympathetically, not knowing what to say. When he asked me out, my first thought was "yeah, sure, why not?" His voice in my head was calling me a cold-hearted bitch from that night—his dad was sick, he was really depressed those past few weeks. A greasy feeling of unease followed me around like a cloud of exhaust smoke, if only I was brave enough to look up.

The Jewish concept/law is called *shomer nagia*. It's a sign of being "really religious," because who would give up on cuddling, hand holding, and holding other things? When a woman has her period and the seven days after that, she is ritually impure. To get rid of this ritual impurity one must immerse themselves in *mikvah* water, which is unfiltered rainfall or a natural flowing source of water. During her time of ritual impurity, a man may not touch her because she is in the *niddah* state. But here's the catch—you can't go to the *mikvah* until you are about to get married because sex was created not just for pleasure but to: a—create a closeness that only exists between two partners for life, and b—create a family. So therefore, you cannot touch anyone of the opposite sex until you get married. And people wonder why religious people get married so young.

I wish I was *shomer* long before the age of eighteen when I took it upon myself, but rather the traditional 13, the year that a Jewish child comes of age. And I wished for it so many times before I did it, every time after I was with some guy and didn't feel any greater about myself afterward. But on most days I would arrogantly say, "that's so not realistic." It's weird to know that something you are doing is not right for you, but not knowing how to do *teshuva,* a return to God, a repentance to your soul for letting your body win.

I couldn't sleep in my bed after I broke up with him, maybe it was because of his few visits to my house, when we would do what teenagers do when they are alone at home. He is six feet and four inches tall, an athlete. We met in a summer program. When he asked me out, my first thought was "yeah, sure, why not?" He was loud, sociable and had a way of talking—like his tongue was a knife. Green slits of eyes, always peering around to make sure he was the strongest person in the room, he was on crew. You quit when you found out your dad was sick again.

The thing that I like about *shomer nagia* is that it's about taking something mundane like touching someone and makes it into something holy. Holiness is a form of romanticism, and we romanticize touching someone—so it was just a thought shift really. Also, I like saying I have cooties.

Maybe it was a comb at a friend's house, or a pair of headphones. My library card? I rifle through my bag, my wallet. My drawers, but there's still something missing that isn't here. I feel dirty—I shower, wash my body four times each shower.

"Shut up Daniel, that's a totally legit reason to break up with someone, and you know you can always talk about it with me," Leor says kindly to me, but her eyes are alight with anger. She's my feminist friend. "It's really good you broke up with him."

In Jewish law, or *halacha,* if a woman is raped the rapist has to pay her father or husband for the damages. I don't know how this amount of money is decided but when I learned about this I thought it was awesome that an ancient culture facilitated for the victims of rape. It's funny how things change. Sexual harassment and not asking consent for anything but sex is another story. There are some things one only gets punished for in the next world.

When he asked me out, my first thought was "yeah, sure, why not?" Lying on top of me, he said that we were ready to take things further. So I said no, that I am not ready. He scowled and held my hands down, kissing my neck, his scruff irritating my skin, the smell of his sweat choking me. I struggled, then I forgot how to say no. He removed my shirt, my bra; I thought I was saying no—is it possible for one's thoughts to take away one's ability to speak? I wriggled underneath him, every fiber of my being screaming NO. I wish I was *shomer* long before the age of eighteen when I took it upon myself, but rather the traditional thirteen, the year that a Jewish child comes of age. And I wished for it so many times before I did it.

I looked away from him—I could barely look at my own body in the mirror, much less let someone else look at mine. He paused to look down at my pale skin, arms draped with scars. I held back my tears, I was so scared he would not like me. He slid his sweaty palm down my body, being fourteen inches shorter and a hundred pounds lighter, there was no way I stood a chance. I looked at my door, a strong piece of wood, custom made just for my house by my father. I knew why my father was so reluctant to put on a doorknob to my door now. There is also a law forbidding two single people of the opposite sex to be together, called *yichud,* singularity. I knew why that was a law at that moment, I wanted it so bad.

Three weeks later he had a girlfriend, she was blonde, thin, and adorable. I was really confused how he could move on so quickly when I was still forgetting something. I cried. There's a buffer period of thirty days in *halacha* from when one can go from one marriage to the next, saying you love someone forever one day to someone else the next. He made his point—he won, again.

In a *ketuva,* or a traditional Jewish marriage contract, one of the requirements of a husband is to sexually satisfy his wife. Yeah, that's right—if a woman doesn't receive proper treatment, she is allowed to go to the Rabbinical courts and demand a *get,* a divorce. Horrifyingly, the man is allowed to refuse to give her one, which gives her the *halachick* status of an *agunah,* a "chained" wife. In recent years, Rabbis have formulated a *halachick* pre-nup that once signed forces the husband to accept the demand of divorce. Women will be chained no more.

His sweaty palms reached into my underwear, he growled "tell me when you are done.".And after three minutes of him pretending like he knows how to stimulate a clitoris and asking me if I was done, I pulled his hand out and somehow got out from the entrapment he put me in, I guess that's just women's intuition.

"Go wash your hands," I said, he went to the bathroom and I composed myself. He came back in, "it's getting late, you better go catch your train."

"I could stay a little longer," he said, hands gripped into boulders at his sides, "I've fingered enough girls to know that they never want to return the favor."

"Next time, seriously, there's a storm coming. This is the last train, look," I pleaded, shoving my computer into his face. I wish I was *shomer* long before the age of eighteen when I took it upon myself, but rather the traditional thirteen, the year that a Jewish child comes of age. And I wished for it so many times before I did it.

We walked to the station in the crisp October air, the whispers of wind caressing my face kindly. He told me he loves me and couldn't wait to see me again. For some reason I could not remember, I knew this was going to be the last time. I showered for a long time when I got home.

And then for years, it wasn't a story to dwell upon. I didn't want to be a victim, I wasn't looking for a monetary reward for damages, I didn't want to ever see myself as chained. So it was an event that rested in the back of my mind until I met Aviva, a now good friend who was following Jewish law with so much purity and happiness I was jealous of her with every fiber of my being.

"Oh, you know him?" a newly acquainted friend of mine whispered to me, her eyes darkening, "how do you know him?"

"We went out for like, three months starting in summer 2011," I stumbled, "it wasn't a big deal."

"Did he hurt you?" She blurted, looking scandalized at her own words.

"I…um…"

"He was dating my sister what must have been a few weeks after you guys. He was really pushy with her, always telling her what to do. He raped her, I hate him." I shook on the inside, feeling horrible for this girl I don't even know. My friend kept on talking, spilling out words she has wanted to say for a long time, as if they were perfectly ripened for this moment. How you ruined her emotionally, how she withered away and became someone else all together. It was my fault, if only I had taught him what NO means. If only I knew how to say NO at that time. "But you probably hate him more than I do."

"He didn't rape me," I said, "I ended it before he could get that far. I'm really ok, I just feel terrible for your sister. I am so, so sorry."

"She isn't *shomer [nagia]* by the way, she stopped going in any direction towards religion after that."

I showered for a really long time that night.

> ### Discussion Questions
>
> - Why would somebody want to read this piece (the "Who cares?" factor)?
> - Can you clearly identify the author's intention for the piece?
> - How well does the author support the intention of the piece? Cite specific details that support or take away from the author's intention.
> - Is there information missing from this piece that would make its intention clearer? What else would you like to know?
> - Does the author portray herself as a round character? How does she do this?
> - Do you trust the author of this piece? Why or why not?
> - How clearly does the author establish a sense of setting/space in this piece? Cite specific details that support your claim.
> - How clearly does the author establish characters other than the self in this piece? Cite specific details that support your claim.
> - Did you learn anything new from reading this piece? If so, what?
> - Are there particular passages with engaging language/description that stood out to you? Describe the appeal of these passages.
> - Would you read more writing from this author? Why or why not?

Brooklyn, Madness, Lust, Death, and the Apocalypse

Chadbourne Oliver

Genny tells me she's finished her first novel. Over the phone her voice is reserved but I can tell she's proud and excited and so am I. "It's almost fifty five thousand words," she says, "I think I'm gonna send it to *McSweeney's*." I know she dreams of being published in that quarterly, a thick hardcover volume that usually incorporates some kind of abstract delivery by means of strange artsy packaging.

"I'll print it out so I can read it on the train," I promise her as I open the lengthy file on my computer screen, not yet realizing that the money in my wallet isn't enough to feed the printer for eighty-six full pages. Never have her prose and beautiful run-ons reached such a length as this. It is called Dust Rules Everything Around Me, or D.R.E.A.M., and the opening page bears a quotation:

"(theory: just like the kingdom of God, hell is within us): and I feel in myself, on certain days, such an overwhelming inrush of evil that I imagine the prince of darkness is already beginning to set up hell within me."

She credits it to a book I do not know by Andre Gide called *The Counterfeiters*. I can hear her voice speaking the words, see her poring over that long sentence. I can see her green eyes flash and her mouth turn involuntarily up at the corners like mine does when she realized how beautiful, how perfect it was.

"What's it about?" I asked her when she first told me she'd decided to work on a full novel. She'd always leaned towards short stories.

"It's about Brooklyn and the apocalypse and lots of lust and death and madness." She paused and smiled as if to say "Don't worry," or "I'm not crazy."

I saw her read a passage aloud to a significant audience in the very borough she wrote about so deftly, without ever having lived there. She stood behind a podium before them, seated in rows of folding chairs under the lofty ceiling of a grand dining room in some posh new hotel. She spoke perhaps a bit too fast, as she's always been wont to do, her thickly written account of darkness projected up like an old movie, a grim tale and a black dress to match.

My sister and I are perhaps the most genuinely happy people I know. I believe it comes from the unbridled enthusiasm for our work that we both possess, and the social confidence that I've always had; that she's learned partly from me. She's been writing since we were children, through all the times I played the younger brother and begged her attention, begged her to stop reading or writing in her little book or typing on the computer and just come play with me for the love of god. She's always had a bit more of the quiet pensiveness I credit to our paternal grandfather than I can bear for lack of patience. In both cases, regardless of our primarily positive outlook on life itself, we both have an affinity for dark things, a fascination that can be seen shining through our dark and yet colored eyes when brought up. Even as I read the opening quotation of her novel I think of a line penciled into one of my lyric books not too long ago. "…Every single thing I do I mean, 'cause I've got a little evil in me…." I snarl into the microphone before moving on to a cryptic song of perhaps love. The words bring a smile to my face as hers do.

I remember reading one of her short stories back when we lived together in the house on Bedford Road, sitting on the double bed of black wood that was once mine. It was about a high school with an overarching thirst for blood. Each year there would be grand ceremony surrounding a bare knuckle boxing match in which one of the contenders was to die. Betting preceded the match, and I remember imagining the basement scene in our own basement, cramped and sweating by the boiler in a press of excited teens. I recall that the reader receives only a small glimpse of the fight and the aftermath and I recall how that made me feel. I felt the same way years later when I read her piece about the devil and the dusty plain and the light in the window as we sat together on the couch at our grandparents' house. The same piece would become the second-to-last chapter of her novel.

"I kind of scare myself when I write" she says as she passes me the joint later that night in our car, the smoke and the steam from our breath clouding the windshield. We wonder if anyone will find out, or care.

She didn't used to smoke, and it seemed to me that pot appeared in her stories before it appeared in her life. Indeed I was not present for her freshman year of college, so it is hard for me to say. I certainly never knew she smoked cigarettes until one night when I pulled out my pack outside the venue in Northampton she'd brought me to for my birthday when I came to visit her at college.

"Don't tell mom," I said over a loud heartbeat or two.

"It's ok," she said, "I have one every once in a while too."

I watched her take a few shallow drags and felt a little guilty for the influence I was sure I had. When we drink I have about three to her every one, something I am only sometimes proud of, but she buys me a seven dollar beer at the concert last spring anyway and we drink them together, cross legged on the floor. I finish mine and with a wry smile hint for another round but they're too expensive and she's probably feeling hers anyway. I'm grateful, to be sure, since she bought the tickets and brought me to the concert, something I hardly do on my own for lack of motivation, or funds. In fact it was she who brought me to my first concert. It was at Rumsey Playfield in Central Park; Summer Stage as they call it during the season. She loved the bands and had thought to bring me along, a young musician and lover of music who needed to lose his concert virginity. I'd only been to local shows for local bands, and I'd marveled at the punk rock aesthetic of those, while she found more pleasure in seeing the big bands who played big places in New York City. We were there early and she brought us to the front row, where we stood stalwart, hands clenched to the rail with white knuckles as the waves of humanity sought to crush us like insects and she held tight her bag and me and shouted over blare something of a coming of age "what do you think?" and I smiled back, glasses in my pocket, sweat and adrenaline on my face. After the first of two bands I pushed back through the throng and bought a soggy boat of french fries." Just take 'em," said the twenty-something-year-old lady at the booth as she handed back my money.

I sat on the tall bleachers in the back and watched the second band. I knew my sister was still in the front row. Just like she would be when we returned to Summer Stage, maybe that same year, for a free show featuring her favorite group at the time. We arrived at around noon, hoping to avoid the inevitable sprawling line that issued like a young and colorful host from the front gates of that huge temporary concert hall. We spent the day in the grass with our sunglasses on, playing a game of cards which I'll never remember. It was hot and when we finally got in it had begun to rain slightly, a prospect that at the time seemed pleasant and cooling. Before long it had begun to pour, and as our wallets, cell phones, and other personal effects were barraged by the liquid onslaught we once again stood fast and waited. My heart nearly failed as the cold began to seep in, and I walked almost to the gates with a swarm of retreating concert goers, only to turn back for the thought that she would weather the storm while I quailed. When I found her again we stood in a pool, inches deep, of brown water and raised our hands to the clouded heavens as they cleared and then advanced once more during the band's set, and we both felt something stir in us then that neither shall forget.

It must have been the shared passion for music that brought us together in our youth. Before we were adolescents we fought incessantly. I the extrovert, she the introvert, we would quarrel as many a brother and sister do. Once, on the walk to school, she struck me with force that knocked my glasses into the high grass and from that sorry void they never did emerge. I remember that afternoon in rage I held up my guitar as an unwieldy bludgeon against her and she probably laughed and turned away. It was not until we both reached high school did we become fast friends. Something clicked then, and to this day I cannot recall precisely what it was. On the subject, she told me once that she saw something deeply respectable in me, a passion or serious part of my persona that had not been clear before. We spent time together listening to the radio and sharing music until our inevitable parting when she left for college a year before me, at which point I tattooed her and I the same symbol and she left the next day.

Fortunately we both have the opportunity to see each other frequently enough these days, as I've visited her at school and she's often come to New York for weeks in the summer to work, or for a weekend away from her busy semester to see a concert. This past New Year's Eve was one such night, and I met her outside the subway station in Brooklyn to walk with her to my friends' party a few blocks away. It was past midnight and I had been drinking most of the evening. When we got to the party we promptly took a seat together on the couch and stayed there, talking and joking as herds of our friends stumbled past on their way out for a cigarette or otherwise. A girl who earlier inquired of me "Where's Genevieve?" sat down with us and joined the conversation. I recall she said "God I love you Olivers" and we smiled.

> ### Discussion Questions
>
> - Why would somebody want to read this piece (the "Who cares?" factor)?
> - Can you clearly identify the author's intention for the piece?
> - How well does the author support the intention of the piece? Cite specific details that support or take away from the author's intention.
> - Is there information missing from this piece that would make its intention clearer? What else would you like to know?
> - Does the author portray herself as a round character? How does she do this?
> - Do you trust the author of this piece? Why or why not?
> - How clearly does the author establish a sense of setting/space in this piece? Cite specific details that support your claim.
> - How clearly does the author establish characters other than the self in this piece? Cite specific details that support your claim.
> - Did you learn anything new from reading this piece? If so, what?

- Are there particular passages with engaging language/description that stood out to you? Describe the appeal of these passages.
- Would you read more writing from this author? Why or why not?

Mommy

Katie Braner

My mother has lived a life of abandonment with abandon. When she was a very small child, the youngest of four, her father walked out to marry another woman and bestow her with another lost little girl. His children have been exclusively female, which I always took to be a kind of poetic justice for the particularly male sorrows he inflicted upon my family. We are a strong bunch of independent women for the most part. But being raised by one sole matriarch has had an effect in that there is something to be said for a complete household with two parent figures to share the responsibility, the fear. All this was exacerbated by extreme poverty in the 1960s. Granny Pauline did the best she could with what little they had, which wasn't much even by poor standards. In the morning, each of the four would be given a slice of bread to eat for lunch. My mother used to smash hers up into a ball and sprinkle salt on top before shoving it into her pocket for later, an action I echo (minus the pocket) every time I'm given a dinner roll. Bread just tastes better smashed sometimes.

Granny took up with the Peace Corps and went off to Africa as soon as my mother was 18, leaving her in New Mexico and newly graduated. Mommy had a J-O-B at Sonic as a waitress on roller skates, and saved up enough money to buy a bus ticket back to Maryland, and the home where she grew up. I can imagine her there, Baby Jane on the hot, dusty Las Cruces bus platform, waiting and wondering what would happen to her next. Not a victim of her circumstances, but a young woman determined to make her own way. The future doesn't always present itself in a linear fashion. My mother's dreams that day were probably worlds different than the dreams she would come to have – after mistakes, after me.

Upon the subsequent meeting, marriage, and divorce of my own father, my mother changed entirely. What happens when the youngest baby of four has a shotgun wedding and a baby all her own? She grows up fast. Mommy had always lived faster and harder than my careful father ever did, which was one of the things that led to their eventual demise as a couple. She loved to drink, party, and play the social butterfly – sometimes she loved it too much. But they were both stubborn, both prideful, and both madly in love with the product of their union. Those early years were not without their rough patches, as is to be expected from two people raising a child who do not belong together, but most of the days were happy. That is, until the Great Move. By this point, we were all living in Tennessee where I was born, and Mommy took it upon herself to transplant the two of us up to Michigan a year after my father had gone there for work. I still saw him one weekend out of every month, but every time he left again I was heartbroken, miserable, and lonely for days. My mother knew that I needed to be close to him. She made an admirable, excruciating, selfless decision that she has paid for in what-ifs every day since. A year later, she went back South and I made the choice to stay with my father. Giving a nine-year-old the responsibility to make that weighty decision on her own was just one sign of how differently my mother probably thought everything would turn out.

We went through a period of time, from when I was thirteen to about fifteen, where we barely spoke. Money was tight from moving twice in one year, and Mommy didn't have the extra funds necessary for plane tickets to come see me. As a selfish teenager, the last thing I wanted to do with my school breaks was get in a car for eight hours and ride to see her. I had friends to focus on, a tenuous social life that depended on my being there for it. When we saw each other, our togetherness was fraught with chasms of reckless blame and long-buried guilt. We had abandoned one another. In the cold north of Michigan, I had crafted a new home and a new life. I had fought hard to win recognition and companionship in the difficult landscape of middle school. My father had taken a job in yet another state as soon as I had become settled in his new home, and I had been left alone, to the devices of a stepmother who didn't understand me. She had no children of her own whose love she could draw upon to emulate with me. I emerged anew, tougher. No longer the sweet innocent child my mother remembered from her rearview mirror, squinting in the summer sunlight. She could recognize herself in me anymore. Spending every day alone with my stepmother shaped so much of who I became in those formative years. If I spent any long amount of time around my own mother, life at my father's would be hell for weeks. At that age, it was impossible to be fully self-aware of the unconscious effects my mother's presence had on me. My stepmother would take offense at the slightest action. If I forgot to make my bed one morning, or was simply too lazy, I was surely just being spiteful because she wasn't my real mother. I was only trying to cling on for dear life as changing winds battered my whole concept of family. My mother chose her own happiness in moving back South, and so we grew apart.

This was never a choice that could have been made less difficult. It was never a cut-and-dry obvious decision with one right answer and one evil answer. Certain circumstances make it easy to see that way, and to lay blame accordingly, but I can't say that if I had been in the same position I would have done a thing differently. It's a fine line to walk between happiness of self-preservation or martyrdom. Mommy spent a year being the martyr, and I don't fault her now for looking after herself and her happiness.

It was a long time before I began to understand the impact my absence would have on her life. Growing up, I used to think that a parent's job was to take care of their children. In my young eyes, my parents were humanity perfected – never making a single mistake or selfish action. Looking back, I'm not sure exactly when that perfect picture shattered and I came to the realization that parents are only human. They need and feel and break. I never imagined that at such a young age, I had played a crucial part in taking care of my mother. With me around, she had a sense of responsibility. Her days revolved around working hard and playing with me. We were silly, happy, and enough for one another. Sure, a rotating cast of men she used to date passed through our home, but we knew it was always us who mattered most. Mommy made sure I did well in school, ate all of my dinner, and didn't watch too much TV. We used to play board games together on the living room floor, cracking raw nuts from the bowl on the side of the table and tossing them up before catching them in our mouths. We watched movies from the pull-out couch and sang at the top of our lungs in the car. Not having much in the way of material possessions forced us to be at home and entertained with one another, and that's something I'm reminded of each time I go home to stay with her now. But without me to look after and take care of, her life lost structure. Suddenly, there were empty hours in the day where she would normally be fixing dinner or dropping me off at dance rehearsal. How she filled them, with a rekindled passion for wine and beer and parties, may become the next bridge we cross together.

My mother can now be comfortably described as "mom-sized." This is a term I coined and take to mean not so skinny like the vegan, SoulCycling New York moms, but also not so fat as to be described as obese. She may have thyroid failure and carry extra weight around her hips and thighs – the product of her nightly drinking habit—but she is strong and can run farther than me without getting winded. She is no longer a fit vessel for childbirth, not a lithe sex object like in the old bikini picture she keeps tucked away in a forgotten drawer at her desk. At 46, she is now likely in the second half of her life, and her figure remains as womanly and beautiful as it was the day she left New Mexico at eighteen. Her eyes are clear and blue, framed by tattooed eyeliner (my mother is, among other things, a badass) and skin soft from years of diligent lotioning. When she kisses my cheek and tells me she loves me, the scent of her Dr. Pepper lip balm lingers long after I've crossed the security barrier in the airport and boarded a plane to elsewhere.

> **Discussion Questions**
>
> - Why would somebody want to read this piece (the "Who cares?" factor)?
> - Can you clearly identify the author's intention for the piece?
> - How well does the author support the intention of the piece? Cite specific details that support or take away from the author's intention.
> - Is there information missing from this piece that would make its intention clearer? What else would you like to know?
> - Does the author portray herself as a round character? How does she do this?
> - Do you trust the author of this piece? Why or why not?
> - How clearly does the author establish a sense of setting/space in this piece? Cite specific details that support your claim.
> - How clearly does the author establish characters other than the self in this piece? Cite specific details that support your claim.
> - Did you learn anything new from reading this piece? If so, what?
> - Are there particular passages with engaging language/description that stood out to you? Describe the appeal of these passages.
> - Would you read more writing from this author? Why or why not?

The Job That You Want

Jeffrey Cheung

You know? I still vaguely remember that time when I did something wrong. My father drove me somewhere far away and stopped the car *(In hindsight, it was probably just a few blocks away from home.)* While my mother was looking bewildered, he told me to get out of the car. When I refused and clung desperately to the chair, he stopped and left me with an ultimatum. Do better in school or next time I'll give you a bowl and leave you here.

Knowledge is important. Therefore, school is important. Learn, learn and grow, else all that awaits you is a life on the streets, dressed in rags and dirt with only a bowl in your possession. Is that? Is that that type of job you want?

....

Alarm rings at 5:50 a.m.

I stop it and continue lying on my bed. I have a second alarm coming up at 6:10; the purpose of the first one is to get me slightly awake. When the second alarm comes I throw my blankets off, hurry to brush my teeth, wash my face and get myself dressed. 6:10 a.m. on a Saturday. That's ten minutes after six o'clock. In the morning. On a Saturday. What is a young boy of only fourteen years of age supposed to do at 6:10 a.m. on a Saturday? Sleep would be the answer. But for the past few weeks of summer, I had been going to work with my father for each Saturday. They were short a person you see, one of my uncles came up with a case of really bad back pain and couldn't work for a while. It's the type of job where that is the norm. It's not uncommon to overexert yourself when working in a Meat Shop in Chinatown after all. I waited with my father at the table for the minivan to come. My uncle drives it over at around 6:40 and we would carpool to work. The car reeks of meat. It was unbearable at first, but this is the fourth consecutive Saturday I have been told to work at my father's store. It would take fifty minutes to get to the workplace, so I shut my eyes and tried as best I can to fall asleep.

We knocked on the glass door behind the partially opened rollup gates. The co-owner of the store comes earlier with some employees to fire up the ovens in the back and oversees them roasting the ducks and pigs for today's sales. He spots us and strides quickly over to open the door and we greet each other. I enter to the same stench of meat that was present in the car, only stronger. The store was a simple place. It had red floor tiles and slightly off-white wall tiles. No doubt those were brilliantly white when the store first opened. Going inside the store you'll see immediately to the left the raw meat display case. The glass where you looked into it was littered with price tags and tape marks of where older tags used to be. On the right side of the store is the small cooked foods section. This is where you'll see the assorted Chinese roasted meats, *Siu Mei*. When the store is opened, Roasted Duck, Soy Sauce Chicken, *Char Siu* and other meats are hung up by the window. Below that would be assorted innards, and hung by the wall would be a large roasted pig and freshly roasted duck waiting to cool. A bit further along on the right side are the refrigerators with various frozen meats *(Sometimes you can spy pig brains in clear plastic containers)* and packaged goods. On the left side is the butcher station, where meat is carved either to the buyer's specifications or for the purpose of displaying it. If you walk back from this area, you'll find a cold storage and a kitchen. The basement houses more cold storages, a door to the back alley and a filthy little bathroom.

I went over to put on a white apron and start the morning task of putting the box of ginger by the front of the store and put the bowl for the bean sprouts on an empty crate next to it. I'll have to dump in the bean sprouts when more customers come in. Afterward I prepare the cooked meats section by bring out the sauce containers out of the fridge and pour the tea eggs back into the warmer. Then tear off some butcher's paper, dampen it with a wet towel and stick it onto trays. I have to do ten of those for placing the packaged raw bird meat on display in the open fridge. That is the first hurdle of the day; the packages were fresh out of the cold storage and freeze my hands while I futilely attempt to distinguish between the various chicken types. Afterward would be breakfast consisting of a bread roll and milk tea from the nearby bakery.

In the butcher area, one of the workers and I packaged the chicken into plastic bags. Those were brought cleaned and gutted. The chickens were covered in the slimy fat and blood, cold to the touch but not as bad as the frozen ones I handled earlier. The feet were stiff. I have to force them into the empty cavity, and it was just as likely to go in as it is to pop out and scratch you. Then reach into a bag of innards, gizzards and livers, and stuff one of each into the chicken as well. Then bag and knot it. The slime sticks to your hands. After I dumped the bagged chickens into the open fridge I hastily went to wash out the oils and blood.

The pig shoulder bone. My father had one of the workers teach me how to carve out the meat from the pig shoulder bone. He says, cut the meat close to the bone without cutting the bone, cut it out in one piece, swiftly and cleanly. So as an example the worker cuts out the shoulder bone swiftly. Try it! Do what he had done! Ah no, he says, that is the wrong way of holding the knife. He cuts another one to show. Try it again! You have seen how he did it? Ah no, he says, if you hold the meat that way, you might overshoot and cut yourself. Here look at this again. The proper way of holding the knife, the proper way of holding the meat; know that and try again. How are the results? Ah no, he says, the meat is ruined, how can we sell something that looks like this? Frayed sides, the product of too many shallow cuts and an unsteady hand. It loses the gleam of a well cut piece of meat, ugly and unmarketable. How many more do I have to cut before it retains that shine? In the end, I was only able to carve a few of them right. I was too slow to do more before the other workers have finished.

Soap and water! You can never have too much soap and water. Hot water is good for washing off the oil and blood. Wash it off, but afterward cut the pork ribs, and it gets bloodied again. Wash it off, and carve the pig shoulder bone and it gets bloodied again. Wash it off, wash it off, and wash it off. It never comes off.

So is that the type of job you want?

....

The morning passes; around 9:00, the store starts getting busy; work at the front counter for cooked meat sales. Nonstop efficiency! The butcher gets the order from the customer, grease flies everywhere! The floor is covered with cardboard to prevent slipping. Prepare the metal tray for the butcher, then when he puts the meat in, hurry and throw the sauce in and close the lid. Bag it and sell it to the customer. Inevitably the grease would get on my hands. I would use the lulls in activities to wipe off the stainless steel countertop, and in the process clean my hands.

The bustle of the marketplace! There is no time to sit, no time to rest. Mandarin customer? Talk to the lady next to me, I can't understand what you are saying! Confusion! What is the price for this item, I ask for the tenth time. I remember the prices of the cooked foods, eight fifty for half a roasted duck, sixteen for the whole, fried chicken legs are a dollar a piece, tea eggs are three for a dollar, and most other cooked meats were by the pound. The raw meats come with a price tag from the raw section when the butcher processes them. But what are the prices for the box lunches? The dried goods? The items in the cold fridge? Half your work potential is lost when you don't know the prices. I was slow, slow, slow!

It is also around those hours that it is possible to spot my father working around the front counter. When the store is really busy, my father would come out from the raw meats area and help out as a cashier. Rarely, he would also act as the butcher in the cooked meats section when the normal butcher needs to take a quick break. As the co-owner he has to know the ins and outs of working at all sections of the store. Know the workers and know the customers! Repeating customers are like friends! He chats with them with his loud voice *(A loud voice, a stigma of working in a loud place. Not so out of place in Chinatown, but so engrained that it follows him everywhere, such that even in quiet places he is loud)* and a smile on his face while keeping an eye on the line. To be curt and courteous!

At 2:00 we are allow to take a quick break to eat lunch. Vegetable and soup is cooked in the kitchen and brought up front, where the workers scoop out rice and cut their choice of meat to go along with it. I scoop out a generous portion of rice for myself and asked the butcher to cut me some soy chicken. This is the only time you are guaranteed to be able to sit. I count down the remaining hours from the clock across the room. Generally we start cleaning up at 6:30, lock the store to customers at 7:00 and close at 8:00. Lunch takes around fifteen minutes, so there is five hours and forty-five minutes of suffering to go, I think as I sat quietly in the basement eating my lunch.

Roast meat! Duck, Chicken and Pork. Oily, salty and sweet. Savory foods with matching aromas. Good food, good food. My father brings it home sometimes for the family to eat. Gobble it up, eat heartily! But my father doesn't eat the meat he brings back. Not the sweet and salty soy sauce chicken. Or the ever popular *Char Siu*, literally "fork-roasted" pork. Nor Roasted Pig that my grandfather is so fond off. He does not eat any of it in the dinner table. Year in, year out, six days a week, for nearly every lunch, he has to eat this meat. I sat eating. How long would it take a man to despise having to eat this every day of his life? How long would it take me?

So is that the type of job you want?

....

At the front counter, besides me and the butcher, my aunt and another woman work as cashiers. How would I describe her? She was a quick worker, fast with her hands, can talk back to the customers. Then again that's moot; they are all more or less like that. You simply can't survive in Chinatown without being fast and quick-witted. When the store is packed, they work at blazing speeds. When the store is less busy, she would take out some 1oz sauce containers. Those are to be filled with the various sauces for the cooked meat. Sweetened soy sauce for the Soy Sauce Chicken and *Char Siu*, ginger scallion oil for the White Cut Chicken, duck sauce for the Roasted Duck. My father left me with one piece of advice when working here, and that is to do things automatically. When having been asked to help once, do it. When having been asked twice, do it. Then afterwards, be of help before being asked. On this cue, I check for customers, and seeing that there weren't so much that my aunt can't handle alone, I go and help her.

Put the cups down and fill with sauce. As she does that, I start lidding them and sweeping them into a container. Slow! For every one I lid, two more takes its place. Customers come and we hurry to attend to them and then hurry back to resume lidding. When the table is full, she starts lidding too. Continue; continue until all the sauces are contained! Continue in monotony, only trying to increase your speed! The sauce is the life blood, do not spill it! It is the work of a machine, so become a machine.

So is that the type of job you want?

....

The day ends as the customers slow to a trickle. Return the sauces to the cold fridge, watch as the workers take away the grease-stained cardboard. The butcher packs all the unsold meat into bags to be refrigerated. A worker pours detergent on the floor and three proceed to scrub it down. Hot water is poured out into every crevice, and stray pieces of meat are washed out from under. Sometimes a penny or a dime would be washed out, which would be quickly be picked up and put onto the countertop. When the whole floor is wet and soapy, that is the cue! Take arms with the squeegee and along with the army of workers, push out the waste water to the streets! A lone worker scoops up the solid waste and dumps it into the trash bag.

The end of the day! Take off the apron and relax your legs. The workers trickle out, my father closes the shop. We wait for our uncle who owns a butcher shop a few blocks away to pick us up. Wearily and tired! Sleep in the minivan until our house appears. The stench of meat sticks to you. The oil, the grease, it sticks to you. Greet my mother! Then rush to the bathroom to take the long-awaited piss and step into the shower. Scrub it off, scrub it off. Scrub all of it off. Scrub it off and think…

…think to yourself, is that the job you want?

Discussion Questions

- Why would somebody want to read this piece (the "Who cares?" factor)?
- Can you clearly identify the author's intention for the piece?
- How well does the author support the intention of the piece? Cite specific details that support or take away from the author's intention.
- Is there information missing from this piece that would make its intention clearer? What else would you like to know?
- Does the author portray herself as a round character? How does she do this?
- Do you trust the author of this piece? Why or why not?
- How clearly does the author establish a sense of setting/space in this piece? Cite specific details that support your claim.
- How clearly does the author establish characters other than the self in this piece? Cite specific details that support your claim.
- Did you learn anything new from reading this piece? If so, what?
- Are there particular passages with engaging language/description that stood out to you? Describe the appeal of these passages.
- Would you read more writing from this author? Why or why not?

Self-Destruct

Danny Gomez

I was a junior in high school, living in Germantown, TN, a rich suburb of Memphis, TN. My family landed in Germantown after my mother lost her parents and my step-dad lost his job. He found a new job in Memphis and decided to move us to Germantown so that I could be a part of the high school's award-winning fine arts department.

Germantown High School was its own stereotype. The school had been around for well over a hundred years by the time I found myself in attendance there. It had been around so long that the mascot was the Red Devils, a mascot that few Christian organizations would ever stand for a high school choosing today.

This fine arts department has a three-million-dollar TV studio (from which I won day-time Emmy awards for producing), showcased $150k+ theater productions, and a reputation for being the best. I was a sophomore when I started at GHS and was full of angst and regret at having been uprooted after my first year in high school from my previous city. I tend to immerse myself in distraction, which is what I used the fine arts department for.

By the time I was a junior I was directing, producing, or anchoring the majority of the television programs produced at GHS-TV. I also held lead roles in every production the school put on. This entailed my arriving at the school at 6 a.m. to do a morning news program broadcast throughout the county, and leaving around 9 or 10 p.m. after rehearsals or set construction or whatever else needed to be done that day. I even had keys to the school. I loved anything that kept me away from home. My mom was a mess and it was the first time in my life that I didn't have my older brother and sister with me. She had thrown my sister out of the house my freshman year for being a lesbian and did the same to my brother for getting his girlfriend pregnant that same year. That's when we moved to Memphis.

My junior year was also a time when I decided to distract myself in other ways. I had met two beautiful girls that year, Angel and Layne. We bonded over our equal love of emo bands. We would wax poetically quoting Dashboard Confessional or Saves the Day lyrics to each other. The three of us were known for our taste in what was considered at the time "good music," although looking back I understand why my step-father never wanted to drive me to school in the car with a cd player. Like all good music does, it eventually led us to begin smoking pot and drinking.

The thing with living in the suburbs is that you either play football or you do drugs. Drugs aren't as readily available to a sixteen-year-old as you might think, so we found other things to supplement our thirst for escape—Coriciden Cough and Cold Pills (or as we referred to them Triple C's). CCC were like nothing we had ever experienced and we were quickly hooked on them. Pop eight to twelve and you didn't know whether you were stoned or drunk or hallucinating. We would write in our journals or cry listening to music together or talk about how we were better than our surroundings—my mom being an abusive drunk, Angel's non-biological Uncle's unwanted advances on her, and Layne's knowledge of her mom's secret affair.

We didn't have much money so often we would go into a Wal-Mart or Wal-Greens or really anything beginning with "Wal" and steal these pills. Often hardly even waiting until we were in the car to start sucking on them, the sweetness overtaking our mouth as the red dye soaked our tongue. Next thing we knew we were in another universe. My parents gave me the family van as my first car, it was a giant Chevy conversion van that I named Geneva. The three of us would often hit up a Walgreens and then stay the night in my van, each telling our parents whatever they needed to hear to allow us to stay out all night.

On a Thursday school let out for the day and I was walking to the theater to help with set constructions for a children's play we were putting on when Angel ran up to me in a huff.

"Anna Claire went crazy today and is in the principal's office. No one knows what the fuck is going on with her. Can you give me a ride home real quick? I'm gonna try to call around and find out what's up," she said. Anna Claire was a friend of Angel's who I would give rides home sometimes.

"Of course. Is she okay?" I responded.

"I have no idea. She needs to get her shit together. She's been so weird lately," Angel told me as we began walking into the parking lot. Upon opening the door to my van I realized the whole car was a mess. I had tons of clothes, blankets, books and CCC packets in the van (it looked like a homeless man lived there). While it was always a mess I could tell someone else had been in there and messing with my things.

"Fuck. Was Anna Claire in my van?" I asked Angel. She looked at me with a blank face. We were both confused. I drove her home and immediately knew that I needed to dispose of the booze bottles I kept in the back of the van before returning to school. Actually, instinct told me that I needed to clean the entire van but my laziness got the best of me. I simply threw the booze bottles out the window and drove back to school to start work on the set. Upon pulling up to the front of the school I was greeted by the principal, assistant principal, and a security guard. They asked to search my van and as I was on school property and had no choice, I allowed them.

They searched through the vehicle grabbing at all of the empty boxes of cough medicine what they were there for.

"My sister's sick," I remember muttering to them. My face drained of blood and shame filled my insides.

There was nothing in the car that was damning so they told me I was free to go about my business.

That night I went home and told my parents about what had transpired. My step-dad told me to go clean the car. I resisted. We were in a fight at the time. I had recently come out to my parents about liking men; they insisted I keep it to myself and my step-father went as far as to tell me I'd get AIDS if I decided to pursue a homosexual lifestyle. Not quite the "I love you" approach I was expecting.

I called Angel and found out that Anna Claire and two of her friends had skipped class, gone to Anna Claire's where they took a plethora of CCCs and then, worried about being caught, returned to school so that they could be counted as present during final period. Upon returning to school they saw the security officer in the parking lot and jumped into my van to hide, utilizing the van's blinds. While in my car they made themselves at home. Drinking my booze and even smoking pot that they had idiotically brought with them to school. Eventually they left my van and went to class where one girl threw up, the other was incoherent, and good ol' Anna Claire ran up and down the hallways screaming.

The next day, Friday, coincidentally Friday the 13th, I went to school. I parked in the teachers' parking lot because the student lot was full and I didn't feel like driving to the annex parking lot. Foolish for a student whose car didn't exactly blend in and had just been searched the day prior.

I want about my day as usual, and was called into the principal's office during third period. They wanted to search my car again. Clearly they wanted to nail me with something. This seemed odd considering I was Junior Class Vice President, a member of National Honor Society, and an all around ideal student. (My outside school persona hadn't yet caught up with my in school persona). I opened up the doors to my vehicle and four people went in the car to search it. The fourth yielded results. He produced a single stem of marijuana from one of the ashtrays. They sent me back to class.

After school that day I went to the studio and directed an idiotic television program called *I Did it Myself*, where a middle-aged divorcee taught DIY projects. After the show ended there was a knock on the studio door.

"Mr. Gomez, you're gonna need to come with me," the principal said. I followed him to the office where I was informed of my suspension.

"You have to be kidding me. Those girls told you the entire story. I was in class, the attendance record shows it. I had nothing to do with them smoking weed or being messed up at school. I only even know one of them," I protested.

"Doesn't matter, we have zero tolerance for drug possession and it was in your vehicle. We're assigning you 180 days of suspension which you will complete at Shelby County Alternative School."

"WHAT? This is fucking ridiculous!"

"Watch your language Mr. Gomez."

"Um, are you kidding me? You just suspended me for 180 days for something that I had no part of and you want me to watch my language. You're completely ruining my future. You do realize that, right? You're completely ruining my future. Look at my record, I've never even been written up," I screamed. The tears began pouring down my face as I imagined spending the next year away from my friends and away from the life that I had just become comfortable with after moving.

No amount of tears or protest would help. I was out. The girls each got eleven days suspension. They weren't in possession of anything.

My parents were outraged. We were having a lot of problems at home and school was the only place where trouble hadn't found me. While they fought the system on my behalf they decided that Alternative School wouldn't be a good enough education for me having just come from all Advanced Placement classes. So they sent me to Daybreak. It's a psychological school. We had group therapy in the morning, followed by an hour of class, followed by an hour of recreational therapy, followed by lunch, followed by thirty minutes of class, followed by an ending group therapy. The final group therapy entailed us having to give our weather reports. Were we feeling tropical, sunny, cloudy, partially cloudy, or stormy that day? I gathered my things from my cubby hole, went home and told my parents I would not be returning. Alternative School started the next week.

My mom drove me, crying the entire time. It's a hard thing to see your mother cry. It's even harder when you know you're the reason for it. I wouldn't see her cry like that again until three years later when I would be sentenced to serve ten days in Shelby County jail for repeated DUI arrests.

I met the principal of the Alternative School. I told him the whole story and he held his hands up to me and made a square with his two forefingers and thumbs and gently said, "If you're not in the picture, you won't get framed." It was then I realized that my outside life had finally caught up with my school life. I wasn't directly to blame for my suspension, those girls were, but I was involved indirectly. Through the friendships I had made and the decisions of my life I brought myself here.

My mom and I became really close after I was suspended. We needed each other. After the death of her parents she had completely fallen apart. She sank into alcohol and Klonopin infused depression that my stepfather refused to acknowledge. Now she had a distraction—someone who was going through as miserable a time as she was. I would fuck up and she would be the shoulder for me to cry on, the voice of reason telling me things will get better, all the while telling herself the same thing.

My parents eventually won against the school. They appealed all the way up to the Commissioner of the Tennessee Department of Education. I spent in all twenty-two days out of Germantown. Despite the work my parents put into getting me back in school, I wasn't reformed. I continued using drugs and getting drunk and shoplifting—I just did it a little bit smarter.

I was chosen for a leadership exchange program the summer after I graduated. I moved to Germany for the entire summer and worked in a TV studio in Frankfurt. The day I returned I was arrested for shoplifting at the mall.

"Why do you always have to self destruct?" my mom said to me.

After high school I took a year off and started using cocaine habitually and would drink at least a bottle of Vodka a day. To my parents' relief I eventually moved to New York City and was accepted into an acting conservatory. The day before I left I got my first DUI as an adult. (During my suspension Angel, Layne, and myself were pulled over while I was driving on CCCs and after having our stomachs pumped I was arrested for DUI. I was sixteen and a minor.)

"Why do you always have to self destruct?" my mom asked me again.

I wasn't much better for the first few years in NYC. My first year in NYC I came home to visit and my parents were out of town with my little brother and sister. I threw a party, took acid, and jumped through my little brother's window completely naked and landed on concrete below. I had watched *Smallville* the whole week leading up to the party and apparently thought I was Superman. I even went so far as to throw my neck brace at the doctors and accuse them of putting kryptonite in my toenails. Miraculously I wasn't injured in the slightest.

My mom had a stroke my second year in NYC and I left school for two weeks to go home and take care of her; my stepdad had found employment in Oklahoma and had to leave my mom in charge of taking care of my little brother and sister herself. The stroke was brought on by the constant mixture of alcohol and pills—her demons hadn't been defeated yet either. My fourteen-year-old little sister told me she had to drive her to the hospital after she repeatedly told her to call Daddy Bob (our deceased grandfather).

During my time being the dutiful son taking care of his ailing mother I racked up another DUI, all while still going to court for the first one. My mom, still recovering from her stroke, was at the courthouse with me when the judge sentenced me. I turned around and she signed, "I Love You" to me, her head shaking and tears falling down her face. This was the last time I would disappoint my mom, and in a lot of ways it was the last time we would ever be this close.

Four years later it's Christmas time and I'm in my Greenwich Village apartment packing to go visit my family in Memphis for the holiday. I only go back once a year now. I open up my Ben Sherman plaid carryall and begin carefully placing my clothes in the bag, making room for my dopp kit and running shoes. All that's going through my head is whether or not I have enough money to take all seven members of my immediate family out to dinner for Christmas Eve. I don't want my mom to cook. Her food is always something along the lines of frozen shrimp she calls hors d'oeuvres and a premade lasagna.

I now work a great job, I go to school full time, and I've fully committed myself to becoming a Manhattanite rather than a poor kid from Memphis. Trauma brings people closer and now the trauma is gone. We're very different people and as a result we're not as close. I feel like a snob. I feel guilty that when she tells me the same stories she told me last week, on the phone, with a few details changed, I will try to feign interest. I feel guilty that I'll have to pretend to like the Men's Wearhouse shirt she buys me for Christmas. I feel guilty that I've come a long way and along with that comes a feeling of superiority that I detest…but can't resist. Mostly though I feel guilty that I don't feel guilty enough. How is it possible that we worked through our troubles together, mother and son, and emerged better people, but aren't as close as we were? The love is still there, but the dependence isn't.

I'm proud of the steps we've made together, but I still miss the days of me needing my mom and her needing me to need her.

Discussion Questions

- Why would somebody want to read this piece (the "Who cares?" factor)?
- Can you clearly identify the author's intention for the piece?
- How well does the author support the intention of the piece? Cite specific details that support or take away from the author's intention.
- Is there information missing from this piece that would make its intention clearer? What else would you like to know?
- Does the author portray herself as a round character? How does she do this?
- Do you trust the author of this piece? Why or why not?
- How clearly does the author establish a sense of setting/space in this piece? Cite specific details that support your claim.
- How clearly does the author establish characters other than the self in this piece? Cite specific details that support your claim.
- Did you learn anything new from reading this piece? If so, what?
- Are there particular passages with engaging language/description that stood out to you? Describe the appeal of these passages.

- Would you read more writing from this author? Why or why not?

The Space or Event Essay: Thirteen Examples

> ### Instructions
>
> Unlike the memory essay, the space or event essay will require you to write about something you will be experiencing for the first time as you write. This does not mean you cannot employ elements of memory as you investigate and discuss your topic. What it means is that you will be writing in "real time," experiencing something with the intention of writing about it.
>
> Until this point, many of our pieces have relied strictly on memories. Going into a new environment or experience with the intention of writing about it will change the way you experience and record the event. I am asking you to enter the moment or space with a writer's eye, using powers of observation to both participate in and find the significance of a space or event you enter purely for reasons of creating this essay.
>
> If you are choosing a space, choose one you have easy access to and will be able to visit readily. If you are choosing an event, make sure it is happening within the confines of the essay dates. Keep in mind that an event need not be something large. It can be something small, a gathering, a visit, or it can be a concert or a lecture. Any of these ideas and other choices will be relevant if written about in a thoughtful and prepared way.
>
> In this essay, whether based on a new experience on not, the space or event should be a main character. Space or event can be important for structuring a narrative, and objects and surroundings can communicate a lot about the experience to the reader. Focus should be on the power of these elements to act as characters in the narrative alongside descriptions of the self and other people. Space and event are not necessarily separate. Your piece may focus on both; do not feel the need to separate these concepts artificially.

Student Samples

These essays went through two drafts. This means that students revised these pieces with peer and instructor feedback.

Mike reflects on a childhood experience involving injury and hospitalization.

Tyana reflects on her childhood neighborhood and family dynamics.

Maria reflects on being an adopted child.

Adriana reflects on her experience attending Coachella.

Will reflects on coming out as a gay man to his family.

Neziah reflects on writing a novel during National Novel Writing Month.

Emma reflects on participating in a gymnastics competition.

Justine reflects on working at a fast-food rest stop.

Anne reflects on her childhood beach home and her brother's struggles.

Hannah reflects on attending Comic Con for the first time.

Jillian reflects on the closing of her childhood church.

Zachary reflects on the death of his grandmother.

Erika reflects on her experiences with basketball and her relationship with her father.

In-Patient
Mike Gomez

When I was seven years old, I dropped a two-gallon pot of boiling water on myself. This story begins earlier that afternoon when my dad picked me and my brothers up from school. He had just gotten off work and wanted to stop by my grandmother's for a quick visit before we headed home. I loved granny's house. There was always company and fun and most importantly, there was always food. You could smell the many aromas of spices and meat from her kitchen from a block away.

We pulled up and a bunch of my aunts and cousins were outside enjoying the new spring weather. I hurried out of the car to see if I could find my cousin Julian, but sadly he wasn't there that day. "Hey Mike! Come here!" I heard my dad call. I hurried through the maze of hips and legs to get to where he was at the top of the stoop. Upon arriving at the front door, I was greeted with a smile and to my delirious liking, a boiled egg. I was starving and could only think about getting home so I could feast on a can of Chef Boyardee while I watched Gargoyles, so when I was presented with such a simple, tasteless treat to break my fasting, you bet your bottom I accepted.

As my dad surfed through everyone giving his farewell before we hit the road, I stuffed my yolk powdered mouth with the last piece of egg. "Just one boiled egg?" I thought to myself was quite the tease, and I was intoxicated with the taste of salt and nothing, so I knew I needed more. " Dad, dad! Do you have any more eggs? I want more." "No that was it son, if you want I'll make you more when we get home. Let's go."

The whole ride there I kept thinking about how much I wanted to eat those eggs. When we finally got home, I rushed inside and quickly threw my things off to get into my inside clothes. I ran into the kitchen to meet my dad. "Alright, Mike how many do you want?" my dad asked. "Mmm I want three!" I told him. "Alright, fill a pot up with water from the sink, I'll get the eggs." I began looking for a small pot but couldn't find one, so I grabbed the next best thing. I started filling the pot we used to make soup and cook noodles in, which could easily fit a newborn inside. My dad left the kitchen and told my older brother, Josh, to watch me in the kitchen because he was going to take a shower. "Stay away from the eggs, Michael. It's very hot and I'm going in the shower. Don't try to get it yourself; when it's done, ask your brother."

About fifteen minutes flew by and I grew highly impatient. My brother was in the living room watching TV and I paced back and forth into the kitchen waiting for my food. "Is it ready yet?" I asked Josh. "Not yet Mike, five more minutes" he responded as he stared at the screen. I looked at the clock and it put me at ease, for five minutes would quickly pass.

Like a strike of lightning, I jolted up and headed into the kitchen. The time was now and I knew the eggs were firmly boiled enough to finally enjoy them. "It's ready Josh! Let's take them out!" I exclaimed. "Alright hold on Mike, the show is almost over. I'll be right there, DON'T touch the pot, I'm coming" he said. But of course, I was far too hungry and a tad too bold for my own good, and I engaged on my own.

I figured I could easily carry the pot of steaming, popping water for I had filled it just moments ago and put it on the stove before my dad put the eggs in. I put on cooking mittens that reached up to my elbow and took a firm grasp onto the pot handles. I had to lift my arms past my head to reach it, and at such an age, I wasn't exactly versed in the etiquette of physics. As I began to lift the pot off the stove, the water inside shifted and swayed in the pot. I stepped back and continued to hold the pot as I tried my best to balance the swiveling pot in my hands. Suddenly I stopped to get a strong stance so as to not fall backwards, but at that very moment, the waves of water were tilting towards me. The force of my standstill thrust the pot towards me and a steaming waterfall poured onto my torso.

The thundering of the pot slamming the floor drew the attention of everyone in the house. Josh quickly stood up and looked into the kitchen. "OH MY GOD! MIKE!" he shouted. I stood there suspended as I lost myself in awe as to what was happening. There was no pain, no noise, no reaction. Everything moved in slow motion. My dad stumbled out of the bathroom soaked, still wrapping a towel around his waist. "WHAT! WHAT IS IT! WHAT HAPPENED" he yelled. "MIKE DROPPED THE HOT WATER DAD!" I pinned eyes with my dad, almost confused as to the excitement around me. His jaw dropped and he quickly came over to me. I stood there with my arms up at my sides and didn't move. My dad took a knee in front of me and grabbed the bottom of my drenched t-shirt. He lifted the shirt, and as the fabric drew up, the first two layers of my skin came off with it. Everyone fell silent in terror. I looked at my dad's horrid expression and then turned my head towards my stomach. All at once the pain, fear, and bewilderment overtook me. "AHHHHHH" I screamed, looking at the white of my flesh juxtaposed against the brown of my skin.

My dad grabbed me by the arms and rushed me into the bathroom. He quickly took my soaked shirt off and shorts and wrapped covered me with a towel. I sobbed in pain and regret for not having listened to the several warnings given to me just moments prior. My brother began to rinse my hands under cold water to soothe and distract my focus from the areas that really needed attention. "You're alright Mike. Just leave your hands under the water, it's gonna help you. You'll be alright man," he told me. "How do you know?" I asked with hopelessness. "Has this happened to you before?" "Yes it has and you're gonna heal and get better, don't worry bro," he confidently replied. My father returned fully dressed a few minutes after with a windbreaker track suit for me to put on. It was light with enough interior room for the burns on my chest and torso to breathe.

The house immediately turned into a state of emergency, and motions to get me to the hospital initiated. In a matter of ten minutes I was carried, undressed, comforted, redressed, sent outside and into a taxi with my dad. I remember the burning cool sensitivity of my raw wounds when it pressed against the jacket I wore as we stormed to the hospital. Everything was moving so fast and deliberately, but I remember how slow and steady my breathing was. I tried not to move much. I kept telling myself I'd be okay, that this would be over soon, to just hang in there a little longer. "We're almost there Mike," I heard my dad say, "Don't worry son, it's gonna be alright, I'll take care of you."

Once we arrived, my dad hurried me into the ER and sought help. He was entirely now in a state of emergency and acted with tenacious urgency. He carried me in his arms as he addressed any medical personnel he saw who could help me. After the process of alerting the nurses, doctors, orderlies, and attending to my injuries, I recall myself lying on a bed while a nurse dabbed and cleaned my burns with a clear cool solution on cotton swabs. I could see my father outside of the room talking to a doctor, him seeming a lot more relieved than before, though still very much concerned for me. They both came in and began talking to me to see how I was doing and reassured me that I'll be fine. I don't remember how the conversation went verbatim, but I'll never forget what the doctor said to me about the burns. "The burns only removed the first two layers of your skin which means it'll heal back with some scars, but I don't think you'll need any grafts. The worst of the wounds is on your hip that was injured the most." He then releases his professionalism and turns to me and says with humor, "But you're very lucky Mike. Any closer and you wouldn't be having kids." As appreciative as I am now for such luck, it was still quite relieving to hear as a child.

I would spend the next two and a half weeks recovering at the hospital, missing schooldays that served as a pleasing vacation, but also missing my family who I longed to play and run around with again. My dad came and accompanied me each night right until I was released. As a kid, I had spent much time in the hospital because of my asthma and its severity, so I was all too familiar with the customs and procedures as a patient. I was a victim of chronic asthma since birth and suffered more than most from it at an early age. When I was two years old, I had caught a really bad fever and it triggered a highly aggressive, violent asthmatic response. My at-home treatments weren't working and periods of normalizing my breath didn't last for more than fifteen minutes. My parents had no choice but to take me to the ER. After several other trials of failed treatments and the growing struggle for air sent my body to the brink of cardiac arrest, the doctors put me into an induced coma for three days. It actually amazes me the amount of times I've flirted with an adolescent demise.

I had developed a liking to being hospitalized; I thought it was fun. Whenever I had been taken into the care of the hospital before, I was sure of two things; eating fast food and receiving a gift. Whoever was sent to stay by my side as I endured another episode was guaranteed to bring me a Wendy's Jr. Cheeseburger and a new little something, whether it was a small book from the gift shop downstairs, or an action figure I requested from home to appease my imagination. This time around was different though. I had never spent more than two or three days in the hospital. And no one was allowed to visit me for the first week except my father.

I was bedridden for a good portion of the time as my wounds crusted over, but every day I would have a man come in from the fitness center there and he would help me walk up and down the hall to get me moving. At the end of the hall, I had discovered a small playroom for the child patients. I would go in there on my own when I was bored and play with the various toys and games. I became friends with the aides who worked there and each time I came in we would play a different board game. I wasn't much for playing board games, simply because, well, they bored me. But one afternoon in particular was the most fun and rewarding time I've ever had at the hospital.

It was one of the last nights I was spending there before I shipped off back home. It was rainy outside and I was terribly bored. No one had arrived to keep me company yet and I was restless. Finally I decided I'd get up to walk around some. The hall was fairly dead and I could only see a few nurses and attendants chattering amongst themselves. Not much was happening to ease my anxious nerves so I headed down to the playroom. When I arrived, I was greeted by two older ladies who were entertaining two other kids playing there. "Hey there, what's your name?" one of them asked. "I'm Mike," I blushed a response. "Nice to meet you, Mike" the older lady said with a smile and handshake. "We're about to get around and begin our drawing contest. Would you like to draw something for a chance to win one of these prizes?" She pointed towards a batch of wooden gift baskets filled with toys, coloring books, and enough candy to sour three stomachs. The immediate glow and growth of my eyes were enough of a response for the lady to laugh and hand me my own sheet of paper with a small pack of crayons. "Alright guys, we want you to draw a picture of anything you want, and the best one shall win one of those baskets to take home over there."

I took a seat and scanned my opponents. There were only two other kids, a boy with a dusty head and pudgy face with a demeanor that seemed to bully me without saying a word, and a younger, more fragile girl with sad, sickly eyes and a faint smile. She was sweet, and I knew she just wanted to have fun. The other kid looked at me and we locked eyes. It was either me or him. I knew he had his eyes set on the same gift basket that I did, the one with the most awesome, boyish, and coolest of toys that were being offered. It was a yellow basket with blue ribbons and a candy-coated bottom.

"Alright kids, you have twenty minutes to finish your drawing. Begin!" The clock began and off we went. The little girl began drawing a flower with the help of one of the ladies. The boy had turned and leaned over his drawing busily as I looked with intrigue to see what my competition was. About three minutes passed and I had yet to begin. I hadn't the faintest idea of what to draw. I liked to draw but couldn't think of any go-to character which would solidify my chances for victory. Then like a soaring rock slamming against my head, it hit me. I picked up a yellow crayon and starting drawing who I thought was the coolest, most clever cartoon kid I had come across in my seven years on the planet; Bart Simpson.

As soon as I realized what I was going to do, I zoned in. I had this spectacular vision of Bart doing what he does best, skateboarding. I drew him zooming past a blue outlined picket fence in front of a tree and single-window house. The women in charge took notice and watched me as I lost myself in the drawing. They were surprised as much as they were fascinated that I had chosen a bit of a mature character to draw with an unexpected deliberate likeness. "Wow that's very good, Mike!" one of them said to me. With the utmost adolescent arrogance and esteem, I knew I had this contest in the bag.

"Okay kids time's up!" exclaimed the older lady as she stood up. She spread all the drawings out across the table and we looked at each other's pictures. The boy had seen mine and unlike the jealous or envious expression I figured he'd exude, he conveyed excitement over what I had done. "Hey that's really cool!" he said and leaned in for a better look. "Well I'd say we have a clear winner" one of the ladies said with a smile. "Congratulations Mike! You can choose one of those baskets over there for a prize!" It's weird, because as set and sure as I was to win, I was still as embarrassed and overwhelmed with modesty as I always was. I walked over to the prizes and chose the one most suiting. Boy was I a happy camper.

Right after I accepted my reward and admiration, I headed back down to my room with a smile and sense of accomplishment. Not too long after my dad arrived with even more gifts and I told him what happened. He was shocked to see how vitalized and jumpy I was, and with such energy, he knew I was ready to go back home.

Two days later, I stepped out of a cab with my dad and bags, well enough to enter my house again. The very moment I opened my front door to get inside, a wave of smiles and overly excited voices welcomed me back. All of my brothers and sisters were there to greet me and express their affection. I came in with warm smile and eased my way over to them all. I was still moving pretty slow and had to take it easy while my wounds healed. "Oh man Mike I can't believe you got all of these toys! Man, I wish I went to the hospital!" yelled my little sister Michelle. I was so happy to play with her again and my brothers, but even more so I was happy to be a part of the whole again. I was home again. I dropped all my things and went over to my sis. "Here Michelle you can play with all of it, let's share the toys. Oh and I got candy too!"

Discussion Questions

- Why would somebody want to read this piece (the "Who cares?" factor)?
- Can you clearly identify the author's intention for the piece?
- How well does the author support the intention of the piece? Cite specific details that support or take away from the author's intention.
- Is there information missing from this piece that would make its intention clearer? What else would you like to know?
- Does the author portray herself as a round character? How does she do this?
- Do you trust the author of this piece? Why or why not?
- How clearly does the author establish a sense of setting/space in this piece? Cite specific details that support your claim.
- How clearly does the author establish characters other than the self in this piece? Cite specific details that support your claim.
- Did you learn anything new from reading this piece? If so, what?
- Are there particular passages with engaging language/description that stood out to you? Describe the appeal of these passages.
- Would you read more writing from this author? Why or why not?

Daringly Different

Tyana Soto

My neighborhood could best be described as a place where if you hear the name, you immediately look at someone a little differently. The people are darker, the accents are thicker, and money is less evident. Kids run through the streets wearing clothes either too baggy or too tight, and while walking on the sidewalk it is expected to get honked at by a group of guys in a loud cantankerous Honda Civic. It's loud, due to the abundance of people, and noisy, due to the freight train that passes through and blasts its horn. This is Haverstraw.

Most people speak Spanish, a language I've never understood. I grew up listening to words race through people's mouths like a motor, flowing through their tongues so quickly and easily that I could feel the passion of their emotions. I always wished that I could understand. After watching Aladdin I would constantly think that one of my wishes would be to understand my native tongue and be able to communicate with my neighbors. The people that were supposed to be my sisters and brothers from my country. The country I could never assimilate in. Not that I wanted to. I blame my grandmother. She never taught my mom how to speak Spanish, who never taught me. And because of her decision I stood one step further from being able to fully belong in the neighborhood.

I mean, I did feel like I belonged, but I was always on the brink of acceptance no matter how hard I tried. I wasn't the typical Hispanic girl getting on the bus going to school. My mother would never allow me to fall in line behind those who had no moral steering. No. I was always too smart, too weird, to ever be one of the South Pole wearing, slicked baby haired girls. I read Harry Potter, had an incredible imagination, always got good grades, and never disobeyed my mother. Instead of playing all day in the park during the summer I was sent away to visit relatives, and given large workbooks to complete. Everyone else was allowed to walk to the McDonald's up the hill or buy a *limbe* from the house down the street, but I wasn't. I was always enrolled in activities, always doing something that separated me from the other kids. I was always different.

I looked different too. Instead of having mocha skin and curly ringlets of dark hair like my mother, I was paler with straight brown hair that turned blonde at the tips in the summer. I was born with a variation in my eye so a triangle of color in my left eye was green compared to brown everywhere else. People looked at me and expected a privileged child, one who didn't grow up in a house that was quite literally falling apart. Then they would glance at my last name and realize Soto, a Puerto Rican name. But no, she must only be half. Her mother must be white. Wrong.

I AM one of them. I do live on those streets.

I lived with my mother and my uncle, in the house that they themselves had grown up in. A townhouse, once big and spacious with three floors, but as time went on, falling apart by the seams. The roof on the third floor was caving in slowly, the bathrooms didn't fully work, and I could never bring anyone over to play. My mother and I did move to an apartment when I was 13, but the townhouse was essentially my place of origin, the house I always placed myself into in dreams and memories. It was a part of me.

I felt like I was living in such a different family situation than everyone that I knew. My parents had divorced when I was young, my mother taking primary custody because my father was in the military and constantly traveling. Many of my friends did have absent fathers, but the fact that I was an only child living with my mom and uncle seemed like a different situation to me. We didn't really have family that we talked to often, and a lot of the time I was raised by my uncle when my mom was busy working or going to school. My uncle was only sixteen years older than me, and on the outside was a G-Unit wearing, cornrow wanting, night shift working older brother who would tease me endlessly. But through the years he would cook me dinner on different nights, always go out of the way to get me something, and take my side on useless arguments with my mom. We were our own little family in the house, as dysfunctional as it was. It gave me comfort to know that I at least had two people in my life that were constant and always caring. A lot of change happened through the years.

Through my uncle we also became close friends with the Canjuras down the street, essentially the headquarters of the neighborhood. They had four kids of all different ages around my uncle, and through the years became the family that always kept their door open to everyone who wanted to come in. They were El Salvadorian, loving, and extremely cheeky. They did a lot for my mother and I; watching me when she had to work, having someone pick me up when I had no ride, or even just inviting us over to their house for every holiday and never letting us leave. Of course they loved to gossip about everyone and had no shame about anything, but that was their way. Through the parties, drinking, and wild stories they were my extended family. I knew that every tease was done with love (even though they tried to corrupt me like crazy), and in their house the neighborhood grew closer. Even though I was an only child and completely different from their delinquent ways, I still had a family and neighborhood of sisters and brothers that I could count on to be there for me. As a neighborhood we were bonded as one through 65 Coolidge Street, and never thought it weird to just walk through the door randomly to say hi or yell from the street into their window. Sometimes I wondered how the Canjuras could stand everyone always taking up their house with space as well as drama, but then again we kind of all were family.

I grew up in Haverstraw, fully believing that the world was what I was seeing. That it was normal to hear music blasting from every car window, for people to just sit in front of their houses talking to those on the streets, to know everyone's stories, everyone's life. Then I travelled to other neighborhoods, neighborhoods with houses separated by lawns and fences, and people that took their kids to soccer practice and play dates. They had a pool in their backyard, they said hello to their neighbors but nothing more, they had a minivan. Everything was so quiet, everything so perfect.

And somehow I never fully understood. Was this how people really lived? Was this how *normal* people lived? To me, the houses in a friend's neighborhood seemed so rich and grand, with their spare rooms and families complete with a mother, a father, and a 50-inch flat screen. Or was I just used to living in a place where you had to fight for a fan because there was never any air conditioning? Which was better? Minivan, Honda Civic. Country, Reggaeton. Organic, fried. Light skin, brown skin.

I would always think about it. Would this place of serenity and clean lines be a better fit for me? I mean my skin was light, I didn't act obnoxious and loud, I felt pulled towards knowledge, not drinking and drugs. Was this the place to be?

I explored, going to different friends houses, travelling to different places, seeing what it was really like to live differently; to live far from the poignant streets and lifestyle of my neighborhood. I loved it. I loved to learn about the different things you can do in life, the paths that were there for you to walk on. The places you could go, the people you could see. I was not forced to stay in the confines of my block, to only have aspirations that included a party next week and a full time job. Who knew? Who knew worlds like this existed? That I could become a part of them, that I could belong in one of them. It was staggering, to say the least.

But despite the fact that I felt pulled to a life far from Gurnee Avenue, the culture I had left behind still lingered, laying dormant in my soul waiting to emerge. I wasn't the girl to paint herself green for Saint Patrick's day, the girl who eagerly awaited her 16th birthday so that she could have Sweet 16. No matter how much I tried I was still that blatant "Latino" girl with skin too light, and a mind too curious.

I think it all came down to a minor instance, a moment that I will never forget. I was travelling through Italy with a friend and we had stopped at a cameo factory to see a craftsman at work. We were looking at the cameos in awe, noting their beauty and intricacy. I stopped to look at one that almost looked like an egg, and excitedly told my friend that it looked like the ring that Selena wore in her movie. When I looked at my friend, she had a puzzled look and asked who Selena was. I stopped, and in awe asked again. She didn't know her. For the rest of the day I was in shock of this minor difference. When I was younger, Selena Quintanilla-Pérez was mine as well as so many other girls in my neighborhoods idol. We all adored her, listened to her music, danced to her songs, and pretended that we were the woman on stage wearing a purple sparkly jumpsuit. How had my friend never heard of Selena's magic? How had she never experienced the twang of pain when hearing about her tragic death? I didn't understand. I didn't understand how such a poignant point in my childhood that I thought was felt by all, was apparently only felt by me and those in Haverstraw. This is what made me different.

I knew that I was different from then on because I may always be that girl who likes to read and write, who always obeys their mother, who likes nature and hiking, who sometimes feels weird and awkward and far away, and who loves to imagine big things in life. I may be all of these things. But underneath these things, lying so far beneath sometimes that I can never find it, I will always be Latina. Spanish may not be my first language, I may never be able to cook arroz con pollo or pernil with as much grace as other women, never talk with as much attitude or be instantly recognized as one from my own race, but these roots that I have are a part of me, stuck permanently to my heart and soul forever. I will always be that girl from Haverstraw. The one who wasn't like everyone else but still was. The girl who would now embrace everything about her.

Discussion Questions

- Why would somebody want to read this piece (the "Who cares?" factor)?
- Can you clearly identify the author's intention for the piece?
- How well does the author support the intention of the piece? Cite specific details that support or take away from the author's intention.
- Is there information missing from this piece that would make its intention clearer? What else would you like to know?
- Does the author portray herself as a round character? How does she do this?
- Do you trust the author of this piece? Why or why not?
- How clearly does the author establish a sense of setting/space in this piece? Cite specific details that support your claim.

- How clearly does the author establish characters other than the self in this piece? Cite specific details that support your claim.
- Did you learn anything new from reading this piece? If so, what?
- Are there particular passages with engaging language/description that stood out to you? Describe the appeal of these passages.
- Would you read more writing from this author? Why or why not?

Two Places, One Home

Maria Beyer

Travel five minutes across the New York State border into a small, suburban town called River Vale, New Jersey. Make a right onto a street called The Plaza, a quick left onto Winding Way, a right up Rolling Hill, and the third house on the left is mine. It sits on the corner of Drake Lane and Rolling Hill; 781 Drake Lane is my address to be exact. Countless birthdays, family dinners, holidays, and laughs all tucked away in boxes filled with photos just in case we forget the good times.

The house itself is a four bedroom colonial with a pool in the backyard for those hot summer days, and a fenced in yard for the family dog to run around in. There is the green L-shaped couch that always has someone fast asleep on it because of the ever-so-soft goose feathers. The newly renovated kitchen is my mother's safe haven where it constantly smells of pasta and homemade meat sauce. The bedrooms echo with the sound of television shows and music played at too high of a volume. But, the one annual event that defines the Beyer household is the Adoption Anniversaries celebrated for my sister and I with posters and desserts.

I had always been Maria Rose Beyer. I had Italian family Sunday dinners and a last name that was of German descent. It wasn't until people started asking me questions about China and my "real" parents that I started to become curious myself.

It was the morning of April 2nd, 2007 when I walked downstairs and stared at a colorful sign that read "Happy Adoption Anniversary Maria" and in the corner the number ten was bolded and underlined. Ten years, the number flashing in my head like a flashlight's bright light that flickers on and off from a dying battery, annoying and constant. Ten years of acceptance, of not asking questions, of just enjoying my perfect bubble of a world in small town River Vale, and ten years of not truly understanding where I came from.

It's funny; I never really cared about my family roots, until it was brought up in a somewhat casual way at the school lunch table. My adoption was always celebrated and it made me feel special. I was able to sit on the makeshift playground throne while all the other kids fought for attention, and I was simply handed it. I played tag, hide and go seek, and had play dates like any other kid. The problems only arose when I was asked questions I couldn't answer myself. Some of the popular ones included: do you remember the orphanage, can you speak Chinese, or, my favorite and most inconsiderate of all, do you know who your real parents are.

I was always caught off guard by this very insensitive, yet genuinely curious inquiry. My response was always somewhat along the lines of "what do you mean, my real parents, my real parents are the ones I call mom and dad" and the follow-up question was always along the lines of "I understand that, but I mean the parents that gave birth to you, your *real* parents" but, my quick response of "oh, I don't really know" usually ended the uncomfortable conversation that wasn't meant to be that way at all. The word "real" blared in my head like the annoying fire alarm that never seems to stop.

So, it was on the morning of April 2nd, 2007 when I decided to ask my parents the difficult questions that I have always subconsciously thought but avoided asking. I first started off with the politically incorrect and definitely hurtful, yet innocent, question of "Who are my real parents?" My mom and dad, startled and confused, sat me down and explained everything. Well, everything I could understand as a kid entering her middle school years.

In March of 1996, Ann Marie and Gary Beyer, the newly married couple, decided it was time to have children and start a family. However, unlike most of their family and friends, they decided to begin the process with a unique approach: adoption. My mom had always made it clear that family wasn't about the biological relationship, but the love and support between people. I think it was her way of putting it simply and making sense of it all to her curious young daughter.

My mom had never wanted us to feel like outsiders in our own home, making celebrating our adoption days a slippery slope. There was always a fine line between the desire to want us to be proud of where we came from, but not praising it so much that we feel too different. I guess my lack of curiosity deemed my mother's approach successful, until this very moment.

On July 4th, 1996 a baby girl was brought into this world, or at least that's what the nurses think is her birthdate, also known as the day she was found on the doorstep of an orphanage. Too innocent and naive to understand the reality of her circumstances, but now, leading a life that may have never been.

There is an orphanage in Nanjing, China that I once called home. However, I am now living in River Vale, New Jersey, a place very different from there. The crowded spaces, created by hundreds of baby cribs lined up with only a few inches between each, unsanitary conditions, and nurses running around doing their best to care for each baby as if it was their own, was my world for the first nine months of my life. Laying in my makeshift crib, fascinated by the motions my fingers made, my version of a mobile, I was swooped out of my natural habitat unknowingly, never to return again.

Halfway across the world, I was lying in a brand new wooden crib, playing with a real mobile that hung at perfect arm's length. The other babies that once surrounded me no longer drowned my cries out, and all attention was on me.

Growing up in a house, with space to throw my dolls across the floor, and a backyard to run around in, inevitably my legs covered in Band-Aids from scraping my knees like every clumsy toddler. But the scraped knees beat the germ-ridden orphanage floor I'd be crawling on. It's just a simple fact that being an orphan in China is a very different life to lead. I can only distantly relate to the potential struggles through my parents' experiences while adopting me.

Meetings once a month to receive updates on the potential baby that's ready for adoption, the anxiety built up over a yearlong period until the phone call announcing them as parents came through, the nearly 24-hour plane ride, the use of money belts stuffed in the waistband of their pants with hundred-dollar bills, and a two week stay in a foreign country, just waiting to hold a baby in their arms. It was the ultimate waiting game and the very real process of adoption, a concept I was just scratching the surface of comprehending.

What I did understand was the parents I was raised by, the siblings I laughed and unavoidably fought with, and the cousins I've vacationed with annually. The Beyer tradition of bringing in a freshly made pizza pie, the cheese melting in our mouths, knowing it was taken out of the brick oven only minutes ago. Jumping into the car at exactly 3:30 p.m. and driving twenty minutes across the New York state border to hug my grandparents and sit down for an Italian family Sunday dinner that always started promptly at 4 p.m. The al dente pasta, and the taste of homemade meatballs were the ethnic foods I was used to. Even Christmas Eve was celebrated with a seafood theme, a spin-off of the ever-sacred Italian tradition of eating seven fishes the night before the birth of Jesus Christ. Chinese food was only consumed at the Jade Village on two days of the year: April 2nd and October 13th, our adoption anniversaries. An important yet seemingly insignificant tradition compared to the many others integrated into my life as a member of the Beyer family.

And while my curiosity still sparked, my sister chose to ignore the place she came from. To her, our four-bedroom colonial is her only home. The crowded spaces, created by hundreds of baby cribs lined up with only a few inches between each, unsanitary conditions, and nurses running around doing their best to care for each baby as if it was their own, was her world for the first eight months of her life, and that is all it is to her, a mere eight months. The homemade signs, mint chocolate chip ice cream cake with the words "Happy Anniversary" written in perfect cursive in blue frosting, and the endless hugs and kisses from our parents was enough satisfaction. Ana Frances Beyer, who attended Italian family Sunday dinners and carried a last name that was of German descent, didn't ask questions when people started asking about China and her "real" parents.

But, on the morning of April 2nd, 2007 I did ask questions. Questions that may only be answered by traveling back to the place that is a part of me. A feeling similar to that of someone who is in love, and cares so deeply for that individual that when apart from that person, a piece of he/she is missing. And while my desire is to find the place that is the essence of my being and the reason behind who I am today, it will never be the third house on the left as you drive up the freshly paved, winding hill. The house that sits on the corner of Drake Lane and Rolling Hill; 781 Drake Lane is the address to be exact, where countless birthdays, family dinners, holidays, and laughs all tucked away in boxes filled with photos just in case we forget the good times, the place that isn't just a place, but my one and only home.

Discussion Questions

- Why would somebody want to read this piece (the "Who cares?" factor)?
- Can you clearly identify the author's intention for the piece?
- How well does the author support the intention of the piece? Cite specific details that support or take away from the author's intention.
- Is there information missing from this piece that would make its intention clearer? What else would you like to know?
- Does the author portray herself as a round character? How does she do this?
- Do you trust the author of this piece? Why or why not?
- How clearly does the author establish a sense of setting/space in this piece? Cite specific details that support your claim.
- How clearly does the author establish characters other than the self in this piece? Cite specific details that support your claim.
- Did you learn anything new from reading this piece? If so, what?
- Are there particular passages with engaging language/description that stood out to you? Describe the appeal of these passages.
- Would you read more writing from this author? Why or why not?

See the World

Adriana Pauly

Oooooh

Some people think they're always right

Others are quiet and uptight

Others they seem so very nice nice nice nice nice oh oh

Inside they might feel sad and wrong

Oh no

29 different attributes

And only 7 that you like, uh oh

20 ways to see the world, oh oh

Or 20 ways to start a fight

—*The Strokes, "You Only Live Once"*

Location: LAX airport, California, USA

Date & Local time: April 18th, around 12:00 p.m.

Finally! I threw my tired and exhausted body into the airplane chair. After having slept for only an hour we had to take down our camp to catch a shuttle at 4:00 a.m. back to **LAX**. Over the four hours that it took the driver to take the eight of us, I drifted in and out of sleep, incapable of resisting my body's exhaustion. At LAX I had another four hours before my plane left, I had found a small couch and had just rolled myself up in my jacket, hugging my purse while holding on to my suitcase. I obviously realize that my soft, sleepy grip would not have kept anyone from stealing my possessions; however I liked to think that it would. Reminiscing about the weekend and the things that happened I was very pleased with my experience.

In about eleven hours I would be reunited with my bed, shower and the rest of the world. I had a feeling my lack of communication had angered several people, even more so since nobody really knew where I was or when exactly I was coming home. I wasn't worried, I had my passport which contains my visa, the only possession with a real value.

Location: Coachella festival site, near Indigo, California, USA

Date & Local time: April 17th, around 6 p.m.

This must be the happiest place in the world. Music, art and freedom—what more could I ask for? I was so glad to have come all the way from New York to Coachella, an annual festival in California. I had just gone off by myself to watch a band while my friends stayed at the beer garden. We had arranged to meet after the concert to watch the last bands of the festival together and finishing off what had been a perfect weekend.

Feeling empowered, free spirited and a little too aware of the fact that I was about to stand in a crowd of people by myself, watching a band by myself, I sat down on the meadow waiting for the band to come on. Buoying myself up and ignoring the cheerful groups of people around me I decided to lie down for a bit, watching the sky turn darker with the setting sun, watching rabbit clouds forming and drifting away. I lay my head on my purse so that in the unlikely event that I would fall asleep nobody would be able to steal my precious possessions, including my phone, camera and passport.

Mid-concert I dejectedly had to admit that watching a concert by myself was not as empowering as I had made it out to be and after making a pit-stop at the "toilets" (I am not sure if these establishments even deserve to be called that since after an entire weekend of 24-hour service under the burning desert sun these little cubicles of disgustingness were more like the entrance to hell than anything else…back to the story) I decided to rejoin my friends. While I was physically moving, mentally I was having a heated debate over female empowerment and why not wanting to be alone at a concert had more to do with wanting to share the experience with a loved one. In a different side of my head I was planning on how I would incorporate this new liberating feeling I had gained over the weekend to my new york lifestyle while still in another aisle I was trying to scout out if there were any potential new acquaintances to be made.

With the intention of getting my phone I rummaged around my bag, eventually dumping all of its inside, on the dirty ground. No phone. I patted myself down, still no phone. I looked up, and around me, no phone just a massive open space and an overwhelming amount of people. My brain quickly tried to reproduce the events of the past 30 minutes. To my own astonishment I realized that I had no idea what had happened. I remembered lying on the meadow and remembered being at the toilets however, I had no recollection of where exactly I had been lying, or how I got to the toilets nor which toilet I was on. I quickly remembered the million times I had cursed myself out, for not paying attention to my surroundings while at the same time hearing my mothers accusing voice:„ "Ay, Adriana!"

I tried to re-create my path, frantically searching the ground, lifting up and touching things that should have remained untouched, opening doors that should have remained locked permanently.

Twenty exasperating minutes later I decided to give up. "Who cares? Pfft. Materialistic things like cell phones are overrated anyways! Who the fuck cares, really? I'll just use my old phone again."

Well it turned out that more people cared than I thought.

Location: Coachella festival site, near Indigo, California, USA

Date & Local time: April 17th, around 7:00 p.m.

Girl finds a phone on the ground. She dials the number of the last person to have called it.

Location: Pawling, New York, USA

Date & Local time: April 17th, around 10:00 a.m.

Nubia Salazar's phone rings while she is about to go to bed. She quickly picks up to not wake her husband who has already been asleep for three hours. She hears a strange voice. She listens but can't quite make sense of what she is hearing. The strange voice tells her that Adriana, her cousin's daughter who she had gotten to know only a year ago when the girl came to New York to study, had lost her purse and should call her phone. Nubia hangs up.

Location: Hoboken, New Jersey, USA

Date & Local time: April 17th, around 10:15 a.m.

Sharlene Salazar's phone rings; it's her mother. She contemplates not answering and decides otherwise. Her mother nervously tells her something about a strange phone call, and that Adriana, her mother's cousin's daughter, was lost somewhere in California without her purse or cell phone. Sharlene patiently listens to her mother, she stays calm. From what she has know about Adriana so far she is not surprised at all, she quickly remembers the two weeks the girl had stayed at her apartment last summer and how she had managed to lose $2000 only to find it an hour later. She gets off the phone, calls Adriana's phone and speaks with the finder. She finds out that the girl on the other line had found her phone somewhere on the festival site and that she wanted Adriana to call it so they could meet up. Only her phone, not her passport, wallet and other valuable possessions as her mother had previously thought. She posts on Adriana's Facebook wall to get in touch with her friends.

Location: Coachella festival site, near Indigo, California, USA

Date & Local time: April 17th, around 7:30 p.m.

Since I had arranged with my friends to meet after the concert at the giant, luminescent mushrooms I decided to just plant myself there and watch out for familiar faces. I was in great company; there was the couple lying on the ground staring at the five meter high installation, tripping on who knows what. Right next to them, a guy with suspiciously red eyes drawing them accompanied by a pill popping long haired individual who every so often attempted what must have been a dance only to stop short after a few seconds. I held on to the few possessions that remained in my guardianship and waited while it got darker and darker. With a professionalism that only TV crime shows can teach you I started planning several emergency scenarios in case I did not find my friends among the other 100,000 people here.

At around 8:00 p.m. I finally saw a familiar face in the crowd. Telling her about my loss, and yes I knew exactly that no one had stolen it, we tried several times to call it. However, since she had a Mexican phone, produced in what seemed like the 1990s, and without the country code for the US (which now I know is +1, of course, how could it have been anything else, bless your heart), we had to give up after several tries. Since I had already gotten over my loss and my interest for any material possessions we decided not to let this ugly event taint our last night.

Location: Coachella festival site, near Indigo, California, USA

Date & Local time: April 18th, around 9:00 a.m.

Girl posts on Adriana's Facebook wall, to call her, meet her and pick up her phone before she leaves at 10 a.m.

Location: Hoboken, New Jersey, USA

Date & Local Time: April 18th, around 1:15 p.m

Monica Jung casually checks her best friend Adriana's Facebook, only to discover that her friend seemed to have lost her phone/purse/wallet. She frantically calls her phone number. A female voice picks up the phone and explains how she had found Adriana's phone, etc. Monica understanding that her friend seemed to be incapable of handling her own life arranged with the girl to have the phone shipped from San Francisco to New York.

Location: New York City, New York, USA

Date & Local Time: April 18th, around 1:30 p.m.

Fabia Neser's phone rings, on the other end her roommate's friend Monica. In a panicked, high pitched voice she quickly gets filled into the issue. Recalling the last summer when she and Adriana went traveling together in California she remembered how Adriana had misplaced her room keys three times in one day only to later throw her jacket into the hostels dirty laundry basket instead of her towel.

She was not worried, she knew her friend and knew that with or without phone Adriana would manage to get home one way or the other. However, she did resent the idea of not having asked for a copy of her travel information.

Location: Marburg, Hessen, Germany

Date & Local time: April 18th, around 7:00 p.m.

Eucaris's phone rings. She picks up to the voice of her cousin Nubia living in New York, her heart automatically beats faster. Nubia tells her that her younger daughter Adriana had been at a festival in California, where she had lost her phone. Eucaris vaguely recalls her daughter telling her about something happening in LA while at the same time cursing herself out for not paying more attention to her surroundings and cursing her daughter out for the same. Why didn't she ask for a copy of the flight information? Why hadn't she asked where exactly she was going and with whom? She started feeling nauseous. Her cousin was telling her that her daughter Sharlene had spoken to the girl who found the phone and that she was trying to figure things out.

After hanging up she goes and tells her husband about the mess her little baby had made accusing him of convincing her to let her baby leave her side and move across the Atlantic Ocean.

Location: Buenos Aires, Argentina

Date & Local Time: April 18th, around 1:30 p.m.

Luis Jesus Murcia reviews his niece Eucaris's Facebook wall. He comes across a post she had made a little earlier on her youngest daughter's wall. Not wanting to intrude into family complications he leaves a simple greeting and a quick inquiry about everyone's well being on his niece's daughter Adriana's wall.

Discussion Questions

- Why would somebody want to read this piece (the "Who cares?" factor)?
- Can you clearly identify the author's intention for the piece?
- How well does the author support the intention of the piece? Cite specific details that support or take away from the author's intention.
- Is there information missing from this piece that would make its intention clearer? What else would you like to know?
- Does the author portray herself as a round character? How does she do this?
- Do you trust the author of this piece? Why or why not?
- How clearly does the author establish a sense of setting/space in this piece? Cite specific details that support your claim.
- How clearly does the author establish characters other than the self in this piece? Cite specific details that support your claim.
- Did you learn anything new from reading this piece? If so, what?

- Are there particular passages with engaging language/description that stood out to you? Describe the appeal of these passages.
- Would you read more writing from this author? Why or why not?

Manhattan

William Rossi

Layering for a Manhattan winter is essential. The winds come from all angles, and if they aren't rushing up the avenues, they're booming down the streets that intersect them. They wrap around the buildings, hugging every concrete curve and bend. The crisp, chilled air blows through the fibers of my thickest layers and sends a chill rushing up my spine. This season was always the worst to come in for; the cold here didn't have the same feeling as the one on Long Island. Here the breeze motivated people; it pushed them to walk a little faster, hold their loved ones a little closer, and focus a little harder.

I was here a week before, to celebrate Thanksgiving in my great-grandparents' townhouse. My mother always likes to make a trip out of Thanksgiving, so before we headed over to conjure with the rest of my family we walked the Brooklyn Bridge. My mother didn't account for two things: the forty mile per hour winds, and the fact that the end of the Brooklyn Bridge leaves us in Brooklyn. We walked the bridge twice, once east and once west. My earlobes and nose were numb by the time we arrived for dinner at the Gramercy townhouse. We all gathered in the basement where my great-grandmother prides herself in her home-décor skills. The whole family knows that she takes advantage of Pier One employees to customize her humble abode.

I sat at the further end of the table, away from the older adults and across from my parents. The draft swirled through one of the windows that my great-grandfather forgot to seal shut with the clear plastic film from Home Depot. We all mumbled along in a grace prayer, knowing that we all only ever say grace before this particular meal. I slugged back the small glass of wine, and braced myself as the row of family members discussed what they were thankful for, a tradition held in the memory of my aunt whose kind-spirit loved to embrace what each member was thankful for.

I wiped my sweaty palms against the red and orange table napkin that had a hand-embroidered turkey on it. It's my turn. "I'm gay," flew out of my mouth in a brash voice, highlighted with a crack. I paused and took in the moment of silence that followed, a silence like that of those mourning a loss. "And—and…I'm thankful that I have a supportive group of friends and I hope that group can include everyone at this table," I muttered out as held back the rush of water that ran to the bottom of my eye. I sat with my head down, acting like I was taking into account what was on the plate in front of me.

My grandmother placed her glass down on the table and spoke before she finished swallowing, "Well—you could not be surrounded by a more supportive group of people, my dear. Hell, you're in Manhattan, you can be whoever you want to be here." This was followed by murmurs of agreement, and softly worded statements of pride that held a slight, uncomfortable air.

My mother has not spoken a word to me since. Instead she's yelled and bolstered her aggravation with the topic and its consequences. I was grounded, in an attempt to keep me away from my boyfriend. My father would enter the confines of my room to try and cheer me up, but it was no use.

But like any rebellious teen filled with angst, I lied. I told my mom I had planned to tour Hunter

College on a day off from school, and I knew she wouldn't be able to excuse herself from work to attend with me. I told my parents the plan: get on the train with Jessica, my friend since kindergarten, around 10 a.m., arrive at Hunter in time for the 11:30 tour, grab dinner when the tour concluded, and then come back home as soon as we could. The plan worked, and I hopped on the train with my boyfriend, Kenny, at the station in our town.

My sneakers maneuvered their way on the concrete, dodging dog shit and trash. The atmosphere that surrounded the city was alluring,; offering escape, comfort, and inclusion. Focused, I concentrated on the streets we passed, the key features of each corner we turned, and the proximity to Central Park. I stayed focused, trying to balance between maintaining a conversation about photography with Kenny, nervous about my mother uncovering my ruse, and figuring out how to get to the Metropolitan Museum of Art. So to stay in the vicinity, the Met seems like the best bet.

We walked along the solid structure that outlined the park, stopping occasionally for Kenny to photograph some aspect of nature that sprung out of the concrete, just as Central Park does to Manhattan. As we shuffled through the chill, we halted at the marvelous steps of the museum. The structure was so large and grand that it stunted the sights around it. The building in the middle of so many that topped it in size, but never in grandeur.

I grabbed his hand, intertwining our fingers instead of grasping his hand fully in mine. This method always seemed most sincere. This action was never so natural, so thoughtless. My body tensed up, and a rush flew to my head, leaving me to slow down a minute as I reached the top of the steps. "Are you okay?" Kenny questioned. I grinned and pushed against the door leading to the center of the museum, still grasping his hand. I tried to stay interested in the boring art that Kenny liked to look at. They all looked the same, some stuck up snob paying big bucks for a selfie. But in silence, I searched the room, for a stare, a glare, and snicker. Nothing. I was never one for PDA, there was always something about it that repulsed me, but this didn't irk me. The deeper we sank into the museum, the less I worried about anyone looking.

We walked around the museum all day. And when we had finished wandering throughout the larger exhibits, we took our excursion to the park that surrounds the colossal structure. Once outside, the thoughts spurred up as my eyes wandered to meet those of passersby who felt confused, or uncomfortable. The only person to meet my eyes was a homeless woman playing the guitar for spare change. The temperature and the wind didn't affect the buildup of sweat between our palms, which had to be smeared on our jeans every couple of minutes. However the inconvenience didn't seem to matter, because it was an action of humility and affection.

Our hands stayed entwined as we crashed through the heavy flow of tourists in Times Square. We dashed through the street and sidewalk to make the train home at a time that would coincide with the end of Hunter College's tour. We left our fingers clasped as we sat together on the train, resting from a long day and analyzing the pictures that appeared on the small digital screen on Kenny's camera. We picked through the pictures we liked, and even the ones of us that we could post to Instagram. We only let go as we arrived at our town's station. When we saw our parents standing together at the ticket booth, all with a glare that stung worse than the icy breeze.

Discussion Questions

- Why would somebody want to read this piece (the "Who cares?" factor)?
- Can you clearly identify the author's intention for the piece?
- How well does the author support the intention of the piece? Cite specific details that support or take away from the author's intention.
- Is there information missing from this piece that would make its intention clearer? What else would you like to know?
- Does the author portray herself as a round character? How does she do this?
- Do you trust the author of this piece? Why or why not?
- How clearly does the author establish a sense of setting/space in this piece? Cite specific details that support your claim.
- How clearly does the author establish characters other than the self in this piece? Cite specific details that support your claim.
- Did you learn anything new from reading this piece? If so, what?
- Are there particular passages with engaging language/description that stood out to you? Describe the appeal of these passages.
- Would you read more writing from this author? Why or why not?

November First

Neziah Doe

(If a person speaks about 5,000-10,000 words a day, how much is 1,667 words, really?) It rings like a promise into my fourteen year old ears. (That amount is not nearly as much as you think it is, I promise myself.) (Yeah, but thirty times over?)

National Novel Writing Month is a month long competition with your mind, health and reality to complete a 50,000 word story in the thirty days that is November. Your account on their website becomes your homepage, as you watch the apathetic brown bar not rise as quickly as you feel you are raising it, piling on words half-senselessly onto a document, shoddily weaving out a story that is nothing like a novel but everything like your own fantastic creation, your magnum opus.

(I am going to write a novel this month.)

A blank screen is the most intimidating thing, the shiny pure white of my dirty old PC glaring at me, daring me to get its face even dirtier with the blather I can produce from my mind. (Word vomit), I smirk as I look down at my pages and pages of notes to write this thing, (it will all be word vomit).

(If I read about one hundred books a day, how hard can it be to write one of my own? All of this reading seems to be passive at this point, compared to writing.) The answer to that is already known—hard. So I begin the hard thing, with my fingers crashing against the keys, fabricating a brutal murder. The salesman with the gun in his briefcase, watching the lovely couple walk into their quaint suburban home. He takes out the gun, he does what is supposed to be done with guns but people insist isn't the reason that guns are made. The man leaves. I twitch, the unfamiliar rush of caffeine surging through me like a tumbling of cheerleaders encouraging me to WRITE WRITE WRITE WRITE. So I WRITE WRITE WRITE WRITE.

November Twenty-Fourth

(Is it one hundred words? After one hundred more I can look at Facebook. For five minutes. Then another hundred. After that I can use *write or die*, shoot out another one thousand. After that I will be caught up to yesterday. Thank God we are not cooking Thanksgiving this year, it is eleven thirty, I have until four until we leave. Write. Thank God I'm not handwriting sections anymore, my hand twitching from overuse as I tried relaxing all my muscles to go to sleep. Write some more.)

(Every day of November is an adrenaline rush, the most invested I have been in numbers since I will be when SAT's come along. My fingers slam against the keys, I get an email from NaNoWriMo. A pep talk email from another famous writer. Awesome. Skim it, read it. That espresso shot of someone else's words sends me back into the abyss of my own design. Where are they going to go to now?)

My mom says, "You haven't showered in two days, go get yourself ready, it's a quarter to four!"

"I'm writing," I say absentmindedly, my mind on one mode: ignore all words that are not yours. Take your words and get them on the paper already, what are you waiting for have you seen the clock? It keeps moving forward, never changing its pace. The clock is your bitch, now make time question itself with your amazing quick writing abilities.

Most writers take years to write their novels, just to have a first draft. They carefully carve each and every word out of a stone that they have meticulously picked, they take their characters out for coffee. I have a scribbled on page of ideas, my flow of words comes only from the gushing stream of my mind, my characters and I eloped about two weeks ago. I am not a writer.

I sluggishly get into the shower, put on the outfit my mom picked while I was gone, I'm too lazy to argue. I pet my computer goodbye and get on with it. Thanksgiving time, I guess.

November Twenty-Sixth

I am the Goliath. I am a beast, a machine, words flow out from my fingers like milk from an udder. My metaphors need work. Me? I slam words onto the computer screen like this is the US Open and this shot will win me my match. I have reached 48,000 words, I feel like crying, my wrists are sore and my fingers are fed up with the marathon dance I have put them through these past few weeks. But my heart, oh! My heart is singing the victory cries of thousands of soldiers, the giant aspiration that I kept deflated, folded up and triple wrapped in the back of my brain, the dream of writing a book.

I speed and I speed, the sky outside turning its colors on me.

November Twenty-Seventh

My whole body trembles as I start writing the final words to my novel. In the other room my brother is working quietly on that project that I am too busy to work on, the only sound in the house the near rustling of my fingers as they fly over the letters, a show to enjoy as the words I have wanted to write down get written. There is a nice thought that whenever you are born, you are only allotted with so many words. I wonder if in these few weeks, I have wasted mine on something that will never come to its true potential. If it has potential at all.

Writers write books all the time that end up being like balloons—they can fly but they are fragile and empty. I don't want a balloon, I want a boulder that slams into a stream and changes the flow as the stubborn waters relent.

I feel an earthquake rupturing inside of me as I look at the word count bar below my writing, my fingers doing the thinking and my eyes stuck to the screen. 49,987…49,992…

50,000.

I finish the scene, put my final number into the NaNoWriMo site, and for what feels like the first time in forever I get up from my desk. I look down at my hands as I walk into the next room to see my brother. I am breathless, all I can do is grin.

"What?" Daniel asks, looking down at his work, the desk lamp lighting his face with a harsh glow in the depths of the night.

"I finished," I grin, "I'm done. I wrote a book."

November Thirtieth

Sitting in the car with my brother and my father as we zip down the highway, I look out at the grey November skies. It's my favorite time of year, my favorite weather.

"Just tell him," my brother pushes me.

"It's not a big deal," I insist, looking away from him.

"Tell me what?" my father asks from the driver's seat. I look down, I don't want my dad to know what I have wasted so much of my time on.

"I wrote a book," I mumble.

"Well it's about time," my dad laughs, "we all knew that was going to happen eventually."

Discussion Questions

- Why would somebody want to read this piece (the "Who cares?" factor)?
- Can you clearly identify the author's intention for the piece?
- How well does the author support the intention of the piece? Cite specific details that support or take away from the author's intention.
- Is there information missing from this piece that would make its intention clearer? What else would you like to know?
- Does the author portray herself as a round character? How does she do this?
- Do you trust the author of this piece? Why or why not?
- How clearly does the author establish a sense of setting/space in this piece? Cite specific details that support your claim.
- How clearly does the author establish characters other than the self in this piece? Cite specific details that support your claim.
- Did you learn anything new from reading this piece? If so, what?
- Are there particular passages with engaging language/description that stood out to you? Describe the appeal of these passages.
- Would you read more writing from this author? Why or why not?

Get a Grip

Emma Suleski

The only way for me to catch my breath at practice was to put my grips on slowly before we began our final event: bars. I was lucky enough to have brand new, two-buckle grips that had a lot of breaking-in to do. After eight years of wear and tear, my old pair had given up, leading me to new wristbands, buckles, stiff leather, and smooth surfaces. All of that had to change, and it had to change in one practice.

I grabbed each wrist and cracked it before sliding a red wristband onto each. Both my wrists and their new protectors were too tight, so I leaned my hands hard against the low bar and looked out over the gym. The sport had chosen me at four years old and hadn't let me go since. I was now twelve years old and living a dual life. I had a home, my place of residence, and a family who all shared my last name. I also had a second home, where I grew up and found myself, with about a hundred sisters and a few coaches, or gym-moms as we call them. Across from me, the floor took on a new appearance. It was old. I thought about its layers, first springs, then wood, foam, and finally the blue carpet and white tape. Stains discolored the carpet, brownish splatters that reminded a few scarred gymnasts of landings gone wrong. They definitely didn't clean it enough.

I pushed myself off the low bar and started to buckle my grips around now-swollen wrists. Buckle one, in the loop, pull to tighten, close. Repeat on buckle two. Go back to one; tighten. Go back to two; tighten. Repeat on left hand. The process became so automatic that I found my focus drifting again. To my right, Janis piked a Yurchenko on vault. In other words, our nationally ranked pride and joy did a really cool trick. She flew through the air, a blur of ponytail and limbs, and stuck a landing on one of our many blue eight inch mats. Each gymnast stopped during her practice at one point or another to watch Janis throw a vault or stick a beam routine. She was our own little inspiration board, a perfection to work towards, a level of achievement the rest of us only accomplished in our dreams.

Janis outnumbered all of us on the famous 9.0 wall. Painted red and blue at the back of the gym, a competitor's name was added after every meet for every score she received of a 9.0 or greater. There was something elitist about being added to the 9.0 wall; it was a recognition, a spot with the greats, or even just physical evidence of your hard work. I held it above any medal, ribbon, or trophy I had ever received. I have never met a gymnast who forgets the day she was added to the wall. Seeing Jen, the Janis of the past generation, and her white paint marker at the wall and knowing you were on the list made the little gymnast inside of you bounce about your body. It was almost like having butterflies in your stomach, except with muscles instead of wings and pointed toes instead of antennae. I smiled reading my name. This was my home, and there was "Emma Suleski" on display for both residents and company to see.

The new white leather of my grips was stiff against my palm and I balled my hand up into a tight fist. I didn't want stiff leather, it was uncomfortable and would slow me down and frankly do the opposite of what I needed, which was to grip the bar. I clenched and unclenched fists until creases appeared like lines in the snow. My middle and ring fingers slid into their respective holes, which rested a little too tightly just below my first knuckles. I pumped my fingers and clenched my fists again, trying to find a comfortable place in my hands' new prison. My head jerked around to the beam as I heard a slip and a bang. Judging by the beam-shaped reddish purple burn down her thigh, Jess had just missed her feet on a back-handspring, one of the most daunting skills to throw on beam. Though the friction the suede beams provide is imperative for limiting slippage, it's a very unforgiving material to slide on any skin softer than the calloused feet of a seasoned gymnast. I watched as Jess stood up and hopped back onto the beam. I cringed with her as she stood tall on the beam, body and pride both aching. Two summers ago, I was working round-offs on the beam. Similar to your average cartwheel, but with a much harder landing; a judge doesn't give the skill credit unless you are entirely airborne at one point. After enough pounding of my dainty feet on a metal-cored beam, the swelling on my left foot stopped healing overnight, stabbing me with pain worse and worse every day. It was sprained and my doctor said two weeks off. My coach said, "Just tape it for support." They say fall down six times, stand up seven, but in the gym we say get beam burn six times; get back on and stick your skill eight.

I rubbed tired hands together and felt the smoothness of new leather. The uneven bars in front of me were a tangle of steel posts, fiberglass coverings, and taut metal wires, standing ominously in a cloud of chalk like mountains in the mist. I rubbed my slick palms against the ridged metal wire, roughing up their surface, stopping every few seconds to pull off shredded leather. Around me my team bustled about, running drills, perfecting routines, and nursing ripped callouses. Sometimes they weren't people, they were messy ponytails, faces a mix of chalk and sweat, bodies hard with muscle contrasted by the shimmer and sparkle of a leotard. They were athletes driven by personal goals, set back by nothing. These girls weren't invincible; they were taped ankles, knee braces, back supports, and Band-Aids. Ripping skin the size of quarters off of their hands didn't bother them, dripping blood down their palms as they finished their bar routines. Landing skills on unhealed fractures, powering through pulls in muscles most people don't even know exist. They could even do it with an infectious smile during a floor routine. They were fighters; they were modern-day warriors. They were climbers, intending to reach every peak with the grace of a ballerina. They were tough. But they were also genuine smiles, hugs, and support. They were my thirteen adoptive sisters.

I flipped my hands and observed my grips. Creased and torn up, they almost looked like I had owned them forever, minus a couple of those inevitable bloodstains. I pivoted my feet and took two steps toward the chalk bucket. I was passed the community spray bottle, which always seemed to be held together by some form of medical tape. I sprayed each grip until water dripped down my arms and stuck my arms and head in the chalk bucket in order to reach the valuable fine dust at the bottom. The chalk seemed to hold all the scents of the gym, making the bucket smell like a combination of sweat and feet that vaguely felt like home.

"What do you guys do, eat the chalk? I don't get it." laughed Coach Lee as she dropped another block into the bucket. I smiled at the opportunity to be the first to use the fresh cut. I rubbed sharp corners onto my dusty grips, caking on thick layers in a methodical fashion. I dropped the block back into the bucket and proceeded to do one of the most famous moves in gymnastics history: the post-chalk clap. Yes, it's necessary to clap off the excess chalk, but the dramatic ritual is more than physicality. It's a beginning. Chalking up before every routine is necessary. If I took a bad fall, it only mattered until I chalked up again. Then I clapped the excess chalk off and it was time for a new routine. I put myself in a cloud of dust, a cloud that smelled like home and made it hard to breathe. I stepped out of it, this time a monster emerging from the mist.

I approached the low bar and rolled ankles over toes, cracking them. You can't point your toes into oblivion if they need to crack. I took a deep breath and jumped. My new hands gripped bars instinctively and I began my routine. It was a mess of friction, hands sliding, body gliding, hips smacking on the bar in the same place they always do. Right above the elastic of the famous "GK" leotard resided two permanent purple-green bruises, resting on top of my hipbones that jutted out like discuses. I paused on top of the high bar, a monster on top of her mountain, a queen atop her throne. I leaned on those bruises and picked my hands up, sliding the grips down my wrists just a little bit. Dismounts were always the hardest part of a routine for me, the free jump off of the mountain I was never really ready to take. The timing had to be perfect, the execution flawless, or I risked ankles smashing into the bar for yet another sprain, tear, or bruise. I looked over my kingdom one more time, tens of girls working at the same time, dancing on blue-carpeted floor, power-thirsty running down the vault runway, focused on beam. Then there was me, observing my home from my balcony of the bar.

Lee called up to me, "Today, Miss Emma-Loo" and I looked over and laughed. Break time was over, my breather was up; it was time to simply face my fear and get a grip.

> ### Discussion Questions
>
> - Why would somebody want to read this piece (the "Who cares?" factor)?
> - Can you clearly identify the author's intention for the piece?
> - How well does the author support the intention of the piece? Cite specific details that support or take away from the author's intention.
> - Is there information missing from this piece that would make its intention clearer? What else would you like to know?
> - Does the author portray herself as a round character? How does she do this?
> - Do you trust the author of this piece? Why or why not?
> - How clearly does the author establish a sense of setting/space in this piece? Cite specific details that support your claim.
> - How clearly does the author establish characters other than the self in this piece? Cite specific details that support your claim.
> - Did you learn anything new from reading this piece? If so, what?
> - Are there particular passages with engaging language/description that stood out to you? Describe the appeal of these passages.
> - Would you read more writing from this author? Why or why not?

Room in the Back

Justine Giardina

There is a room in the back of the Ramapo Travel Plaza McDonald's restaurant on Route 17 that is the only room in which Ramapo Travel Plaza McDonald's employees are allowed to eat McDonald's. "That must be the saddest room in the whole entire world," my boyfriend said one night over a meal paid for by real, McDonald's minimum wage earnings. "I can't think of a more depressing purpose for a room." He was right, the room was approximately six feet wide and seven feet deep, decorated solely with white, 8.5-by-11-inch papers bearing policies concerning what was included in a free employee meal, the criteria for being promoted from a minimum wage cashier to a minimum wage crew chief, and one printed photo of a manager with a man dressed as Ronald McDonald in a decrepit New Jersey mall. The tiles on the floor were the color of brick and occasionally someone would bring a stack of napkins from out front to put on top of, but never in, the empty napkin holder. "You should be damn grateful for that room," I giggled. "Because if we could take the McDonald's out of the room I would be bringing it back here and we would be eating that."

A primary goal of working the front counter was to make it look nothing like the back room. If the manager said, "make sure your station looks spotless," I always felt the subtext was, "make this place so clean that they'll never even guess about that weird fucking room in the back." I never thought there was much sense in that request, the customers were either truckers who wouldn't mind the break room or were Manhattan dwellers on their way home from a summer house who shouldn't have been eating McDonald's anyway. The floor behind the front counter was the same brick-colored, tile floor, only differing in the way that, with the exception of the corners, it was swept more often. The front counter was a good place to get yelled at for leaning on something, as the manager of Ramapo Travel's Carvel, Sbarro's, and Lavazza Coffee section, Louise, truly thought she was clever in the development of the phrase "cleaning not leaning" and applauded herself by stating it often. She disappeared often, preferring to inhabit the break rooms or flirt with coworkers in the McDonald's kitchen. As soon as she was out of earshot, my favorite coworker, a small Hispanic woman named Virginia would squeak out, "*perezosa* lady." Louise was a harsh woman who worked in the military before she worked at McDonald's. She seemed to regard the authority aspect of her managerial McDonald's job about as seriously as a military position and felt herself above doing any of the tasks that the minimum wage workers or other managers did. She took an interest in holding screaming matches with the sixteen-year-old crew chief and entertained the petty power plays that took place on the floor. With the exception of my second-favorite coworker, Robyn, no one really liked her.

It's impossible to say where one could typically find Robyn, mostly because Robyn was all over the place. Robyn was fifty-four and always wore her hair in three braids tied together into one ponytail, earning her the nickname of "Crazy McDonald's Grandma" by my mother. I have never met anyone who loved anything more than Robyn loved the Ramapo Travel Plaza McDonald's. She cleaned the Carvel ice cream machine every Thursday with a concerning amount of tenderness and care and one day when the machine broke she was devastated enough to sulk for four days. She also liked to do things we weren't allowed to do, like move all of the condiments from the storage room under the front counter and put half and half in cappuccinos instead of two percent milk for customers who preferred it. Robyn would dance Chubby Checker's twist every time someone requested a chocolate-vanilla twist cone and gave away teeny tiny ice cream cones to customers with babies for free. Robyn would even hide in the storage room once her shift was over so that the manager wouldn't make her go home. All of the new employees, myself included, adored her because she was entertaining and just as nice to new employees as she was to everyone, but the other workers all seemed to have a problem with her, which I never thought of as more than anything but a silly jealousy of how much customers liked her.

I was hired to work at the Carvel, Sbarro's and Lavazza stations, and usually worked at all three in any given shift. Virginia worked with me, and she worked hard, late and often by herself when it got past midnight. Usually when she came in it was after having already worked a shift at Boston Market, where she received the same minimum wage salary that she did at our job. She had worked at McDonald's for a couple of years, longer than most of the employees. Two months after I began work, on a day that Virginia didn't start her shift until five, a manager decided to send Danielle, a girl who had been working the McDonald's counter, to our side of the store to learn the Lavazza Coffee stand so that Virginia could have some help on my days off. Louise had been present all morning and, seeking to drift into the break room, requested that I teach Danielle the coffee stand. Danielle had worked on the other side of the store for about seven months, but had taken a month off for her finals at community college and a half of a month off to go on two vacations, one with her family and one with her boyfriend. I understood she had been trained to work at the coffee stand in the past but, as far as I knew, hadn't been asked to work there again after her first day. "Joe trained me and he told me I could pick a drink that I wanted as reward for learning," she explained to me, fair hands folded delicately on the counter. "So I put it next to the cash register and when I came back *someone* has thrown it out." She exhaled dramatically. "I was *so* pissed that Joe told me he would make me another one." She pushed a strand of her red hair behind her ear and put an extra espresso shot into the drink she was making, looking prickly when I pointed out her mistake. Danielle wore rings on every finger even though it was against the dress code and her hair was unbound for the most part, something Louise would have made a fuss about if she hadn't been so quick to leave.

"Do you want to work the register?" I asked, my patience running short. "Sure," she answered coolly, not catching my tone. The McDonald's side had touch-screen cash registers with pictures of the food for the cashiers to choose from rather than having to memorize and punch in designated number combinations for orders. Our side wasn't afforded this luxury, but there was a list of numbers printed, laminated and taped down onto the side of the cash register.

"What's a small chai?" Danielle asked. I moved over to the cash register to show her how to put the order into the cash register, as it wasn't listed on the sheet. Chai had an unordinary key combination, so I went over to show her how to enter it into the register. "Oh, also," I nonchalantly added as the drawer opened, "the bills should all face up."

I looked back to what I had been doing, not thinking it odd that I had received no acknowledgement in regard to the last statement. After I had made the chai and the customer left, Danielle hissed out my name.

"Justine," she said bitterly. Surprised at her tone, I turned to face her, eyes meeting hers in what I found was an unflinching glare. "I have worked here for almost a year," she said once she had my full attention. Her tone was unwavering, and she spoke slowly and deliberately, as though I wouldn't be able to understand her if she didn't. She continued with an air of condescension, "I know the way the bills are supposed to face." She raised her nose in the air just slightly as she turned to push the register drawer shut.

Taken aback, I felt myself shrink. "I didn't know if it was different on the other side." I muttered, and, realizing she was not going to break eye contact, I spitefully turned away from her, refusing to meet her challenging gaze.

"Why would it be different on the other side?" she questioned boldly.

I didn't answer her. Instead, I began washing the counter and glared at the brick colored floor. Danielle stood idly and leaned on the counter. As we continued to stand there, still in the positions we had argued in, I began to feel very small. No customers came for several minutes, and when the silence was finally broken I was startled.

"Oy, chica!"

I looked up, excited to see Virginia on the other side of the counter. "Where is *perezosa* lady? Isn't she supposed to be training the new girl?"

Danielle, surprised, turned to Virginia. "I'm not new Virginia! Don't you remember working with me?" Danielle asked accusingly, as though Virginia were being rude. "I've been here for a long time," she emphasized.

Virginia cracked a wide, crooked smile but didn't give an answer. "*Perezosa* lady said you can work on McDonald's side, it's time for my shift on cashier." Danielle smiled back at Virginia, mistaking her cheeky grin for a genuine one and, with a flamboyant flutter of her fingers, walked back to the side with the touch-screen registers.

Virginia pulled Danielle's untouched rag from the side of the cash register and began washing the spot she was in, started to wipe the surface of the register. "Why she giving you a hard time?" Virginia asked me. Unaware that she had heard the exchange, I turned to her, surprised and a bit relieved.

"Everyone thinks they better than everyone else here," she sighed, absentmindedly. "Why she care? Don't need a promotion. White, no babies to feed, lives with her *mami y papi*."

The tension began to leave my body as my anger with Danielle began to leave my mind. I looked to Virginia, now not just my coworker Virginia but also immigrant, single mother, homeowner, Virginia. I exhaled shakily, embarrassed at my overreaction to such a petty spat.

"And still no *perezosa* lady." Virginia sighed. I gave her a weak smile.

I left my job a couple of months ago, but the last time I was in town I stopped in at a quiet hour and leaned on the customer side of the coffee counter, cheekily showing off for Louise. Louise grinned at me, rolled her eyes and shook her head, wandering off like she usually did. Virginia came out from the storeroom behind the coffee stand, having heard my exchange with Louise.

"No help for you?" I asked, noting that Danielle had failed to take up my position next to Virginia. She grinned at me, explaining that Danielle hadn't been asked back.

"Too many *perezosa* lady already," she said and disappeared into the storeroom.

> **Discussion Questions**
>
> - Why would somebody want to read this piece (the "Who cares?" factor)?
> - Can you clearly identify the author's intention for the piece?
> - How well does the author support the intention of the piece? Cite specific details that support or take away from the author's intention.
> - Is there information missing from this piece that would make its intention clearer? What else would you like to know?
> - Does the author portray herself as a round character? How does she do this?
> - Do you trust the author of this piece? Why or why not?
> - How clearly does the author establish a sense of setting/space in this piece? Cite specific details that support your claim.
> - How clearly does the author establish characters other than the self in this piece? Cite specific details that support your claim.
> - Did you learn anything new from reading this piece? If so, what?
> - Are there particular passages with engaging language/description that stood out to you? Describe the appeal of these passages.
> - Would you read more writing from this author? Why or why not?

Aging Not so Gracefully

Anne Ehart

I'm digging my toes into the sand, feeling the breeze getting cooler as the sun begins to set. Goose bumps form on my bare body and I reach for my t-shirt in the multicolored beach bag. I shake the sand off of my gray t-shirt and pull it over my fading yellow bikini. I stare out at the distant horizon and listen to the soothing crashing of the waves as the breeze blows strands of salty hair across my face. I can tell I have been here for hours by the receding tide that was once nearly pulling my flip-flops out to sea, and by the long, slow arc the sun has made across the sky. Removing myself from my reverie, I turn around and look up the stretch of white sand toward the dunes and down the path that leads to the street. I scan the silhouettes of the distant figures for the limping walk of my grandmother, but don't see her. My dad emerges from the water, grabs the pale orange beach towel, and dries his salt and pepper hair vigorously.

"Any sign of them?" he asks.

"No, Michael said Grandmom took an hour to finish the potato salad," I replied. My dad had asked Michael to stay behind to help Grandmom get down to the beach.

"Well, she is getting older."

"Yeah," I say, thinking about Grandmom struggling to get around and tiring out more than usual. Every summer we come here to visit her, and for the last three years my dad has said Grandmom will have to give up the place soon. Up until this year I have shaken off the idea of parting with the beach themed décor of the condo in Brigantine, New Jersey just a few steps from the beach, not wanting to think about a summer without a visit to the condo and not thinking the day would ever actually come. The whole island is like home to me. I've grown up on the white sand of the 39th Street beach. Here I dove through the waves for the first time: my cousin taught me to put both of my arms above my head, take a deep breath, and plunge through the wave and come up on the other side, the cool water cascading down my body in delicious refreshment. Here Michael and I built countless sand castles.

"We need to build a moat!" he would shriek, as a wave got dangerously close to our castle. We dug tirelessly, until the moat began to fill with water. Once our castle was safe and dry, we would add the finishing touch.

"I got a bucket for sand dribbles," Michael said, carrying a small yellow bucket with water spilling over the edge. We would dig our hands into the bucket of water and sand and let the mixture drip onto the castle and dry almost immediately, creating tiny towers of delicate sand. Then we would sit back and admire our work, wondering if our sandcastle would still be there when we come back tomorrow.

Here I fell in love with the ocean, its ability to put me in a state of pure happiness, its vastness enveloping me and taking me away from the rest of the world. I lose myself here for hours, lost in the serenity of the shore.

"Is that them over there?" My dad is looking back toward the dunes and I'm pulled back to the present.

I turn to look. "Yeah, that's them."

My dad goes to meet them halfway between the dunes and the water. They're slowly making their way toward us, Michael slowing his pace to match Grandmom's. He's carrying two beach chairs and stops to readjust his grip. My dad reaches them and takes the bag that Grandmom had been carrying. After a few minutes I hear my grandmom's sing-songy voice behind me.

"Oh, what a lovely day, this is my favorite time to be on the beach. Thank goodness I've finally made it down here, I'm very tired." Her black hair is windblown and fading to a brown since it hasn't been dyed in awhile and her purple-rimmed sunglasses sit slightly crooked on her face. Her white cotton pants are printed with beachy designs of seashells and ripple in the breeze. My dad unfolds a chair for her,

"Here, Mom, why don't you sit down?"

"Okay, that would be lovely," she begins to turn herself around but loses her footing on the downward slope of the sand and tumbles down face first. For a moment there's a freeze in time where none of us are fully aware of what just happened. Michael and I look at each other in disbelief, knowing that right now would be a really bad time to laugh. My dad is the first one to snap out of it, bending down to help her up. I hesitantly move to her other side and we lift her up with a hand under each arm and the other holding her hand while Michael stands awkwardly not knowing how to help.

My dad sees Michael looking lost and says, "Michael, why don't you hold the chair steady for your grandmom." He holds the back of the chair as we lower her into her seat. We're all holding our breath, not yet sure what to say or what she will say, and then she starts laughing. Her face is covered in sand from the fall, and she's laughing. We laugh with her hesitantly, unsure of how to react. "Mom, there's some sand on your face," my dad tells her.

"Oh my, there is sand on my face, isn't there?" She laughs again and pulls a paper towel and a water bottle out of her beach bag and begins dabbing at her face with the wet paper towel. The wet paper towel only makes the sand stick to her face even more, but she doesn't realize and continues to dab her face. I've never seen her so disheveled and helpless before this visit. I start to wonder what will become of the condo, which family member will take on the responsibility, or what type of people will inhabit it next. I wonder if they will rinse the seashells they find at the beach in the sink with bleach so they don't smell, like Grandmom showed us when we were kids. Before her hip surgery, she would take us on walks down the beach, where the water meets the sand and leaves shells washed up on the shore, like treasures waiting to be found. We would make our way down the beach slowly, stopping to pick up and examine each shell that caught our eye. She would tell us the name of each shell that we picked up.

"That one you have there, Michael, is a razor shell," she said, pointing to a long, thin, slightly curved, sand colored shell.

"What's this one, Grandmom?" I asked, holding a black rounded shell, perfectly intact, with ridges radiating out from the bottom.

"That's a scallop shell, my favorite. Look how beautiful this one is, what a good find."

She explained how some of the clamshells have tiny holes in them from the seagulls using their beaks to eat the flesh of an unfortunate clam. She called the pieces of shells with a million tiny holes in them moon rocks, because they looked like the cratered surface of the moon. We would collect shells until we all had full hands and then we would rinse off the extra sand in the ocean. When we returned to the condo, Grandmom would be sure not to let us play with the shells right away. She showed us how to fill the bathroom sink with warm water and add a splash of bleach. She put our shells in the sink and let them soak for ten minutes.

"You have to be patient," she would say. "You don't want smelly shells, do you?"

While waiting for what seemed like an eternity, Michael and I would get distracted with other games, like mischievously feeding the seagulls. We would steal a piece of bread from the cupboard when no one was looking and run outside on to the balcony, giggling. We would tear the soft bread into seagull bite sized pieces and throw one over the railing onto the black pavement of the parking lot below. For a few seconds the lone piece of bread would sit on the pavement, waiting for a seagull to notice it. It wouldn't take long for one to swoop down and devour it, then more would join as we threw more pieces over the railing until a whole flock would be squawking for more. Our fun would last until the piece of bread was gone or someone told us to stop, whichever came first.

After our slow trek walking Grandmom off of the beach after her fall, I've showered off the saltiness in my hair and skin and put on some dark skinny jeans and sandals and a flowy white tank top for dinner. I walk into the living room and see her sitting on the blue striped couch with nautical accent pillows, waiting for us to be showered and ready. She's treating us to dinner at our regular spot, Andre's. My dad still reminisces about the days when it was the Pizza Palace and all they served was pizza and hoagies for takeout. Now, Andre runs an overpriced Italian sit-down restaurant.

"Oh, hello, Anne. Won't you be chilly in that top? You'd better take a sweater. Look at these old pictures I found." She hands me an envelope and I take out the first picture, of Michael and I with our grandad sitting at the table eating ice cream. I look about seven years old, my short hair and bangs wild and blond from sunny days on the beach. I'm wearing a pink Minnie Mouse t-shirt from that year's trip to Disney World. I'm gripping an ice cream cone and grinning widely with ice cream dripping down my face. Michael is about four years old, dark hair and big dark eyes, he's focusing intently on his ice cream cone instead of the camera. My grandad is looking at Michael's ice cream cone too, gesturing as if he's in the middle of saying something. Maybe telling Michael to lick his ice cream before it drips.

In ten years my brother's chubby innocent hands holding the ice cream cone would grow and elongate, and one day take a blade to his own arm and cut over and over again. Slashing away the frustration and confusion. He would be careful to slip away to the bathroom without us noticing, careful to not let any blood drip onto the counter and hide the tissues he used to stop the bleeding. He would hide the cuts by wearing long sleeves in all seasons, even on the beach. One day it would be just us on the beach, and he would take off his long sleeves when I ask him if he wants to go for a walk. He would try to hold his left arm close to his body, but I would already know. He would forget, and reach down to pick up a seashell, revealing the deepest cut he's made, so deep that the healing skin is bumpy and raised. I would be crushed inside, defeated. I would ask when he did it, why he did it, if he's okay. He would shy away, back into his shell, close back up, tell me he's okay. I wouldn't ask any more questions, I would try to coax the smiling, laughing boy back out of his shell. I would look down at my feet squishing into the wet sand as I walk and wonder what happened to the little boy with the chubby hands.

Discussion Questions

- Why would somebody want to read this piece (the "Who cares?" factor)?
- Can you clearly identify the author's intention for the piece?
- How well does the author support the intention of the piece? Cite specific details that support or take away from the author's intention.
- Is there information missing from this piece that would make its intention clearer? What else would you like to know?
- Does the author portray herself as a round character? How does she do this?
- Do you trust the author of this piece? Why or why not?
- How clearly does the author establish a sense of setting/space in this piece? Cite specific details that support your claim.
- How clearly does the author establish characters other than the self in this piece? Cite specific details that support your claim.
- Did you learn anything new from reading this piece? If so, what?
- Are there particular passages with engaging language/description that stood out to you? Describe the appeal of these passages.
- Would you read more writing from this author? Why or why not?

There and Back Again: A Comic-Con Tale

Hannah Lajba

"TARDIS?! Is that you TARDIS?! I have been looking ages for you, what is your name TARDIS? Vanessa?! It's been over a hundred years and I finally know your name!!"

His first words, I almost cry with excitement at hearing the most fake British accent coming from the eleventh Doctor cosplayed by a 14–32-year-old boy (you really never know at these things). I try to catch a closer glimpse, to see the face that matches the voice, but the hoards of nerds push me through the entrance. *"I'm here, I've arrived."* Quest Log Updated.

"Making My Way Downtown" starts to play in my head as I go from fourteen to one on the elevator and I try to get into my cosplay character. I am King Thranduil of Mirkwood, son of King Oropher of Greenwood the Great (the former name of Mirkwood), and ada (father) to Prince Legolas Thranduillion (the blond elf from the *Lord of the Rings* [LOTR] movies), but you can call me Fab Thrandy. In other words, I am that elf in *The Hobbit* movies who has the long blond hair and rides an elk, but not the blond elf that shoots a bow and arrow. My brows are as thick as two caterpillars and my elven [sic] skin is flawless, it's almost as if I was wearing pounds of foundation and bronzer. My ears come to perfect points with my prosthetic attachments, and my short hair perfectly matches the explanation that I lost a bet to Lord Elrond (king of the elven [sic] realm of Rivendell, or the elf with the brown hair in *Lord of the Rings*) and in my drunken state he cut off all my long platinum locks. My beautiful silver robe is gleaming, and as I exit the elevator my face is beaming, my crown made of branches is straight, and my dress fits me like a glove. I am so ready. *"Just quickly walk past the security guard and he won't ask questions."* That is my thinking until I stop dead in my tracks as soon as I reach the door.

"It's raining??" I groan out loud to no one in particular. I should have seen this coming; it's been raining almost every weekend since I started college here in New York City. I turn to the security guard, he just stares, that plan turned out *so* well. "I'll be right back," I say before hopping back in the elevator to grab my umbrella. *"OK Hannah, just walk out, no convos."* I exit the elevator and pass the security desk, but I'm abruptly stopped.

"You going to Comic Con?" he asks. I'm surprised he knows, but then again I can totally imagine him sitting on a couch reading comic books. We begin to converse, he tells me tricks of the Con and I know now that my quest has begun. It's like in Lord of the Rings online (LOTRO, a computer game that has a virtual world even larger than World of Warcraft), he had the Flaming Ring above his head, I knew it would be bad to go in without a plan, to go into uncharted territory without any knowledge of the beasts and creatures that inhabit it, like those wretched Longbeard dwarves on the other side of the Misty Mountains…I digress. In LOTRO the Longbeards are the first foes one must face as an elf, so for my own safety, I click accept and I'm sent on my way.

Quest Log Entry One: Walk to New York Comic Con in the pouring rain. Foes lie between here and the Javits Center, be wary traveler for 8th Avenue is treacherous. Before stepping out into the wild I put in my earbuds. I quickly scroll through my phone and find all three LOTR soundtracks. Soon the sweet sounds of "Lothlorien" home to Lady Galadriel and her husband Lord Celeborn (pronounced Keleborn, this is the third elven [sic] realm in Middle Earth). I close my eyes as I make my way from 27th and 7th Ave. to 46th and 11th Ave. using my imagination to turn the buildings into trees and the sidewalks into the moss paved, winding pathways of Mirkwood. I am a king on a walk in my kingdom; all the stares are just my lovely red headed elven [sic] peasants astonished by my magnificence. The wind whips up my robe, my slit in my dress exposing my leg with each stride, I feel on top of the world, oh wait, I already am (I'm really getting into character). I keep walking for what seems like hours…wait I'm an elf, I keep walking for what seems like thousands of years (elves are immortal, to quote Thranduil, "A hundred years is a mere blink in the life of an elf…") until finally I see someone. He too has a flaming one ring above his head. I look closer to see it's Jake from *Adventure Time*, and a word bubble appears from atop his head, "Follow Me," it says, and I do.

Quest Log Entry Two: You have successfully made it to Comic Con; you get $100 coin, +2 in morale, but a -5 in confidence. Your next task is to establish panel locations and explore artists' alley. Be on the lookout for friends and foes. I am in cosplay and afraid. I really shouldn't have gone alone. Underneath my umbrella, I look up and see the five giant, inflatable teen titans, all greeting me with smiles, except Raven of course. I look around me and everyone is rushing to a bin…"*Does that say free lanyards?*" I power strut (a king never runs) to the bin and grab one. "*Would you like to equip yourself with a basic black lanyard?*" I select yes and attach my ticket/pass to it and wrap it around my wrist. First rule of quests: Always good to leave as much room as possible in your utility pack. I finally open the doors and I'm immediately met with the warmth of bodies, which actually feels nice after being in the chill of the air for so long, too bad I wasn't lucky enough to have been given one of the cloaks of Lothlorien (though paper thin, these cloaks are waterproof, warm as ten down coats, and can make you look like a rock). I take out my earbuds and close my umbrella, putting both in my utility pack. "*Which way should I go?*" I tried to find the map the security guard told me about, but no luck, they were all gone. Questing rule two: It's never safe to travel without a map, tracking skills required otherwise. Following the rule of Gandalf (The Grey wizard who is in the company of the ring, this is a reference from a scene in *The Fellowship of the Ring* when they are lost in the Mines of Moria) I followed my nose and headed toward where it smelled less like middle-aged man sweat and that took me down the White Moving Stairs of Javits (it was an escalator) to where the panels occur. The line for the Walking Dead panel had already started two hours prior to the Con, but all I was concerned about was Video Game High School (VGHS) and The Hobbit (I mean duh, I'm freakin dressed as Thranduil). Seeing that there was nowhere else to explore down here, I make my way back up the treacherous climb and there it was in front of me, my second questing location. I head straight toward the sign, staring in awe at some of the cosplays: you have your deadpools, spidermen, batmen, slutty superheroes, Bumblebee, Sailor Moons, Anime schoolgirls, shirtless Gokus, men as princesses, 1–12 Doctors, TARDISes, sexy TARDISes, the Avengers, anyone from *Game of Thrones*, and of course anyone from the *Walking Dead*. The time people have on their hands just amazes me. Of course then you have middle-aged men in way too tight fitting t-shirts…I'm just going to leave that at that.

As soon as I arrive in artist alley I see a familiar red head with a bow, and we make awkward nerd eye contact, it's sporadic and uneasy.

"Tauriel!" I say with open arms as I make my way toward her, "You're the first Hobbit person I've seen today." She smiles and replies that there has been a Thorin also…stupid dwarf princeling (elves and dwarves HATE each other, especially Thranduil and the Durin's Folk, it all dates back to the war, Thrandy not getting his precious gems, some lack of payment on both sides…all the details are lost but the hatred remains). I smile and grab a quick picture before walking the aisles of artists. Quest Log Update.

Quest Log Entry Three: You have gained +2 in conversation and +1 in morale. Explore the upper level, but be careful not to get lost in the winding maze of booths. En route with my quest I ascend to the Area Gateway, and I see him in the distance. That Pale Orc, Azog the Defiler, that very orc who killed Thror (Thorin's, the dwarf princeling's, grandfather). I strut, my exposed leg being shown to all those middle-aged men, but I don't care, I only care about *The Hobbit*. The closer I get I soon see Smaug (the dragon who live(s/d) in Erebor, the only creature to have more greed than a dwarf) with his fire eyes even mechanically blinking. I try, I try so hard to contain my excitement but I can't. I practically run to the Weta booth (New Zealand company that did everything from prosthetics to animation for *LOTR* and *The Hobbit*). Their display almost had me in tears as I examined the rock cutout of a door to Erebor (home of the Durin dwarf bloodline under the Misty Mountains, i.e. Thorin, Thrain, Thror) and Smeagol aka Gollum who was sitting quietly by himself on a rock holding his latest meal. I, in pure awe, take as many selfies and pictures I can of the props you can purchase and the miniature porcelain figurines. Once there was no one taking pictures with Gollum I swiftly moved in to capture the moment of Thrandy moving in to kiss Gollum, "*This is going on insta.*" I sadly leave the place where I felt at home to continue on with my exploration, vowing to the Valar (Middle Earth gods) that I will return to buy something. Quest Log Updated.

Quest Log Entry Four: You have successfully encircled the entire upper level, you receive a +1 in your tracking skills but a -1 in agility. Do not forget about the VGHS panel at 5 p.m., but be wary, friends may turn out to be foes, travel with caution. I'm not quite sure where I am, I've wandered deep into the comic book section, and for being at Comic Con, I really don't know much about comics. Suddenly an arrow appears on the floor in front of me instructing me on which way to go. I follow it until I come across another Flaming Ring. I strut over to get a closer look as another word bubble pops up, "Free Lip Makeover and Goodie Bag. Do you choose to accept?" "*Did I read free?*" I quickly click accept and get into line, a copper lip will be the perfect finishing touch to my cosplay. While waiting I insta my Gollum picture, minding my own business when suddenly, out of nowhere, I hear the second fake British accent of the day.

"Excuse me my Lord, but I believe your ear is coming off."

I turn around and look down to see non other than a stereotypical member of the Slytherin House (doubt this needs a footnote, but *Harry Potter*) with a tree branch for a wand.

"Oh, thank you, yeah they're just not made for my ears, but they're definitely stuck on," I smile and turn back around…"*Is this supposed to be my friend?*" She speaks again, any English person would be appalled, and I answer back…regretfully.

It has been two and a half hours and I'm still stuck with her, at least she's dropped the accent, but she insists on holding my hand as we walk so I seem more "royal." I have been dragged around to all these booths and at my current age estimation how is a fourteen-year-old girl allowed to buy throwing knives? I look to the ground and see that my quest arrow is pointing the other direction. "*How am I going to get out of this?*" I already tried once with the whole bathroom thing, but she waited for me. I look at my phone and see that it's almost three o'clock. We line up for her to get her book signed, but I can't even go in because I didn't pre-purchase a ticket. This is my chance…"*don't screw it up now,*" Hey, I realized I want to get that poster from the Weta booth. I'll go and then meet you back here when you're done."

She smiles and says ok, and I'm off, trying my hardest not to look like I'm running. "*I'm free precious, FREEEEEE!!!*" I've now returned to my strut, gliding across the red carpeted floor to claim my Tolkien prize (get it, token…Tolkien…). I arrive at the booth and wait in line, why get a poster when I can get a replica of the Key to Erebor…or is it the real key…definitely the real deal. I finally make it to the counter and I'm met with the beautifully charming, real, New Zealand accent of the woman, wife to the head of Weta.

"Can I get a picture of you?" she asks and I, of course, agree, then as if it was written in the stars the other worker, who I've seen on the over eighteen hours of extended *LOTR* footage, says, "Let me get Thranduil's staff out for you to hold."

Reader, I don't know if you will ever understand what this moment means to me. I shakily extend my hand out to grip the staff, "*this feels so right.*" I can't stop smiling, it's so out of character but I don't care, I physically and mentally can't care, I'm holding the Staff of Thranduil, THE STAFF, I'M HOLDING HIS STAFF!! I quickly give my phone to the first lady who offered to take my picture. It turns into a mini photo shoot with all the con goers taking my picture. By this point I'm hyperventilating, I can feel my heart beating out of my chest, I think I'm going to puke rainbows. I finally let go, a smile still on my face as I leave the booth after thanking the patrons for the hundredth time. "*I'm here, this is my con.*" I put my key in my utility pack, Quest Log Updated.

Quest Log Entry Five: You have received a +10 in morale, a +9 in confidence, and a -2 in agility. Your day is halfway over, explore more booths (Star Trek and anything with plushies) and get in the panel line for VGHS (which I end up not getting in to, long story, but if you've ever read A-Relief, it relates to that) and then get in line for The Hobbit: Battle of Five Armies Panel. (For a guaranteed spot, I go in two panels ahead of time to secure my seat in the second row. I know so many spoilers reader, who dies, when they die, how they die, it's great.) After panels, successfully make your way back to your dorm, be wary of foes, for the paths are not safe at night, don't follow the lights.

Congratulations, you have completed Quest: First Comic Con. Your rewards: one Star Trek t-shirt dress, one cute pin, one free bag and lanyard, one iron on patch, three free stickers, one Key to Erebor, multiple cute pictures, and many compliments. I sadly click the log off button, "Are you sure you want to quit?" I sadly click yes and close my eyes. "*And she lived happily ever after, for the rest of her days.*"

Discussion Questions

- Why would somebody want to read this piece (the "Who cares?" factor)?
- Can you clearly identify the author's intention for the piece?
- How well does the author support the intention of the piece? Cite specific details that support or take away from the author's intention.
- Is there information missing from this piece that would make its intention clearer? What else would you like to know?

- Does the author portray herself as a round character? How does she do this?
- Do you trust the author of this piece? Why or why not?
- How clearly does the author establish a sense of setting/space in this piece? Cite specific details that support your claim.
- How clearly does the author establish characters other than the self in this piece? Cite specific details that support your claim.
- Did you learn anything new from reading this piece? If so, what?
- Are there particular passages with engaging language/description that stood out to you? Describe the appeal of these passages.
- Would you read more writing from this author? Why or why not?

Sundays
Jillian McDonnell

"Jillian, let's go. Time for church." For years those were my Sundays. Wake up later than expected, hop out of bed, throw together an outfit clad in a sweater and dress pants, shove a granola bar in my mouth and go. Always show up late, run in and sit next to Baba, and let the hour begin. An hour of mass weekly was not only a part of my routine, but my family's. St. Nicholas of Myra Byzantine Catholic Church was built in 1892, and my great great grandpa helped build it. Our family line had stayed there through the turn of the century. My great grandmother was raised in the church, as well as my Baba, my mom and aunt, then all the way down to my sisters and me.

The church was old, very old. It was beautiful, with icons lining the walls telling different biblical stories. Detail was found in every nook and cranny of the church. From the pew ends with wood carvings to each and every pillar lined and curved. My favorite was the ornate glass windows. There were about twenty windows. Each window had the same pattern with different colors and names. A window dedicated to every man who helped build the church. That was why we sat in the row three up from the back every week, no exceptions. That was the row that stood next to the glass window with the name JOHN YURINA FAMILY. The family name on my Baba's side. Despite all of the detail and beauty in each of the carvings or the icons or the windows, there was damage. Time had done its part. If you looked past the wall trimming in teal and brown paint the wall itself was chipping. If you looked past the windows and followed up to the ceiling, large masses like tumors formed due to water that the roof could no longer keep away. The church was beautiful, yes, but was also so hurt and damaged, in constant need of repair. But for the remaining twenty to thirty people it held during my generation's time it was still just as beloved. Just as loved as when it was full and jam packed, with aisles filled with fold out seats because it could not hold everyone. Though numbers had dwindled as the years passed it was just as loved for, and I loved it too.

I had loved the church, but only the building. As we shuffled in each Sunday all I thought about was what I was doing next. Assignments due in school, friends I would see in the upcoming hours, when I could check my phone again, everything but what I should have been thinking about. Every time I was caught stuck in my own daydreams I got a squeeze of the hand.

"Jillian Mary, *stop*." We would go through the hour's routine. Pray, sing, sit, stand, Communion, kneel, sit, stand, and out we would go. We would leave and I wouldn't think about church again until the next Saturday when I was reminded to go to bed early once again. Despite my inability to sit still or focus in church, I was proud to tell anyone who asked what I practiced. Kids who would run off to CCD (Confraternity of Christian Doctrine) for the Roman Catholic Church every week would give me a confused look when I would say, "Yes, I am Catholic," and, "Yes, I was confirmed as a baby." Byzantine Catholicism is a religion that derived from Orthodox Christianity. A group of priests from the Orthodox broke off and swore their allegiance to the pope, a tradition the Orthodox had abandoned. So while we still had almost exactly the same beliefs as Roman Catholics, I took pride in our deep traditional roots to Eastern Europe and always enjoyed it when a kid in school would look at me with complete confidence and say, "You're not Catholic."

There was not just one building to my church. Right next to our church was the carriage house.

The "reception hall" for holidays and luncheons. That's when we would be excited to go to church, or better yet, get out of church. Because following church would be the *best food ever*. Etta and Martha were the two Hungarian ladies in a parish of Slovaks. Rather than hide among the crowd, they shone and brought their food to the top. It was the most desired. They were truly the best chefs around. While we all sat in church, the two Hungarian sisters went to town and finished cooking the great feast they had begun preparing weeks in advance. We would get to the hall, sit in our assigned seats (usually with a temporary frown because one of our names was always spelled wrong) and we would wait. With forks in our hands and nothing in our stomachs, we would sit patiently and then not so patiently.

"Can we please help them? It'll bring the soup out faster."

With a reply from Baba, "Don't be foolish. Sit down and put your napkin on your lap and quit shaking your leg!" But alas the first course had arrived. Three carts rolled out from the kitchen, each with soup on their trays. This was not a "save the best for last" type of meal, because the best was certainly served first. With broth so warm and perfectly salty with noodles cut by the Hungarian sisters' hands, the soup was the best part. You always filled up with two or three bowls, as many as you could get your hands on. But it would finish and the next course would come. Chicken, pork, mashed potatoes, and cabbage all lined the tables and were eaten just as quickly as the soup. Then dessert would arrive. The lightest yet sweetest Krezchiki: a fried dough with powdered sugar sprinkled on top, it would melt in your mouth or break in your hands because it was so thin yet so delicately scrumptious. But food was only a small part of the festivities. By the time my sisters and I were born, we were one of maybe two or three families with kids in the parish. That was compared to the dozens of kids my grandma and mom had when they were our age. So with no one to really entertain us, we turned to entertain ourselves. We would explore for as long as we could in between courses or in between announcements, try to get our feet onto as many new places as we could. Each time would be a new discovery. Once we found an upstairs with an old map falling off the wall. There was a desk but the rest was empty. We took it as our own and sat on the dusty floor with cards in our hands. Another day we found an old bar. Yes, the church had had its own bar for social events. We would climb up behind it now and giggle as we ordered our cosmos and Old Fashioneds. These were measly findings compared to what we found one day. After climbing the bar and playing our cards we wanted to see more. So we kept looking. From this room to that closet, we left nothing unturned and nothing untouched.

And then, gasp, "No way, guys check this out."

We had found a bowling alley. Not only did our church have a barren room with a map falling off the wall and a parlor with a bar inside, but a bowling alley. Just one single lane, but just as official as one at Lucky Strike or Homefield Bowl. It was a lane just as nice, or better yet, it had been. I looked at the alley and got mad and ran upstairs. "Baba how could you let a bowling alley get so…*ruined*?! We come here every Sunday and you never thought to tell us there was a bowling alley!?" I could not believe that this small church with all of its little treasures had this truly *awesome* treasure, and they had let it run itself into the ground. Like time's toll on the church itself, the alley was completely unusable, boards coming up, and probably not turned on in decades.

"We used to use it at coffee socials like this Jillian, but who can play now? You, Jenna and Jolie? That's it. There's no one else to play on it so there's no use in keeping it up." I knew she was right.

This was why the church was run down too. Of course the oldest things anywhere can be kept nice, look at museums with pristine artifacts dating from centuries before us. But museums had a leg up, they had money. With a diminishing parish almost all over eighty now and priests who had lost the will to bring members in, the parish was decreasing by the day. With each parish member's wake I attended as a little girl, there was no one to refill their seat. As one left, no one returned, and the numbers went down and down and down. I look at pictures of the church in black and white and see the carriage house jam packed. Tables so close together I don't understand how anyone got into their seat. But now we are small. Tables filled at these luncheons only by family members forced into eating with us, a measly attempt to look united again. But I don't know these people like Baba knew her parish. Her parish was her family, mine is just a group of eighty year olds, those who either tell me I'm an "Adorable little one" or yell at me to, "Stop touching that. Don't play with that!" Awkward encounters with people that I don't know as well as I should. As well as Baba knew her parish, friends she holds dear to her heart now, I don't have that. Baba's best friend today was her best friend when she was four, and now when her grandkids come and we see a desperation in their eyes for us to be friends. There is nothing, nothing to really talk about other than answering our parents' questions of, "So how's school going?" It's forced. A lot of it's forced. Yes, there are some members of this church that I do consider family, those like second sets of grandparents. So when we have lost them I feel like I've lost a grandma or a grandpa. Mrs. Lash whose wake that I attended I had cried at because I was scared for Mr. Lash, who died a few years later. Mr. Russo whose cross I still wear, it's my favorite. I get close to some but not many. The Hungarian sisters or the Valkos, but still it's not the same as Baba. My church family is quite different than hers, I won't have mine when I'm the eighty year old in my parish.

"Baba who are those people?" I whispered one day at mass.

"Hush we'll talk about it later." So I kept turning my head and looking every so often, quite curious. Like I said, we don't get new members, and if we do they're usually another elderly couple in New York on vacation thinking that it's a Roman Catholic Church. But when we do, they don't look like these two. One in a pastor's uniform with a white band on the collar sitting next to a friend or something, but they're young, really young. So I wait until we process out of the doors, wait for mom to throw her shoes back on after another successful cantoring and look at Baba again, waiting for an answer.

She sighs, "They're looking to buy the church."

Then I think out loud, "Why would anyone want a church that isn't theirs? Are they even Byzantine?" I shouldn't keep pushing questions but I do. "No, we think they're Baptist, but Father Hospidar refuses to tell anyone." And then, like the bowling alley, I'm mad again. I don't get how these strangers feel okay coming and taking this church from me, it's *mine*. It's my family's, I'm a part of the JOHN YURINA FAMILY remember? And what are they going to do when they have a mass? Ignore the three bar crosses and the icons, accept the details in the wall and the benches but not understand how old they are, or how I looked at it for an hour every week? It's not fair this is our church. Yes I'm not as close as Baba is but I'm there, I still like seeing all the old ladies shuffle out of church and touch my mom's shoulder to tell her she has the voice of an angel. I like to run gifts around at coffee socials. I like seeing the cats because I see the same three every time. And it's *beautiful*. My church is truly beautiful. I get it, it's old and needs a lot of repairs that we can't afford but what are these new people going to do? I'm sure any repairs they can afford will involve tearing down beautiful wall details and icons, and I bet when they clean up the empty room we played cards in they'll throw out the map that hangs itself up with only three corners.

As upset as I am, Baba's heartbroken. She tries everything. Petitions and e-mails to the Bishop but they do not do anything. It's simple, we can't afford repairs and these people can. We can put money into the more lucrative church at White Plains. So that's it, there's nothing we can do. So she does the next best thing, and calls the local news to come on our last Sunday. I sit in the church that day with two buttons. Two big red buttons. This was when I was in my button phase. I sewed them onto bags and wore them on my neck so I thought, what better way to leave my mark here than to hide a button somewhere that no one can find it. I hold both in my pocket the whole mass shifting the two in my thumb and forefinger. Usually I squirm and wiggle, make one bathroom trip too many anxiously waiting to leave and go back home, but not that Sunday. That Sunday I dreaded every turn of the page of the hymn book and every step up to receive communion. And as my mom sings the last song to close the mass, Baba's eyes well up with tears. I look up and mom closes her book and puts on her shoes, that's it. It's over. Baba whips out a camera trying to capture everything she can, then insists on a picture of my sister's and me at the JOHN YURINA FAMILY window. But it doesn't work, the camera's not working well with the light.

"Why can't we take the window Baba? They don't even know who John Yurina is!"

"Uncle John wanted to but I said no."

"Really why wouldn't you let him it's his grandpa too-"

"That's enough Jillian let's go." I hold my buttons as we walk away. Baba's holding a tissue in one hand, holding my hand in the other, and I hold the buttons in my other hand as my eyes search frantically to stash the button. And then, I just stop. I turn back around and look into my church and then I quickly turn and walk out. What's a button going to do, either I'm here or I'm not. We go out and Baba gets interviewed by the news reporter. I hug Baba tight after the interview and then we drive away, drive away from the little church on Ash Street. St. Nicholas Byzantine Catholic Church, 1892-2012.

Discussion Questions

- Why would somebody want to read this piece (the "Who cares?" factor)?
- Can you clearly identify the author's intention for the piece?
- How well does the author support the intention of the piece? Cite specific details that support or take away from the author's intention.
- Is there information missing from this piece that would make its intention clearer? What else would you like to know?
- Does the author portray herself as a round character? How does she do this?
- Do you trust the author of this piece? Why or why not?
- How clearly does the author establish a sense of setting/space in this piece? Cite specific details that support your claim.
- How clearly does the author establish characters other than the self in this piece? Cite specific details that support your claim.
- Did you learn anything new from reading this piece? If so, what?
- Are there particular passages with engaging language/description that stood out to you? Describe the appeal of these passages.
- Would you read more writing from this author? Why or why not?

Family Ties

Zachary Volosky

I buttoned the last button on my sea-foam green shirt. Luckily for me, it was one of the shirts that my grandmother had ironed the night before. It was a little too tight around my shoulders and about two inches too short to stay tucked into my pants, but it was good enough for school, plus, it matched perfectly with the blue and green tie that was draped around my shoulders. I opened my closet to grab the light blue pair of pants that went so well with the rest of the outfit. I stepped out of my closet as a knock sounded from the other side of the door. I knew it was either my brother or my mom, so I didn't care that I wasn't wearing pants.

"Yeah?" I answered.

My mother opened the door enough for her to respect my privacy but still enough that I could see her face. Her eyes were puffy and her voice was soft, exactly how she was every morning after she just got up.

"Can I come in?" She spoke in a quiet tone filled with grogginess.

I decided to tease her a bit because she was never that polite about coming into my room when I was only in my boxers.

I mimicked her drowsy voice, "No, no, no. You cannot come in." I smiled at my own silliness as my mom came in anyway.

She looked up at me and my smile instantly fled. She wasn't groggy. She wasn't drowsy. She had been crying.

"Grandma died last night," she choked.

My first reaction was to hug and comfort my mom. I knew how close she was to her mother. We were all close to her. She lived next-door to us, so around eleven o'clock every day she would shuffle down the sidewalk in her little slippers and quietly walk into our house. When I say little slippers, I mean *little* slippers.

The woman was five-foot-two and barely a hundred pounds. Every evening at dinner she would yell at my father for how much food he would put on her plate when she asked for a spoonful of potatoes, or carrots, or peas. Truthfully, the helpings were barely large enough to fill me up when I was nine. She had your stereotypical short, white grandma-hair and a thin pair of glasses that she was always afraid of losing but never did. After she would shuffle her way to our house, she would put on her headphones and turn on the AM radio that she kept in her pocket so that she could listen to the local news station while she did our chores. She would empty our dishwasher, fold and put away our laundry, and then sweep the kitchen floor. She would even leave five dollar bills on my dresser for me to find after she left for the night. I never thanked her for those.

I held my mom for a brief minute or two and then come to the sudden realization that she wasn't crying. She wasn't the one that needed comforted, I was. The minute I realized this I started to sob uncontrollably.

"I saw her last night," were the only words that I could manage to say.

I got home from practice the night before in the usual bitter mood. When you're on a rowing team in March, things aren't exactly at their best. Practice would be from 5:30 until 8:00 in temperatures that are forty-five degrees or below, so when practice ends it's already dark and cold and, because it takes almost an hour to get home, when I finally did it would be darker and colder. So now, because it's 8:30, I have less than an hour and a half to eat, shower, do two hours' worth of homework, and get ready for practice the next day because getting your daily eight and a half is the only way I would survive school tomorrow. This was especially frustrating because I never had time to iron the balled-up dress shirts that came out of my gym bag earlier that week. Time and time again, my grandma would offer to do it, but I always refused because it wasn't her responsibility. I should have to take care of myself.

Anyway, like any other night, I came home and burst through the door, bitter and crabby. After I closed the door, dropped my bags, and began to plan the rest of the night, the door behind me opened and a little woman in slippers holding eighteen freshly ironed shirts was standing there looking up at me with a tiny grin on her face.

My grandmother laughed her usual raspy, lung-congested laugh and said, "I ironed all of them for you so you wouldn't have to worry."

I smiled, thanked her quickly, and took the shirts. Truthfully, I only wore about four of those eighteen shirts, but I still appreciated the thought. A gesture like this was so typical of her, I really didn't think twice about it. She came in and chatted with my mom in the kitchen over a glass of wine while I ran around upstairs trying to get my work done so I could get to sleep on time.

Five hours later the blood vessels in her lungs ruptured from the pressure of the mucus and sputum that was built up in her airways due to an illness called bronchiectasis. Her right lung began to fill with blood and no matter how much of it she coughed up, the blood continued to fill the lung until she became asphyxiated and slowly but painfully stopped breathing. Six hours after that, I would learn all of it before I put pants on.

I became painfully aware that I was standing in the middle of my room holding my mom and sobbing while wearing nothing but a shirt and underwear. It occurred to me how ridiculous I looked.

Trying to choke back tears so that I could talk normally I said, "I'm going to put pants on."

"Okay," my mom replied. "Are you going to be okay?"

"Yeah, I'm okay," I answered. I wasn't.

I finally put on my pants and continued my morning routine because it was the only thing that I knew how to do. When I came downstairs to eat breakfast, my mom informed me that she had arranged for me to come into school late. Any high school sophomore would jump at the chance to miss a little bit of their school day. I wasn't exactly jumping.

I got to school during my second period. I sat in the art room and drew the same line over and over again, erasing it just to draw it again. When I went to Chemistry the following period, I was relieved to remember that the kid who sat in front of me was twice my size in both directions so it was virtually impossible to see me behind him. The teacher usually forgot I was there. Just when I was about to get into a comfortable and hidden position to fall asleep and forget for a while, a student with a note from our Assistant Principal's office came in looking for me. I was being called to the principal's office. I was never called to the principal's office.

When I got to the office, I walked in and saw our vice-principal, Mr. Bernot, a tall bald-headed man (or did he shave his head purposely?) who had a passion for following the rules. If you followed the rules, you were always good in his book. I was also surprised to see my brother sitting in one of the two chairs in front of the desk. He looked about as gleeful as I did. The person that surprised me even more was standing behind our principal: Dr. Petrone, the school's therapist. I suddenly knew why I had been called into the office that day.

"Have a seat Mr. Volosky." Mr. Bernot motioned toward the only empty chair in front of his desk. I sat down next to my brother who half-grinned at me as I rested in the chair. "Now, I don't know if you gentleman are familiar with Dr. Petrone, but he is part of our support services here at Central Catholic." Mr. Bernot motioned to Dr. Petrone as he stepped forward and sat on the front corner of the desk. He looked exactly how one would think a psychologist looks. He was balding (definitely no shaving there), he wore thick black glasses, and had an impressive assortment of sweater-vests.

"Now boys," Dr. Petrone started, "I understand that you guys had a loss in the family recently. Your grandmother?"

My brother and I nodded in unison. The air of the room suddenly felt awkward and I could tell that my brother felt it too.

"Was it unexpected?" Mr. Bernot asked.

I looked at my brother to see who would answer. He stared back blankly and I could tell that it was going to be me.

"Yeah, we saw her last night."

"Wow…" the two adults replied, both trailing off. There was an uncomfortable beat.

Dr. Petrone picked it back up, "You boys should know that Central Catholic has many resources that we offer to students who need help in times that their lives become complicated. Please don't be afraid to come talk to me whenever you need some extra help or if you just want to say 'hi.'"

Dr. Petrone seemed like a remarkably nice guy. He always had a content smile on his face and the students who knew him never hesitated to say "hi" when they saw him in the hallway, whether they were walking past him or heading up a stairwell and saw him far below on another landing. I wanted to be that friendly with him but not now. Not under those circumstances.

My brother and I both said "thank you" to Dr. Petrone's offer and were excused. We stepped outside the office.

"That was weird," my brother said, trying to force out a chuckle.

"Yeah, really," I replied, faking a smile. We both stood there and looked at each other for an uncomfortable minute. Before we went our separate ways back to class, I gave him a pat on the shoulder for one reason or another. Maybe it helped him, or maybe I wanted to feel like it helped him.

When the final bell rang that day, I picked through my locker and got whatever I needed to get out of school as quickly as possible. I don't know why I was rushing home. I didn't want to be home because I knew that she wouldn't be there. I closed my eyes and slept the entire way to my house.

My brother and I didn't say a word when we got home. My dad was sitting in his armchair when we walked in. I had never seen him cry but I could tell that he had been. The television was off and he was just staring forward. He stood up when we walked in and hugged us as we entered. Displaying emotions with my father was always an uncomfortable experience, but I knew that this is what families did when an important member passes. He smelt of his usual musk of Brylcreem and beer. His embrace was so warm and comforting that I wanted to let out the tears I had been holding in all day. When I remembered that this embrace was with my father, I became uncomfortable again and held the tears in.

"I love you guys," he said in my ear.

"Um. I love you too, Dad." The sentence came out awkwardly, and I cringed at my inability to show affection toward my father. After he let go, I slowly went up to my room where I spent the rest of the night failing to distract myself from what was happening downstairs.

I knew that my mom was on the phone with either her brothers or her aunts or any of the number of people that you call when you are organizing a funeral. Unfortunately, the planning was thrown upon her because she was the closest to my grandma. She was the youngest of four kids and the only girl. One brother, my Uncle Bill, was a police officer who lived about half an hour away, and another brother, Dan, lived in Illinois. They would both be knocking at our door in the next couple of days. Her third brother would not.

When I was about eight years old, I used to sit on the first step of the stairway to the second floor of my grandmother's house. I would doodle on a yellow legal pad that my grandma would keep in the same place for me when I felt like drawing. I used to sit there for hours trying to draw superheroes over and over again.

Every now and then, she would come and check on what I was drawing and say, "You're just like your Uncle Tony. He loved to draw. He was such a good boy." My mom always got quiet and changed the subject when she would say that to me.

That night, I heard the phone ring and my mother's groggy voice answer it. She didn't know that I was still awake because she stood outside my bedroom door and had the volume on the phone loud enough that I was able to make out the whole conversation.

"Hello?"

"Joanne?" the voice asked.

"Who is this?"

"It's Tony," the voice replied

"Who?" my mom asked, both confused and frustrated.

"Tony…," he repeated. "Your brother."

"Oh." I expected my mom to say something after this but she was silent.

"I heard about mom," Tony said. "I just wanted to say that I'm sorry."

"Okay," my mom said. Still nothing more than a word.

"I won't be able to make it to the funeral. I'm sorry. I have to go now though. Goodbye, Joanne." Tony rushed out these last words because I think he could feel my mother already growing weary of the conversation. He was right. Without saying another word, I heard the electronic beep of the phone hanging up and my mom slamming it down on the charging dock.

My mother hadn't the faintest idea that I heard the whole thing. After she went downstairs, I closed my bedroom door and sat on the floor, leaning up against the side of my bed with a blanket my grandma had made for me wrapped around my shoulders. I sat there for a while, crying and cursing God. He never said anything back.

Through my teary eyes, I noticed my alarm clock turn from 11:59 to 12:00. That miserable day had ended but I didn't feel any better. I actually felt worse. Not because it was the first of many days without my grandmother, but because right then I remembered that it was her birthday.

Discussion Questions

- Why would somebody want to read this piece (the "Who cares?" factor)?
- Can you clearly identify the author's intention for the piece?
- How well does the author support the intention of the piece? Cite specific details that support or take away from the author's intention.
- Is there information missing from this piece that would make its intention clearer? What else would you like to know?
- Does the author portray herself as a round character? How does she do this?
- Do you trust the author of this piece? Why or why not?
- How clearly does the author establish a sense of setting/space in this piece? Cite specific details that support your claim.
- How clearly does the author establish characters other than the self in this piece? Cite specific details that support your claim.
- Did you learn anything new from reading this piece? If so, what?
- Are there particular passages with engaging language/description that stood out to you? Describe the appeal of these passages.
- Would you read more writing from this author? Why or why not?

Focus

Erika Veurink

"This summer, instead of getting a job, I want you to focus on basketball."

I looked up at my dad, my best friend, my coach for many years, and my biggest fan since forever. He towered over me at six feet and five inches. His hands were raised in expression. Large, swollen knuckles from decades of gripping spheres of leather moved expressively as he spoke. When he talked about basketball, his eyes grew a darker shade of blue and the corners of his mouth turned in ever so slightly. I don't remember him being any happier than when I ran off the court after my first game on Varsity freshman year, embracing him with my sweat covered body as I hear him whisper, "I'm so proud of you, Erika." He would recall his teammates of past like familiar friends. He talked of winning the state championship as a senior or the Duke Men's Tournament with clarity and enthusiasm. I loved the way he spoke about basketball. I loved the way basketball made him light up. But I could never feel the same way.

"Do you play basketball?" When I committed upwards of twenty-five hours a week to the sport, I took pride in this question.

I would always answer with a, "Ya, big surprise, I do." Basketball became an expectation when I was the tallest kid in my kindergarten class. Or maybe it was when I smiled innocently at the blinding bulbs of studio lights as my first baby pictures were taken with me holding a plush basketball. But maybe it was even before that, when my mom, the quiet freshman volleyball player, fell for the star-studded basketball player in college.

I shift uncomfortably in my seat. A montage of endless nights out back shooting free throws until I made ten in a row and early morning drives to the gym suddenly overwhelm me. I smile weakly at my dad and nod. He pulls dramatically from behind his large back a poster board. Drawn across it are rows and columns each belonging to a unique basketball drill. My eyes enlarge and I look up in confusion. He explains that it's just a guide to help me "work on my game." I know he means well. He means better than well, in fact. He means to help me guarantee a starting position on Varsity next season. He and I know that if this happens, I'll get the attention of the coaches. By junior year they'll come flocking to my tournaments with scholarship offers in hand. Then we'll all be able to say it was worth it, when I too shine on the court and dribble, pass, and shoot my way through college.

I take the poster from him, overwhelmed, and agree to do my best. I wasn't scared of my dad. I was scared of playing the sport I hated for at least the next eight years. It felt like a prison sentence.

From its designated place in the laundry room, I grabbed my basketball. Worn, soft, and extra bouncy. I remembered picking it out from the variety of options with my dad a few years earlier.

"You can take them out of the package and try them out, Erika," he spoke knowledgeably as he popped one out and tossed it to me.

I caught it, examined it, and threw it back, "I don't like the color."

He laughed and rolled his eyes, the same way I do, and reached for a higher shelf, the same way I reached for rebounds, extending from my hips, lifting my long arms with purpose. The next ball came as a surprise and I hardly caught it. It felt comfortable as I transferred it from one hand to the other. I smiled and dad smiled back. He pulled his faded leather wallet from his Saturday jeans and "invested in my future."

"You made Kingdom Hoops? Erika, do you know how many scouts are at those tournaments?"

I nodded as my homely, information driven, semi-close friend, Renee, listed off NBA and Division One players who played for the team in high school. I was shocked to have made the team after an informal tryout late in the season. I thought that maybe if I didn't get selected, it would be a sign and I would quit once and for all. But mom got the call and called dad at work and we all went out for dinner. They were proud of me. I sat on the edge of my bed just moments before leaving for my first practice on the team. I bent over and ran my fingers over the Nike symbol on my brand new shoes. I laced them, slowly and tightly. I sighed, hoping to clear the butterflies. I pulled my hair back tightly, too tightly, and snapped the rubber band. I nervously sifted through my drawer looking for a replacement. I smoothed my t-shirt into my new shorts and headed up the stairs, basketball in hand.

The drive to the facility dragged by as my mother spoke, her words mute to me. I imagined all the possible drills. In my head, I ran through pieces of advice my dad and I talked over the night before. In my bag I found a note Ashley had drawn of me dunking over what looked like my entire team. I read, "I know you'll do so well. Love you! Ash."

"Do you want me to come in or just drop you off?"

I scoffed and laughed nervously as I lied with a simple, "No Mom, I'm fine." I walked to stairs to the gym focused and brave. The smell of sweat hit me as I opened the door. The sound of shoes squeaking and whistles blowing and plays being called and coaches swearing filled my ears. I froze. At that point I didn't hate basketball, I was terrified of it.

Three minutes into practice we were both running lines for a "lack of hustle." My coach lectured us as we ran back and forth base line to base line. Our eyes darted to each other in silent moments of encouragement. Finally, we heard, "start the drill over." We each moved to our spots, panting, but grateful to be finished. At water breaks I would sit on the floor chugging water, too tired to socialize. Counting down each minute, slowly as the numbers changed on the scoreboard I endured the first practice at Kingdom Hoops.

"It was good. Really good coaching," I would remark to my parents. They seemed happy, so naturally I thought I should feel the same. The practices didn't get easier, but I got tougher. I learned how to turn off emotion when doing wall sits for three minutes or running sprints by myself in front of the entire team. I learned to nod when my coach asked me if I really wanted this, if I really wanted to be a college player. I learned plays and would record them in my homemade playbook right after getting out of practice and review them at night in fear of messing up.

This fear of failure dragged me through that season. I would come home from an evening of first my high school practice and then my Kingdom Hoops practice and fall asleep the moment my sore muscles slammed against my bed. I would come home early on Friday nights in order to prepare for Saturdays filled with tournaments and team dinners. I remember the exhaustion that followed a day full of running up and down and across a court vividly. I can recall the achy pain after landing on my feet thousands of times after gathering all my strength to block a shot or grab a rebound.

But I can also remember my dad, sitting on the third row of the bleachers, hands propping up his head in concentration. The way his eyes darted with my movements on the court, analyzing my reactions in order to create a game plan for improvement for the next game. I can so easily remember the way he would smirk and shake his head, as if to say, "Well done," when I would block a shot and turn to look back at him.

After a weekend of two tournaments in a row, both out of state, I remember dragging my bag across the carpet into my room and collapsing on the floor. Shoes laced, ankle braces tight, jersey reeking of sweat, I cried. I cried deeply and for a long time. I cried because I knew I hated it. I couldn't deny the fear it stirred up in me, or the constant feeling of pressure every time I stepped on to the court. I was tired of fitting expectations bestowed upon me and just plain tired. My body and soul ached. As I cried, alone, pathetic, and ashamed, the dread filled me, the dread of destroying the dream my father had for me the moment the doctor mentioned my unusual height moments after my welcome into this world.

I angrily zipped open my bag and, through my tear filled eyes, saw my playbook. I ripped out the last page, turned it over and wrote. In rage I blamed my dad for everything. Lines came and paragraphs followed until the entire page was filled. I read it to myself over and over. I read it out loudly. I stood up and paced my room reading it. I opened my bedroom door with momentum, convicted and ready to speak my mind and then stopped. Scenes of my dad lifting me on his shoulders to slam the rubber ball into my five-foot hoop at a young age faded into view. Late nights throwing shots from half court and screaming in celebration when one of us made it followed. Scenes from our trip to the NBA stores in New York ushered in remembrances of the tears of joy I saw out of the corner of my eye when we leaped in celebration as Duke won the National Championship in Indianapolis. Slowly, quietly, and purposefully, I stepped back from the door. I sat on the edge of my bed, holding the note. I folded it once, twice, three times. I pulled out the faded shoebox from under my bed. I slid it in. I sat back up. I wiped the tears from my eyes and slowly unlaced my dirty, worn shoes. I slipped each brace off with caution. I didn't bother with the jersey; a sort of comfort came from being in it. I lifted my legs to the edge of my bed and I slept. I endured the rest of that season. I listened to lectures from my dad about how I didn't show enough passion or drive on the court. I decided that my relationship with him was more important than my relationship to basketball. I played basketball for the college offers, for the strangers that insisted on asking me if I did, for my terrifying coach, for my younger brother, in his matching jersey, but more than anything else, I played basketball for my dad.

Discussion Questions

- Why would somebody want to read this piece (the "Who cares?" factor)?
- Can you clearly identify the author's intention for the piece?
- How well does the author support the intention of the piece? Cite specific details that support or take away from the author's intention.
- Is there information missing from this piece that would make its intention clearer? What else would you like to know?
- Does the author portray herself as a round character? How does she do this?

- Do you trust the author of this piece? Why or why not?
- How clearly does the author establish a sense of setting/space in this piece? Cite specific details that support your claim.
- How clearly does the author establish characters other than the self in this piece? Cite specific details that support your claim.
- Did you learn anything new from reading this piece? If so, what?
- Are there particular passages with engaging language/description that stood out to you? Describe the appeal of these passages.
- Would you read more writing from this author? Why or why not?

The Autoethnography: Ten Examples

Instructions

Choosing a Topic

For our final project for the class, you will be asked to select a subculture that you have currently chosen to be a part of or one that you will choose to connect yourself to and to investigate this subculture in a larger research paper called an autoethnography.

For this immediate assignment, I would like you to identify two subcultures that you are currently a part of and that you would find interesting to research. For each of the subcultures you identify, I would like you to give a brief description (three to four lines or more if necessary) that gives an overview of what the subculture is and your position in the subculture (how long you've been a part of it and how you feel about it).

From these two options, you will be choosing a topic for your final research paper. We will be sharing these ideas with the entire class. Please be as specific as possible. Your topics must fulfill the following criteria:

You must be able to do background and preliminary research on your topics. In other words, written and visual material must be readily available for analysis.

Topics must be local and accessible.

There must be a place, field site, or event space for the topic that you will be able to visit at least twice during the semester.

There must be at least two people you can interview who have different roles relevant to the topic.

Topics must be new and cannot overlap with research topics in any other course work.

Interviewing

The purpose of the interview is to help you gain insight into the perspective of another member of your subculture. This can be valuable on a number of levels and for a number of reasons. It can help you understand the subculture more as an outsider, offer additional information you can use to examine your own positionality, and provide interesting narrative content for the final project.

As you plan for your interview, consider what information you would like to get out of the interview, and write out your questions accordingly.

For this assignment, write up a minimum of ten questions you plan to ask your interviewee. Make sure the questions are in an order that is logical. This will allow you to know what you intend to get out of an interview and enable you to adapt when an interviewee inadvertently answers more than one question at a time or shares information you would like to ask about in greater depth.

Make sure you ask leading questions rather than questions that can be answered with one-word responses. It is helpful to incorporate phrases such as these into your interview questions: "Tell me a story about the time…"; "Can you explain in detail when…"; "Describe your favorite memory about . . "; "At length, describe…."

This kind of questioning will help your interviewee to feel comfortable and willing to share more information about which you can then ask follow-up questions.

Interviews can be conducted in various ways: through online chats, via telephone or in person. Each method has its own plusses and minuses, so be aware that they will yield different products.

In-person interviews are usually the most productive in that they allow you to take notes on the interviewee's manner, dress and composure in addition to getting your verbal answers. The benefit on online interviews conducted in writing is that they are already written up for you, and the task of writing up in-person interviews is time-consuming. You will miss out on observation details, however, in any form that is not face-to-face.

Please bring to class at least one set of questions with a brief description of whom you will be interviewing, what you already know about that person and what you would like to learn from her or him. Ultimately, you will be picking two people to interview and writing questions for each interview.

Observations

When we engage in autoethnographic writing, it is important to try to re-create the spaces we are visiting—in other words, to explore the field sites where we are spending our time.

As part of our larger assignment, you need to identify a field site that will be relevant for your subculture. This can be a location where it meets, a place where history, event or memory is held.

For this assignment, I want you to walk into a space or event related to your subculture and spend at least twenty minutes there. You will be engaging in a stream-of-consciousness freewrite, making notes on everything you experience with your five senses. As in earlier assignments, I will then ask you to create a narrative from the details you have noted.

Rely on all five of your senses to convey not just what the space looks like but what it feels like. Sight, smell, touch, sight, sound are all important to consider as we try to re-create an environment we are experiencing for an outsider. Do not edit! Just write for the entire twenty minutes in the space without picking up your pen or pencil or relinquishing your keyboard, and see what you come up with!

As you did with earlier assignments, you should write the narrative version of your notes as close to the time of observation as possible.

Putting It All Together

When trying to incorporate your research into a final paper, it is important to realize that you will not be using all of it. As in our essays earlier in the semester, you will be drawing on important pieces of it to make your larger arguments (parts of the observation, pieces of the

> interview, etc.). You should not try to use all of the information you gathered in the final paper. Any kind of personal and qualitative writing is about making choices and creating narratives and subtext while maintaining your own voice as a participant-observer.
>
> The most important thing to do is to find common threads in your research, identify your main themes and use the information you have gathered, combined with your own narrative understanding or experience, to create your final piece.
>
> Your final paper will end up being roughly six to ten pages long, given the amount of data you have collected. It is important to ask questions as you go through this final drafting process, so please feel free to contact me at any point about concerns and ideas.
>
> When transcribing interviews, please include only your questions and the full responses that will appear as quotes or paraphrases in your final paper. Since transcribing is time-consuming, this will be the most efficient use of your time. I ask you to attach these documents as well as the observations you completed to the final paper.
>
> You will be asked to present your findings and read a brief piece of your project on the last day of class.

Student Samples

These essays went through multiple drafts at each point. Observations, interviews, and the final draft were all peer and instructor reviewed.

Adriana explores Anarchism in New York.

Tyana explores the group Student Activists Ending Dating Abuse (SAEDA).

Hannah explores the world of computer programmers.

Heather explores the world of Bronies.

Jillian explores modern artistic taxidermy.

Emma explores a religious institution for the first time.

William explores the world of Manhattan Drag.

Joomi explores National Novel Writing Month.

Justine explores the world of Manhattan-based metal band Steel Paradise.

Neziah Doe explores science culture on YouTube.

On Anarchism in New York

Adriana Pauly

> Every time you treat another human with consideration and respect, you are being an anarchist. Every time you work out your differences with others by coming to reasonable compromise, listening to what everyone has to say rather than letting one person decide for everyone else, you are being an anarchist. Every time you have the opportunity to force someone to do something, but decide to appeal to their sense of reason or justice instead, you are being an anarchist.
>
> David Graeber

I was in a small makeshift kitchen in what can only be described as a makeshift apartment. From the big window that graced the long front of the apartment, the sound of raindrops crushing against glass filled the room with their melody. A light smell of humidity with a hint of industrial paint and plaster lingered in the air. From a faint distance I could hear the sound of a waterfall crashing, followed by more water, and what sounded like the piping system exploding.

I set my cup, covered with Russian advertising, of hot, delicious espresso on the table. The kitchen was bordered by an industrial metal shelf, separating it from the couch, a relic from Jonas's grandmother, that made up the living space in the sparsely decorated apartment. The walls, naked, in their original state of plaster waiting to be dressed in paint.

It's still unfinished. We have a lot of work to do," Jonas had said somewhat apologetically and awkwardly upon entering the apartment. "Tomorrow I'm going to paint my room. I'm thinking about black and green." Every nerve of my body cringed at the thought of his shoe box room covered in black and neon green paint.

I took a closer look at my immediate surroundings. The high ceilings of the old factory building had been decorated with several posters animating to come together for noise manifestations at prisons. The kitchen was sparsely equipped with a stove, a wooden table, and a few more industrial shelves, not exactly creating the most comfortable and relaxing environment. "Well, I guess that fits." I thought to myself, Jonas not being exactly comfortable and relaxed himself.

When Jonas came back from the bathroom, he proudly explained to me that they had just got it running a few days earlier after having moved in almost two months ago. The move-in apparently had been the result of an agreement with the landlord who allowed the two boys to utilize the space for a low price under the condition that they built the entire interior themselves.

I met Jonas earlier this year at one of his after hour parties in a dingy lower east side restaurant. A friend, his "business partner", introduced us after having told me earlier "Yeah, he is an anarchist. Everything he earns he reinvests into his newspaper about anarchist stuff. It's really crazy, the Fed has been to his place more than once…". My curiosity was immediately awakened.

I excitedly anticipated a mohawked man covered in tattoos, leather, and studs. What I was actually introduced to ended up being not only a normal white boy but a rather nervous, to the extent of socially awkward, normal white boy. After exchanging the regular "What's your name? What do you-do? Where are you from? Germany. Oh really?" part of what has become my regular introductory conversation, he surprised me by telling me that last year he had visited Berlin and had stayed at a squat across the street from my sister's apartment. I took this as the gateway to making myself known as at least somewhat well versed in young activism. I felt like a dog being sniffed by its kind in order to figure out what category to be put in, friend or foe.

He recognized my rambling about the neighborhood in Berlin as a sign of kinship, or maybe I had cracked the code into the secret club. In any case, after that night of animalistic sniffing, I was regularly invited to parties and dinners.

Back in the kitchen I asked Jonas, "What is anarchism to you?" Seeing that he was starting to go off on one of his tangents about the cruelty of today's society and the controlling and oppressing reign of all corrupt governments I interjected, "No, I mean what is anarchism to *you*? I am just confused…what kind of impact does it have on your life or what exactly does it mean to you?"

Jonas paused for a second. "Do you know the movie *Amélie*?"

I nodded, trying to conceal my annoyance, expecting him to go off topic once again.

"So, you remember the way she broke into her neighbor's apartment to fuck with his head so he would leave his slightly dumb assistant alone?"

"Yeah that's my favorite movie, so?"

"Well, that is exactly it. Anarchism. Taking your own approach to help people, not caring if it is socially accepted or not or illegal. Amélie helps the guy to fight his oppressor and then goes on banging her way through Paris."

Throughout my research I came across many definitions and explanations of anarchism, anarchy and anarchists, but only one reflected what I believe to be the essence of it all. "Anarchists are simply people who believe human beings are capable of behaving in a reasonable fashion without having to be forced to," the Anthropologist David Graeber states in his explanation. He continues explaining the two basic assumptions, "The first is that human beings are, under ordinary circumstances, about as reasonable and decent as they are allowed to be, and can organize themselves and their communities without needing to be told how. The second is that power corrupts."

That evening in the small kitchen, sipping my espresso, I was reminded of my thirteen year-old self, her braces, her limbs too long for her child-like body, and her oily, bumpy puberty skin. With my hormones going through the roof I had decided to change my look for the x-time. Inspired by the German punk-rock band "Die Ärtze" I wanted to give myself a more radical edge, dying my hair purple, purposefully ripping my jeans, and adding a vast variety of patches, bells and dangly shit to my backpack. The variety of patches included some against racism, Nazis, and one with a circled A for anarchism. When asked by one of my friends about what the A stood for I usually replied with some vague rambling about no government, no rules and stuff, not really knowing what the meaning was.

Sitting opposite Jonas I smirked at my ridiculousness and my mother's patience for my identity crisis. Jonas had gone far off topic, explaining to me that Haiti was originally an island for prisoners and slaves, and how lighter skin people in Mexico still hold better jobs than dark skinned.

While my naive thirteen-year-old self could only refer to banal stereotypes, I was emerging deeper and deeper into the topic. I had started following blogs that report on anarchist activities in all of North America and was shocked to see that what I had thought to be more of a teenage phase like punk rock, was actually an entire community of people. Looking at Jonas across from me I was once again amazed at how normal he looked. His black polo, dark denim jeans, and black sneakers did not allude to any political orientation in particular, nor did his bike or his backpack. The backpack itself was his constant companion, a habit he acquired during his stay in prison he had told me. With a Mary Poppins-esque magic he continuously whipped out treasures that so far had included, several pairs of socks, overnight gear, boxing attire, a computer, tobacco plus several additives, beers, water, and several crumpled up issues of the last edition of his magazine.

Sitting in the kitchen, the outside growing darker and darker and the rain heavier and heavier, I pictured a younger version of Jonas, who as a young boy struggled to fit into the social structures of regular suburban high school life. Frustrated with what to him felt more like a prison than an educational institution, Jonas did not get the tolerance or open-mindedness to freely express his points of views but instead was faced with many disciplinary actions. During his sophomore year he was sentenced to six months in prison. Usually open about his life and his experiences, Jonas was hesitant to reveal the reason for his sentencing, and even thought my curiosity was flaming up like a wildfire I did not ask.

The sense of injustice and the abuse of power he experienced during his stay only strengthened his anti authoritarian way of thinking.,, Feeling secluded and forgotten by society, he connected with the anarchist notion of solidarity that tries to break through the isolation and alienation created by an external structure of power and oppression and the authorities who hide behind badges, titles, and the power of the states.

After Anarchism had given him a sense of belonging and purpose he dropped out of high school and started moving around the country, finding friends and like-minded people all over the country and the world. He finally settled once again in New York where he started his own publication with the help of a friend. Taking the belief of solidarity to the next level, the publication aims to unite people who live in conflict with the social order, reporting on different forms of domination with the intent to achieve absolute freedom. Connecting to like-minded people over social media platforms and anarchist forums, the magazine publishes articles from many sources besides their own. All sources are kept anonymous, not striving for private recognition but together pushing toward the greater goal, awareness of any kind of oppression happening around the world. The wish to create insight, connect to different people, and making the topic accessible to anyone is also the reason why it is available as a free PDF download online, besides the print copies in several small bookstores.

Thinking back once again, looking at the thirteen year old girl who embarked on at least twenty more journeys of self discovery only to find herself, after having finished high school, at twenty-three in major she does not really care for, with no goal in life, no passion and nothing to strive for.

And there, in the dark kitchen, illuminated by a cold and naked light bulb, right in front of her was a high school drop-out, ex-convict who openly admitted to being high all day, telling her that he was flying to Thailand in a couple of weeks, then to China, followed by Japan, maybe Europe, maybe even Germany. With the confident, borderline smugness of someone who had found his calling in life, Jonas leaned back in his chair, casually resting his feet on the table.

"Now I am free. I work whenever I want, I work where ever I want, yes I know I will never have a career, but I also don't want one. Now I can go on vacation whenever, I can explore the world, I am not bound to anything."

With growing admiration I felt myself becoming more and more attracted to Jonas's lifestyle, my heart being pulled like a magnet to this notion of limitless and absolute freedom. Suddenly the dark kitchen seemed lighter, the naked light bulb dipping it into a warm and cozy yellow, the rain drops outside started playing a soothing melody, the darkness outside appeared less menacing. I could see how this apartment, once it was painted in friendly colors, could create an escape, an oasis from the pressure, restrictions, and expectations from the outside world.

Almost instantaneously a blanket of heaviness was spreading over my heart, a result of the same connection in our brains that makes us realize that happiness is fleeting and that no moment can last forever. But my heaviness was unrelated to fleeting happiness, it was the discouragement that I was not prepared for a lifelong struggle for acceptance, a lifelong fight against social norms, a lifelong battle against narrow minded people. My lack of bravery to break free from society's strings only made it all the more apparent how much control traditions and social acceptance have in our everyday lives. Discouraged, I slumped back into the heavy, wooden chair. It was only then that I realized I had been sitting up straight this whole time, listening to Jonas's monologues like a child to a fairy tale.

Jonas, having moved on already, was busy telling me about the twelve-people squat he had been living in the past three years while balancing on the back legs of his chair, the chair letting out screeches of pain. A phone call interrupted his monologue about rent prices in New York. From the living area I overheard a one-sided conversation with one of his friends, Jonas for once being the silent one.

"Sometimes I wish I could just go to the hospital and tell them to put me under anesthesia for like a week. Just knock me out. Just one week to get a break from my own head," he said coming back into the kitchen, rubbing his temples. With an expression of confusion, anxiety, and irony he explained that the cops had raided one of his friend's apartments, looking for evidence on suspicious activities. Jonas's paranoia sparked up immediately. "Do you think they are going to come here too? I mean I really don't have anything important here, besides the printer. And my computer is encrypted…". This was followed by several minutes of nervous rambling about shoving his belongings in the basement, smoking up his stash of pot, and angry outbreaks of cursing out the police.

He told me that the police had raided his apartment several times, a few years earlier. The feeling of violation and impotence had only strengthened his opinions, and the fact that they were paying attention to people like him showed that they were getting somewhere.

"In a weird way it can, at the same time, be incredibly empowering to see those fucking idiots frantically going through your shit and not finding anything."

When asking Jonas about what his family thought about his chosen path, he paused for a moment. For a split second I believed, or for my own sanity hoped, to have seen a shadow on his blue eyes. Feeling myself getting enthralled with the topic, I hoped that I could find an excuse for myself why I should not leave my current lifestyle behind and join Jonas on his quest for justice.

"They worry," he said after a while, " but I feel like they know that this is the path I have chosen and that there is nothing they can do about it, so, it makes them proud, or at least my dad. But, they worry."

I tried to envision a future, aged Jonas, maybe with a few wrinkles under his mischievous, boyish eyes and a few gray strands in his blond curls. And yet, how would future Jonas sustain his lifestyle? Would he still organize events, "taking money from rich guys?" He surely would not have succumbed to a 9-to-5 job?

"I don't really worry about the future. We'll probably all be dead so why bother? I am free to decide what I want to do, and for now I want to live every day to my own standards. I want to share my passion, knowledge, and support with people who share my beliefs and those who don't I want to prove them wrong, constantly, until they understand. But most importantly, I want to give those who can't speak a voice, make their stories heard."

Discussion Questions

- Why would somebody want to read this piece (the "Who cares?" factor)?
- Can you clearly identify the author's intention for the piece?
- How well does the author support the intention of the piece? Cite specific details that support or take away from the author's intention.
- Is there information missing from this piece that would make its intention clearer? What else would you like to know?
- Does the author portray herself as a round character? How does she do this?
- Do you trust the author of this piece? Why or why not?
- How clearly does the author establish a sense of setting/space in this piece? Cite specific details that support your claim.
- How clearly does the author establish characters other than the self in this piece? Cite specific details that support your claim.
- Did you learn anything new from reading this piece? If so, what?
- Are there particular passages with engaging language/description that stood out to you? Describe the appeal of these passages.
- Would you read more writing from this author? Why or why not?

Works Cited

Publications:

Fifth Estate [Detroit] Spring 2012, Vol. 47 No. 1 #386 ed. Print.

FTTP [New York] Spring 2011, Issue #11 ed. Print.

Articles:

"On Building Dangerous Bonds." *FTTP* [New York] Spring 2011, Issue #11 ed.: 5-7. Print.

"School." *FTTP* [New York] Spring 2011, Issue #11 ed.: 28-29. Print.

Web:

"Anarchist Neighborhood: New York City." Infoshop OpenWiki. Web. Spring 2012 <http://wiki.infoshop.org/Anarchist_Neighborhood:New_York_City>.

Anarchist News. Web. Spring 2012. <http://www.anarchistnews.org/>.

Chuck. "An Anarchist FAQ." Infoshop.org. 22 Jan. 2012. Web. May 2012 <http://www.infoshop.org/page/AnAnarchistFAQ>.

"Featured Essay." CrimethInc. Ex-Workers' Collective: Home. Web. Spring 2012 <http://www.crimethinc.com/>.

Graeber, David. "Are You An Anarchist? The Answer May Surprise You!" *NYMAA*. Web. Apr.-May 2012.<http://nymaa.org/surprise_anarchist>.

Libcom.org. Web. Spring 2012. <http://libcom.org/>.

Trends in U.S. Corrections. Publication. The Sentencing Project, May 2012. Web. 19 May 2012.<http://sentencingproject.org/detail/news.cfm?news_id=1304&id=107>.

United States of America. U.S. Department of Justice. Office of Justice Programs. Correctional Population in the United States, 2010. By Lauren E. Glaze. Bureau of Justice Statistics, 2011. Web. 18 May 2012.<bjs.ojp.usdoj.gov/content/pub/pdf/cpus10.pdfhttp://>.

Allies, Advocates, Activists

Tyana Soto

The line stretches across the room in an uneven sprawl. Everyone is shoulder to shoulder, and their faces are furrowed with curiosity.

Alma steps forward and says to the group, "Okay, now I want everyone to get in order according to their birthday and birth month. You have forty-five seconds, and can't speak…Ready, set, GO!"

Everyone pauses for a second and then immediately springs into action. Hands begin waving with various hand motions, mouths begin to sound out dates and letters, and finally with a swirl of frenzy everyone is in line. Alma stops the clock, checks to make sure everyone is lined up properly, and makes three simple demands. "Point to the ceiling. Point to the floor. Now point to the front of the line." With confused faces, everyone does so, finally pointing to the left side as the front.

Alma then looks around and says, "Now I want you to line up alphabetically by name. You can't speak, and this time you only have thirty seconds…GO!"

Everyone rushes through the room again, this time mastering the hand motions and silent language barrier and finishing just as Alma says, "Times up!" Once again she demands the group to, "Point to the ceiling, point to the floor, and point to the front of the room." Everyone once again chooses the left side as the front, this time looking less confused and more eager for the next task they would have to complete.

"Okay guys this is the last one, and you don't have to do it if you're not comfortable. I want you to line up according to your skin color. You have fifteen seconds, but you CAN speak…GO!"

This time everyone swirls around the room with anxiety, comparing arms while yelling and arranging people. Finally, the clock stops and everyone cheers for completing the task in the short amount of time.

But then Alma turns to everyone and says one last time, "Point to the ceiling. Point to the floor. Now point to the front of the room."

Everyone does the first two mechanically, but then when pointing to the front of the room, everyone and stares. Through the chaos and mayhem, it wasn't noticed until then that the lightest students were placed at the front of the line. Everyone begins to look around in shock and realization that subconsciously no one had given a second thought to something so blatant.

Everyone then looks at Alma in awe when she says, "You now have an example of internalized racism."

The room goes silent.

This, is SAEDA.

SAEDA (Student Activists Ending Dating Abuse) is a youth group offered in my county through the Rockland Shelter. Its mission statement declares that SAEDA is a youth-led education and prevention program dedicated to celebrating diversity, challenging social norms, promoting leadership, and inspiring youth to ultimately end gender-based violence. Simply put, SAEDA is a program like no other. It transforms youth into people who care about the world and want to change it in any way that they can. It inspires and educates, and brings alive a new generation of people who will fight for their rights as well as others. I can proudly say that I was a member of this group all through high school.

To become a member of SAEDA, you must first complete a four-day training session where you learn about a slew of topics concerning dating abuse, oppression, gender roles, and a multitude of isms. In these few days, barriers are broken and it's likely that you may begin to think differently about what you have thought to be true. After you have completed the training you are welcome to attend the weekly subgroup meetings where you have a direct hand in planning everything for SAEDA. You can bring up ideas for meetings, collaborate with other members, help run the meetings every month, and much more. It seems simple, but really the most important thing to focus on is that it is a *youth run group*. Yes, we do have an advisor, but essentially she is just doing that. Advising. Everything done at SAEDA comes from a student. Every idea, every plan. We all collaborate and work together for one goal. To educate young people and be allies to all.

I began SAEDA as a meager freshman in high school. At the time I really didn't want to be involved with anything, but I was beginning to feel pressure from my mother to start having "extracurricular activities" for college. The advisor was a family friend and my mom signed me up for the winter training session. In my opinion it was too long and I didn't want to be there. I learned about a lot of new things, but I felt like I could be doing something better with my time. I didn't even think that I would attend monthly meetings after the training. I was mistaken, though, because every month my darn dedication would fail me, and I would go to the meetings and sit in the back quietly. I never really took an active role, and was always just waiting for it to end.

When I reached my junior year, things changed when we got a new advisor, James. James changed the dynamics of SAEDA into a more youth-led group by adding weekly subgroup meetings and trying to get more of the youth involved. After getting to know James he began to persuade me to come to a few subgroup meetings, and even offered to give me a ride. Through these meetings I realized that I had a lot to say. I could give input; I had an opinion and ideas. One idea that I had could be the focus of an entire monthly meeting. I never knew that something like this was even possible and it was staggering. I was always the quiet kid in the back of the room, but now I was able to present at monthly meetings and facilitate trainings. I had a voice, and with my group's help I could make a change.

After speaking with Alma Reyes-Evans, the current advisor of the group she agrees fully. She says, "SAEDA is a way for young people to have a voice and become leaders in their community. They learn that it IS possible for them to work together and make a change, no matter how small." She then goes to explain the impact that SAEDA has. "In the small community it's often hard to cultivate a new generation of leaders. But through SAEDA one becomes informed and feels the need to tell others. That's why I think SAEDA is wonderful not just for the community, but for each and every student."

These words ring true, because it is what SAEDA does. It helps the community as well as every member. Through collaborations we have done big things like bring Shine the Light to certain high schools, screen a movie and attempt to bring the filmmaker to the event, create a petition in support of a New York State Bill, and much more. All of these things were done by us. We would sit through subgroup meetings and pin purple ribbons on cards for Shine the Light, endlessly email and contact people to attend our events, and tirelessly write and promote petitions that can help others. In meetings we would bounce ideas off of each other, such as spinning an idea about advertising and the media into a "Media Literacy Hunt" in which students had to walk around the local mall with cameras looking for pictures of offensive advertisements. Or even in general, just speaking out against certain issues. Every meeting we would discuss certain moments or observations that we had found offensive, and coin them an "oops" or "ouch". An "oops" would be when you said something offensive and caught yourself, and an "ouch" would be when you heard or saw something offensive and wanted to let the person know that you were hurt by it. Small things, but still effective.

Internally as well, SAEDA concentrates on the inner person. Valerie Passanante, a dedicated member in her senior year once said, "I feel like you go into SAEDA being one type of person and come out completely changed and empowered." She was right, because even if you don't become a regular member you will still have gained some sort of information and feel the need to tell it to at least one person. That's all that matters. Spreading the message. Because once your eyes have been opened to certain issues, it's hard to close them and walk away. This is even what another student, Samantha Vasallo, said. She only attended one monthly meeting and claimed immediately after, "I feel like my mind has just been opened to something that I had never even thought to wonder about. I feel like I'll never think the same way again about racism."

I think that even in myself I've found such a change through the years. I used to just be that girl who loved art but had no real passion. The girl who didn't feel strongly about anything and just lived life not knowing. After I joined SAEDA and began to put my ideas forth, I felt like I was doing something worthwhile and learning things that I wanted to let the world know. It ignited something in me that I can't explain. It's only a feeling that can be described as empowering. Through SAEDA I was able to do so much that gave me great experiences and knowledge for the future. I created the logo, brought Shine the Light to my high school, won their poster contest, was part of a panel for the county newspaper about teen dating violence, published articles in the SAEDA newsletter, completed two trainings, and then facilitated at another one. None of this would have even been possible without SAEDA.

In essence SAEDA is just a stepping stone for all the youth that go through the program. We go to the training, learn from it, take something away from it, and go on our merry way. But as we go we feel the need to change what's around us. We become a force of nature, a swirling mass of people from all different backgrounds and lifestyles that stand together as people who want to make a difference in any way. We become youth with a mission, youth with a goal, and will stop at nothing until we get a world of acceptance and peace. Or even just a more understanding one.

I guess SAEDA could best be described as its logo. It's a simple circle with three hands of different shades inside creating a triangle (or the delta symbol). They all connect, and have an equal sign in the middle. The colors of everything but the hands are teal and purple. These things show the true ideals of SAEDA in a straightforward way. We are all different people coming together for change and equality. We are allies, we are advocates, we are activists. Simple as that.

> **Discussion Questions**
>
> - Why would somebody want to read this piece (the "Who cares?" factor)?
> - Can you clearly identify the author's intention for the piece?
> - How well does the author support the intention of the piece? Cite specific details that support or take away from the author's intention.
> - Is there information missing from this piece that would make its intention clearer? What else would you like to know?
> - Does the author portray herself as a round character? How does she do this?
> - Do you trust the author of this piece? Why or why not?
> - How clearly does the author establish a sense of setting/space in this piece? Cite specific details that support your claim.
> - How clearly does the author establish characters other than the self in this piece? Cite specific details that support your claim.
> - Did you learn anything new from reading this piece? If so, what?
> - Are there particular passages with engaging language/description that stood out to you? Describe the appeal of these passages.
> - Would you read more writing from this author? Why or why not?

Unicorny, the Only Way a Coder Will Define Rails

Hannah Lajba

Every day we use apps, check our social networks, and peruse various other websites in our idle time. It is said that the fast-growing technical world is consuming our lives and that our youth is so obsessed with technology they've even forgotten what it means to speak face-to-face. Everyone always wishes for the underdog to fight their way to the top, and what used to be those so-called "nerds" at the bottom of the high school food chain have now risen up as the single power that defines and creates the world. Through their own language they program their own ideas and thoughts into every piece of code they touch; they can turn our minds to conform with theirs through the simple selection of a specific background color like Tumblr blue. Don't you wonder why you can't get off once you've gotten on? Coders are always the future and yet the majority of the world still thinks they are losers who live with their parents and can't get a girlfriend or boyfriend to save their lives. Now this might be true in some cases…OK the majority of cases, but there are indeed a lot of coders who experience the opposite. These programmers make up over half of the workers at Ketchum, a software development firm in the heart of Times Square and the location of the meet up group known as the VTS Hackers. Think support group, but with less talking, laptops, and a very excited camp counselor.

The Ketchum office is a space built to ensure a technical, creative environment. My eyes take time to adjust from the dim lit, eleven-floor ride in a wooden elevator to the all white, glass, and steel work environment. This is a far cry from a parent's basement or a college dorm room equipped with more than one monitor. (As what some would say "nerdy" as that sounds, Brian, a college coder you'll met later, has in fact just equipped his tiny dorm room desk with two monitors plus his laptop, but isn't that how all computer geniuses start out?) This is the optimal coding space where employees spend their days rewriting, improving, and innovating code for their current assignment. Like that of a typical 'modern' architecture, the inner workings and the air ducts are exposed and the floor is left in concrete, creating a blank canvas void of distraction that allows for the coder mind to be completely consumed in a twenty-four inch wide computer screen with an LCD display while sitting in one of those high quality rolling chairs. (You know, the ones with the almost mesh-like back that gently conform to fit the user's back. This space clearly indicates that commercial coding will pay the big bucks)

"Go to your logs…. ok ctrl-C, ctrl-C!!" I am taken out of my laptop by the excited exclamations of Karl. His frantic face hovering over Brian's shoulder as his left hand tightly grips the mug containing his Vitamix smoothie that he recently pulled out of his L.L. Bean camo lunchbox and has been sipping on through a straw ever since. (This man lives for multitasking, taking in all his meals through a straw while he helps people code, though I'm not sure how much help telling everyone to download Rails is) I keep a steady gaze from the corner of my eye and here the bad news, "I'm going to have to reprogram all of that, aren't I?" The defeat in Brian's voice crushes me. I see him work endlessly in the basement of our dorm and just as we walked to the venue today he said to me he only had a few touch-ups to make before it was finished. "Yeah, it looks like it, but…ohhh you don't have a Mac…I don't know how this is going to work on your laptop, but try downloading Postgres, that'll make this a whole lot easier next time," Karl replies with a smile and a pat on the back. That positive energy—it just exudes from him. To put the image of his personality and physicality in your mind, think of Chris Treager from Parks and Recreation (aka Rob Lowe). He's that overly excited, overly enthusiastic man trying to come off as a no other than a cool dad. (His success in achieving "cool dad" status has yet to be confirmed). His baggy, worn out jeans (clearly due to weight loss, an explanation for all the smoothies and his side comment to another employee, "Yeah, I'm going to go for a run when I get back home") combined with a polo and quarter zip, pullover sweater show he has not bought any new clothes since the early 2000s. His hair is gelled and spiked with blonde frosted tips, it's as if he's been so involved in the advances in coding that he's forgotten about the advances in everything style related. (Or he just likes the way those clothes and hair look. I'm not one to make judgments; I'm just making assessments based on evaluations.) He is a software developer and the creator of the VTS Hackers (Hackers being the newest and hippest term for programmers as confirmed by Brian). They are a mixed group of thirty- to fifty-year-olds with Brian at eighteen being the youngest and, in my opinion, taking on the biggest programming feat in the group; he is, after all, creating his own social network. Like a support group they all sit in a circle of sorts defined by Mac, Mac, PC, Mac, Visio, Mac, IBM. (Props to the IBM user for using the dinosaur of laptops. I used those laptops to code when I was in junior high and this man is still using one today to code. Maybe he just really likes that red dot in the middle of the keyboard.) There isn't much talking, though the customary "Hi, I'm Hannah," to which all respond "Hi Hannah," did occur and then it was back to the sound of hands flying over the keyboard typing over and over in a somewhat therapeutic way the lines of code that all start the same.

The Fashionista. I say this not only because she is working on a fashion website, making adjustments to the format and color, but she is also well dressed. She wears a business chic ensemble with a black pencil skirt and even kitten heals that can be slightly seen under the jean-and-sweatpant-clad legs of all the other members. She is, however, not the only fashionably dressed person. While there was downtime during which Karl wasn't telling another story that I just had to overhear, I would focus on those workers at Ketchum, who were still working even though office hours were over. About half of the persons I saw had on button-ups and slacks and that signature long winter coat that through outside observation I have found is a sign of wealth in New York City. So this leads me to think, (Of course as a fashion design student I would think about clothing) well-established coders in their thirties have a sizable income and are pretty well off, but what happens to those younger than thirty and those older than forty-five, why have they given up on style? Why would they conform to the stereotype? I discovered it isn't about conforming; it's about work ethic. "It's hard to be productive if I have to think about what I'm going to wear and then get to work when I can just throw something on and get right to work." Brian is exactly right in saying this; the more casually someone is dressed, the harder they are working, in the coding environment at least. Coders aren't trying to fit into a stereotype because the stereotype isn't in fact a stereotype; it's a reality. It takes a certain type of person to code, or at least a certain type of person to be good and successful at coding, and they just happen to dress very casually in a t-shirt and jeans. (Having a boyfriend or girlfriend is completely based on work. Many coders do have a partner, but others like Brian are so caught up in their work that he can't even tell when a girl is trying to flirt with him; he just thinks everyone is being really nice to him.)

Next, we have the eldest member of the group who that very day was learning JavaScript, the language of the Internet. I bet you can guess what he's wearing, none other than worn out Levi's and a sweater. I am just about to pass him off as someone trying to "get back in the game" when Karl comes over to him and the older man strikes up a conversation as he pulls out his iPhone and puts his reading glasses back on his nose from their perch on the top of his head. "Look at this new app I just got. It's just a trial version so you can't buy it yet, but isn't this cool?" I instantly saw a light sparkle in his eyes. Maybe it was the reflection of whatever was happening on his iPhone into his glass lens, but I think it was a hidden excitement that all coders share. "Coding is all about changing the world and creating ways to make lives easier and tasks more efficient." When a coder finds something they're passionate about, they strive to make what they love better for themselves and for the people, and there is no better example of this than Mark Zuckerberg…I mean Brian Gainer. I'm sorry; sometimes it's easy to get them confused.

Brian strives for change. He not only codes, but also is highly involved in student government. His passion is to make the places wherever he sets foot in better for those who walk there every day. Brian is not afraid to voice his opinion; his own personality is what sparked the creation of his coding project; his code is literally a piece of him as any code of any coder is. It is a description of personality in the language of JavaScript, and Brian's personality is all about informing and pushing for change. It's called The Painted Web (you know what else started with "the"? The Facebook) and it is a means of informative information. "I love Twitter; I think it's genius. I want people to be able to share ideas like that but in a longer format, and anyone can see anything. Maybe even scientists and theorists will want to post essays on here. Maybe it will be a platform for events. It can really be anything once it goes live, and that's what I'm excited to see." Brian is the ultimate definition of a coder; he fits his own defined stereotypes perfectly: "no girls, virgin, antisocial, (well I used to be, but now that I'm networking my social network I've had to break that barrier) terrible clothing (basic clothes, comfortable), unreasonably logical, bad social skills." On our walk back from Ketchum he gave me some insight into his past, that would define him as a secret genius. He was not your typical high school student. Instead of doing his assignments or going to class he would sneak off to the library to study what he wanted to study. It is that way that he taught himself how to code and how he became interested in politics and social change. He barely graduated high school and he's still not sure how he managed to get into college, but then again he did get in as a fashion design major. (I know what you're thinking, a fashion design major?? It's true, and the secret of success; you can't be a singularly talented designer and expect to make it and Brian is a prime example of that).

The best way to define Brian, and all coders is by calling them risk takers. They spend hours on websites and lines of code that in the long run, after everything is finished, may have a glitch or might not catch on with the popular culture and be left in the dust. But coders are willing to take that risk because they always have hope that something positive will come from their hard work. I commend these coders, and think so much more of each piece of technology I touch because I'm not just playing a game; I'm making someone's vision come true.

Discussion Questions

- Why would somebody want to read this piece (the "Who cares?" factor)?
- Can you clearly identify the author's intention for the piece?
- How well does the author support the intention of the piece? Cite specific details that support or take away from the author's intention.
- Is there information missing from this piece that would make its intention clearer? What else would you like to know?
- Does the author portray herself as a round character? How does she do this?

- Do you trust the author of this piece? Why or why not?
- How clearly does the author establish a sense of setting/space in this piece? Cite specific details that support your claim.
- How clearly does the author establish characters other than the self in this piece? Cite specific details that support your claim.
- Did you learn anything new from reading this piece? If so, what?
- Are there particular passages with engaging language/description that stood out to you? Describe the appeal of these passages.
- Would you read more writing from this author? Why or why not?

Friendship Is Magic

Heather Brackman

The wind whipped my face as my extremely long hair danced in the air. I shoved my hands into the pockets of a long blue coat that was wrapped around my shivering body. I fingered the pen and folded up piece of paper, both of which were vital to the mission I was on. My boots tapped on the ground with each step I took, producing a sporadic rhythm as I quickly dodged people who meandered back and forth on the sidewalk. The bright lights of Madison Square Garden glowed on my face as I passed. Halfway there. With each street that I crossed, my stomach sank lower. Pulling my phone out, I rechecked the address for the tenth time, trying to ease my nerves. Nearing my destination, I looked up at the numbers marked above four glass doors. I grasped onto the gold handle and leaned back, pulling the door open with all my weight. The walls of the lobby were painted a stark white and the pillars that lined the perimeter towered in an antique gold. My steps echoed off the black and white marble-like floors as I neared an attendant standing behind his desk.

"Hi," I said, trying to let go my nervousness in a single breath. "I'm here for this Meetup thing tonight?" My voice raised, hoping he would know what I was talking about.

"Ok, do you know which floor it's on? And can I see some identification please?"

I pulled out a card and handed it to him. "I think it's the 12th floor," I replied.

He smiled, and I could feel him judge me, like he knew exactly where I was going. "Walk straight back and take a left. Use the leftmost elevator. It only goes to the fourth, sixth, tenth, and twelfth floors." His eyes crinkled as he smiled and gave me my I.D. back.

"Thank you." I quickly shoved the card back in my pocket.

****

Only a few nights prior, I was sitting in my dorm scrolling through the documentary section on Netflix, in desperate need of something to keep my attention. With my blue fleece blanket wrapped tightly around me, the TV clicked every time I pressed the arrow button. I started pressing the button faster, annoyed at the lack of interest in any of the documentary covers. About to give up, a documentary titled *A Brony Tale* caught my attention. In the center of the cover was a blond woman holding her head as if it were about to explode while in the background sprouted rainbows, fluffy clouds, and some sort of pony all mixed with the heads of some very masculine guys. Confused, yet intrigued, I pressed play. Not even five minutes later, a roommate of mine walked in.

"Yo, what are you watching?" She held a tortilla in her hand; a few bite marks already showed from where she ate.

"It's called *A Brony Tale*? I guess it's about My Little Ponies." I looked up at Sam as she froze, mid-chew. "Have you heard of it before?"

"Please. Don't. Tell. Me. You're. A. Fucking. Brony."

I shifted in my chair, "You know what a Brony is?"

"Well yeah. They're weird as hell. It's like all these grown ass men who watch a little girl's show. They're all pedophiles. Or gay." She stared at me in disapproval. "You're so fucking weird for watching this." Sam shook her head before leaving me in silence. Don't get me wrong, I'm not one to make hastily first judgments, but at first glance something did seem a little strange about the Brony culture. The term Brony started a few years back. It's typically described as a group of men in high school and college who enjoy watching the little girl's show *My Little Pony: Friendship is Magic*, but the documentary followed both adult men and women of ages ranging from thirteen all the way to people in their forties and fifties. The thing that struck me about Bronies is how comfortable everyone was being weird about a little girl's show together. The concept of an adult interested, if not obsessed, with such a childish thing sparked an interest in me. Feeling adventurous, I found a Brony meeting just a few blocks down from where I live and RSVP'd to it.

But now, I was thinking it wasn't such a good idea. My side was pressed against the white, freckled wall. I couldn't shift an inch. Ten people were squashed in an elevator that comfortably fit six and the second the doors opened to the twelfth floor, I was shoved forward as everyone swarmed around me. The hallways were dimly lit and every twenty feet was a door leading to a dance studio looking room. As I walked down the stark white hallway, I could hear Spanish-sounding music coming from one room, and then hip hop blasting from another. The doors opened and closed as people came and left as they pleased. My stomach flipped and I started to realize that I was in the wrong place. I turned the last corner to find one last door tucked away. Brightly colored balloons bobbed next to the handle and I peeked in the small window to see a larger man sitting at a table dressed in a bright red shirt with black pinstripes and black suspenders. A black newsboy hat sat on top of his slightly greased hair, hiding the small beads of sweat that started to form at the top of his forehead. I pushed the door open and was immediately greeted by the man.

"Hello! Welcome! What's your name?" He was clearly excited at the position he had been appointed to.

I smiled at his enthusiasm. "Hi my name's Heather. I didn't pay online so how much do I owe you?" He looked up at me stumbling on his words. He wasn't prepared for that question.

"Oh, um, one? That would be, um, fifteen dollars." His eyes followed my hands as I pulled each bill out of my wallet and placed it in his hand. "Thanks. Enjoy!" He mumbled.

I smiled at him. Brony Meetups hadn't been going on for more than a few years. The Brony culture itself was fairly new, too, but you wouldn't know that by going to a meeting. There were maybe sixty people there and they all seemed to know each other, comparing different merchandise and joking around with each other. The room wasn't too big; it was long but not too wide. On one of the long walls, mirrors hung from the floor to the ceiling but only peeked through the cracks of the black curtains that hung in front of them. Lined along the same wall were banquet tables covered in tablecloths and cluttered in My Little Pony t-shirts, playing cards, and fan art, all for sale. A few people stood behind the tables, pulling items out of clear and blue Rubbermaid bins, excitedly chattering amongst themselves. I walked toward the tables as a girl sporting a powdered blue wig jumped in front of me.

"Hi! How are you? I haven't seen you before? What's your favorite pony? What's your name?" She spit out questions faster than I could comprehend them.

"I'm Heather." I extended my hand to shake hers. She just stared at it. Pulling my hand back in my pocket I said, "I don't really have a favorite pony, this is all pretty new to me actually."

"Oh. Well, ok. Have fun!"

"Thanks, I will! I love your blue hair, by the way." I complimented her, trying to make friends in the unfamiliar place.

"It's actually a wig." She twirled her fingers through the plastic looking strands, as if I actually thought it was her real hair. "I got it at the Comic Con a month ago."

Finally. I thought. *Something I can make conversation about.* "Did you go to the one here in the city?" She nodded her head ferociously. "That's awesome! My friend went, too. She loved it."

"Yeah, it's amazing! Ok, well, bye!" She quickly turned on her heel and made a beeline to a group of guys standing on the other side of the room. Slightly shocked, I sat down in one of the many tan, metal folding chairs lined up in the middle of the room, facing an organically-shaped screen. Next to the screen were three computers and what looked like a D.J. booth. A man hovered over all the technology, connecting wires, testing the volume of a microphone, and changing the colors of the picture projecting on the screen. Pushing one last button, he walked to the middle of the room, cleared his throat and put the microphone close to his lips.

"Hello, everypony! Welcome to the monthly My Little Pony Meetup! We have some exciting stuff going on tonight. In just a little bit, we are starting our Super Smash Bros tournament." The man gestured to the opposite wall where there was yet another large screen hung up projecting a video game. "And we'll also start playing some of our favorite episodes of *My Little Pony*!" This was followed by cheering from every person in the room. "Also, we have a webcam set up tonight, so later on we'll be Skyping other Brony Meetup groups tonight from all over the world! There's a group from Germany who wanted to talk as well as Bronies from Salt Lake City and Nashville! So that'll be cool. Anyways, I'm finishing up some techy stuff but in the meantime, get your gaming on, and check out all the tables with merch and awesome fan art. Episodes will be playing in a sec. I promise! OK, bye!" The man hastily waved to everyone and shuffled back to his computers as they cheered for him, eager to watch their favorite show. As I was sitting in the chair, others began to sit down as well. A very tall man plopped down in the chair next to me. His shoulder length, curly brown hair cascaded over a majority of his face and he did nothing to move it out of the way. As soon as he sat down, he pulled a Nintendo DS out of his backpack and popped his thumbs into the holes of his sleeves before turning the power button on and pulling its matching stylus out from its hiding spot. He kept the DS in his lap as he crunched over it, hiding the screen with his hair. He saw me watching before he angled his body in the opposite direction of me, afraid to make any sort of human contact. Next, an older man sat down a few rows behind me. He was in his mid-fifties and wore a light brown cowboy hat. His jacket matched, embellished with fringe along the breast seam, and underneath his jacket was a t-shirt printed with a horse splashing through water. He sat by himself, but person after person would pass and pat him on the back saying their hellos and how are yous. He would just raise his hand, nod at them and smile, acknowledging their greetings. All of a sudden, a very large, pudgy woman ran, or waddled rather, flailing her hands in the air, a box in hand. If there was one thing I observed, it's that these Bronies come in all shapes and sizes. Some members of the group were high school students, while others were classical music experts or employed by NASA. There was even one guy who would come to meetings occasionally who was an Air Force pilot in Afghanistan but has since returned to the States to deep sea dive and participate in amateur racecar driving. A loud shriek rippled through the air.

"Bbbrrrreeettttttt!!!! Brett! Look at this! Look what I ordered and what just came in the mail! Oh, my god you're going to die!" The woman stopped, out of breath. The woman's stomach wiggled its way from the waistband of her pants and hung out underneath her blue t-shirt.

"Brett." Gasp. "Look. At. This." She raised the clear box she was tightly gripping.

A man with rainbow-colored hair gasped as his eyes grew wide. "No way! You have got to be kidding me! My Little Pony curtain hangers?" He jumped up and down as he clapped his hands. "Those are absolutely amazing. I can't believe you finally got them!" The two huddled together, whispering and giggling about the new My Little Pony gear. I felt a tap on my shoulder.

"Hey! How are you? My name is Wyatt." He smiled. "You don't go to many of these do you? I haven't seen you before at least."

"No, this is actually my first time here!" I turned around to talk to him.

"Well, welcome to the Bronies!" He threw his hands up in the air and leaned back in his chair as he grinned. I smiled right back at him. Wyatt was only in high school, yet he looked to be about 23. He had been a Brony for only a year but became extremely involved in the Brony Conference in New York City fairly quickly. It all began for him when he went on vacation to Florida and a tropical storm hit. He was stuck inside all day with nothing to do but look on Facebook. My Little Pony memes popped up in his newsfeed and that's what sparked his interest. He found the memes funny so he watched the show, curious to see if it was funny too.

"I was like wow, this is awesome. So I watched more and then some more of it and more dramatic things happened and there are funny bits and references to like, *Star Trek, Star Wars, Apocalypse Now*, all hidden within." He wrung his hands together, recalling the vacation. After talking to many Bronies, I started to see a pattern. Not a single one of them found the culture, they just fell upon it. Whether it be from Facebook or via friends, they all unintentionally found it and loved it. Most of them hid it from friends and family, afraid of the judgment. My Little Pony was like their dirty little secret that they indulged themselves in but didn't allow anyone else to know about.

Wyatt and I sat in the metal chairs as more and more people started to file into the room. The Super Smash Mario Bros game was picking up attention and there were small groups of people huddled in circles next to the tables, discussing the latest Dr. Who season. While this meeting was for people who love My Little Ponies, I started to realize that as a group, My Little Pony was only one similar interest that everyone shared. Next to all the Pony merchandise were also *Dr. Who* and *Star Wars* items too. Almost all the Bronies knew these other shows just as well as they knew My Little Pony. Wyatt explained that although the show was for little girls, the amount of adult references there were pertaining to shows like *Dr. Who* and *Star Wars* was huge. The writers hid small phrases within each episode that a small girl wouldn't think twice about but made complete sense to an older group of people. I started to realize that *My Little Pony* is much more than just a little girl's show to these Bronies.

A man dressed in all black started to walk towards us. He looked about mid-twenties as he shuffled his way toward us. The man was lengthy with short brown hair and he seemed to always have a smile on his face. He stopped right in front of us, lifting his hand to wave.

"Hello!" I warmly greeted him. "How are you?"

The man just kept waving with a sheepish grin on his face. After about a minute he walked away, following the perimeter of the room. Confused, I looked towards Wyatt.

"There are a lot of people who come here who are of the autistic spectrum. Some are more obvious than others. The guy who walked up to us usually doesn't talk, but he's always happy when he's here." Wyatt chuckled as he explained. Up until the man in black came up to us, I hadn't even noticed. Everyone bonded with everyone. When I looked closer, some seemed more awkward than others, but their awkwardness was accepted with open arms. Not a single person seemed to feel out of place. Although Bronies come together to celebrate the show itself, I realized that they focused on the friendship aspect of *My Little Pony: Friendship is Magic*. The idea is that any person, no matter shape, size, race, or sexuality, is welcomed and accepted as who they are. Almost every single person who I walked by made sure to say hello and ask how I was doing. Judging someone was a concept they never used.

Toward the end of the night, I began to see Bronies as something other than what Sam would call pedophiles and weird, creepy people who found children's shows amusing. It was much, much bigger than that. The Brony community is a welcoming place where little to no judgment is made. It's a place to build friendships around multiple hobbies and enjoyments other than My Little Pony. The show, the characters, and the lessons hidden within helps those who have disabilities as well as those who don't. Being a Brony doesn't mean being an adult who loves a girly little kids' show, although that's how it started. Being a Brony means embracing who you are and who others are without judgment. It means welcoming everyone with open arms and creating an environment to grow in.

Discussion Questions

- Why would somebody want to read this piece (the "Who cares?" factor)?
- Can you clearly identify the author's intention for the piece?
- How well does the author support the intention of the piece? Cite specific details that support or take away from the author's intention.
- Is there information missing from this piece that would make its intention clearer? What else would you like to know?
- Does the author portray herself as a round character? How does she do this?
- Do you trust the author of this piece? Why or why not?
- How clearly does the author establish a sense of setting/space in this piece? Cite specific details that support your claim.
- How clearly does the author establish characters other than the self in this piece? Cite specific details that support your claim.
- Did you learn anything new from reading this piece? If so, what?
- Are there particular passages with engaging language/description that stood out to you? Describe the appeal of these passages.
- Would you read more writing from this author? Why or why not?

Gin and Tonic: A Look into the Subculture of Taxidermists

Jillian McDonnell

Taxidermy is generally viewed as the reanimation of an animal form after it has passed. Whether seen as a hobby, an art form, or the creepy heads lining southern houses and quirky antique shops, taxidermy has existed for centuries, and along with hunting and farming had lost popularity in the most recent years. Quite recently, taxidermy has moved from the expected Midwest or South and has begun a movement in New York City. Moving from "log cabins to hipster havens," taxidermists as a subculture have begun holding classes and shows in Brooklyn and have had individuals get articles in *The New York Times*. Taxidermy and taxidermists have been a subculture for decades, but now many subsets have grown tight-knit groups of people. These entities have created a really unique and unexpected variance within the subculture due to factors such as location, but why now? Why has taxidermy just begun to gain interest in Brooklyn while it's been common for decades to see a deer posted on a wall in Texas? Why has taxidermy been more apparent in movies such as the Wes Anderson films or "Dinner for Shmucks" now? What brings this newfound interest to taxidermy so recently is the same reason a fascination has grown for thrifting and steampunk. It is a way to reconnect with older times, a way to connect back to an American tradition usually done by the hicks in flannels but now done by New York City artists. To taxidermy an animal means reanimating an animal that is no more. In the taxidermy of an animal, a preservation of life or legacy is created, similar to the portraits of dead babies when infant mortality was high in the 1800's. Taxidermy is both a connection to the past, and also a connection to the memory of those who passed.

The first time I was ever introduced to taxidermy I was only six or seven. The Italian kid a year older than me, Joey Verastro, said, "Hey! You wanna see *Bambi*!?" and to my horror saw a deer head sitting in a box. Roadkill gave me the chills and I refused to touch the frog we dissected my freshman year of high school, but last Sunday I sucked it up and walked into a building full of Bambi's and frogs. I had entered the Morbid Anatomy Museum, home to the new interest of taxidermy in New York City.

Set in Brooklyn, you did not expect to see a building as peculiar as this when walking through the neighborhood. In fact, this part of Brooklyn felt much less like the city to me and much more like Yonkers. With apartments lining the streets, a few restaurants across, and a New Millennium Motors right across, the Morbid Anatomy Museum stuck out among everything else. It was a black brick block on the corner of 7th and 3rd. There was no mistaking it because the building's two sides had "Morbid Anatomy Museum" painted in huge white letters. Even before walking in I let out a giggle. "What?" my friend Helen asked, and I pointed. Two statues of saints stood in the glass windows to greet you as you walked in. Just like the ones in a church, only these greeted you to a house of the dead. "Here we go," I thought, and already had my fingernails digging into my palms.

Just as expected, the first word that popped into my head was "weird". A whole room lined in taxidermy, but not just taxidermy, there were books and trinkets as well, like any other museum's gift shop. One box at the register was labeled, "Random Old Photos…$1.50 each." In fact, a lot of the taxidermy in this opening entrance was for sale. From stuffed animals to skeletons to canned fetuses, the museum had certainly filled the room. The fetuses were the most difficult to look at; I felt my nails dig a bit deeper when I saw those. There were fox tails and antlers, framed bats and four mice spinning on a wheel, and two possum heads, one with its tongue sticking out. On top of one of the sets of shelves that held ducklings and sea life and framed butterflies there were three huge bones—parts of an elephant, I learned after reading the card.

The best way to describe the Museum was as a hole in the wall. Though it was a large space, you could tell that after only being up for five months they had appreciated the pipes in the ceilings and the stairs in the basement that led to nothing but a wall. It all contributed to the scene, a scene in which people of all sorts gathered to look at dead things while eerie music played in the background. One employee there stood out among many. Along with her bright fuchsia hair tossed up into a bee's nest of a bun was a necklace of bones and a 50's skirt and shoes. She held a vaporizer in one hand and a bottle of gin in the other (gin was free that day thanks to a killer sponsor). If you looked closely you would see that under the necklace of bones a tattoo of a set of wings stretched over her chest. I watched her as she ran around the basement in a tizzy helping this presenter and that, then sitting down again, exhausted, pulling out her vaporizer and gin to sit back and relax. Another woman who looked like she was in her 50s or 60s had light lavender hair with bangs chopped rather short and wore all black—a black shirt with a thick black belt, a black fur coat slung against the back of her chair, and a black maxi skirt. Her hair was tied up into a scrunchy decorated with bright and big flowers. While my eyes moved past a woman wearing chickens for earrings, I also saw a man. With a gaunt face and shoe polish black hair, he wore a dark grey satin scarf and held a glass of gin in his hand. He looked like a character out of a Mafia movie.

Though I had gone for the taxidermy, many other topics and fascinations were being presented that day. I ran up the stairs to catch the last few minutes of a Victorian Hair jewelry tour being given by my jewelry professor. Once I arrived, the scene had totally changed. Rather than dead animals it had switched to portraits of babies. I watched the tour and looked in admiration at the little hairs woven into ornate and beautiful broaches and bracelets. When we arrived at another wall, the dead babies had been explained. Back when babies died more frequently in the 1800s, it was common to have portraits done of the dead children. I had not noticed this before because the dead infants were being held by their mothers or fathers, and just looked like they were sleeping. I shuddered and shook my head in disbelief, but one word kept bouncing around in my head, "common". It was common to die at an early age and, of course, memorial was common as well. After the end of the tour we walked into a room off the main and saw, yes, more taxidermy. Some were a bit more avant-garde this time, like the duckling with a little hat, the mouse holding a sign that read "Morbid Anatomy Museum" in script, and a duckling with two heads. There were more canned fetuses, and canned bones that were died purple or blue so that they stood out in the water. Other trinkets laid here as well. Also, there was a shelf of books dedicated to sex, my favorites being *The Look of Love* and *The Anatomy of the Female Pelvis*. After sitting in on two lectures, "Seductive Drugs" and "The Not-So-Fun Funhouse," we went back upstairs to meet Divya, the woman who is allowing me to visit her studio. In her 20s or 30s, she stood tall in her heels. She wore black leather pants, a pink sequin kitty cropped top, and cat ears to top off the look. We met and she looked so excited to have me. Afterwards we left and made our way back to the subway. As we rode back to school my friend Helen said, "Open-minded. You had to be very open-minded to stomach what we saw today."

I chose to delve into taxidermy because my jewelry professor is involved with it. She not only introduced me to the museum, but to Divya as well. Although connected to each other by taxidermy, both had studied at Pratt and had jobs in the fashion and jewelry industries. Divya compared taxidermy to the tanneries, "It's so interesting when I told people I was a shoe designer and I worked with leather and snakeskin they were very fascinated by it and they'd picture this glamorous job, but a lot of the tanneries I went to then were *way* grosser than any tannery I've visited for taxidermy. Way more disgusting than anything I have to work with now. You're using so many of the same raw materials but when you say taxidermy some people are really grossed out." (Anantharaman) Divya and Karen were not the people one would expect to see taking a dead animal and stuffing it. Karen, a mom with round glasses and a dirty blonde bob, could be a bit more expected to but only after you saw her wearing a necklace of donkey teeth. Her connection to the Morbid Anatomy Museum was strong not only for taxidermy but also for Victorian Hair Jewelry. Divya, however, in her 20s or 30s dressed in black or sequin cropped tops would never be expected to, but she was a self-taught professional. Karen did not sell much of her taxidermy, but instead kept most of it around her house. I asked, "What does your family think about the taxidermy, are they ok with it?" She answered, "The taxidermy is all over the house, I have a pretty tolerant family. They don't necessarily like to taxidermy. They're kind of…used to it as much as they can be. They're certainly not squeamish." (Bachmann) She also spoke about her favorite piece, "The raccoon heads on a plate are my favorite. I'm forever working on this installation piece called 'Road Kill Banquet' in which I take taxidermy I've done and stuffed it into my mother-in- laws ugly china which I will never goddamn use. As old ladies will in this country she had the ugliest little teacups and what not. My husband wouldn't let me throw it out so I kind of got around that by stuffing it with roadkill."(Bachmann) Divya however had turned taxidermy into her career. After working in the fashion industry and running back and forth from China to the US, the few classes she had taught on taxidermy had gained enough popularity overtime that she had made the move and became a professional taxidermist. Most of her work was sold, but both Karen and Divya explained to me that taxidermy pets could not be sold. While Karen told me about the Chihuahua her student plans to give to her after it has passed, Divya told me about a pet rat and its owner. "Pets are so personal. I've done a pet rat that was really funny. When the lady dropped her off she was really calm and collected and wanted a really simple mount with it just sleeping on a pillow. When I gave her the mount she was super happy. But then she started texting me. Weeks later she'd be like, 'I miss Dolly.' And this went on for a couple of months and I thought, ok, maybe I need to start screening these people because she needed a therapist. And I can't be the therapist but I can be the taxidermist. So it came to, OK, I can't keeping doing this, like I'm at a party, it's my birthday!" (Anantharaman)

Helen, who lived in Texas all eighteen years of her life until coming to New York this year for school, said it well, "Divya's not the type of person you see taxidermying in Texas. At home everyone has at least one deer on their wall and that's because the big guy with a beard and a flannel shot it. I see a lot of taxidermy in antique shops but not like this," (Minor) referring to Divya's studio in Greenpoint. A few blocks away from the G Train on Java and Provost, Divya's studio was on the third floor and was set in a small room, not even to herself as she shared it with a friend who was a painter. We walked in and were immediately greeted with a "Sorry for the mess, guys," to which Helen and I glanced at each other with a perplexed smirk. When Divya had warned us of the mess in her studio, Helen expected vats of chemicals while I assumed the worst (as in animal guts on the table). So, as she showed us around and allowed us to take pictures I watched with much appreciation. This studio was no bigger than the size of my room and she only had half of it to work with. There was a table with tools on it similar to the pliers I use for jewelry and there was a pig with two heads on it. As you looked from wall to wall everything was covered in taxidermied masterpieces. Unlike the classic deer mountings, these were fairytales. A fawn standing in a patch of flowers; the deer had eyelashes long and silver, similar to ones you buy at Forever 21, and the flowers continued up to the fawn's mouth and covered it delicately. "It was way in the beginning when I just started. And this guy said he had two deer fawns that he had found in his dad's freezer. He said one of them was a tanned skin and the other one was whole. After calling me back a few months later and changing his mind saying that both deer were tanned, he sent them but didn't send them overnight. So my doorman gets this dripping box and luckily knew what I did and put it in the employees' freezer for me and even texted me a picture because we were so close. But I get this box and immediately know that they weren't both tanned. So I just threw the box in my freezer and didn't want to look at it for a while but finally just did it. The tanned skin was destroyed; all the hair had fallen off but the whole surprisingly worked out. It was a mess to clean; it was dripping with all sorts of body fluids. But, yeah, so after that disgusting bloody bodily fluid mess I got to make that beautiful blooming little cute guy over there." (Anantharaman) Across from the deer was another fairytale scene but this time a young fox. Two pheasants, many skulls painted with the galaxies, and little mice lined the rest of the workshop. Nothing phased me until a rat laying on its side on the table caught my eye unexpectedly. After we looked around for quite a while I finally asked, "How do you keep it so clean?!" and she looked at me confused and said, "No, I already apologized, it's really quite unorganized." I replied, "Not that, the smell!" I could not understand how a room full of dead animals could not smell terrible, but it did not. The room smelled like Divya did, a bit like perfume. She laughed, "Oh, I understand. Yeah, it's really not that bad if you skin the animal quickly; that's really the only time you smell anything bad. The first time I skinned an animal it maybe took three hours, but now I can do it in fifteen minutes." "It was really hard to find something in Florida that I could try because of the heat. So when I was up in New York for school, I went on this hike upstate and I found this tiny frozen squirrel. I thought, "This was meant to be!" So then I took him home and skinned it. It took forever and I was exhausted, so I left the skin in salt and thought I'd see what happens. A couple days later I mounted it and it didn't turn out any way I wanted it to, but I was totally hooked." (Anantharaman)

Karen had told me to research rogue taxidermy and later brought up ethical taxidermy. I thought they were the same, and that being ethical was what made you rogue. What I discovered later was that rogue and ethical were two totally separate things, and you did not have to be rogue to be ethical. While talking to Divya, I realized there was not really a large gap between the taxidermists in Brooklyn compared to the taxidermists who were hunters at all. When asked if taxidermy were an art form, Divya answered with a strong yes, but, to my surprise, when I had asked her to put that into context with location, she still explained it as an art for *every* taxidermist, "People don't think it's an art for the hillbillies in the flannels that shoot the deer left and right but it is. They have to have an understanding of the anatomy. It takes a steady hand, it takes finesse, and, of course a strong stomach, but it is the art of taking something 3D, making it 2D and then making it 3D all over again. In terms of location it's different but the same. It's really like any profession; it changes as the old people die and the new people come. A lot of people talk about a divide but there's a real respect between the rogue and the traditional. The people know it's such a small crowd so they want to stick together." (Anantharaman) Both women showed their ethics of animal rights differently. While Karen explained that she was an animal rights activist who only wears fake fur and eats meat that is sustainably sourced, Divya told me about using the entire animal, "I have ivory as a jeweler that I received and worked back with way in the 80's when it was less regulated. But now I have this ivory from the elephant that has passed so long ago I will not work it because it creates demand. I wear fake fur and I won't wear old real fur because it creates demand from people that see you wearing it and are maybe less ethical and don't even give a crap about where it comes from." (Bachmann) "My personal ethics is using the whole animal. So I eat the meat and even feed my cat the organs. I mean I use everything but the poop. If my fiancé and I get a deer, it's like we're set for the whole year; it's just so much meat." (Anantharaman) What I learned after talking to both Karen and Divya was that ethical taxidermy was as undefined as ethics; there was no one answer and a lot of gray areas. While Divya supported the taxidermy done by hunters, Karen did not appreciate it as much. Divya explained, "A lot of people think that the traditional guys like the ones who go hunting shooting stuff left and right are unethical, but they're doing it within the law. It's a very regulated thing. I think it's very unfair for people to come up to me and say, "You're ethical and they're not" but the law itself is ethical. I think the whole field's ethics, whether you're rogue or traditional, are overlooked." (Anantharaman) Karen has mostly found her animals as feeder animals, such as mice, and roadkill. "I must be the weirdest parent at my daughter's school. I was picking my kid up from school one day and I saw a pigeon on the road. So I started doing the happy dance and I had a bag with me and I picked it up, wrapped it up, and put it in my purse, and my daughter's librarian saw me doing it. Yeah she doesn't talk to me the same way"(Bachmann). While Divya also gets roadkill, she also has many connections with farms and is able to taxidermy many animals through them because they are stillborn. "The farmers sell these stillborn animals and, yeah, they make a buck but then I get to turn it into art." (Anantharaman)

I asked each woman, "What tool do you think every taxidermist needs and why?" Karen answered with a smile, "Scalpel to open up the animal, your fingers to peel off the skin, and a needle and thread to sew that thing back up," (Bachmann) and so did Divya, "A good set of knives. They do everything…like *everything*." (Anantharaman) I questioned, "How do you think the general public views taxidermy?" Divya answered, "A lot of people think it's like, oh, you must want to kill everything, but I didn't say I'm a sociopath; I just said I have this job. I went on a hike with some girls and a flock of ducks flew by and one of the girls said, 'Do you just want to shoot all of them?' and I thought, no, I just want to enjoy my fucking hike. If one of them drops then that's that but c'mon, do you think I'm that terrible of a person that I want to kill everything? I think it really speaks to this curiosity and this discomfort that we have with death. We'll go and buy the chicken from Whole Foods and it's in this beautiful package with a nice story but if you really think about it someone has to kill it; it doesn't just grow on a tree and then fly into the container featherless and ready to eat…Yeah, people don't think death exists in the world. That's a change that's happened over the last 50–100 years. No one recognizes that death exists; It's crazy." (Anantharaman)

"The whole appreciation for things from 100 years ago or 150 years ago and the fascination with the Victorian Steampunk revolves around a less modernized and less technological age—that's appealing." (Bachmann) I was surprised when Divya had a similar response to Karen's, "Everyone wants to revisit old times." (Anantharaman) When Karen and Divya answered my question about why taxidermy was gaining popularity now, I thought back to the Morbid Anatomy Museum. I did not think about the taxidermy, but instead the room with the portraits of the dead babies. Though I had already gotten a better understanding of taxidermy when I was there, Karen's answer had given me more understanding. These taxidermists were artists; they were not these gruesome people looking to shred and stuff an animal. You had to know the body of the animal, and with that knowledge you were able to reanimate that animal, and almost bring it back to life. That was why I had thought of the babies. Here were parents who had to hold their dead child, but they did it to have that memory. These parents held their dead children so that they could later look at the picture and think of their child, and think of holding him or her. That was the legacy given to these animals as well—to give that dead mouse on the side of the street a new purpose or give the stillborn who never even saw life a place in a museum or a person's home adorned in flowers from a fairytale. That was why I could stomach this paper. I thought of the act of having to cut open a dead animal and reshape it, but I was taught to see beyond that and appreciate the art and reconnection to life that went with it. "When I started taxidermying that first mouse the first thought was, 'Oh, my god, it's coming back to life'." (Bachmann)

Works Cited

Anantharaman, Divya. "Interview with Divya Anantharaman." Personal interview. 10 Dec. 2014.

Bachmann, Karen. "Interview with Karen Bachmann." Personal interview. 5 Dec. 2014.

Minor, Helen M. "Talk with Helen Minor." Personal interview. 10 Dec. 2014.

Discussion Questions

- Why would somebody want to read this piece (the "Who cares?" factor)?
- Can you clearly identify the author's intention for the piece?
- How well does the author support the intention of the piece? Cite specific details that support or take away from the author's intention.
- Is there information missing from this piece that would make its intention clearer? What else would you like to know?
- Does the author portray herself as a round character? How does she do this?
- Do you trust the author of this piece? Why or why not?
- How clearly does the author establish a sense of setting/space in this piece? Cite specific details that support your claim.
- How clearly does the author establish characters other than the self in this piece? Cite specific details that support your claim.
- Did you learn anything new from reading this piece? If so, what?
- Are there particular passages with engaging language/description that stood out to you? Describe the appeal of these passages.
- Would you read more writing from this author? Why or why not?

Don't Judge the Bible by Its Cover: An Honest Story with a Cliché Title

Emma Suleski

Steven looked down at his hands that were neatly folded loosely around his coffee. "We suffer the same struggles and temptations as everybody else," he said. "We are human. We gain connection through our beliefs and through what we work to abstain from together…there is community in that we are all striving for the same goal."

I considered what he said while chewing my lower lip before choosing careful words, "That makes sense. I get it. I always thought about it like a school, simply just teaching. I never considered that it's just like any other club or team or group, you're all working to achieve a goal."

Steven knew me well enough to know all about the labyrinth of walls I had built up around my opinions of religion. I didn't have a lot of personal experience with it, but that which I did was not positive. I had a bad attitude and a wicked mindset that to have faith simply does not make sense.

To put it bluntly, I watched my parents lose their religion. Maybe it was the fact that my church was home to a priest involved in the sexual abuse scandals, or that my two older brothers were altar boys under his direction, or maybe it was the growing string of family members that died too young, I don't know. As a child, I kept absorbing their anger and disappointment, turning it into information that I based my opinion of the church on: it had betrayed us and everyone who still trusted in it was only fooling himself or herself. All I was left with was a cynicism for religion that never seemed to stop hardening.

Steven and I threw out our empty coffee cups and began our walk to the Regal Cinema. He walked in front of me, an eighteen year old of average height with a frame that was filled out with bulky muscle. He wore old black Converse and fitted jeans with worn knees and small tears. His black hair was spiked and crunchy with gel underneath his gray beanie that flopped lazily on his head underneath the hood of his sweatshirt. His leather jacket was well loved and stained from the salt of Boston winters.

"In you go!" he laughed, pushing me up the concrete steps. Steven believed I had to experience this on my own in order to gain the most pure knowledge so I was to go in first, and he would follow in a few minutes, picking a seat a few rows behind me.

The smell of buttery, rich, movie theater popcorn wafted into my nose. I smiled as I walked up the steps, following families, couples, and friends. I had never thought of a movie theater as anything other than a place to pay way too much money in order to watch a movie, but that was clearly about to change.

As I approached theater seven, I felt my stomach roll a little bit inside me and I wiped sweaty palms on my sweater. I hadn't been to church myself since I was six or seven years old and my vague recollection was only of being silent in my pew, following instructions to sit and stand, and trying to understand the complex hymns I was singing. I was a child seen not heard, wearing one of my best dresses. It had always been serious.

In front of me was a movie theater transformed. Members of the church sat in seats, while a podium and tables lined the front of the theater, right in front of the screen. Projected onto the screen was "Mosaic Boston" in big bold letters. I looked around, kind of baffled at the things I was seeing. Everyone was laughing and smiling with one another, greeting fellow church members with big hugs, not stiff handshakes. I immediately felt the knot in my stomach loosen. There was an air of friendship, a welcoming aura that took me by surprise, drawing me to sit in the middle of the theater, not the back corner as originally planned. From the hall entered a band of five members. Two guitars, a base, drums, and a singer began to play. I listened as they carried on a pop-rock melody, feeling the knot loosen yet again as the music comforted me.

The greetings slowed down and the talking ceased. Now there was only the beauty that comes from many voices joining together to sing the same words. Many people stood at their seats, keeping time with their bodies, dancing with their children or swaying back and forth with their companions. Unity had taken hold of everyone in that room, and though I knew I was an outsider, I didn't feel like one.

After two songs, the Pastor Jan stepped up to the microphone, iPad in hand. He was a young man, maybe in his early thirties. He wore thick-rimmed glasses and a smile that was contagious. Between the iPad and the genuine smile, this church already felt like a completely different world than I had expected. It appeared to be a very fresh take on practicing religion, modernized and efficient. Jan began to speak.

"Welcome to Mosaic Boston. We are a new interdenominational church, and we are so happy to have you with us today. We have members here from more than sixteen different countries!" I raised my eyebrows. To me, that was an incredible fact. There were people here from all over the world, yet they choose to come together under this roof all for one purpose.

"We are a Mosaic, built of many different pieces, to come together to create something beautiful." I felt as if I was being read poetry. Sure, it was a blaring metaphor, but it did wonders to help me to understand what the goals of this church were. They simply wanted to unite people based on their beliefs. I didn't feel like an outsider because it didn't matter who I was; I was going to be accepted, just like many had been before me.

"Today we are going to talk about what unites us." I froze. Was this a joke? Seriously, it was way too perfect. I adjusted in my seat and listened.

"It is not only our belief in Jesus, but our love for Him. Love is what brings us together. And not only the love for Him but also the love we give to others. The love I give to you, the love you give to me, the love we give to friends, family, and neighbors, even strangers. Love brings us together." I looked around me as many nodded in approval. The couple in front of me looked at each other, and he planted a kiss on her forehead.

Steven's words echoed in my head yet again. He was explaining to me how people have so many stereotypes for those who are practicing Christians. They are often expected to be gay hating, judgmental, bible thumpers. What people often forget is that love is the most important, fundamental part of Christianity and that's what he strives to live by.

As the sermon went on, I found my attention being held by the endearing way that Jan spoke about love and the Bible. Plus, the way that each bible verse was projected onto the screen helped me to follow along. I felt as if I was learning about Jesus, but also about myself as many parts of the sermon were introspective. He lightened tense moments with stories about his young daughters, one of which claimed he loved her because she is obedient, smart, and of course beautiful. The entire theater laughed because kids say the darndest things and all, but we were transitioned into a discussion about selfless love. Jan seemed to reach peak intensity as he challenged us to live a more selfless life, and the knot in my stomach tightened once again.

The band made its way back out onto the floor and began another catchy song with a jazzy swing. I stood up with the rest of the crowd and tapped a toe along with the beat. The joyousness still bounced among all that had gathered and children laughed and danced, rewarding themselves for having been silent and still for so long.

I looked around. I was standing in the center of a diverse group of human beings. I saw people from different towns, countries, and religious backgrounds; people with different levels of wealth, religious interest, and education. At the brunch, just a few hours later, Mosaic's devoted volunteer Eric explained to me how he and the other volunteers work tirelessly to make Mosaic inviting for everyone. They focus on what these people are here for, to strengthen and celebrate their faith, and then use that initial connection to help members build friendships with outside activities.

He told me, "...they [church members] would probably never meet each other without Mosaic. And if they did they probably wouldn't form the bond they have...we try to build off of that." Again, things started to make sense to me. This church wasn't simply a place of worship, but a catalyst for members to build relationships with people of like values. This church was not about following rules about when to sit and stand, it was about building up more than one part of your life to be stronger in order to meet that ultimate goal. This goal changes from person to person; it could be strong faith, everlasting life in heaven, or maybe simply happiness. The common thread was the ways these people worked to achieve their goals, by working in their faith.

Eric confirmed my thoughts when talking about the struggles of being Christian and how to pull oneself out of a dark time. He said simply, "...our brothers and sisters have a huge influence in helping us see our way out of difficulties, especially when it comes to our own relationship with God." The Church members weren't there to judge me or anyone else. They were there to strengthen their own faith and help give strength to those around them.

We began to slowly exit the theater as the band slowed to a stop. Outside theater 7, I recognized Jan standing, shaking hands and giving hugs as devoted members exited on their way to Sunday brunch.

"Excuse me, miss!" I turned around. Jan stood in front of me with a smile on his face. "I don't recognize you, I just wanted to say welcome to Mosaic." I grinned, feeling the love he had so solidly preached about just a few minutes before.

"Thank you very much," I answered, shaking his hand before turning to go. I walked towards the exit, the smell of rich butter in my nose, and an honest smile stretching across my face.

Works Cited

James, Eric. Personal interview. 19 Dec. 2014.

"Mosaic Boston Church: A New Church in Boston, Fenway and Allston." *Mosaic Boston Church.* N.p., n.d. Web. 29 Nov. 2014.

Scott, Steven. Personal interview. 15 Nov. 2014.

Discussion Questions

- Why would somebody want to read this piece (the "Who cares?" factor)?
- Can you clearly identify the author's intention for the piece?
- How well does the author support the intention of the piece? Cite specific details that support or take away from the author's intention.
- Is there information missing from this piece that would make its intention clearer? What else would you like to know?
- Does the author portray herself as a round character? How does she do this?
- Do you trust the author of this piece? Why or why not?
- How clearly does the author establish a sense of setting/space in this piece? Cite specific details that support your claim.
- How clearly does the author establish characters other than the self in this piece? Cite specific details that support your claim.
- Did you learn anything new from reading this piece? If so, what?
- Are there particular passages with engaging language/description that stood out to you? Describe the appeal of these passages.
- Would you read more writing from this author? Why or why not?

Autoethnography on Manhattan Drag

William Rossi

"Well, Drag is whatever you want it to be—drag is…if you're going out as business man one day and you're in your business suit, that's your drag. Also, drag is random gay men in dresses, who are debatably beautiful, dancing to Kylie Minogue," expressed Giovanni Palandrani, my roommate/drag performer. Drag has always been a form of entertainment; but with the growth of drag in pop culture, drag has become more expressive. Some drag queens go for artistic endeavors, while others aim to transcend the crowd with a character. Overall, the drag community is widely diverse, and behind each queen is a unique motivation. No one wakes up one day and says, "I'm going to do drag today." Drag takes more than time, money, and networking—it takes dedication. With the community growing in the public eye, it takes a true passion to stay true to oneself and continue to make one's *own* drag.

I used to scroll through eBay, clicking through all types of links and tabs relating to wigs. Ordering off of Visa gift cards so that my mom wouldn't find out. For me, the wigs were the best part of drag; with every wig, the look, the attitude, and the persona could be something different. Altering a wig can make anyone feel new and revamped. My sophomore year was full of drag parties, and RuPaul marathons. When the wigs arrived after their long voyage from China, it was time for a party. Everyone would show up with new hair, new costumes, and new identities. It was always key that we got ready in order: the makeup, the costume, the tuck, the heels, and then the wig. Once the wig was on, we were done; aside from touching up the lipstick that stuck to beer bottles. Jesii was our "drag mother"; he had already created a name for himself online but not as a man, as a queen. Reina Vanity, his drag persona, had fans on Twitter, Instagram, and Tumblr. He never did so well finding the right costumes, due to his full figure and lack of knowledge in sewing. Nevertheless, Jesii knew a good wig when he saw one. His collection was massive; the hair hung on his wall on hooks to keep them in their finest condition. He would take special care of them, always brushing and bending them delicately until she performed. She would whip the hair, swirl it in the air, always making sure that the glue had firmly secured it to her skin.

For our group of misfit teens, performing in drag was fun. It was a playful act that became personal and exciting when in an intimate setting. We laughed and giggled at the performances of others. Occasionally, shouting a "*yaasss*," or "turn the house down," as we sat on the small sofa and admired each other's performances. It was simply for the joy of performing and enjoying the company of those around us. Nothing was ever rehearsed and often the song choice was made on the spot.

I was nothing close to the standards of Reina Vanity. I never developed a drag name or a persona to model myself from. I didn't publicize my drag or make it an identifiable part of me; I was never *Will the Drag Queen*. My last time performing in drag was in March of my junior year in high school. I performed as Lady Gaga in the powder puff challenge of the school's class competition. It was my first and last public performance, my *au revoir* to drag. It was an ultimately fun performance; even though synchronized dancing was never my thing. The thirty-second performance went by so quickly that I never had time to really process what I was doing. I had exposed drag to a town that wasn't fully liberal and had ousted myself as a drag performer, whether I was or not. Although the performance brought us 1st place and tons of praise, the love of doing drag had ultimately diminished afterward. As the group of friends began to move on to less grandeur expressions of our individuality, we grew away from the essence of drag. It became redundant and our wigs were traded for booze and better clothing.

Although the physical attributes of drag were cut from my life, I still admired the performance and expertise displayed by the queens on RuPaul's Drag Race. Friends and I would watch the show religiously, betting on who would survive the lip sync and who had the best outfit. I never thought I would come across drag of such a high caliber on a personal level, until I found my college roommate, Aquaria. When we moved in, the name hadn't been made official but had been in the works. After reaching out to other drag queens, Giovanni settled on the name so that his career as a drag performer could begin to have some solidarity. It not only took time and effort to acquire the name but also to apply her look.

The light above Giovanni's desk flickers on while he preps the desk for the timely process of applying her face onto his. He mumbles along to himself as he pulls out the brushes he will use to apply powder after powder. He wraps his hair back and the project begins. He battles with gray contact lens in the bathroom. Occasionally yelling a "shit" or an "ohhh my godddd." Once he manages to pop the lens in, he sits down in his seat and fumbles through his array of sponges and begins to pat. First lightly, then quickly like the wings of a hummingbird. The powder that didn't stick to his primed skin fluttered in the air, hovering in the light in front of him. Prior to the application, he made sure to remove every fiber of hair from his face, chest, armpits, and eyebrows. Since he has such a skill with the art of makeup he decided recently to shave his eyebrows off completely, and draw them on everyday. "It'll be easier to do my drag eyebrows because now I don't have to wait to glue them down," he said as he ran the razor across his hard brow bone. Next brush, next color, and now let it sit. He turns on his blow dryer and the roar fills the air with the dust has coated his desk. The particles dispense further and become invisible to the naked eye. "Should I do a red or a nude lip?" he asks. "Red," I reply. He follows my advice, as he does with many others. He seeks the approval of others before most of his decisions, and this trait is heightened when he becomes Aquaria, his drag persona.

He continues to apply coats of lipstick and lip liner, making them look plumper than they are. He moves up to his eyes drawing on his new eyebrows and then going to work on the liner. He moves the brush swiftly, assuring to make soft, concise lines that he will fill in with more eyeliner. As he finishes his last wick of liquid eyeliner, he places the bottle onto the desk. He gazes into the mirror, viewing from all angles the face he has painted onto his skin. The contour curves that cut into his face and the accentuated shadows on his nose to slim it down and hide its masculinity. It's a true art form, contorting the face by using shades and highlights, masking the masculine with the feminine.

He works away at the accessory he created to stand out amongst the queens attending the same event. He finishes the last knot, clips the thread and places the silver outlining around his face. He removes the piece and looks into the mirror again, finishing the job he didn't before. He rubs a couple more brushes into the tubs of powder and finished with a click of the brush onto the desk. Not made by the placement of his hand but gravity taking the brush as he released it from his grasp. Almost done.

It's crunch time; he darts in and out of the room, fumbling with the door each time before finally wedging the door open. He runs his arms through the drawers under his bed to grab a hairbrush and multiple pairs of tights. He places all his items on his bed and grabs the platinum blond wig, his favorite. He flips it upside down; spraying it with hairspray to keep it from losing its wild up-do. He slips his feet into the massive platform heels without looking down and stands tall. The massive heel almost erases the masculine structure of his thighs, smoothing the lines of muscles under his tights and fishnets. Observing himself in the mirror, he bends his knees and arches his back to get a full view of the completed look, stopping at the eyes because his wig has not been glued on yet. It's time for the tuck.

He walks behind his bed ducking to assure that his crotch is hidden as I stare away at my computer screen. He squats and slings back his last element of manhood up and in between his tights. He perks himself back up; adjusting his legs and settling into the most comfortable position a man can when his testicles are in small sockets above his penis. He turns back to his wig grasping the hair to ensure that it has enough hairspray. It's good; he closes up the aerosol can and tosses it under his bed.

He clips his hoop earrings in and turns into the mirror for one of his final gawks. Then the wig goes on, covering his head in another identity; she's finally completed. She ties the laces up to her mid calf and begins to work away at applying nail glue. She has just a few minutes to get her three-inch metallic nails on. Just before 7:15 p.m. she grabs her phone and struts out the door, clicking into the hallway and knocking at the neighbors door to show off tonight's look.

It never took me this long to get ready. Thirty minutes was around the usually time for all of my friends and I to squeeze into the bathroom and get ourselves together. The epidemic that Aquaria goes through to get ready was insane. It took around two hours of time to turn Giovanni into Aquaria, and this look was done in a hurry. The hard work did, however, pay off. The pride in her completed ensemble was featured on Instagram multiple times that week, with over 200 likes and a range of comments applauding the queen.

"…I feel very powerful and important [in drag] because people pay a lot of attention to you because you don't look like them, you look cooler than them. I feel like it's easier to go out in drag because people care about you more than if you're just another gay guy at the bar or club," he admits. To some, like Giovanni, it's a love for attention and admiration. He is aware of his talent and knows that he can use his performances to increase both his social status and self-confidence. After all, with RuPaul's Drag Race Season 4 Winner, Sharon Needles, as his drag mother, he has learned from some of the most prominent queens on the circuit. However, that doesn't stop him from admiring his work even after it's completed. It isn't uncommon for him to re-watch his performances the next day to pick and poke at what he could improve on and what he was happy with. His drag lacks the essence of humility; although he draws humor into her performances and nature, it is all rehearsed. Aquaria's performances are that of a dancer – rehearsed, practiced and strategic. If something goes wrong, her Rolodex of recovery techniques flips through her head to try and make the absolute best of the situation. After the performance she will sit and run through what went wrong, harping on negative attributes of the performance and shedding light on them on the walk home.

Although he is no stranger to the stage, from performing with his high school dance ensemble since freshmen year, his priorities have shifted focus to gain a foothold in Manhattan drag. As a Philadelphia native, Giovanni explains the difference between the drag cultures of both cities:

"NYC drag is…in the words of drag-icon Madonna, reductive. You can go to a drag show and find a handful of blonde bombshells– with the same wig, in the same look they wore last week, at the same gig and it can just be very repetitive.

Philly drag is definitely more about theatre, concept, and mixing comedy with glamour and entertainment. I think in NYC the drag scene is more paycheck oriented. Meaning they do what they can because they have to. In Philly they don't limit themselves for their performances, in terms of monies & theatrics. But it's because they don't have to be; the same crowd always comes out in Philly. NYC brings tourists and unfamiliar faces a lot of times," (Palandrani, Interview).

As the crowd fills into the club, men and women climb onto the high barstools. Aquaria has been in the back prepping for the past thirty minutes while the guests order drinks and wait in anticipation for the show to begin. The small spotlights highlight the wooden railing and nicked up boards that serve as the queens' stage. Boots & Saddle serves as the start up spot for aspiring drag queens. The "little drag bar that could" has been supporting queens for fifteen years (Hernandez, "The Little…"), and Tuesday's are reserved for the up-and-coming queens of Manhattan. As the bar fills up, a spunky queen in a green jumpsuit hops on the small stage and begins interacting with the guests. She cracks jokes and curses up a storm, laughing along with the crowd as her curly black wig shakes. She introduces herself as Yuhua Hamasaki, the master of ceremonies and queen of queens for the night.

Four queens perform, each two numbers with brief entertainment from Yuhua to give the queens prep time. With all the elements of hair, make-up, wardrobe, performing, MC'ing in one, Yuhua says she found her job. "When I started, it wasn't about the money…it was more about expression, and fun, and celebration of me. Then realized if I enjoy doing it so much, why not get paid for it as well?" Yuhua told me during her interview.

She sprints into the back to change her hair, coming out shortly after with a vibrant fierceness. The long red wig trails behind her as she walks, ending at the middle of her thigh. Before snapping her neck to whip her new wig, she grabs the microphone and greets the guests for the final performance, hers. She lip-syncs along to 'All About that Bass' as she slaps her padded butt and shimmies around the tiny stage. Her performance displays her expertise in the elements of drag, as well as her love for the fun and enjoyment of performing in drag.

At the 3 a.m. arrival to the dorm, Aquaria's heels are the first to go followed by the half the nails and the outfit. Aquaria is put to rest before Giovanni because she cannot live without these material items. At night the queen is taken to rest and the character is a separate entity. As a young adult, Giovanni is searching to establish himself in two fields, fashion and drag. Many older queens intertwine the two, coming from artistic of fashion backgrounds and using that in their drag. However, for Giovanni it's hard to devote to one completely at this point in time.

The queens of Manhattan devote themselves to a work that is so diverse it's only real factor is men in dresses. Portraying a female character through drag is often taken as a lack of masculinity but the queens are truly turning the masculine into the feminine. They blend creative natures with artistic attributes and performance allows these queens to make drag their own. Performing their own drag is often what makes these queens so approachable and boosts the enthusiasm of the individual to pursue a career that may sometimes be difficult or excessive work.

Discussion Questions

- Why would somebody want to read this piece (the "Who cares?" factor)?
- Can you clearly identify the author's intention for the piece?
- How well does the author support the intention of the piece? Cite specific details that support or take away from the author's intention.
- Is there information missing from this piece that would make its intention clearer? What else would you like to know?
- Does the author portray herself as a round character? How does she do this?
- Do you trust the author of this piece? Why or why not?
- How clearly does the author establish a sense of setting/space in this piece? Cite specific details that support your claim.
- How clearly does the author establish characters other than the self in this piece? Cite specific details that support your claim.
- Did you learn anything new from reading this piece? If so, what?
- Are there particular passages with engaging language/description that stood out to you? Describe the appeal of these passages.
- Would you read more writing from this author? Why or why not?

NaNoWriMo

Joomi Park

NaNoWriMo. I played with the words on my tongue as I rode the One train to 79th Street. I anxiously opened the door to Irving Farm Coffee Roasters, afraid that the write-in group would be very exclusive and unwelcoming to those who do not have the experienced hands that have typed 50,000 words. A calming whiff of coffee beans pulled me into the café and I found myself plopped down at the nearest one-person table. I glanced at my surroundings and felt an odd déjà vu. The wooden tables, red brick walls, and modern lighting designs made the place feel like a cozy café plucked out of a romance movie. "NaNoWriMo—National Novel Writing Month" signs were placed on various tables in the front of the café so participants (and a certain subculture observer) could find each other.

I was not sure what to expect from a subculture of writers, but I looked around and saw some people boot up their laptops while others ordered warm drinks to thaw their insides and get their gears going. I didn't know it then, but Alexis's (the municipal liaison for Manhattan) words would hold true: I had chosen the safest and most normal group of people for my subculture essay. There was no specific trait that classified them as the type to partake in this writing event. It seemed like an everyday winter scene with people clad in flannels and sweaters, all enjoying a coffee after a long day. To my surprise, the most common occupation in the group this year was lawyers; however, their determined typing figures gave nothing away.

Other than the normalcy of their attire, everyone seemed to be in their mid twenties to thirties. At eighteen, I couldn't help but feel like an awkward outlier. Later when I asked if there were any younger participants, Alexis and Clarice (the municipal liaison for Brooklyn) recalled a few teenagers at the Brooklyn write-ins. "One time we had a girl come in and say that her dad thought she was at swim meet right now. And we said 'oh, you shouldn't do that!'" Clarice laughed at the memory while Alexis carried on.

As I soaked in my surroundings at my one-person table, two men by my side greeted me with the warmest of smiles. When I asked who was in charge they pointed me to Alexis, who was seated at the end of a large table with other NaNoWriMo writers. She gave a surprised chuckle when I asked if I could sit and observe, and I was swiftly seated beside her. The people around the table noticed me as a new face and they smiled and introduced themselves. I shyly opened up my notebook to begin my observing process, while Alexis supplied me with an incredible amount of information that I didn't know if I'd have enough paper to jot it all down on. The ladies around me pitched in as well, and I was overall blown away by their kindness. It radiated through the room with a warm and comfortable feeling.

When I tell someone that I observed NaNoWriMo, the question I get asked most is "How intense are the write-ins?" Many assume that the month long event is all work no play, but what I experienced at the café was an unmistakable bond of friendship and chatter. I overheard people talking about how tearful, yet amazing *Big Hero 6* was, and other conversations wandered off into methods of getting rid of hand cramps. At another corner of the room I could hear writers exchanging ideas on their stories thus far. A woman exclaimed, "I don't want to be the arsonist upstairs!" and it made me wonder what her story could possibly be about. So it wasn't hard to believe when I asked Alexis about the relationships within the group and she proudly mentioned a couple who met through NaNoWriMo and got married, and a group of people who became roommates. "We even join book clubs together," she added. I realized that the dynamic of this group was welcoming and enthusiastic. It reminded me of a close-knit group of true friends who are genuinely supportive of each other. I asked Alexis to describe NaNoWriMo as a subculture, and she claimed that the group would not be one if it weren't for the write-ins. "A woman from Denmark moved to New York for a month to participate in this! She wanted to be in a community where people are really engaged and active." My jaw dropped at the fact that the woman took a leave from work just to participate in NaNoWriMo.

Suddenly a man in a red and white gingham button up yelled from behind, "We're starting a ten minute sprint…NOW!" A tremendous hush fell over the group and all I could hear was ferocious taps on the keyboard. It dominated the clamor of customers at the back of the room, to the point where even the café music became a dull hum. A few sighs escaped the lips of those who were frustrated at either their writer's block or their fingers that would not move fast enough. "It's a writing group. They do this every year or something." A barista clarified to a curious customer. "It's so quiet," a few passerby's whispered as they made their way to the door. I looked at the faces of those around me and was appalled at their level of concentration. Knowing that I was clearly a little lost, Alexis leaned over and explained what a word sprint is. "Basically everyone starts typing whatever they can during a certain amount of time, and at the end we shout out our word counts. Back when the group was smaller, we used to give prizes for the winner, like buy them a cup of coffee or give them all the change we have in our pockets." I nodded in understanding and was surprised by the activities that the group did to motivate each other to write. I also found out that there is a Twitter account for NaNoWriMo word sprints, and topics and times are tweeted on a daily basis. It seemed intricate and well-thought-out so that everyone could join in no matter where their location. When the timer rung, everyone went back to their normal chitchat mode. The average word count seemed to be around 320. Then one woman shouted, "1195!" I couldn't believe my ears until people around me explained that she always had the highest counts, to which she chuckled and said, "At this point I think we agree that I don't count. I'm not here, I'm the NaNoWriMo ghost."

I realized that a great part of this subculture has to do with technology, whether it is in the form of a smartphone or a laptop. One observation is all it takes to show that it is an obvious artifact in this subculture. Almost everyone types his or her novels—although, I was told a funny story about those who brought typewriters to quiet write-in locations and were forced to move to somewhere else and type—and the 50,000 word count happens online, as well. The website is really a collective source of useful devices and information. There they have a forum where participants can communicate, a chart that graphs how much they have written so far and how much they have left, and a calendar where people can add their own write-in days with or without a municipal liaison present. Without the Internet and technology, NaNoWriMo would be a desolate event with no sense of community at all whatsoever. I also noted how the forums are used on a frequent basis, and many receive feedback and ideas through them. One exemplary situation is when the woman sitting diagonal to me asked if anyone had a different word for "volunteer." She read her sentence out loud as people pulled out their smartphones and searched on their thesaurus apps. "How about 'missionary?' What about 'helper?'" The options flew around the table and she nodded or shook her head at each one. After a while her fellow writers told her to move on. "Don't get stuck on one sentence. It'll probably come to you when you're in bed at 2 a.m. and you'll have to fly out of bed and write it down before you forget." This advice was given in a silly tone, but I personally took a lot from it too. Had the smartphones not been around, these NaNoWriMo writers would have had to lug around an actual thesaurus and hope for the best. Technology has certainly made life easier, and for participants, much faster too. Many of the people there found out about NaNoWriMo through the Internet, specifically LiveJournal. I interviewed those around me, and they giggled as they remembered the fan fiction they started off with on that site in their younger years.

Towards 9 p.m. the write-in began to come to a close, and many started to pack their laptops and say their goodbyes. "Email me your drafts" and "I'll see you at the next write-ins," were exchanged and slowly the front of the café became empty again, excluding some of the few writers who stayed behind to continue their writing journey.

A week after my observation, I attended another write-in at Whole Foods where I spoke to Alexis more in-depth about herself. When I got there another girl was already interviewing her, so I sat beside them and listened in. Alexis has been a municipal liaison for eight years, and her role is essentially a cheerleader and event planner. She and the other municipal liaisons send out pep talks through email and motivate others around them. She works as a writing tutor so she's constantly around writing regardless of NaNoWriMo. It was evident that she was great at both roles when she talked me through a lot of what I could write about for my observation and the ways I could steer my essay, all while educating me on the basics of the group. I asked her to describe a moment when she felt most accomplished through NaNoWriMo. Alexis replied, "When I wrote my zombie apocalypse novel. I reached 75,000 words and that's when I knew what I was capable of." 75,000 words felt like an impossible milestone, but seeing her beaming face made me realize that she was a good representation of the subculture. She was outgoing, friendly, and she had a real knack for writing. It encompassed her life even while she taught writing to others. NaNoWriMo is more than just reaching an end goal of 50,000. The subculture is a welcoming force that develops writers, novels, and the meaning of community.

Discussion Questions

- Why would somebody want to read this piece (the "Who cares?" factor)?
- Can you clearly identify the author's intention for the piece?
- How well does the author support the intention of the piece? Cite specific details that support or take away from the author's intention.
- Is there information missing from this piece that would make its intention clearer? What else would you like to know?
- Does the author portray herself as a round character? How does she do this?
- Do you trust the author of this piece? Why or why not?
- How clearly does the author establish a sense of setting/space in this piece? Cite specific details that support your claim.
- How clearly does the author establish characters other than the self in this piece? Cite specific details that support your claim.
- Did you learn anything new from reading this piece? If so, what?
- Are there particular passages with engaging language/description that stood out to you? Describe the appeal of these passages.
- Would you read more writing from this author? Why or why not?

Steel Paradise: The Hardcore Metal Aesthetic

Justine Giardina

Tony Gorta is the artist for a metal band. He has long red-blond hair, hair that comes down past his shoulders and ends in ringlet curls a hairdresser would spend hours just trying to replicate. He's thin—wiry almost—and grandly tall, standing at 6'4". His glasses, rimmed with thin wire, slide halfway down his nose and rest there, as though the contours of the fixture were molded just to hold them in place. His eyes are wide and glassy, a gorgeous teal color that's repeated in his shirt, which is every color. The shirt is pinstriped and buttoned up, evocative of a psychedelic poster. His skin is a chalky white and almost all covered, with the exception of his hands and face. He wears Doc Martens, the kind that only go up to the ankle and could be mistaken for regular dress shoes if not for the signature yellow threading along the outsole. The dark denim of his jeans is patched only in one place, right under the front left pocket, "It's because I lit them on fire," he tells me, for the fourth time. The first time he told me was the night I met him, on the edge of the water on the Upper East Side at four in the morning. The second time was on a subway to Brooklyn, and the third time just a bit earlier this very night in a sparsely populated diner. He's very proud of the incident, as it's very edgy to set one's own pants on fire. He's even more proud that he sewed up the pants himself. The band that Tony is the artist for is the recently signed Manhattan-based metal band called Steel Paradise. "I met Christian through Moise and I met Moise in high school," he explains. We're sitting on a bus stop on a Tuesday night, lit by the passing cars and street lights, and I am asking him questions. "That was when Moise still had his afro," he continues, as though I should remember this seemingly important nugget of information that apparently divides Moise's entire life into Before Afro, During Afro and After Afro. His left arm lays across his lap, fingers curled around a cigarette the way a pencil might be grasped. His legs are crossed and he's slouched over, just slightly. Tony went to LaGuardia High School for the Arts, where he met a whole slew of eccentric ruffians which he can, and will, talk about for hours. Mostly he likes to talk about the ones that he smoked with before he got arrested, but also he likes to talk about the ones that he gave baby animal themed nicknames to. Moise Scott, who Tony has taken to calling "Mouse," is a muscular 6'2" musical performance major who plays drums for Steel Paradise. In high school he played the flute. Christian Realmuto is the lead guitarist of Steel Paradise, and probably the only person I've ever met who is taller than Tony. The three of them are a bit frightening upon first glance, but after you've seen them talk about baby animals for twenty minutes the hardcore metal aesthetic doesn't seem quite as intimidating.

Christian is the center of Steel Paradise, and is thus the center of the local community that has risen around it. Steel Paradise, according to Moise Scott (sans afro), started as a project of Christian's in middle school. "Yeah he was like, 'I'm really serious about learning guitar,'" Scott says as he flips a pancake on the stove of his mother's Washington Heights apartment. He's making me breakfast while we talk. "And I was like, 'Yeah, sure, whatever Christian, because I know Christian isn't serious about shit. But I went along with it and I guess he kind of was because we're still doing it." He wrenches the pancake out of the pan and unceremoniously drops it onto an empty ceramic plate. "I knew Christian for a while because he was friends with my best friend in elementary school." Moise goes on to explain the complex intricacies of elementary school social circles, taking care to explain the weight of the word "best friend" several times before telling me that they didn't really become close until they were in high school band together. They both play flute.

The band has changed members several times, and several members have left and come back. The members of the band and the friends and fans that have flocked to it have formed a sort of intimate group that participates in activities centered around the band's performances and events. Not everyone is directly connected to the band, like Tony, who creates all of their promotional art, or Moise, who is a member of the band. The majority of the people in this group are just fans of the band's music, actively attend their shows, or are associated with other local metal bands that come into contact with Steel Paradise. Members of this small community include a variety of interesting factions, including "Christian's Neighbors", "Art Girls from LaGuardia", "People Christian Works with at the Deli", and "People Who Have Dated Someone We Know", which is probably the largest faction. There is also, always, a small faction of people Steel Paradise is currently dating, the only member of which right now is Emma Montgomery, Christian's girlfriend.

"Emma is a saint" Tony tells me, sitting all the way back in his seat and looking upward toward the heavens with an expression of ultimate gratitude. Every time someone says that, which is often, it's always followed by a story about Christian pissing on something.

"One time Christian was pissing on a car and he didn't check to see if it was empty first—which it wasn't, there was a family in it—and he's drunkenly cursing at the top of his lungs and we were all yelling at him and Emma just goes over to him and touches his arm to pull him away—and he just stops!" Tony sighs, leans forward in his seat and kind of smiles, peacefully. Emma has also ignored antics such as the 24" x 36" poster of Megan Fox that is hanging on his wall, his firm stance as a Republican despite his liberal beliefs, his long, uncombed hair, and the fact that his name is also her brother's name. Emma can stop Christian from doing things that Christian does while he is drunk and for that reason she is the unknowing savior of the Steel Paradise group.

"Emma is a saint," Moise says, breathlessly, when asked about the subject. He stares blankly into space for a couple of moments, probably recalling horrors unbeknownst to common folk such as you or I, and lets the pancake currently in the skillet cook slightly past golden-brown before taking it out. I don't question him further. "The Steel Paradise Crew," as Moise refers to the group as, is typically recognizable by their typical metal aesthetic, sporting all sorts of black band t-shirts, double-grommetted belts, lace, wristbands, ripped jeans, and everything obtainable that is black and covered in studs. Other notable clues include Metallica paraphernalia, large, bulky instruments thrown over their backs in black cases, long, tangled, unruly hair, and the repeated use of the phrase popularized by the adult cartoon *Metalocolypse,* "Metal as hell." There are, however several notable exceptions. Moise, the drummer, likes to wear patterns and bright colors, and is often in athletic-wear and shirts with rappers on them. Tony is usually wearing a colorful button-up, and sometimes what the Art Girls from LaGuardia refer to as "Dad clothes," a pair of thicker-rimmed glasses combined with a tweed jacket that Tony has never been carded in a liquor store while wearing (this is the only reason I have uncovered that explains why they all call him "dad"). My favorite example of this is a smiley, clean-cut boy named Weston who is always wearing salmon-colored, tailored clothing that looks like it's from a J. Crew catalog. He lives on the Upper East Side and doesn't like metal music, but seems to enjoy drinking as much as metal kids do. The Steel Paradise shows are most notable for being loud, sticky, and erratic. They typically take place below the ground floor in some hole in the wall, and no matter where it is the same people go every time. Any venue they play in reeks strongly of beer and is dimly lit. The last show they played was in a bar on Lafayette Street with walls painted black and colored lights that reached over the span of the room, flooded the entire scene. The audience wasn't generously populated, but the male crowd still managed to cause some sort of commotion with a frivolous show of violently throwing themselves into one another in some sort of display of support of the band. This had to be explained to me multiple times and I am still not sure that I can properly articulate its purpose.

Local music shows aside, drinking is the most notable Steel Paradise event. Usually this is set in some poor kid's dirty New York apartment, but it really can happen anywhere and they are not very discriminant about it. Currently, the most frequented place for a Steel Paradise drinking event is the Chelsea Galleries, specifically on Thursdays between six and eight when free wine is given out.

"I think this is about how life always changes," Moise says, looking quizzically at a painting. It's a series of smudged paint strokes that don't really seem to form much of anything at all. We are on a 25th Street gallery and he has one cup of free—presumably Trader Joe's—wine that the studio is giving out, in each hand. He's trying very hard to seem interested in the art. "And about old people. And death probably." He notices his empty glass and, abruptly ending his analysis, goes back to the wine table. I am treated with these gorgeous, half-assed analyses all night. "I think this is about sex," he says, looking at a black and white photo of just an erect penis. "And about how it's art. Is there only white wine here? Because if there is then we should go to the next one."

At the galleries where beer is served everyone collects a can and, upon remembering they hate beer, pass each one to Christian. He puts them in his messenger bag and walks around with six open beer cans under the buckled canvas flap.

At eight o'clock, after the wine is done being served, they usually go to a liquor store and dedicatedly continue to drink through the night. On every occasion that I have had the pleasure of being present, this has meant a night of cheap whiskey being poured into a plastic red cup with store-brand soda, someone vomiting in timely intervals for three hours, metal music by different bands that I virtually can't distinguish from one another blasting from a cheap iPod docking station, Christian drunkenly screaming at innocent passersby and urinating on something that is public property, Emma somehow calming him down, and Tony whispering "Emma is a saint" the whole way home.

Typically there are some delightful surprises that come with a night spent with Steel Paradise drinking crew. Once a radio station promised to play one of their singles but played the song "This is Halloween" from the soundtrack of some Tim Burton movie instead. Another night I entered a room to find Christian wearing women's Guns N' Roses leggings. One night, a night that I wasn't there, they found out that a recording studio liked their work and wanted to fly them out to California for a month to record an EP. I didn't get to witness it firsthand, but Moise says the excitement and celebration that night held can be measured in the sheer amount of things Christian pissed on that night.

"California was great," Moise confides in me. "There was this restaurant there. Oh man, I would fly all the way back to California just for the hamburgers at that restaurant."

From what I understand, Steel Paradise had a very wonderful experience in California, but I couldn't elicit much from Moise, or anyone else for that matter, other than two subjects that he was very, very passionate about that he dabbled in quite a bit during the trip to California: the food and the weed.

And, oh, how they love to talk about the weed. "California...is a different way of life," Christian says, reclined on a musty couch in an apartment that belongs to some poor soul who got suckered into hosting thirteen kids looking for somewhere to smoke after a metal show. He goes on to explain things very specifically, such as accessibility societal acceptance, and drug culture, but he does so in such an aimless, unacademic, ridiculous and nonsensical way that it's not even worth noting. He closes his eyes, and then, losing track of what he was talking about, mutters again, "California was really different."

Tony sits at a table nearby with some of the Art Girls from LaGuardia. They're fumbling with some sort of vaporizer that was legally purchased online from a site with some statement about only endorsing the use of legal aromatherapy as though they don't know who their audience are. Two of the art girls are piecing the contraption together, attaching some sort of nozzle and sliding batteries into it. "There's really no need for this," Tony is telling them, "Weston and I once smoked out of a bell pepper and it worked fine."

America's real engineers are not at Princeton.

In accordance with their views on marijuana, the Steel Paradise group is also, for the most part, unified by their liberal social and political views. Much of the Steel Paradise group advocates queer rights and feminism, and most all members, like in any Manhattan-based group, identify with either the Democratic Party or some sort of liberal party. "Ben and I are basically socialists," Tony explains to me as we sit on the bus stop. Ben is Steel Paradise's bassist. He grows visibly frustrated and his tone changes as a thought passes over him. "It's just Christian who's the problem."

Christian, Tony explains, "thinks he's a Republican just because he believes in God." Tony grows visibly upset as he delves further into the subject. "And I've tried telling him, 'Christian, you play rock music. You don't hate gay people. You don't hate black people. You like smoking weed, you aren't a Republican.'" Impressed at this Official List of Qualities that, according to Tony Gorta, invalidate a Republican identity, I nod my head wordlessly. "I think hopefully Emma's gonna change him," Tony confides in me. "She's liberal; she goes to art school for Christ's sake." I nod my head again, taking in this Official Qualification for a liberal identity. There is a silence invaded only by the sound of passing cars and then, as I expected him to, Tony gratefully mutters, "Emma is a saint."

Despite the fact that going to art school isn't quite *directly* correlated with identifying in a liberal way, liberal viewpoints are certainly common in artists and art students, and a good portion of the Steel Paradise community are artists and art students. Often too, it seems, that the community is a place where eccentrics and misfits often fit in. Having the connecting factor of interest in the same musical genre opens opportunity to participate in an assortment of events on a regular basis, and the opportunity to meet other people in the group.

Regardless of whether or not they agree with liberal views, the group seems to be deeply rooted not in a shared belief, but in a familial, communal sort of way. Despite the differences within the subculture, it seems as though they are all ready and willing to support each other. "These are just really open and accepting people," Tony tells me. "There's a lot of support between friends here."

And he's right, the community has provided a support system for a lot of people who have felt otherwise lost when times are bleak. As in any group of people, there have been tragedies faced by participants throughout the years, and they are always met with an overwhelming show of compassion and sympathy. Most recently, Vironika, the lead singer of Steel Paradise, suffered the loss of her older brother. All of the band members shed their ridiculous garments on November 6th to attend the wake and support her.

"Vironika is like a sister to me," Moise tells me, sincerely. "There's nothing I wouldn't do for her."

The band is currently on hiatus until Vironika feels ready to come back. In the meantime, Tony is currently working on a new logo design for the band, and the other members are looking forward to the release of more music, maybe even a full album. The band will continue to hold practices once per week once their lead singer is well enough to return, and hopes to continue performing local shows.

"The group is still going to see each other even if there aren't any shows," Tony says, now walking along the edge of the sidewalk, Doc Martens scuffing against the cement. "It's not like we aren't friends outside of band [functions]."

As I finally get ready to say my goodbyes and take myself home, Tony gives me a quizzical look.

"It's dark out. I'm taking you home," he says, plainly. I can't help but laugh at the tall, scary metalhead that will pay the extra fare to make sure a girl gets home safe at eight o'clock on a Tuesday night. Gladly accepting his offer, I consent to hearing about how Emma is a saint and a tentative list of things Christian has pissed on for another thirty minutes.

Works Cited

"Steel Paradise." Steel Paradise. ReverbNation.com. Web. 10 Dec. 2014. <http://www.steelparadise.com/about-us>

"Steel Paradise." *Facebook*. Facebook. Web. 10 Dec. 2014. <https://www.facebook.com/steelparadiseband>

"Let's Talk About Metal Kids: The Interview." Personal interviews with Moise Scott and Anthony Gorta. 11/2014.

Discussion Questions

- Why would somebody want to read this piece (the "Who cares?" factor)?
- Can you clearly identify the author's intention for the piece?
- How well does the author support the intention of the piece? Cite specific details that support or take away from the author's intention.
- Is there information missing from this piece that would make its intention clearer? What else would you like to know?
- Does the author portray herself as a round character? How does she do this?
- Do you trust the author of this piece? Why or why not?
- How clearly does the author establish a sense of setting/space in this piece? Cite specific details that support your claim.
- How clearly does the author establish characters other than the self in this piece? Cite specific details that support your claim.
- Did you learn anything new from reading this piece? If so, what?

- Are there particular passages with engaging language/description that stood out to you? Describe the appeal of these passages.
- Would you read more writing from this author? Why or why not?

YouTube: Science Isn't Just for Geeks Anymore

Neziah Doe

The average color of the universe is called a "Cosmic Latte"

The Internet is Miley Cyrus—it will never be tamed and the more you tell it to stop making you feel uncomfortable, the more it will come back at you like a wrecking ball with ten more heads than before and it will win awards while obsessing over genitalia, insisting that it cannot stop. For many young people, the Internet is their medium of finding people with similar interests and exposure to what life has in store.

Within the abyss of cat videos and illegal downloads of music and films, on YouTube there are dynamic and creative creators curating content for the curious mind. Strongly believing that any creation could be used for the good of society, I have become obsessed with the idea of these informational YouTube channels and the endless wonder they provide for people every day. This genre of videos is usually presented in a list format, to explain how it was founded and what it means for us.

This community on YouTube is one of the most accessible and interactive sources of information on the Iinternet. Many people agree, including Nava Maynard, who is a huge fan of these videos, "I think that the information side of YouTube attempts to open viewers up to as many new types of information as possible. It expands the brain and in that manner, your social circle as well. It comes down to the realization that the world is bigger than just yourself. It also teaches a lot about agency and that you can make a difference even in just a local manner." Many people complain that the authentic process of education has been deteriorating since the Internet was established—with everything I have experienced with this bright community of people, I believe that something beautiful has arisen.

An ostrich egg would take four hours to boil

Given the nature of the Internet, it's debatable how this community really began. Many would say it began with the likes of Vi Hart, who made instructional videos on all things mathematical for Khan Academy. While Khan Academy is most certainly the granddaddy of this community, there was an interactive element missing from their very helpful math tutorials. 2011 brought the channels Veritasium, MinutePhysics, and CGP Grey. While they had created videos that people adored, they did not reach a broader audience until the Internet's famous had brought them and their educational tools to light.

In came the Green brothers, already YouTube's "nerdiest" duo (with a huge fanbase called "Nerdfighteria") with a new channel called CrashCourse. The dynamic duo created full series of educational videos based on what the viewers were asking for—physics, biology, world history and psychology, just to name a few topics covered. This branched into the video channels Mental Floss (a channel comprising only lists of facts), SciShow (experiments, asking the "big questions", astronomy, biology, chemistry, physics, and more…), Sexplanations (sex/gender studies), and Healthcare Triage (medical findings, medicine, and the healthcare system), inspiring others to create exciting videos about the things that we are supposed to learn in class and the things that we never had the opportunity to learn.

There is more real lemon juice in Lemon Pledge furniture polish than in Country Time Lemonade

This fandom seems to be following me wherever I go. Assembling Lego with my boyfriend Aryeh in his school lounge, a group of friends began to accumulate around us to watch us play (and by us I mean my boyfriend dictatorially demanding me where to put each piece to his design, while I got to make it look all pretty in the end with all the dot pieces we collected).

"You guys are not actually playing with Lego, are you?" asks Rivka, an old friend. We grinned at her knowingly as we assemble the spaceship car.

"If this isn't how our first car looks like, I will break up with you" I tease.

"You guys are such nerds," says Ian, a friend of Aryeh's, plopping his thin self on the couch with over-priced salads for himself and his girlfriend.

"We did meet because of Nerdfighteria," I said.

"Well, you should know that Ayala is writing her paper on educational YouTube videos," Aryeh says. "You're into that kind of thing, right Ian?"

"I write for Mental Floss," he says casually.

"Wait, you're kidding me, right?" I say.

"I tweeted the director if he had any internships and he said he needed writers. That's all there is to it, you should get a Twitter."

"But I don't want a Twitter, social media is the devil," I say in earnest.

"Then you're just not going to get these opportunities. Twitter is where it's at! Also, you should talk to Nava—this kind of stuff is Nava's life."

Because so many of these videos are related to John and Hank Green (the founders of CrashCourse, SciShow, Mental Floss, Sexplanations, and Healthcare Triage), many would say that this is not a community of its own but a sub-fandom of what their following—called Nerdfighteria—is. A fan named Jenna described it as "a branch from the same tree."

"Nerdfighteria serves as an introduction for those people to the other aspects of online culture and the search for information. It is more of a central, wide-reaching, introductory branch that tends to stay close to the heart," said superfan Nava.

Every day more money is printed for Monopoly than the U.S. treasury

On most SciShow, Mental Floss, and CrashCourse videos, one thing is pretty much the same—the abundance of questions pertaining to the video in the comment sections. "If we know why mint feels 'cool,' then why does one's mouth seemingly freeze when drinking water?" When people post questions like that, it gives the community a chance to discuss things and do their own research. It's very hard to not see this as a modern classroom.

With technology wildly changing classroom dynamics, there is a question, "Is this the future of education?" With the common-folk procrastination tools of BuzzFeed, Cracked, and online magazines of the sort, people are obtaining information for fun—from fun and relatable people. No wonder people sneak onto other websites while they are in class—YouTube is interactive; channels like SciShow are only answering questions that come from the comments. In a world of instant gratification, the amount of information that YouTube provides on real questions is astounding. Why does asparagus make your pee smell bad? Do I only use ten percent of my brain? What's the deal with eating disorders?

When asked what this community means for the future, CrashCourse enthusiast Jenna had this to say: "students who know about these resources are starting to use them more and more—like Khan Academy. With CrashCourse, [John] Green caters to AP History students, but I just watched them for fun. That said, they will not take over the classic classroom setting; there is still the need for a teacher."

I love school—the smell of fresh pencils, the crisp hopeful feeling of September days, seeing everyone after the summer. I like using my computer, but I like having a person in front of me, talking to me. Someone who knows my name. I like going on the journey of education with the people around me. But there is just something appealing about this extra help—short, humorous, and free.

Asking YouTube nerd Nava about this was delightful, though. For the whole interview she was practically falling off her seat, her eyes alight with the passion that fired her making this part of YouTube such a huge part of her life:

YES. Watching the way CrashCourse has been embraced by educators and students alike is the first indication of this. I think education is steering more towards personal choice rather than institutional education, or at least much of society is pointing out those flaws and inaccuracies in the system.... Taking the issue into their own hands is validating and freeing—this can be achieved through 'joining' this subculture.

I think that this will hit a threshold and then become institutionalized as a standard of education, but not before it sees a backlash. Also, ease of access to information that you *want* to learn, rather than being *forced* to learn, is a huge factor, particularly the voluntary aspect. Another huge factor is the visual experience rather than the textual experience. Society is moving towards this visual theme must be embraced by ALL aspects of culture—education included—or else those nonconforming aspects will fail.

A scientist who weighed people immediately before and after death concluded that the soul weighs 41 grams

Scrolling through the videos produced by Mental Floss and SciShow, I do not even know where to look first. They have multiple series going on at once—I could just binge. The religious person inside of me is tickled by the title, "What is the meaning of life?" Wow, I knew science was good, but not *that* good. The second I hear Hank Green, one of the hosts of SciShow, say, "Don't die—have sex!" I smile, happy that that question is still being asked and will never be properly and universally answered.

I compiled a Survey Monkey to ask people in the community some questions, similar to the ones that I asked fans Jenna and Nava. Most of these channels hold surveys at least once a year, trying to get feedback from their viewers as to how to better themselves. "[These videos] showed me how naturally curious we all are, how we have this big desire to know things." Another viewer said, "These videos also sparked my curiosity, and made me realize my passions in life."

During the movie "The Silence of the Lambs," Hannibal Lecter never blinks while talking on screen

It's a cold October day and as I approach Madison Square Park, I look down occasionally on my phone, ensuring that I reached the right destination. The destination in question is SciShow, one of the leading informational YouTube channels. The event is titled "What is Energy?" The mysterious title leaves a lot of questions. I walk my way down the winding path, the autumn wind blowing through the defenses of my sweater.

In the corner of the park is a giant clear cube, with multicolored balls jumping up and down in its different sections. Each section is color coded, and the viewers have to attempt to make the balls fly up using different methods, giving the person an interactive understanding of what different units of energy are, compared to one another, and how much power does it take to produce them. A young group of people is surrounding the tablets scattered around, trying to make the balls go up. Some are laughing during their attempts. A child with a particularly determined look on his face is turning a crank like it is the last thing he will ever do. People are in clusters, looking over at the real life "episode" going on before them as they talk excitedly to the producers.

Circling the event like a hawk on its prey, I don't feel uninvited, but out of place. I like science, but even after starting to watch these videos, I need to look up some things on Google before it all really comes together.

"Hi!" a gawky, tall volunteer in a sterling white lab coat says to me friendlily, "Would you like to try this?"

"Yeah, sure, of course," I say, taking the crank the child was playing with before, "What's the record?"

"Five point eight," he says, "No one is going to beat it though." With the steel determination of a racehorse I hit 5.8 in a second, trying as hard as I can to get to 5.9, after a few minutes I give up, the volunteer looking at me like I'm silly. People around me are not noticing, they all must have tried the same thing.

"So, why did you decide to volunteer here?" I ask, hoping to alleviate the awkward display of arrogance.

"Well, I really like the show. When they were asking for volunteers in the area, I knew that was something I wanted to help with."

"Do you feel like you're a part of a community?" I ask him.

"Yes," he automatically replies, "If it wasn't we couldn't have events like this." His comment gave me the courage to begin to speak to all the other strangers there. Each and every person I talked to was friendlier than the next, more excited by my idea for the project than the now-not-strangers before them, nearly falling at my knees to answer my questions.

"THAT IS THE COOLEST IDEA FOR A PAPER EVER," exclaims one of the girls I meet, already bundled up in her winter coat. I laugh, asking her the same questions I asked everyone before, but the answers are all the same. I do not know if that reinforces their sense of community or just proves that they are all clones or brainwashed. Yes, this is a community and a subculture—a lovable one at that. Yes, I love learning new things through this new way of introducing information. Yes, I do think this is the future of education. Yes, I think that this community is a beast of its own, separate from the other projects that the founders Hank Green and Michael Aranda have curated. Yes, I am involved in the STEM fields, but still love these videos.

"Do you want to talk to the producer?" someone asks me. I twiddle my thumbs nervously. I am playing with the big boys now.

Meredith, one of the producers, is as kind and enthusiastic as everyone else. When I ask her questions, she also gives me the same answers.

"Did you think that this project was going to be as successful as it is?"

"If you told me five years ago that I could work full time for an informational YouTube channel, and we could have events of this magnitude in New York City and ads in the subway systems, I would have thought you were crazy. But look, it happened. And it's brilliant and I love being a part of it."

The Bible has been translated into Klingon

Whether you love listening to John Green writing letters to historical figures on CrashCourse, or walking to the supermarket ensures you also return with a bag full of questions, there is a channel on YouTube for you to satisfy your curiosity. So, as Lindsay Doe of Sexplanations says—stay curious.

Discussion Questions

- Why would somebody want to read this piece (the "Who cares?" factor)?
- Can you clearly identify the author's intention for the piece?
- How well does the author support the intention of the piece? Cite specific details that support or take away from the author's intention.
- Is there information missing from this piece that would make its intention clearer? What else would you like to know?
- Does the author portray herself as a round character? How does she do this?
- Do you trust the author of this piece? Why or why not?
- How clearly does the author establish a sense of setting/space in this piece? Cite specific details that support your claim.
- How clearly does the author establish characters other than the self in this piece? Cite specific details that support your claim.
- Did you learn anything new from reading this piece? If so, what?
- Are there particular passages with engaging language/description that stood out to you? Describe the appeal of these passages.
- Would you read more writing from this author? Why or why not?

Works Cited

Barnard, Ian. "Anti-Ethnography?" *Composition Studies* 34.1 (Spring 2006): 95-107. Print.

Bartholomae, David. "Writing with Teachers: A Conversation with Peter Elbow." *College Composition and Communication* 46 (1995): 62-71. Print.

Bishop, Wendy and Hans Ostrom, eds. *Colors of a Different Horse: Rethinking Creative Writing Theory and Pedagogy*. Urbana: NCTE, 1994

Bishop, Wendy. *Ethnographic Writing Research: Writing It Down, Writing It Up, and Reading It*. Portsmouth: Boynton/Cook, 1999. Print.

Bizzell, Patricia. *Academic Discourse and Critical Consciousness*. Pittsburgh: University of Pittsburgh Press, 1992. Print.

Bochner, Arthur P. "Criteria Against Ourselves." *Qualitative Inquiry* 6.2 (2000): 266-72. Print.

Bradway, Becky and Douglas Hesse. *Creating Nonfiction: A Guide and Anthology*. Boston: Bedford/St. Martin's, 2009. Print.

Brodkey, Linda. *Academic Writing as Social Practice*. Philadelphia: Temple University Press, 1987. Print.

—-. *Writing Permitted in Designated Areas Only*. Minneapolis: University of Minnesota Press, 1996. Print.

Brown, Stephen Gilbert and Sidney I. Dobrin. *Ethnography Unbound: From Theory Shock to Cultural Praxis*. Albany: State University of New York Press, 2004. Print.

    Gaillet, Lynée Lewis. "Writing Program Redesign: Learning from Ethnographic Inquiry, Civic Rhetoric, and the History of Rhetorical Education." Brown and Dobrin 99-114.

    Hanson, Susan S. "Critical Auto/Ethnography: A Constructive Approach to Research in the Composition Classroom." Brown and Dobrin 183-200.

Charters, Ann, Ed. *The Story and its Writer: An Introduction to Short Fiction*. 6th Ed. Boston: Bedford/St. Martin's, 2003.

    Kincaid, Jamaica. "Girl." 320-1.

Clark, Virginia, Paul Eschholz and Alfred Rosa. *Language: Readings in Language and Culture*. New York: St. Martin's Press, 1998.

    Cunha, Edite. "Talking in a New Land." 3-11.

Cofer, Judith Ortiz. "More Room." *Silent Dancing: A Partial Remembrance of a Puerto Rican Childhood*. Houston: Arte Público Press, 1990. 23-28. Print.

Dailey, Sheron J., ed. *The Future of Performance Studies: Visions and Revisions*. Annandale: National Communication Association, 1998. Print.

   Conquergood, Dwight. "Beyond the Text: Toward a Performative Cultural Politics." Dailey 25-36.

Denzin, Norman K. and Yvonna S. Lincoln, eds. *Handbook of Qualitative Research*. Thousand Oaks: Sage, 2005. Print.

   Jones, Stacy Holman. "Autoethnography: Making the Personal Political." Denzin and Norman. 763-91

Didion, Joan. "On Keeping a Notebook." *Slouching Towards Bethlehem*. Seattle: ScriptorPress, 1967. Print.

Elbow, Peter. "Being a Writer vs. Being an Academic: A Conflict in Goals." *College Composition and Communication* 46 (1995): 72-83. Print.

Ellis, Carolyn. "Maternal Connections." *Composing Ethnography: Alternative Forms of Qualitative Writing*. Eds. Carolyn Ellis and Arthur C. Bochner. Walnut Creek: AltaMira Press, 1996. 240-43. Print.

—-. *The Ethnographic I: A Methodological Novel About Autoethnography*. Walnut Creek: AltaMira Press, 2004. Print.

—-. "Evocative Autoethnography: Writing Emotionally About Our Lives." *Representation and the Text: Re-Framing the Narrative Voice*. Eds. William G. Tierney and Yvonna S. Lincoln. Albany: State University of New York Press, 1997. 115-42. Print.

Ellis, Carolyn and Arthur C. Bochner. "Telling and performing personal stories: The constraints of choice in abortion." Eds. Carolyn Ellis and Michael Flaherty. *Investigating Subjectivity: Research on Lived Experience*. Newbury Park: Sage, 2002. 79-101. Print.

English Course Descriptions: Spring 2008 University of Illinois Urbana-Champaign. http://www.english.illinois.edu/undergraduate/courses/sp08/rhetoric/, August 2009.

English Course Descriptions: Fashion Institute of Technology. http://catalog.fitnyc.edu/undergraduate/courses/en/, August 2009.

Ethnography of the University Initiative. "About: From the Directors." University of Illinois at Urbana-Champaign, n.d. Web. http://www.eui.uiuc.edu/about.html, August 2009.

Fontaine, Sheryl I. and Susan Hunter. *Writing Ourselves into the Story: Unheard Voices from Composition Studies*. Carbondale: Southern Illinois University Press, 1993. Print.

   Bishop, Wendy. "Student's Stories and the Variable Gaze of Composition Research." Fontaine and Hunter 197-214.

   Clark, Carol Lea. "Student Voices: How Students Define Themselves as Writers." Fontaine and Hunter 215-28.

Hunter, Susan. "The Dangers of Teaching Differently." Fontaine and Hunter 70-85.

Forche, Carolyn and Philip Gerard, eds. *Writing Creative Nonfiction*. Cincinnati: Story Press, 2001. Print.

Lopate, Philip. "Portrait of My Body." Forche and Gerard 214-22.

Lopate, Philip. "Writing Personal Essays: On the Necessity of Turning Oneself Into a Character." Forche and Gerard 38-44.

Gutkind, Lee. "What's the Story #6: The Five 'R's of Creative Nonfiction." *Creative Nonfiction* 6 (1996). Print.

Kerouac, Jack. *On the Road: The Original Scroll*, New York: Penguin Books, 2008. Print.

Kirklighter, Cristina, Cloe Vincent, and Joseph M. Moxley. *Voices and Visions: Refiguring Ethnography in Composition*. Portsmouth: Boynton/Cook, 1997. Print.

Branscomb, H. Eric. "North Northwest: Ethnography and *The Making of Knowledge in Composition*." Kirklighter, Vincent and Moxleycunha 1-10.

Kirsch, Gesa E. *Women Writing the Academy: Audience, Authority, and Transformation*. Carbondale: Southern Illinois University Press, 1993. Print.

Kothari, Geeta. "If you are what you eat, then what am I?" *The Kenyon Review*. Vol. 21. No.1 (Winter, 1999). 6-14.

Lu, Min-Zhan. "Reading and Writing Differences: The Problematic of Experience." *Feminism and Composition Studies: In Other Words*. Eds. Susan C. Jarratt and Lynn Worsham. New York: MLA, 1998. 239-51. Print.

Lunsford, Andrea and Jenn Fishman. "Performing Writing, Performing Literacy." *College Composition Communication* 57.2 (2005): 224-52. Print.

Madison, D. Soyini. *Critical Ethnography: Method, Ethics and Performance*. Thousand Oaks: Sage Publications, 2005. Print.

Maher, Frances and Mary Kay Thompson Tetreault. *The Feminist Classroom: Dynamics of Gender, Race and Privilege*. Lanham: Rowman and Littlefield, 2001. Print.

Miller, Susan. *Textual Carnivals: The Politics of Composition*. Carbondale: Southern Illinois University Press, 1991. Print.

Minot, Walter S. "Personality and Persona: Developing the Self." *Rhetoric Review* 7.2 (Spring 1989): 352-63. Print.

Moss, Beverly J. "Ethnography and Composition: Studying Language at Home." *Methods and Methodology in Composition Research*. Eds. Gesa Kirsch and Patricia A. Sullivan. Carbondale: Southern Illinois University Press, 1992. Print.

Newkirk, Thomas. *The Performance of Self in Student Writing*. Portsmouth: Boynton/Cook, 1997. Print.

North, Stephen. *The Making of Knowledge in Composition: Portrait of an Emerging Field*. Upper Montclair: Heinemann, 1987. Print.

Paley, Karen. *I-Writing: The Politics and Practice of Teaching First-Person Writing*. Carbondale: Southern Illinois University Press, 2001. Print.

Phelps, Louise Wetherbee and Janet Emig, eds. *Feminine Principle and Women's Experience in American Composition and Rhetoric*. Pittsburgh: University of Pittsburgh Press, 1995. Print.

   Hays, Janice. "Intellectual Parenting and a Developmental Feminist Pedagogy of Writing." Phelps and Emig 153-90.

Phelps, Louise Wetherbee. "Becoming a Warrior: Lessons of the Feminist Workplace." Phelps and Emig 289-33.

Richardson, Laurel. "Evaluating ethnography." *Qualitative Inquiry* 6.2 (2000): 253-255. Print.

Schneider, Pat. *Writing Alone and With Others*. New York: Oxford University Press, 2003. Print.

Skloot, Rebecca. "When Pets Attack: The Truth About Cops and Dogs." *New York Magazine*, 2004. Web Aug 10 2015.

Smith, Sidonie and Julia Watson, eds. *Getting A Life: Everyday Uses of Autobiography*. London: University of Minnesota Press, 1996. Print.

—-. *Women, Autobiography, Theory: A Reader*. Madison: The University of Wisconsin Press, 1998. Print.

   Miller, Nancy K. "Teaching Autobiography." Smith and Watson 461-70.

Smith, Sidonie. "Autobiographical Manifestos." Smith and Watson 433-40.

Sunstein, Bonnie Stone and Elizabeth Chiseri-Strater, *Fieldworking: Reading and Writing Research*. New York: Bedford/St. Martin's, 2003. Print.

Tinberg, Howard B. "Ethnography in the Writing Classroom." *College Composition and Communication* 40 (February 1989): 79-82. Print.

Tombro, Melissa. *"Performance Studies and the Reinvention of "I" in Composition: Moving Myself Beyond a Textual Model."* Diss. University of Illinois at Urbana-Champaign, 2010. Print.

Turner, Victor. *The Ritual Process*. Chicago: Aldine Press, 1969. Print.

Wallace, David Foster. "Consider the Lobster." *Consider the Lobster And Other Essays*. New York: Little, Brown and Company, 2005. Print.

Williams, James D. "Counterstatement: Autobiography in Composition Scholarship." *College English* 68.2 (November 2005): 209-25. Print.

About the Author

Dr. Melissa Tombro is an Associate Professor of English at The Fashion Institute of Technology in New York City. She is the recipient of the SUNY Chancellor's Award for Excellence in Teaching for her work on a wide range of courses from Creative Nonfiction to Theatre Arts. Her research interests include autoethnography, ethnography, personal writing, creative writing and performance studies.

Outside of FIT she runs volunteer writing workshops for at-risk and underserved populations through the New York Writers Coalition. In her writing, teaching and volunteer work, she encourages other writers to use self-reflection and community engagement as a way to create meaningful, informed, and inspiring prose.

www.ingramcontent.com/pod-product-compliance
Lightning Source LLC
Chambersburg PA
CBHW080411170426
43194CB00015B/2776